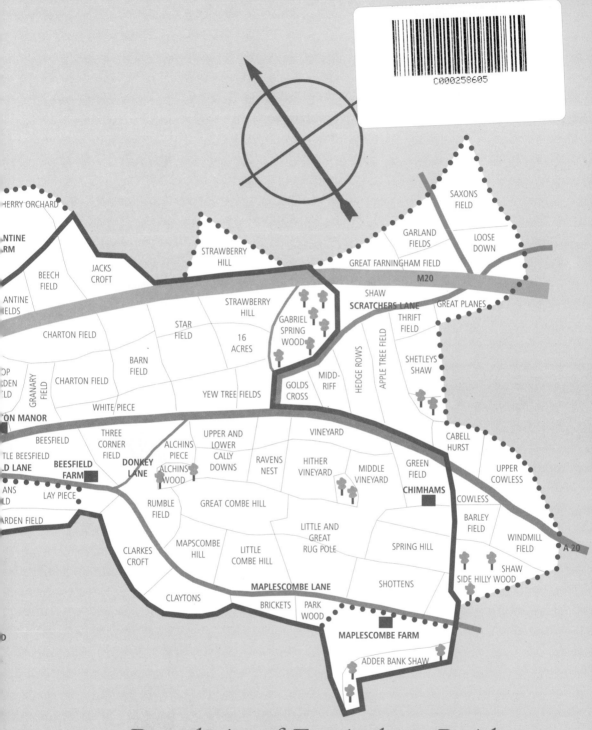

Boundaries of Farningham Parish

· · · · · · · · · · 1840

——————— Today

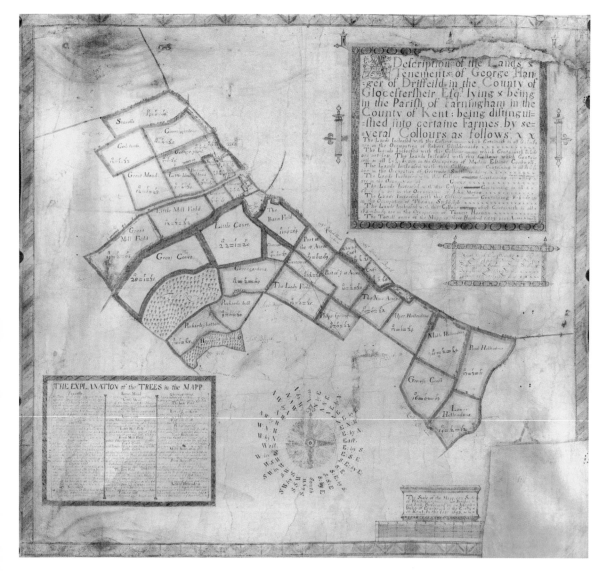

The Hanger Manor Estate map 1693, by permission of The British Library.

Farningham and its Mill

For Wilfrid

Farningham
and its Mill

A history of a village in Kent

Hilary Harding

Wadard Books Farningham Kent

Acknowledgements

I must thank Zena and Frank Bamping, local historians, without whose assistance and encouragement this book would never have been written, Martin Finch, my publisher, for doing all the hard graft of origination and design and for his imaginative work with illustrations and captions, Reg Nightingale, for his untiring and uncomplaining work on the index. Many thanks also to the librarians at Swanley, Sevenoaks, Maidstone and the Centre for Kentish Studies, Dartford Library and Museum, Canterbury and the Cathedral Library, Lambeth Palace Library, the British Museum and the British Library, the Public Record Office, and the Science Museum. Thanks also to Nigel Snelling Colyer, Malcolm Goldsworthy, Caroline Gould, Lady Ann Reid and the late Bishop Frank Horner West for allowing me access to family papers, Malcolm Rose for information about the Roper claviorgan and Geoffrey Copus about the Fuller and Waring families, the Farningham and Eynsford Local History Society and the Dartford Historical and Antiquarian Society. I must also thank many others, too many to mention, in the village and elsewhere who have helped me in conversation. I must also record my gratitude to the trustees of the Kent Archaeological Society History Fund and the Allen Grove Fund for their generous grants towards publication costs. And lastly to my husband Wilfrid and my daughter Alice for their active support and encouragement.

First published in Great Britain in 2005 by Wadard Books
6 High Street, Farningham, Kent DA4 0DG

ISBN 0-9550858-0-2

Designed by Martin Finch FCSD

Typesetting and origination by
Matthew Finch Design Consultants LimitedFarningham Kent © 2005
Printed in Great Britain by
Woolnough Bookbinding Limited Irthlingborough Northants

Introduction

Many years ago, when I first came to Farningham, I used to tend my landlord's graves in the churchyard. Mrs Guthrie, éminence grise of village society, had suggested this arrangement which pleased both her old friend, my landlord, and integrated her new one, myself, with village life, and also helped to keep the graveyard tidy.

My landlord's family, the Colyers, had owned the village water-corn-mill for six generations and I was living in one of their mill cottages. They had a lot of graves to tend. The original miller, my landlord's great-great-great-grandfather, had a stone Georgian sarcophagus. His son, the second Colyer miller, had a Regency tomb with an urn on top and, next door to him, was the grave of the family cook, "In Grateful Memory of Faithful Service". Later members of the family were in more mundane Victorian graves requiring a lot of finicky work with the shears.

The churchyard was a quiet and private place, but it hummed with history, and I was soon drawn into curiosity about the countless generations of villagers lying all around. One day two old ladies, having asked where I lived, told me that they used to go gleaning in the fields as children and take their bags of corn to be ground at the mill. This was in the 1960s and, as the mill had closed for grinding in 1900, it seemed an extraordinary link with the past.

Sometimes, indulging my proprietorial interest in the miller's family and my new found fascination with churchyards, I would find other Colyers lying in some foreign field a few villages away. Who were these exiles? My landlord, pleased to find a budding genealogist among his tenants, lent me a copy of his Family Tree. Perhaps I would get a grave like the cook.

The Tree had a coat of arms with a crest of a black African holding a spray of oak leaves. "We had no blackies in the family", Mr Colyer assured me, "perhaps it was a slave from the Crusades". In view of their surname I thought to myself that maybe the founder of the family had been associated with coal mines. I looked up the arms and discovered that the original owner was a Robert le Collier, a collar or saddle maker from France who had married a Staffordshire heiress in 1500 and quite possibly had no connection with the Kentish millers who had, maybe, simply adopted his crest.

I also found a number of discrepancies in the Tree.
A black sheep, with three wives and an illegitimate son
had crept away to die bankrupt in Calais. Worse still,
there was a whole branch of poor relations, agricultural
labourers, who did not feature on the Tree at all. Other
missing persons who should have been in the churchyard appeared to have gone over to the Baptist Chapel.
"You'll be saying we were RCs next" groaned my
disappointed landlord.

My hopes of a fine grave were fading so I turned my
attention towards getting to know my neighbours.
I discovered a network of old families who had lived in
this or neighbouring villages for many generations.
It seemed amazing that a village 20 miles from London
could have such a core of people who had lived within
such a small radius for so many centuries.
I was only just in time to catch a passing world.
Few children of the old families can afford to live here
now. The history of the village was too big a subject to
write about, but the mill itself seemed small and safe.
How could I have known that it could only be understood in relation to the village, and the village in relation
to the country, and what about the rest of the world?

Bread of some kind has been the primary diet of the
people of the village for two thousand years, and so the
history of the arable fields is a necessary part of the
story of Farningham Mill, as is the history of the manor
which would own it, the river which fed it, the people
who lived and worked here and the church next door
which would order their lives. They are all inextricably
linked. I have plodded on with this story over the last
thirty years, partly in gratitude to a kind landlord who
now, sadly, lies with his ancestors in the churchyard, but
mainly to celebrate a place that has given me so much
happiness.

Hilary Harding
Bridge Cottage
Farningham
November 2005

Part One Ancient

Bread signifies true love
Abbot Aelfric (circa 1000 AD)

Chapter One pp. 8-23

Farningham / The Earliest Landscape / The First Settlers /
Early Milling Methods / Corn Festivals and Milling Legends /
Six Roman Settlements in Farningham / Roman Villa 1 / Early Watermills /
Roman Watermills / Villas 2 and 3.

Chapter Two pp. 24-41

Anglo-Saxon Invaders / Anglo Saxon Farningham and the First Place Name /
Wood Pasture / Ethelbert of Kent 560-616 / The Grinding Women /
Christian Anglo-Saxon Kent / The End of the Kingdom of Kent /
The Charters / Vikings / Alphege / Aelfric / Status / End of the Era.

Chapter Three pp. 42-60

The Normans and Domesday Book / The Four Domesday Manors in
Farningham / Ernulf de Hesdin / Dering of Farningham Mill /
Charton Manor / Wadard / Wadard's Mill / The Village Mill / FitzHelte and the
de Cheritons / The Church / Tithe / Gavelkind or Partible Inheritance The
Village / William Fitzhelte's Mill / John Scot.

Chapter Four pp. 61-76

13th Century Farningham / Odo de Cheriton / The de Freminghams /
Farningham Castle / Farningham's Jews / Farningham Market and Fair /
Statute Pistoribus / Feast Days / The Fair / The Assize of Bread and Ale /
The Market / John de Fremingham / Ralph's Tomb /
The Manor of Franks or Little Farningham / Mills as Prisons.

Chapter Five pp. 77-89

14th Century Farningham / The Black Death / Vicar Thomas and his Vicarage /
The Second Ralph and Second John de Fremingham /
Chaucer's Mill / The Peasant's Revolt.

Chapter Six pp. 90-103

15th Century Farningham / The Farningham Font / Roger Isley's Mill /
Jack Cade's Rebellion / The Pastons / The Farningham Landscape /
John Isley / Gilbert Carleton.

Chapter Seven pp. 104-118

16th Century Farningham / The Ropers / Wyat's Rebellion / Anthony Roper /
The Theewes Claviorgan / Law and Order / Assizes / Murder /
The Poor Laws / The Inns / Titles / The Roper's Manor House.

Chapter Eight pp. 119-140

17th Century Farningham / The 1616 Terrier / The case against Sir Anthony
Roper / Civil War / The Bull Inn / John Kemp, Miller / The Hearth Tax and the
Inventories / John Kemp's Mill / The Poor / Sir John Beale /
Early 18th Century Farningham / The Woods /
The Craykers of Charton Manor / William Ebbutt.

Chapter One

Farningham / The Earliest Landscape / The First Settlers /
Early Milling Methods / Corn Festivals and Milling Legends /
Six Roman Settlements in Farningham / Roman Villa 1 / Early Watermills /
Roman Watermills / Villas 2 and 3.

Farningham

In the 1778 edition of his great *History of Kent*, Edward Hasted wrote 'Farningham is a most pleasant, healthy village; having every conveniency, both for profit and pleasure. As you approach it from the hills, especially from the North, it forms the most beautiful, picturesque landscip that can be imagined. It stands on the high road from London, through Wrotham to Maidstone, which crosses this parish from West to East, and the river Darent directs its course through it from South to North'.[1]

It is a clear, affectionate description by someone who knew the village well. Hasted must often have ridden through from his home in Sutton-at-Hone. He even rented a house in Farningham for two years in 1763.[2]

Ten years later, in the 1788 edition, his language has been polished, which is a pity because this is the edition that most people read. The river Darent now 'meanders its silver stream across the parish northward in the midst of a valley of fertile meadows' and the spelling of landscape is updated although Hasted may originally have meant that the scene looked like one of the newly popular 'landscip' paintings by, among others, the miller's son John Constable.

Today the M20 and A20 roads closely bypass Farningham, leaving the village in the valley below, an island of red and brown roofs with the grey flint church and white mill at the centre. It is still a pretty sight, even if not the most picturesque imaginable.

The proximity of the village to London, about twenty miles by road, has contributed to its prosperity since the middle ages. Farningham not only stood on the old road from London to Folkestone and Hythe via Maidstone, but the parish was also bisected by the road from Dartford to Sevenoaks.

There was once a medieval stone bridge here,[3] a small castle[4] and a weekly market and annual fair,[5] so the village was quite an important crossing and meeting place. Both roads were turnpiked in Hasted's time, an event that brought profit and pleasure and left behind some buildings with facades of late Georgian elegance.

There has been a water mill here for at least ten centuries,[6] and the descendant of those mills, a splendid late 18th century white weatherboarded building with an adjoining grey brick mill house and white weatherboarded cottages, is the focal point of the village. It has not ground corn for a hundred years and most of the milling machinery is now missing but, thanks to the Colyer family who have owned it for 270 years, it still looks much as it did at the last rebuilding in 1790.

1–Edward Hasted (EH) *History and Topographical Survey of the County of Kent, (1778-1801)*
2–Centre for Kentish Studies (CKS) *p.145/12/1*
3–British Museum (BM) *Add MS 32362f195*
4–B&E Philp, *Archaeological Excavations in the Darent Valley (1973)*
5–Public Record Office (PRO) *Charter Rolls 1270*
6–John Morris, ed. *Domesday Book, Kent (1983)*

There is little change today between the Mill shown above circa 1904 or from the earliest known photograph below. Note the miller just visible in the doorway.

Farningham Mill, as we see it today, is largely the work of two millers, Charles and Henry Colyer. Charles came to the village from Southfleet in 1735, rebuilt the existing mill and mill house and constructed the present layout of waterways. His son Henry embellished the property with a new bay-windowed facade to the house, a larger mill and a 'Garden and Grove' of extravagant fantasy which included a castellated folly, hanging gardens, shell grotto and 'gothick' stables and counting house.[7]

Henry also acquired the Lion Hotel[8] opposite and is probably responsible for the enlargement and Regency features of that building. The changing fashions of the time, already reflected in Hasted's two descriptions of the village, can be seen in the work of the Colyer father and son. The functional simplicity of the first and the fanciful imagination of the second in turn reflect the tastes of the leading father and son of the day, George III and the Prince Regent.

Today, looking at the mill from the road, we see Henry's grey brick facade of 1790 on the left, with steps up to the splendidly porticoed front door. The large, four-storey, white weather-boarded mill building on the right also dates

7-CKS p.145/5/1
8-CKS U36/T448

9

from Henry's time as, probably, do the Napoleonic eagles on each cornice and the great urns beside the steps.

Up at the fourth floor of the mill is the locum, or pulley house, with its little gothic revival window. Sacks of grain would have arrived by horse drawn waggon to be hoisted up here to begin the descent, floor by floor, through the milling process to emerge on the ground floor again as sacks of flour.

The remains of Henry's Folly can be seen above the mill on the cliff to the right. Sadly, most of the hanging gardens, the shell grotto and the grove with its statue of a wood nymph, are overgrown at present but the little towers, often presumed by passers by to be the remains of an ancient castle, can still be seen. Although the little castellated towers appear ornamental, they are in fact chimneys to convey air down to the storage caves below, where it seems likely that grain was hoarded against times of shortage.

The waterwheel is now missing but a turbine, probably installed in the nineteenth century, remains set in the river as it flows through the building between the sluice gate and the mill race. The race still falls into a deep pool below the mill, to flow along the channel constructed by Henry's father who is commemorated by a plaque saying 'Charles Colyer Miller, 1773' on one of the bridges above the mill stream.

Flanking the entrance to the mill drive are two groups of cottages, the ones on the right form part of a medieval half-timbered house, disguised by 18th century weather boarding. The Victorian 'cottage orné' on the left has a false front added by Henry's son to beautify the terrace of workmen's cottages built by his grandfather Charles in about 1770.[9]

The earliest landscape

Professor Alan Everitt in *Continuity and Colonization, the evolution of Kentish settlement,* says 'the landscape itself is our most important historical document'[10]. To understand the history of a place we must first understand the nature of its landscape.

As one walks the fields round Farningham one begins to understand that the hidden landscape, the geological bed under the blanket of fields and woods, is not only important to the history of the village settlement, but explains the nature of the scene. Chalk and flint and clay tell the story of the houses, church and mill. The look of the place is determined by the soil; chalk-land trees, flowers, birds, butterflies, even the fish are chalkland fish. Richard Fortey has written 'geology has the same role in landscape as does the unconscious mind in psychology; ubiquitous but concealed'.[11][12] The geological map of Kent is like a multi-layered cake. It is these different formations that give the county such contrasting aspects. From North to South there are the Foothills of the alluvial Thames, clays, brickearths, sands and pebble beds, the chalk Downlands, then the gault clays and greensands, then the Wealden clays and sandstones and lastly the alluvial deposits of the Marshland.

9-'CC 1866' on front door
10-A.M.Everitt, *Continuity and Colonization; the evolution of Kentish Settlement, (1986)*
11-Richard Fortey *The Hidden Landscape (1993)*
12-Dartford District Archaeological Group (DDAG) *Under Your Feet, the archaeology of Dartford District.* Mike Draycott, *'the Geological Background'. (1993)*

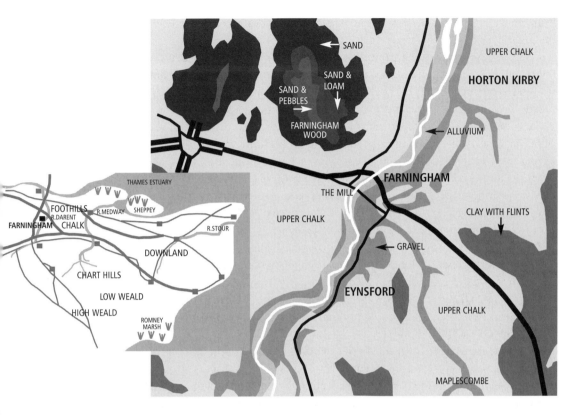

The geological map of Farningham parish is also beautifully varied, although it is naturally not as rich as the whole slice of Kentish cake.[13] The river Darent cuts the parish neatly in half from South to North in a valley of alluvium and flood plain gravel. This is fertile Foothills country. The Upper Chalk Downland rises steeply on either side, not so fertile, but on the other hand not too difficult for the early settlers to clear and till. The nature of the chalk, laid down by the Great Chalk Sea so many millions of years ago, means that one may be lucky enough to find fossilized sea urchins among the flints on the fields. The woods are overlaid with sea-washed pebble beds and, in the East, towards Brands Hatch, the chalk is overlaid with clay-with-flints. It is easy to see the attraction for the early settlers of a river crossing where the Downland dips and the flood plain widens to make a ford.

Farningham is in the middle section of the Darent Valley, made famous by Samuel Palmer in his early 19th century landscapes. He called it his 'Valley of Vision', and his early etchings of semi-mythical subjects are idealisations of the way the valley might have looked many centuries ago.

The first people to see this landscape may have been the contemporaries of Swanscombe Man, or rather Woman, one of the earliest British human fossils, discovered less than ten miles away. Although the lie of the land that these first people saw was much the same as today, the flora and fauna were quite different. Swanscombe Woman was alive during a warm interglacial

13-British Geological Survey, Dartford, *Sheet 271*

11

period, and fossil bones of this date found in the Darent river beds are of animals such as cave lion, woolly rhinoceros and mammoth. However, Swanscombe Woman seems to have had little effect on her environment and does not appear to have grown grain or ground it for bread.[14]

After the last glaciation, most of Britain became covered with natural forest but none of this original wildwood exists today. Human activity and natural changes in the cycles of vegetation mean that today's 'Ancient Woodlands' such as Farningham Woods, have been 'managed' for their produce since the Iron Age and possibly before that.[15]

Early Stone Age flint tools have been found in many parts of Farningham parish, although not in any particular pattern. There is more evidence of the mysterious Neolithic people who built the Medway megaliths and used a network of trackways across the Downland. To judge by many random finds near Calfstock Lane, this was possibly one of these early roads. These people were probably the first to make clearings in the Farningham wildwood for pasture, building materials, firewood and, most important of all for this history, to grow the first crops of grain. Neolithic saddle-quern stones, the first mills for grinding flour, have been found at Lullingstone.[16] 'Flour', in fact, was a later refinement, 'Meal', from the word to mill or grind, is a better description for the gritty stuff that made the first bread for the first square meals.

The neolithic agricultural revolution meant that people's lives began to be dominated by the cycle of growing crops and nurturing domestic beasts, and there would be new gods of the food supply, such as the corn gods, found in every Western culture.

Boundaries began to be important and apparently stones had a great significance for the earliest settlers. Sarsens, those strange rocks scattered on the surface of the chalk downland and often used in the building of Stonehenge and the megaliths, probably became meeting places and boundary markers. Lulling's Stone was maybe a later name for such a place, as was Axstane, or oak stone, as the area round Farningham became known. There must be many hundreds of places called Stone in Britain.

Bronze Age people continued the colonization of the Darent Valley. Some itinerant smith or trader, or cautious householder, buried a fine axe-head and an ingot of bronze in Farningham Woods about three thousand years ago;[17] the only evidence in the parish so far of the early Celtic, or Central European, people who were contemporary with the great classical civilizations of the

Top left,
Early Bronze Age
unfinished arrow head.
Top centre,
Neolithic/Bronze Age
blade.
Above, Neolithic wood
working implement,
chisel cutting edge and
engraving point.

All found locally and
courtesy of Geoff Burr

14-DDAG, *Under Your Feet*(1993) Sharon Mitchell *'The Prehistoric Period'*
15-Oliver Rackham, *Ancient Woodland,* (1980)
16-Sharon Mitchell DDAG
17-Dartford Museum exhibit

Eastern Mediterranean. The hillfort at Hulbury in Eynsford was partially excavated in 1915 and it was said to be impossible to walk over the site without stumbling across Bronze Age pottery, loom weights, bones and broken quernstones.[18]

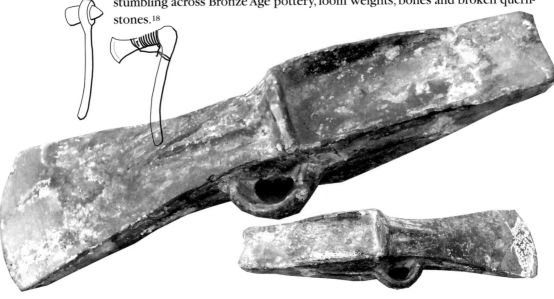

The first settlers

Bronze Age axe-head found near Farningham Woods
Courtesy Dartford Museum

The first known settlers in Farningham belonged to an Iron Age community which has been dated to sometime between 100BC and 100 AD. Their hut farmstead with a ditched livestock enclosure was excavated below the woods on Farningham Hill in 1973,[19] and is now buried under the M20 motorway.

When Julius Caesar made his two, not entirely successful, campaigns through Kent in 55 and 54 BC he described the settlements of these Celtic people, the so-called Belgae, as very similar to those of the people of Gaul. He considered the people of Kent to be the most civilized of the Britons and saw the countryside as thickly settled with homesteads, although he was probably only seeing the more populated areas.[20] [21] Tacitus, who came to know the people better, said sharply 'Who the first inhabitants of Britain were, whether natives or immigrants, is open to question: one must remember we are dealing with barbarians'.[22]

18-Dartford Museum, *Farningham Archaelogy envelopes.*
19-B.J.Philp, *Excavations in the Darent Valley, (1984)*
20-Peter Salway, *Roman Britain, (1981)*
21-Peter Salway, (1981)
22-Tacitus, *The Agricola,* trans H.Mattingly (1970)
23-Geoff Burr, metal detectorist, personal communication
24-Barry Cunliffe, *Iron Age Britain, (1995)*
25-Philp de Jersey, *Celtic coinage in Britain, (1996)*

Maybe he used the word to mean alien or foreign. The Farningham Iron Age farmers may not have been highly civilized by Roman standards, but they were far from barbarians in today's sense. Sophisticated and beautiful Celtic coins have been found in Farningham parish,[23] probably used as gifts rather than in a money market, although there was by now plenty of trade with the continent of Europe in the shape of British grain, metal, slaves and hunting dogs in exchange for luxury goods such as wine, pottery and jewellery.[24] [25]

Farningham is very lucky to have a resident metal-detectorist in Geoff Burr, whose scrupulously recorded findings have contributed so much to our understanding of this period The social organization of these Celtic Iron Age people may have been centred on the hillfort at Hulbury where an Iron Age field system has been traced on the downland above Lullingstone which probably extended as far as Farningham Woods. Their religion is believed to have been associated with sacred oak groves and shrines beside rivers or springs. Adherents of this old religion are thought to have built the cult room devoted to water goddesses underneath the Christian chapel at Lullingstone. Two early Farningham place-names, Puckard's Bottom and Puckard's Hill, (now known as Perget) at the highest point of Farningham Woods and very close to the Iron Age settlement, may possibly derive from the Saxon word 'puca' meaning goblin, and suggest the possibility of a magic place or shrine here.[26] Readers of Kipling's Puck of Pook's Hill might like this tenuous connection. The river itself has the Celtic name Darent, Derventio or oak-tree-river.

The Farningham Iron age farmers kept sheep and span wool and used commercially produced pottery and jewellery. Animal bones indicate that they had work ponies and hunting dogs and occasionally ate deer and wild boar as well as domesticated beef and mutton, although their lives were likely to have mainly been hungry, short and harsh. Most important of all from the point of view of the history of local milling, they grew varieties of wheat and barley which they ground for flour with saddle and rotary quernstones. The remains of charred corn found in their storage pits indicates that the grain was parched or burnt out of the ears before grinding.

Top, 65BC Gallic War type, imported gold stater struck by the Ambianie tribe of North East France/Belgium. Disjointed horse right.

Above, 40-35BC Gold quarter stater, late Weald type, Cantii tribe minted in Kent-Celticised horse left.

All found locally, courtesy of Geoff Burr

Early milling methods

Grinding stones, or querns, had been in use throughout antiquity. The milling of corn is one of the oldest activities. ('The Daily Grind'). Egyptian terra cotta figures from the tombs of 3000 BC show millers kneeling behind saddle stones and leaning forward over the stone to crush the grain with a kind of stone rolling pin.[27] Saddle querns such as these are still used in many countries, as are pounding stones and mortars, other early methods of milling.

The earliest crushing device used in prehistoric times was simply a rounded stone pounded on a hollowed stone, and the earliest word for 'mill' in the Indo-European languages means an apparatus for crushing. The Latin word 'pistor', which came to mean a miller-baker, meant 'pounder', as in pestle and piston. In Biblical times millers, or operators of querns, were usually slave women. Moses, in Exodus, speaks about 'the maid-servant that is behind the mill', and Samson, eyeless in Gaza, is said to have ground at the mill with the slaves in Delilah's prison.

26-Eilert Ekwall, *English Place Names*, (1960 ed.)
27-Elizabeth David, *English Bread and Yeast Cookery (1977)*

14

The next development was the rotary quern which came into use in the Iron Age. Professor Barry Cunliffe[28] says that it appeared in Britain in the 3rd or 4th century BC, 'long before, it would seem, it became known in the Mediterranean'. The rotary querns consisted of a pair of round granite or lava millstones turned by hand with a wooden handle and, as Elizabeth David says in her history of bread, they sometimes looked like small bee-hives, or 'like two roughly made, misshapen cheeses standing one upon another'. The coni-cal beehive shapes were the earliest variety, querns became flatter as time went by. The concave upper stone was hol-lowed to fit the convex lower one and, in time, an iron spindle was added to hold them together, with a disk known as a rynd to keep it in place. There was a hole in the top through which the grain was fed. The mill was now a machine.

Samuel Palmer's beloved classical writer, Virgil, has been attributed with a description of a rotary quern in the late 1st century BC. The peasant 'summons his two hands to the work, the left is bent on serving, the right on the toil of the mill, this turns and drives the disk...and now and then the left takes over from her mealy sister. On a little shelf above is his lamp to light him through the night'.[29] The Farningham Iron Age farmers used these querns, presumably in this fashion. Although they used the river as their main water sup-ply, they did not as yet have the technology to harness the river to drive a watermill. The first prime-movers, or sources of motive power, were human and animal.

Animal mills appeared soon after the invention of the rotary quern. Donkey mills were recorded in Rome by 160 BC and there were several at Pompeii. Sadly no traces of any survive in Farningham. They looked like giant hour-glasses and the donkey walked round them pushing a lever. Apuleius, in the *Golden Ass* gives a description of life in a donkey mill in the 2nd century AD.[30] Transformed into an ass, Apuleius is bought by a baker-miller and put to work blindfolded in a mill. The baker's wife in this story was a wicked woman, perhaps the first in a long line of villainous millers.

Corn festivals and milling legends

Vesta was the Roman goddess of the hearth and of ovens and mills. She was always associated with the asses of the donkey mills, and there is a wall painting at Pompeii of her festival, the Vestalia, and the miller's festivities with garlands of bread round the asses necks. There was a Vestal temple at Janiculum where the Roman water-mills were situated and the perpetual fire in the temple was tended by the famous Vestal Virgins.

Ceres was the Roman corn goddess and her festival was the Cerealia, as in cornflakes. The Greek corn goddess was Demeter and she is still followed in Sicily, albeit in a Christian metamorphosis. The inhabitants of a Sicilian town, Calatafimi, which once had twelve water-mills, still have a yearly church procession, carrying the silver crucifix donated by the town's millers, where little sun-shaped loaves are thrown to the crowds.[31]

Mills and milling have become part of mythology all over the Western World, presumably ever since bread first became seen as the staff of life. Corn spirits appear in most mythologies.[32] Early myths have avenging gods grinding bones in their querns. They are ancestors of our own Jack and the Beanstalk, where the bloodthirsty giant is a miller; 'Fie, Fie Fo, Fum, I smell the blood of an Englishman, be he alive or be he dead, I'll grind his bones to make my bread'.

Other myths use the symbol of the rotating mill-stone and later, the mill wheel. Mythical mills often break and fall to pieces. Sometimes they are stolen by sea-gods and taken down into the depths to grind salt until they create the Maelstrom, a whirlpool that appears in Homer's *Odyssey*.[33] Odysseus himself met twelve women plying twelve mills. Mill legends are legion.

A Celtic calendar of the 1st century BC shows the four great agricultural festivals which would have been celebrated by the Farningham farmers.[34] Their year began with a ritual feast on November 1st, when summer fattened beasts were killed for winter food. It celebrated the dark season and has survived as Halloween. The Saxons were to call November 'Bloodmonath'. February 1st, later Candlemas, celebrated the beginning of the growing season, and Mayday was the great spring festival. The feast of interest to millers was August 1st, held in honour of Lugh, a great sun god, later translated into Lugh mass, or Lammas, the Saxon Loaf Mass when the first corn was ground and baked.

The carbonised grains discovered in the pits of Farningham's Iron Age farm were varieties of wheat and barley. Owing to its high gluten content wheat had been recognised in the Western world as the best variety of grain for bread. Emmer wheat, the ancestor of European grain, is believed to have first been grown in Mesopotamia and arrived in Britain by the Neolithic period.

The wheat grown on the Farningham farm was Triticum Spelta, a new variety which could be sown in the autumn. Emmer may also have been

31–L.Accardo, P.Boni, S.Palmeri, *I Mulini di Calatafimi, (1996)*
32–Sir James Fraser, *The Golden Bough, (1922)*
33–Graham Hancock, *Fingerprints of the Gods, (1995)*
34–Barry Cunliffe, *op. cit. (1995)*

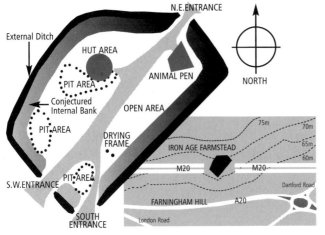

present, probably for spring sowing.[35] The barley was also a new variety which could be sown in the autumn. Both crops matured about the same time, but the slow maturing winter wheat was considered the best. Barley was regarded as an inferior grain for bread, 'food for slaves', and was used for malt brewing.

The small Celtic fields, about 64m square, could be ploughed in a day. The corn was reaped with iron reaping hooks.[36] The ears were then dried and parched over heated flints or pot-boilers to loosen the grain from the husk. The corn might be stored in granaries but there was no trace of one at Farningham. The seed corn would probably be sealed up in one of the pits until the next sowing time.

The south facing slope, just below the skyline, on which the iron age farm was located.

Photograph circa 1936 courtesy Malcolm Goldsworthy

Six Roman settlements in Farningham

The river name, Darent, and the place name, Kent or Cantium, were apparently the only local words of the Celtic language adopted by the Roman conquerors, who seem to have left very few local place names themselves.[37] We have no idea of the names of the six Roman settlements so far discovered in Farningham, or the names they gave their local roads and fields, let alone their own personal names.

The Farningham Iron Age farmstead was apparently abandoned at about the time of the successful Roman invasion of 43 AD. Nothing was found on the site belonging to a later date, and a number of good pots were found dumped in one of the ditches, perhaps indicating a hasty exit. The site had probably been chosen for its sunny, south facing, position half way up the hill, rather than for defensive purposes, and would have been easily taken by the invading army, although the Roman policy was supposed to be to assimilate native Britons as far as possible.[38]

35-B.Philp, *op. cit. (1984)* Barry Cunliffe, *Iron Age Communities, (1974)* 37-Margaret Gelling, *Signposts to the Past, Place Names and the History of England, (1978)* 38-Peter Salway, *op. cit. (1981)*

17

By the end of the 1st century AD the Darent Valley was beginning to be thickly settled as a Romano-British colony of riverside farms and villas. The first occupation date given to the Lullingstone villa is between 80 and 90 AD, and the early part of one of the Farningham villas has also been dated to about this time.[39] Two small Farningham Roman sites, one at Calfstock Lane and one at Eglantine Lane, belong to this early period. Both these farmsteads are on the Downland above the river at about the same contour line as the Iron Age settlement. The Roman Calfstock site is very similar to the Iron Age farm in so far as it was apparently the house of a native British farmer. The finds include British copies of Roman pottery and oyster shells, indicating that this family had already developed Roman tastes.[40]

A third, now lost, Roman site near the Folly in Farningham Woods, was reported in 1866[41] and has been searched for in vain by Lt.Col.G.W.Meates and others. It indicates the use made by the Romans of woodland. As Oliver Rackham points out in *The History of the Countryside*, Roman settlements often extended deep into woods. They managed woodland for timber to build ships, houses and bridges and the firewood was needed for baths, hypocaust heating systems, corn-driers, iron, lead and glass. Badgers have thrown out Roman tiles in several places in Farningham Woods.[42]

The Romans are believed to have introduced the sweet chestnut which grows in such abundance in these woods and, although much of this is due to the 18th and 19th century's demands for hop-poles, it possibly represents a much older tradition. One of the arts of woodmanship, coppicing, is to crop the wood without felling the tree, and the giant chestnut stools, or tree stumps, from which the coppice wood sprang, are considered the oldest living organisms in the woods and may be a link with Roman times.

Roman Villa 1

The best known Roman villa in Farningham was discovered in 1925 and is now buried under numbers 36, 37 and 38 Oliver Crescent.[43] This was a small but comfortable house with a hypocaust and a bath. Several broken quern stones for milling were found on the site, among them a sarsen used as a saddle quern, a lower millstone suggesting use as a donkey mill and rotary querns made of mill-stone grit and continental lava. One specimen was from the top stone of a bee-hive pattern quern made from Herefordshire pudding-stone with holes for the wooden pin and the corn hopper. The earlier quern stones found on the Iron Age farm site had mostly been made from local greensand and sarsen stone.

Perhaps this is the place to say something about mill-stones. The Roman villa stones, as might be expected, came from further afield than those from the Iron Age farm. Lava, often from Etna, was popular, but the most highly prized stones in the ancient world came from the island of Nisyros in the Aegean. Millstone Grit, quarried in the Pennines, was to be the most usual,

39–*Archaeologia Cantiana LXXXVIII (Arch. Cant, 1973),* Lt.Col. G.W.Meates, *Farningham Roman Villa II*
40–Brian Philp, *Excavations in West Kent 1960-1970, (1973)*
41–*Gentleman's Magazine 1866*
42–Chris Ferris, author of *The Badgers of Ashcroft Woods, (1990),* personal communication
43–S.Priest & A.Cumberland, *Translations of the Dartford District Antiquarian Society (TDDAS,1931)*

and cheapest, British source. It is a hard sandstone, cemented together by quartz. The great house of Chatsworth is built of Millstone Grit and the Bronte sisters walked on the Gritstone Moors. In later years the best stone was considered to come from France. French burr-stones, Dutch Blues and 'cullen' stones from near Cologne were all highly prized.[44] Millstones needed to be 'dressed' regularly. They have been cut into a pattern of grooves to provide cutting edges since the fifth century BC.[45]

Lower part of a turned column cut from a solid block of oolithic limestone

Box flue tile scored to provide a key for mortar (for hypocaust or heating hot air system)

Both found at Roman Villa 1, Oliver Crescent in 1925

Courtesy Dartford Museum

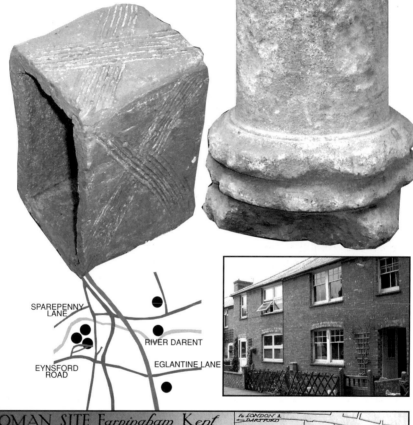

Sites of Roman settlements

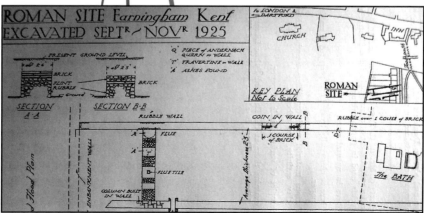

44-L.A.Moritz, *Grain Mills and Flour in Classical Antiquity,* (1979)
45-Martin Watts, *The Archaeology of Mills and Milling,* (2002)

Early Water-mills

Although some Roman watermill sites have been discovered in England, none as yet have been found in the Darent Valley. The Romans were apparently the first people to develop the vertical water-wheel for grinding corn in the 1st and 2nd centuries AD. The technology was first described by two classical writers, Vitruvius and Antipater in the late 1st century AD.[46]

Other less intricate waterwheels had existed in antiquity. The Noria, a wheel with a chain of pots for raising water for irrigation, may have originated in the Middle or Near East and is still in use in many countries. Another waterwheel used for grinding corn was the horizontal 'Greek' or 'Norse' mill which was also in use from an early period. Richard Holt, author of a book on medieval mills argues that this should really be called the Irish mill because it was the predominant mill in Ireland, and there is a possibility that it originated there.[47] He says that 'undoubtedly both types of mill, (vertical and horizontal), were known to the ancient millwright, and knowledge of both spread to all parts of the Roman Empire and beyond'.

The Norse/Greek/Irish mill had a horizontal wheel which lay flat on the river bed and turned millstones above it by means of a vertical spindle. It required no gearing and so was economical to build and run, but was possibly less efficient. It is still in use in many places, especially on fast running streams. Richard Holt says that 'the horizontal mill flourished everywhere that peasants were legally able to operate their own mills, being the least expensive design; the vertical mill on the other hand, with its far greater costs of construction and maintenance, was everywhere associated with large scale milling'.

The Greek poet Antipater addressed an epigram to the milling women. 'Oh stay your busy hands, ye girls that grind at the mill, let not the cock that heralds dawn disturb your sleep. The river nymphs are bidden by Demeter's will to do your work; and on the topmost wheel they leap and turn the axle's winding spokes, upon whose coil concave Nisyrian millstone's weight revolves anon'.[48] L.A.Moritz, writing on classical mills in antiquity, gives the above translation and points out that the verses not only indicate the novelty of the invention, but describe it accurately as the logical order of wheel, axle, gears and stone, and also suggests that this was an overshot wheel. There were three varieties of wheel from early times, an undershot, an overshot and a breast high wheel.

Writing at about the same time the Roman engineer Vitruvius described the vertical waterwheel, with its gearing to drive millstones.[49] He says that it consisted of a paddled wheel set vertically in the river on an axle which, when driven by the current, turned a vertical toothed drum or cog wheel. 'Next to this larger drum', he continues, 'there is a smaller one, also with teeth, but set horizontally, and this is attached (to the millstone). Thus the teeth of the

46-N.A.F.Smith, *The Origin of Water power, Transactions of the Newcomen Society No 55, (1983)*
47-Richard Holt, *The Mills of Medieval England, (1988)*
48-L.A.Moritz, *op.cit. (1979)*
49-Vitruvius, *De Arcitectura*

drum, which is fixed to the axle, make the teeth of the horizontal drum move, and cause the mill to turn. A hopper, hanging over this contrivance, supplies the mill with corn, and meal is produced by the same revolution'. It is generally accepted that Vitruvius has described the classic, Meccano-like, mechanism that would remain unchanged for the next two thousand years.

Water power has been described as the first important prime-mover in the history of technology. Lewis Mumford[50] uses geological metaphors to describe three eras of technological advance. His 'Eotechnic' phase was the era of wood and water power. The 'Paleotechnic' was of iron, coal and steam and the 'Neotechnic' was of electricity. The Dutch historian of technology, R.Forbes, gave the history of prime-movers five eras. First, human muscle; second, animal muscle; third, water power; fourth, steam power; and fifth, nuclear power.[51]

The milling women, who were told by Antipater to sleep late, were probably still slaves. Slave mills, as well as donkey, horse and ox mills, remained in use throughout the Roman Empire. It is hard to imagine anyone other than a poet caring much for the wellbeing of slaves at this period, which perhaps explains the slow adoption of the watermill. Women and donkeys were much cheaper than the expensive new device. Given the expense of building and maintaining a watermill compared to maintaining an animal or a slave it is not surprising that the new invention took time to become popular.

Domestic milling with quernstones turned by slaves or animals would continue for many centuries, but in Rome and other cities, the watermill now began to take precedence. At Janiculum, the traditional Roman milling and baking place, the mills were fed from the Tiber by the Trajan aqueduct.[52] According to Bennett and Elton in their great *History of Corn Milling* the citizens of Rome were supplied with free bread for three centuries and the Emperor Trajan founded a College of Pistores or miller bakers.[53] Locally, the Roman town at Springhead on Watling Street is believed to have had a public bakery with a miller-baker, a shop, an animal mill and a granary.[54]

Waterwheels
Left, horizontal
Right, vertical

50-Lewis Mumford,
Techniques of Civilization,
(1934)
51-Terry S.Reynolds,
Stronger than a Hundred Men,
a History of the Vertical Water
Wheel, (1983)
52-Paul N.Wilson,
Watermills, an introduction,
SPAB
53-Bennett & Elton,
op.cit.note 30
54-W.S.Penn, *The Roman*
Town at Springhead,
Gravesend Hist.Soc. 1966

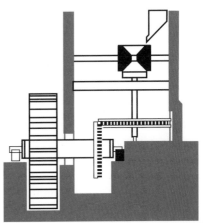

Roman Water-mills

The Romans were moving from human and animal power to that of water, but probably only where large quantities of corn needed grinding. Although no watermills have yet been discovered in the Darent Valley, everything indicates that a great deal of corn was grown here. The great granaries at Lullingstone, Horton Kirby and Darenth point to this, and it has been suggested that much of the grain was exported to the Continent, some of it as flour. The valley was fertile country and the Romans farmed it intensively. Until the late 19th century nobody believed that Roman watermills had ever existed in Britain. Bennett and Elton, writing in 1898, spoke about the watermills in the Roman Empire but, at that time, no archaeological evidence for Romano-British mills existed. Since then several sites have been discovered, two of them at Ickham in Kent, described by R.J.Spain in *Archaeologia Cantiana*.[55] Watermills, by their situation, are unlikely to survive for much archaeological research. As Mr Spain says 'Watermills, probably more than any other building, have suffered most from the forces of nature...Ancient roads do not move; rivers do'

The luxurious lifestyle of the occupants of the valley's Roman villas must have been maintained by many servants and slaves, so perhaps there was no incentive yet to build watermills. The quern stones in the Oliver Crescent villa certainly confirm the survival of this form of domestic milling, but it seems possible that the other, riverside villa developments had small watermills.

As well as the 'gentry' in the villas there was surely a large population of farm labourers from the original Celtic/British population living in more modest dwellings. No peasant's houses have survived. Some writers have suggested that the 'aisled' buildings associated with many of the villas, such as the one at Horton Kirby, were communal houses for workmen or slaves. Others believe that the remains of Romano-British dwellings lie underneath the present day village settlements.

Corn and other commodities were probably exported by barge to Dartford and the Thames. Imports such as amphorae of wine and oil came back. The farmers may have used slow ox-waggons along the valley lanes but they are considered more likely to have used flat bottomed boats as the Darent is believed to have been navigable as far inland as Riverhead. Britain now had a money economy for the first time. London was rapidly developing as the centre of trade, the hub of a network of roads and a major port.

Villas 2 and 3

Many of the villas in the valley were built on the alluvium and flood plain gravel. Some, including two of the Farningham villas, were built so close to the changing course of the river that erosion has washed away part of the buildings. There seems a strong possibility that there were watermills on these two sites. One of these villas, (villa 2) in the fields at the back of the present day Manor House, was excavated by Lt.Col. Meates of Lullingstone in

55–*Arch.Cant.C.1984*, R.Spain, *Romano Brirish* Watermills

1948, but not fully reported in *Archaeologica Cantiana* until 1973. Occupation was dated to between the 1st and 4th centuries AD, beginning with a thatched barn-type house divided into nine rooms.

More rooms and a hypocaust system, bath house and verandas were added in the second century and, in the fourth century a much grander house was built. 'A luxurious riverside retreat' as Lt. Col. Meates put it. There was a loggia with 'a pleasant aspect over the river', floors of red tesserae, decorative mosaics and all the trappings of the Roman good life. The site is close to the weir that divides the river from the canal or leat leading water to the present day mill.

In 1981 Brian Philp of the Kent Archaeological Rescue Unit excavated another Roman building in the same manor-house field which he identified as a large bath-house, also two very large Roman ponds.[58] This particular field is very rich in Roman remains, there is also a system of Roman ditches and a long boundary ditch containing Roman domestic rubbish.

The other Farningham riverside villa, (villa 3) in the watermeadows southwest of Franks Hall, was excavated by J. Ritson in collaboration with Lt. Col. Meates between 1960 and 1962. This site was dated to between the Ist and 4th centuries, with the observation that Belgic pottery and Celtic coins suggest a continuous occupation since the Iron Age. This appears to have been a smaller house with a range of rooms, a hypocaust system and a veranda or loggia.

Roman tilemakers mark found at Franks
courtesy Dartford Museum

In his *Roman Britain*, Professor Peter Salway mentions the possibilities of ecological changes brought about by Roman activities in Britain, including making roads and clearing watercourses. He also says that climatic changes in the 2nd and 3rd centuries affected the sea levels and caused flooding in the river valleys. Maybe there are still some Roman watermills waiting to be discovered underneath the flood plain alluvium, especially in these two riverside villa settlements which would probably later become the sites of the two Farningham watermills.

Brian Philp's excavations of a water channel at the Darenth Roman villa in 1972 and a discovery of a water channel in a Roman site near the river in Eynsford by Col.Meates in 1971, are the only suggestions, to date, of Darent Valley watermills. Brian Philp and his team, while examining the Darenth villa site, commented that the water channel resembled the ones at the fourth century watermill at Ickham[59]. Col.Meates examined a site in Eynsford in the grounds of the Social Club, next to the ford and the bridge. He found it to be a Roman building, 61 feet long, with a heavy platform of flint and mortar at the southern end with an apparent cutting for diversion of water. His 'tentative interpretation' was of a 'water channel perhaps to activate an undershot water-wheel'.[60]

56–Alan Everitt,*op.cit.1986*
57–*ArchCant.LXXXVIII (1973)* Lt.Col.Meates *op.cit.*
58–Brian Philp, *Archaeology in the Front Line, 50 Years of Kent Rescues (2002)*
59–Brian Philp, *Excavations in the Darent Valley Kent (1984)*
60–Lt.Col.Meates, *unpublished typescript Dartford Museum*

Chapter Two

Anglo-Saxon Invaders / Anglo Saxon Farningham and the First Place Name /
Wood Pasture / Ethelbert of Kent 560-616 / The Grinding Women /
Christian Anglo-Saxon Kent / The End of the Kingdom of Kent /
The Charters / Vikings / Alphege / Aelfric / Status / End of the Era.

Anglo-Saxon Invaders

In the mid-fourth century AD Kent was part of a rich province of the Roman Empire. The villas of the Darent Valley were at the height of their prosperity. A hundred years later they were apparently in ruins. Nobody really seems to know exactly what happened.

At the end of the fourth century the Romans began to withdraw their troops from Britain to contend with barbarian invasions in Gaul, leaving the Romanised Britons to deal with their own barbarian raiders. In 401 AD there was a final administrative severance from Rome. Many historians believe that life went on for a while much as before. Visitors to London such as St Patrick and St Germanus in the early 5th century describe a normal scene of urban life. It has been suggested that the brilliantly dressed landowners who greeted Germanus may have looked much like the people in the colourful wall paintings at the Lullingstone villa. This villa itself was burnt down in the early 5th century and was never rebuilt.[61]

Life in the country seems to have run down slowly, but the lack of archaeological evidence for this period makes it hard to describe the sequence of disintegration in the Darent Valley. Coins ceased to be minted in about the year 400 and there is a dearth of dateable pottery. As J.N.L. Myres says 'the sub-Roman Britons of the fifth and sixth centuries appear to have enjoyed, if that is the right word, a culture almost as completely devoid of durable possessions as any culture can be'.[62]

The story of the Saxon conquest of Britain has been told many times.[63] Anglo-Saxons had already been hired as mercenaries by the Romans and a few had already settled here. Abandoned by the Romans and harassed by their northern barbarian enemies, the Britons turned to these new allies for protection in return for more settlements. Soon a great wave of land-hungry invaders arrived. The historian Bede describes them as 'warriors from the three most formidable races of Germany, the Angles, Saxons and Jutes'. He continues that it was not long before such hordes of these people crowded into the island that the natives who invited them began to live in terror.

The conquerors devastated the land and slaughtered the inhabitants. The Britons fought the legendary Saxon chieftains Hengist and Horsa at Crayford where four thousand Britons perished, and the Britons then deserted Kent and fled to London. London probably survived as a ghost town, racked by famine and disease.[64] Kent was to be ruled for the next three hundred years by the descendants of Hengist's son Oisc.

61–Lt.Col.Meates, *Lullingstone Roman Villa (1963)*
62–J.N.L.Myres, *The English Settlements (1986)*
63–Bede, *A History of the English Church,* trans L.Sherley Price (1955)
64–Myres, *op.cit. (1986)*

The history of the Kingdom of Kent in Saxon times has been fully described by Keith Witney.[65] It was quite unlike the rest of England and came to an end with union with Wessex in the ninth century. The period divides roughly in half with a first, pagan phase, succeeded by the return of Christianity in the seventh century.

Christianity had been recognised as the state religion of the Roman Empire in the year 324 and had arrived in the Darent Valley soon afterwards. The Lullingstone villa shows that Christian rites were practised in the chapel on the ground floor while the pagan shrine to the water spirits in the room below remained in use.[66] That Christianity and paganism co-existed for some time can be seen in another Darent Valley find, the 5th century Darenth glass bowl, which has a Christian Chi-Rho symbol, but was excavated in a late 5th century pagan Saxon grave.[67]

Bede says that Kent was colonised by the Jutes and it is generally agreed that the culture of the settlers in Kent was predominantly Jutish. However, as the majority of settlers west of the Medway were Saxons, and as the only site discovered so far in Farningham of this date was a Saxon cemetery, perhaps it is simplest to call the local colonisers Saxons, although they belonged to the Jutish Kingdom of Kent. Later, the Angles would become the dominant group and England would take its name from them.

The early Saxon settlers of the Darent Valley kept close to the pattern of the Roman villa estates. It is not thought that they actually inhabited the Roman buildings; they were warrior-farmers and had no time for mosaics and hot baths, but there is some evidence, both at Darenth and at the Franks Roman villa, of the sunken Saxon huts, or wooden barn houses, known as 'grubenhauser', built inside the perimeters of the Roman ruins.[68] The houses were dug about three feet deep and so are believed to have been built over boarded cellars.[69]

The Anglo-Saxon poem, *The Ruin*, describes the feelings of awe experienced by the invaders when they saw buildings like the Roman villas which they called the works of giants.[70] The oral tradition of poetry and song of these illiterate people which led to the survival of such stories as *Beowulf*, means that most people know about the heroic life style of the Anglo-Saxon warriors and their mead-halls. The halls were communal timber-framed barn houses with a fireplace in the centre, round which were ranged trestle tables and wall seats. Outside, but within the same enclosure, were the huts or 'bowers' for women and their activities, such as weaving and food preparation including grinding and milling.

Very little archaeological evidence of these earliest settlements survives, and even less of the methods of milling. It must be assumed that the saddle stones and querns of the Romano-British were adopted by their first English successors and used again, as later evidence shows, by slave women.[71] It is not likely that these early Saxons had the technical competence to keep the watermills going.

65-K.P.Witney, *The Kingdom of Kent (1982)*
66-Meates *op.cit. 1963*
67-Gavin Kitchingham, *The Saxon Period, DDAG Under Your Feet (1993)*
68-Susan Tyler, *Anglo Saxon Settlement in the Darent Valley, Arch.Cant.CX (1992)*
69-D.A.Hinton, *Alfred's Kingdom (1977)*
70-R.K.Gordon ed. *Anglo Saxon Poetry (1954)*
71-Christine Fell, *Women in Anglo Saxon England (1984)*

Anglo-Saxon Farningham and the first place-name

Although there is so little evidence of dwellings, eighteen early Anglo-Saxon cemeteries have been discovered along the Darent valley, including one above Charton Manor in Farningham which may have been the burial ground for the people who lived in or near the present day village.[72] These pagan burial grounds were all on high ground, well away from the settlements. It was only in the later Christian era that churches with graveyards were built in the village centres.

One large cemetery of over a hundred burials was found at Riseley,[73] on the boundary of Farningham and Horton Kirby, which was possibly associated with a settlement below, near the site of the Roman villa at Franks. Part of a sunken Saxon building was found at this site. There was another cemetery with sixty graves, less than a mile away, at the site of the Farningham Homes for Little Boys.[74]

The name, Farningham, is believed to derive from the name of the group of Anglo-Saxon people who settled here; the home, or village, of the Fernings or Fremings. It is considered one of the earliest forms of place-name, although there are disputes about which came first, the 'hams', the 'ingas' or the 'ingahams'. A 6th or 7th century date seems most likely.[75] Wallenberg, in *Place Names of Kent*,[76] suggested first that the name might mean 'people who live in a ferny place' and second, the Freoningas or 'free people'. Most people now settle for the less romantic 'fearn' or bracken; useful stuff for fuel, bedding and thatch. Bracken grows freely in most parts of the parish. Fern may also have had a mystic significance. Fern spores appear to have been magic and hallucinatory and are now considered carcinogenic.

In Domesday Book the name is spelt variously as Forningeham, Ferningeham and Ferlingeham. Whatever the meaning, it seems likely that the people buried up on the hill at Charton in the seventh century used a version of 'Farningham' as their collective name. As a tribal kingdom however, they kept the Celtic name of Kent, from 'canto', coastal or border-country, and called themselves the Cantware or Kentings, as the Kentish Romans had called themselves the Cantiaci.

The practice of burial with grave-goods, which continued well into Christian times, provides the few surviving clues to the lives of the people buried at Charton. The grave-goods found there include a shield boss, a throwing axe, a dagger, knives and spearheads. These are thought to indicate people of the warrior class but not necessarily noblemen. The Kentish ceorl, or free peasant farmer, is considered to have been rich enough to possess arms and to have been called out to fight when needed. He also had arms for self protection in a violent society. The highest ranking warriors would have carried a great two edged longsword, but none were found here.

The burials at Risely included not only longswords but fine gold and silver jewellery and glass, copper and bronze artefacts. This graveyard may also be

72-S.Tyler, *Anglo Saxon Settlement in the Darent Valley,* Arch Cant.CX.(1992)

73-A.Cumberland, Saxon Cemetry, Riseley, TDDAS.No8, (1938). & Arch CantCX,(1992) Susan Tyler, *op.cit.*

74-Gavin Kitchingham, *op.cit.*

75-J.N.L.Myres, (1986) *op.cit.* M.Gelling, *op.cit.* (1978)

76-J.K.Wallenberg, Kentish Place Names, (1931) & The Place Names of Kent, (1934)

Artifacts from the Anglo-Saxon
cemetery Charton Manor, excavated
by E.Greenfield in 1938.
Spear with remains of wooden shaft.
Throwing Axe.
Ceramic globular urn
Shield Boss.
Courtesy Dartford Museum

Anglo-Saxon coin
Courtesy of Geoff Burr

considered with Farningham because, although it is in the neighbouring parish of Horton Kirby, it is on the parish border and is believed to have been associated with a settlement at Franks manor which, again, is on the border. Indeed, Franks at one time in the early 15th century, was known as 'Little Farningham'.[77] Most of the gravegoods in the Darent Valley burials are Saxon, although some of the Risely jewellery is Jutish. Objects belonging to women included combs, chatelaines for keys, sewing boxes and weaving needles, but no articles associated with milling.

So, although these were the so-called Dark Ages, with no written and little archaeological evidence of everyday life, we know quite a lot about the Farningham Anglo-Saxons. They lived the tough life of pioneer farmers, ready to fight for their territory if need be. They also enjoyed themselves, dressing up for feasts and telling stories and bawdy riddles.[78] Best of all, they had the warm weather of the meteorological age known as the Little Optimum to ripen the fruit and grain.

Woodpasture

The Kentish Downland was still heavily wooded country in Anglo-Saxon times. Farningham Woods, at the top of the downs to the west and Gabrielspring Wood to the east, are the only survivors of these woods in the parish. It is always assumed that Farningham Woods were never cleared because they lie high on an outcrop of gravel beds which would have been unrewarding and difficult to till. Both woods are full of the indicator plants of ancient woodland. A few other small copses and shaws in the parish, such as Alchin's Wood, Side Hilly Wood and Adder Bank Shaw, are also vestiges of the earlier woodland.

It is possible to trace the Anglo-Saxon wood pasture culture in some of the place-names of fields and wood compartments in the parish, names such as 'denn' and 'leah' and 'stoc'. Calfstock, as the woodland stockade for calves; Hollanden, the holly tree swine pasture; Cow Leas, a clearing for cows. And just across the parish border the name 'Swanley' meant the woodland clearing for swine. Woodland pasture for animals was practised across the whole of Kent.

From the accession of Oisc in 488, to the death of the last of his line in 762,

Anglo-Saxon woodpasture. From the Julius Work Calendar (British Library, ref Cotton MS. Julius A.VI) c.1020 AD

77–S.K.Keyes, *Further Historical Notes, (1938)*
78–John Porter, *Anglo Saxon Riddles, (1995)*

there was comparative peace in Kent and an opportunity for people such as the inhabitants of Farningham to turn from warfare to agriculture. No doubt young men of the warrior class still looked for glory defending and extending their territory, but the bulk of the population were now farmers.

Historians say that the dispersed Kentish settlements were now gradually divided into a series of agricultural 'estates' or provinces which later became the county divisions known as lathes. Each lathe was centred on a royal court. The lathes were much later sub-divided into hundreds, which possibly represented the amount of land needed to support a hundred families. Farningham by the time of Domesday Book would be in the Lathe of Sutton, or 'South Town', and the Hundred of Axstane, or 'Oakstone'.

Professor Everitt says that the Darent Valley 'has long been recognised as one of the earliest cradles of English settlement in Kent', and he suggests that it was probably the riverine estate of a later lathe which was centred on a Kentish royal court at Darenth, taking its name from the river. In later Christian times Dartford or 'Darent Ford', became the ecclesiastic centre and Sutton, the south town of Dartford, took the name 'at Hone' or 'at the Stone', and became the administrative centre of the lathe.[79]

The half lathe of Sutton from the autograph of Domesday Anno 1086 as depicted in Henshall's map of Kent published in 1798.

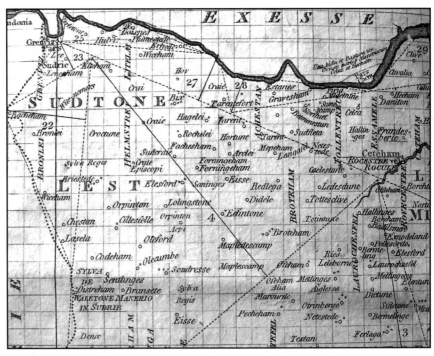

With Darenth as the primary estate of the lathe, secondary estates were soon formed along the valley, often corresponding to the earlier Roman villa farms. One of these was probably based on Eynsford, which may have then included Lullingstone and Farningham. The boundaries of this estate may

79-A.Everitt, *op.cit. (1986)* have even corresponded not only to the earlier Roman territory, but possibly also to an earlier Celtic territory centred on the hill fort at Hulberry. These agricultural estate divisions often hold clues to the later ecclesiastical parish boundaries.

As W. Hoskins says in *The Making of the English Landscape*,[80] 'a commonplace ditch may be the thousand year old boundary of a royal manor, a certain hedgebank...the boundary of a Celtic estate'. There are clues on the maps and on the ground. A very early earthwork, the Faestendyke, or fortress ditch, in Joyden's Wood near Swanley, may have been part of the boundary to our own territory.[81] Each estate had its own Downland cattle and sheep pastures, and pastures for swine down in the Weald. Pasturage of beasts far away from the home farm was a feature of the Jutish tradition of transhumance. Sheep to the marshes and cattle to the downland in summer and swine to the Wealden commons for the pannage of the oak trees in the autumn.[82]

Transhumance, or the seasonal movement of livestock, is still practised all over the world, often with ceremonies such as decking the beasts with flowers and bells on their journeys to and from the summer pastures. The shape of the lathes of Kent, long strips running from north to south down into the Weald, probably came about from the necessary inclusion of as rich a slice of the geological cake as possible, so as to provide not only arable land but also pastures, meadows, woodland, fisheries and marsh for the communities.

Farningham had woodland pastures within its own territory. The Hollanden fields, in a 17th century estate map,[83] cover 70 acres and are on the edge of Farningham Woods, which would have been continuous woodland through Birchwood to Joydens Wood. Holly was valuable as a dense evergreen cover and shelter and it was also, extraordinary as it may seem, considered a nutritious winter diet for animals.[84] Browsewood grazing had been practised since the Iron Age and the lower leaves of the larger holly trees were, it is said, smooth as camellias.[85] The woods had also never ceased to be used as a source of timber and coppice wood. The Farningham farmers also had common swine pastures down in the Weald in part of a great, 695 acre forest common also called Hollanden, near Leigh.

Much has been written about the Jutish Forest and its communal swine denns. It is a romantic story with the flocks of swine following their master's horn along the steep droveways leading down into the Weald, or Wald, which was still a wildwood full of deer and wolves. Unfortunately it is a pastoral story, not a ploughland one, and so has little to add to the history of mills and milling. For the arable history of the fields and their crops and the farmers who sowed and reaped and milled, we need to go to the laws of the Anglo-Saxon king, Ethelbert I of Kent.

80-W.Hoskins, *The Making of the English Landscape*, (1955)
81-Kent Arch.Soc.Records, (KASR) VolXI, *A Kentish Cartulary (1930)* G.Blaxall. pers.comm.
82-K.P.Witney, *The Jutish Forest, (1976)*
83-BM *Cart.Add Mss 23, 196b*
84-Martin Spray *Holly as Fodder in England, The Agricultural History Review, 29, (1981)* J.Radley, *Holly as Winter Feed, Ag.Hist Rev VolIX (1962)*

Ethelbert of Kent 560–616

Ethelbert, a pagan, was married to Bertha, a Christian from France, so he stands at the cusp of the transformation of Kent to a Christian country. Ethelbert was one of the few tribal kings described by Bede as a Bretwalda, or ruler of all Britain south of the Humber. Northumbria was another country. He was converted by St Augustine who brought his Christian mission to Canterbury in 596. The conversion of Kent followed, but it was a slow process and pagan burials with grave-goods continued in the Darent Valley until the mid-8th century.

Ethelbert died in 616, having had, as Bede observed, 'a glorious earthly reign of 56 years'. He had lived far longer than the majority of the Darent Valley inhabitants, whose life expectancy was about 25 years. He left a Code of Laws which indicates the structure of Kentish society. Each person had a wergild or blood price, the compensation to be paid in case of death or injury. The price was paid in golden shillings or silver sceattas.[87] The highest wergild belonged to the eorls or hereditary noblemen. Next came the ceorls or free peasants. On the lowest rung of the elaborate social scale were the slaves, who had no wergild of their own, but their owners were entitled to compensation for their loss or injury. There was only one category of male slave, the 'loaf-eater' or dependent, but there were three types of female slave, the serving maid, the field woman and the 'grinding woman'.

The Grinding Women

Women grinding slaves are mentioned in three types of household, the king's, the eorl's and the ceorl's, and the wergilds or penalties for killing or raping a slave woman varied according to the status of her owner.[88] In this way the king's grinding woman was worth 25 golden shillings, while a ceorl's grinding woman was only worth 50 silver sceattas. The laws also show that the grinding women were slaves of the middle category; the lowest were the field women. They were well protected by their owners and could marry, in which case the honour of their husbands doubled their value. It was later decreed that slaves might be entitled to their own dwelling, and to keep anything they earned in their free time.[89] It is not likely that this was carefully observed, nor that they had much free time.[90] These slaves, in Farningham as elsewhere, were likely to have belonged to the former British population.

Some grinding women may even have had the misfortune to have been used as grave-goods themselves in order to continue working for their owner in the afterlife. One history of Anglo-Saxon England mentions a Yorkshire excavation where a female skeleton, weighed down by a quern stone, had been thrown on top of a rich woman's coffin.[91] Life for the loaf-eaters and grinding women was probably very precarious.

Grinding and milling had apparently returned to a primitive Biblical sim-

87-D.Whitelock,ed. *English Historical Documents, (EHD) Vol.1 500-1042*
88-K.P.Witney (1976) *op.cit.*
89-Ibid.
90-EHD *Vol.1*
91-R.I.Page, *Life in Anglo-Saxon England. nd.*

plicity in England after the departure of the Romans. Release for the grinding women was not to come for several centuries. The manumission, or freeing, of slaves was a Christian obligation, but it was one to which many Christians turned blind eyes, as can be seen by the number of slaves still listed in Domesday Book. However, it becomes an increasing feature in late Anglo-Saxon wills that the testator frees his or her slaves 'for the love of God and the need of my soul'.

Christian Anglo-Saxon Kent

There is little written evidence of the early years of Anglo-Saxon England. Literacy only came back to Canterbury with Augustine's mission and his Christian scribes. As time went by, Ethelbert and his Christian successors endowed the new church with land, and religious foundations, such as Christ Church in Canterbury, became great landholders.

These endowed monastic foundations were not only rich in arable fields of corn, they were also the leaders of moral behaviour. If it was a Christian duty to free the grinding women, and if it was also an economically attractive thing to do, then the monks might start to build watermills. The Benedictine rule specified that 'the monastery should be so arranged that all necessary things, water, mill, garden....may be within the enclosure'. Watermill technology had never died out in continental Europe, but it is not until the late 8th century that the first documentary evidence of an Anglo-Saxon watermill appears.

The period after Ethelbert's death was a good time for the agricultural communities of the Darent Valley. Trade was expanding and London was well on its way to becoming 'the great emporium for many nations' described by Bede. Coins were minted again by the late 7th century. A hoard of a hundred golden shillings discovered in Hampshire is believed to have been the wergild of a Kentish ceorl.[92]

Although the Kingdom of Kent suffered many setbacks and a slow decline of power, the church in Canterbury never died out again. Archbishop Theodore of Tarsus, that 'aged scholar from Asia Minor',[93] arrived in Britain in 669 and set about a reorganization of the church. He also founded schools of Latin and Greek at Canterbury and introduced the 'age of the charters'. From now on there would be written evidence of the organisation of the county.

These written land charters were originally intended to confirm grants of land from the king to the religious communities. They were later used as land grants from the church to secular tenants whose lands would eventually become the '4manors' of Domesday Book. The charters often include land boundaries which hold many clues to the later landscape and are of the utmost importance to local history. Margaret Gelling, in *Signposts to the Past* gives examples of Anglo-Saxon boundaries which closely correspond to modern parish boundaries and suggests that it is reasonable to suppose that they were already of some antiquity when they were written down, which would put the later parish boundaries back into Roman and even pre-Roman times.[94]

92-K.P.Witney, *op.cit.* (1976)
93-F.M.Stenton, *Anglo-Saxon England,* (1971)
94-Margaret Gelling, *Anglo-Saxon Charters,* (1968)

Theodore united the church, held councils or synods and appointed new bishops, but the division of a bishop's diocese into parishes served by a parish priest was still in the future. A bishop had his seat in a 'head minster' or cathedral, from which he and his mass priests set out to preach and to baptise in the lesser churches, or 'ordinary minsters', or at simple field crosses. It is believed that places of pagan worship were often adopted by Christian priests as field churches. What could be more natural than to meet at the traditional boundary stone or oak tree, and what more useful for baptism that the sacred river or well. The pagan festivals were also often adopted by the Christians. Christmas came at the winter solstice, or Yule. The goddess Eostre gave her name to Easter, and of course some of the days of the week remained dedicated to the gods Tiw, Frig, Thunor and Woden.

The end of the Kingdom of Kent

The last king of Kent, Ethelbert II, died in 762. By 774 King Offa of Mercia was calling himself Rex Anglorum, as England was now known. In 776 there was a last wave of resistance by the Kentishmen at the Battle of Otford but by 785 the charters show that Offa had annexed Kent and was rewarding his thegns with lands in his new province.

The earliest Kentish mill charter was made by Ethelbert II shortly before his death and is a grant made in 762 by himself to the Minster of St Peter and St Paul at Canterbury, in which the Canterbury community of monks were to give the use of half a mill at Chart to the royal ville at Wye in exchange for the right of the miller to pannage a herd of swine in the Weald 'for ever'.[95] This is the first English miller to emerge as a real person, neither a slave, nor a god, nor a giant. An ordinary independent Kentish man with his own herd of pigs. He is a tenant miller, a ceorl no doubt, who is neither a slave nor a tied farm servant, the forerunner of the free medieval tenant millers. It is also interesting in relation to the Kentish custom of woodpasture for swine in the Weald and, lastly, perhaps tying up with the later Saxon ownership of 'half-mills', frequently recorded in the Domesday Book.

Offa, the new ruler, 'a name to conjure with', is remembered mainly for his Dyke, the boundary earthwork between England and Wales. Stenton calls him 'the first English king to play an independent part in Continental affairs', an early diplomat, capable of dealing on equal terms with Charlemagne of the Franks.[96] He is also of some interest to the history of milling. One of the few 8th century watermills to have been excavated is at the site of Offa's royal court at Tamworth in central Mercia.

Curiously, this mill had one of the more primitive horizontal 'Norse' water-wheels, although it was apparently constructed with a high degree of craftsmanship. It seems to have been a two storey building with window glass and a main mill bearing of steel.[97] Michael Wood, in *In Search of the Dark Ages*, questions whether the fragments of imported lava mill stones discovered on

95–P.H.Sawyer, *Anglo-Saxon Charters*, (1968)
96–F.M.Stenton, (1971) op.cit.
97–P.A.Rahtz, *Medieval Milling, Council for British Archaeology Research Report No.40* (1981)

the site might be part of those referred to in a letter from Charlemagne to Offa in which he says 'As for the black stones which your reverence begged to be sent to you, let a messenger come and consider what kind you have in mind, and we will willingly order them to be given over, wherever they are to be found, and will help with their transport'[98][99]

Offa was succeeded by Cenwulf who crushed the last feeble rebellion of the Britons in Kent, and 'mightily devastated' the province with 'a grievous pillaging almost to its utter destruction'.[100] No doubt these were bad days for the inhabitants of the Darent valley. Cenwulf continued Offa's practice of giving or selling grants of land in Kent to his thegns. These lands, formerly the royal inlands, became known as booklands, or lands granted by charter, as opposed to the folklands of the free tenants which were held and inherited by the Kentish law or custom known as gavelkind.

The Charters

During the time of Cenwulf's successor, Ceolwulf, a strong new archbishop, Wulfred, began to buy back lands in Kent from the crown, both for himself and for Christ Church, Canterbury. By the time of Domesday nearly a third of all the lands in Kent would belong to the archbishop or to the Christ Church community. An interesting charter was made in 822 between Ceolwulf and Wulfred in which the king granted the archbishop five ploughlands at Mylentun near Kemsing. Keith Witney describes this land as the nucleus of the great manor of Otford.[101] The name Mylentun means mill settlement, 'mylen' being the Saxon word for mill.

In the charter Ceolwulf gives the land, 'so devoutly,...chiefly for the love of Almighty God and for the venerable...pontiff...and also for his acceptable money'. The estate comes with the usual rights of 'fields, woods, pastures, meadows and rivers'. This is the formula generally used in the early charters but now, in the 9th century, includes 'mills' as well as 'fisheries, fowling and hunting grounds'. As is also customary in grants of bookland, the estate is freed of all servitude 'from entertainment of king, bishop, earldormen or reeves, tax-gatherers, keepers of dogs, horses and hawks'. The only services demanded, and again this is a usual formula, are the three public duties of 'military service against pagan enemies, the construction of bridges and the fortification or destruction of fortresses'.

The most interesting part of the charter is the description of the boundaries which would have been walked by some, though surely not all, the witnesses. The signatures include the king and the archbishop, four bishops, six earldormen and five, presumably local, other men. People were expected to know their territory and its boundaries intimately. The bounds are a most important part of a Saxon charter. The natural features often include such lost landmarks as 'the crab apple tree', 'the wolf's pit', 'the stone ford', 'the muddy torrent' and the 'wild garlic wood', as well as the local hamlets, fields and woods.

98-M.Wood,
In Search of the Dark Ages,
(1981)
99-D.Wilson,
The Anglo-Saxons, (1972)
R.Holt, *op.cit. (1988)*
100-EHD *Vol.1*
101-K.Witney, (1982)

In this charter the lands are described by boundaries such as the Darent river, Shoreham, Kemsing and the great wood of 'Andred' or the Weald in the south. 'Also, in Andred, food and pasture for swine, cattle or goats'. In D. Clarke and A. Stoyel's history of Otford they give an account of present day hedge-dating on the Otford/Shoreham borders which appears to identify the vestiges of some of these boundaries.[102] The Sevenoaks historian Dr. Gordon Ward identified the Mylentun of the charter with a field south of Shoreham known in 1305 as Meleton, and in 1840 as Milton Mead.[103] One thing that is clear from these charters is that by the early 9th century there were several watermills on the Darent. Two hundred and fifty years later, at the time of Domesday, there were to be at least thirty.

The agricultural estates that were now beginning to be defined along the valley, fall roughly speaking, into three parts; 'demesne', 'inland' and 'outland'. Demesne was the king's, and later the lord's, own land around their courts. The occupiers of the inland were tenants who were tied to their lord and the land by service. The outlands were occupied by the free ceorls, who paid for their land with rent and some obligatory service, but held it by the peculiarly Kentish custom of 'gavelkind', and were free to sell or lease their property and to leave it at their death in equal shares between their sons or daughters. Their lands were known as gavellands.

The origin of this custom of partible inheritance, the 'Custom of Kent' as it became known, is obscure. It was once presumed to be peculiarly Jutish but may have been prevalent in many parts of Celtic Britain. This, and the practice of transhumance, had the effect on the countryside of the predominantly scattered settlements of pastoral people.

Although outland was often outlying land, and inland was grouped near the demesne, both in fact are often interwoven on any one estate and were legal terms of tenure, unrelated to topography. Another puzzling legal term is the Kentish unit of land known as the 'sulung' which was to become a very important feature of the Farningham entries in Domesday Book. The word is derived from the Saxon 'suhl' or plough, so sulung and ploughland say the same thing, but the legal definition of sulung may mean something different. At first the sulung apparently meant sufficient land to be ploughed by a team of eight oxen. In the same way a 'yoke' meant a quarter of a sulung, or land for a single yoke of two oxen. 'Yoke' had been a Roman land measurement, the 'jugera', intended to provide subsistence for one man.[104] The legal definition of sulung for purposes of taxation came to mean an area of roughly 160-200 acres, depending on the quality of the land. In time sulung also became a definition of gavelland or outland, and 'yokeland' was often used to describe a small independent farm.[105] The ceorls of the outland sulungs were the original free Kentish farmers, descendants of those warrior husbandmen buried at Charton and forerunners of the rich Kentish yeoman.

The last years of Anglo-Saxon rule in Kent saw a steady increase in the numbers of watermills mentioned in the charters, although there is little archaeo-

102-Dennis Clarke & Anthony Stoyel, *Otford in Kent*, (1975)
103-Gordon Ward, *The Making of the Great Park at Otford*, Arxh Cant, XKI (1929)
104-Cambridge Ancient History, *Vol.XII* (1939)
105-K.P.Witney, *Kentish Land Measurements of the 13th Century*, Arch Cant (1991)

-logical evidence of them in the Darent Valley. It can only be assumed that, as the new settlements grew beside the earliest churches in the river valley where they remain today, evidence of the earliest buildings have been buried under today's village.

Vikings

The first Viking raids on England took place in the late 8th century but did not affect Kent until the 830s when, according to the *Anglo-Saxon Chronicle*, 'Heathen men ravaged Sheppey'. For the next century and a half, the Kentish countryside would suffer from random raids by the Norsemen. The clause in the Mylentun charter of 822 referring to military service against the heathen enemy, and fortification or destruction of fortresses, meant that local men could be called up to fight and to work on the network of defences set up across the country. Much later, after a treaty concluded by Alfred the Great, the Vikings would be, more or less, confined to the north-eastern territories to be known as the 'Danelaw'.

The story of Alfred and the cakes is a little sub-plot in the history of milling. The king was said to be sheltering incognito in a peasant's hut near Chichester during one of his campaigns against the Danes. The peasant, a cowherd's wife, was making bread, not cakes and the king, left in charge but with his mind on other things, allowed the loaves to burn. As a cowherd the peasant was probably paid with an occasional sack of corn which his wife might carry to the mill or grind herself at home with a quern.

Refined flour for cakes did exist, but surely not for cowherds and not in a time of war. According to Bede, the second month of the heathen year was called Solmonath, or the month of cakes. He also relates a story about three heathen princes, sons of a Christian king, who demanded the white bread kept for the mass from Mellitus, the first bishop of London. Mellitus told them 'If you will be washed in the waters of salvation, as your father was, you may share in the consecrated bread as he did, but so long as you reject the water of life you are quite unfit to receive the Bread of Life'.

In 886 Alfred occupied London and 'all the English people who were not subject to the Danes submitted to him'.[106] London now became one of his chief fortified burghs and a centre of trade. It was a boom town with wharves and a street plan still traceable between Cheapside and the Thames. Such an important market must have meant some short lived prosperity for the nearby Darent Valley.

Alfred's Laws give a useful picture of country life in the 9th and 10th centuries.[107] Life was not quite as harsh as we might imagine. All free men were to have holidays for the twelve days of Christmas; fourteen days at Easter; several saint's days; at All Saints and at harvest time. Even slaves had four days to sell anything they had been given or had made. Matters of crime and punishment however were severe. Witnesses to a crime had a duty to call out the 'hue and cry' for a citizen's arrest, then the fugitive would be brought before

106-F.M.Stenton, *(1971) op.cit.*

107-EHD, *Vol.1 op.cit.*

a public assembly, the 'folk moot', and justice would be dispensed by the ordeals of boiling water, burning iron or immersion in a river or pond.[108]

In the early 890s a great Danish invasion came through Kent and laid waste much of the county before retreating again to the Danelaw lands. Saxon kings followed kings in quick succession, culminating in the wretched Ethelred the Unready who was blamed for the vast increase in the custom of paying tribute to the Danes to get them to go away but, as Kipling was to say 'if once you have paid him the Danegeld, you never get rid of the Dane'

In 999 the Danish army 'came again round into the Thames and turned then up the Medway... and they then destroyed and ravaged almost all West Kent ...and went about as they pleased'.[109] Again, in 1006 'the great fleet came to Sandwich and did just as they were accustomed, ravaged, burnt and slew as they went', and again Ethelred negotiated for peace with tribute and provisions. It is hardly possible that life in the Darent Valley, so close to these terrible events, was not affected.

Alphege

1006 was the year that Bishop Aelfheah, or Alphege as he is more usually known, became Archbishop of Canterbury. He is responsible for the only two appearances of Farningham in the Anglo-Saxon charters. The first charter is a mid-11th century confirmation of lands in Farningham belonging to Christ Church, Canterbury. The second is part of a grant of land at Warehorne in Kent made by Archbishop Alphege to Christ Church in 1010, to which a note is added of a previous grant, 'in his days' of lands at Farningham and Wooton.[110]

The two charters are not complete or conclusive, but later sources certainly confirm that Archbishop Alphege gave land in Farningham to Christ Church, Canterbury some time before 1010. How he came to own the land is

Bishop Alphege from portraits of the Archbishops G.M.Bevan 1908 -from an illuminated manuscript in the British Museum

108–ibid
109–ibid
110–P.H.Sawyer, A.S.C. *op.cit.*

37

another question. Perhaps it was part of the Canterbury archbishop's Eynsford estate, and maybe he gave it to build a church here.[111] [112]

The possibility of Alphege building a church here actually seems unlikely. The gifts of land were to provide food rents for the community at Canterbury, not to build churches. That was usually the responsibility of some local thegn who might put up a small wooden church as he would build a watermill. Both brought in income. Some time before 1086 two churches were built at Farningham and Eynsford but we do not know exactly when or by whom.

The establishment of parishes is one of the most interesting items of local history. How did these scattered farms become organised into parishes and who decided the peculiarly shaped boundaries. Was it, as has already been suggested, a case of using the earliest boundaries of first the Celtic and then the Romano-British estates, already existing as named rivers, dykes, hedges, trees and stones.

The organization of a parochial system was beginning to be made in Edgar's time. His codes of law set out four classifications of churches. First came the head minsters or cathedrals. Canterbury and Rochester had been established in Augustine's time by Ethelbert I, who had also founded St Pauls in London. Second came the ordinary minsters, or mother churches, of a district. Third were the lesser churches with a graveyard, and fourth, the field churches without a graveyard, often wayside crosses or preaching places. A later category of church came with the manorial chapels, or churches built by private landlords for their domestic use.

Churches were being built all over the country and the church collected money from the people in various ways. Church Scot was the basic tax paid by all free men according to their means, often in grain or hens. Soul Scot was an offering made at the graveside. Plough Alms usually consisted of a penny for each plough team, paid at Easter, and every free man had to pay Peter's Pence, a penny due to the Pope in Rome on St Peter's day. The new, lesser churches, were probably first served by a visiting priest sent out by the mother church. Later, each church would need to maintain a single priest and he would be given a piece of glebe land to farm for himself. By the 10th century he would be entitled to receive tithe, the tax of a tenth of the produce of land in his parish.

The parishes were created by dividing the lands of the mother churches or ordinary minsters. In the Darent Valley these were at Dartford and Shoreham. Sometimes the secondary churches with graveyards had daughter churches of their own and it is Everitt's theory that Farningham was a parish carved out of an earlier parish at Eynsford and so was Eynsford's daughter church.

A source of evidence for an early church in Farningham is the *Textus Roffensis*, a collection of Rochester documents which contains a list of the chrism oils used for baptism due from churches in the diocese.[113] This list is believed to date from about 1077 and so is assumed to be a list of Anglo-Saxon churches. A church paid nine pence chrism dues and a chapel only six pence.

111-F.R.H.Du Boulay, *The Lordship of Canterbury*, (1966)
112-Colin Flight, *4 Vernacular Texts*, *Arch Cant.CXV*, (1995)
113-Dr Gordon Ward, *The List of Saxon Churches in the Textus Roffensis*, *Arch Cant,XLIV*, (1932)

As Farningham paid nine pence it can be assumed to have had a church at this date. There is no evidence of Anglo-Saxon stonework so maybe this was a small wooden church.

Alphege, the first named person in the history of Farningham, is believed to have been born in 954. He entered a monastery near Gloucester and later lived as an anchorite in a hut near Bath.[114] In 984 he became bishop of Winchester and in 1006 he was chosen as Archbishop of Canterbury. Apart from his later gift of land, there are no apparent connections with Farningham in his life. He was considered a good and holy man; legend said that he fasted so much that the sun shone through his hands when he held them up in celebration of the mass.[115]

Aelfric

A lively contemporary of Archbishop Alphege was Abbot Aelfric who was one of the few writers of Anglo-Saxon prose to give us some idea of the lives of ordinary people. His *Colloquies* were a series of imaginary conversations designed to teach Latin, the language of the church, to his pupils at his monastic school in Cerne Abbas.[116] [117] One dialogue is with a ploughman, another with a fisherman who says 'I catch eels and pike, minnows and burbots, trout and lampreys and whatever swims in the rushing stream'. He might be describing the Darent which would have known all these fish. The shepherd describes guarding his flocks 'lest wolves devour them', and milking them twice a day to make the cheese and butter. The shoemaker describes how he buys hides and skins for slippers and shoes, leggings and leather bottles, straps, halters, bags and purses. The fowler traps birds with nets, snares, lime or with a hawk or a trap or just by whistling. Unfortunately there is no dialogue with a miller although there is a rather lowly conversation with a cook. 'We don't need you' say the schoolboy monks. 'Then you will all be servants' replies the cook. And a baker tells them 'You cannot live long or well without my craft...I make people's hearts strong, I am the stamina of men'.

Aelfric was very conscious of the almost sacred nature of bread. He was also very familiar with watermills and, in one sermon, he said that 'the rotation of the heavens around the earth is swifter than any mill-wheel, and as deep under the sea as overhead'. The most important feast of the year was Lammas, or loaf-mass, on August 1st, when the first grain of the year was baked into a loaf and blessed in church. 'The ploughman feeds us all', said Aelfric, 'he gives us food and drink', meaning flour and barley for the everyday ale. His sermons dwell on the living Bread which came from heaven. 'Just as leaven changes substances...so sins change the nature of man...so do not feast on the leaven of corruption but on the unleavened loaves of sincerity and truth'. This ancient attitude to leaven, or yeast, continued through the centuries. Most Anglo-Saxon bread was tough and flat.

His sermon for Rogation week, the old magic festival of blessing the crops and praying for abundance, as well as beating the boundaries of the parish,

114–The Compact Edition of the Dictionary of National Biography, (1975)
115–Dr Gordon Ward, Arch Cant. LXIX, (1953) The Witan meets at Canterbury
116–Kevin Crossley-Holland, The Anglo-Saxon World, (1982)
117–M.Swanton trans. Anglo-Saxon Prose, (1993)

tells the congregation to pray for 'the Three Loaves' of faith in the Holy Trinity. 'Then you have food for your soul....What father would give his child a stone if he asked for bread. Bread signifies true love'.

In 1009 a Viking army again attacked Kent and were again paid off. In September 1011 they besieged Canterbury and took archbishop Alphege captive back to their ships where, according to a contemporary chronicler, they 'ill treated him with chains and hunger and indescribable torments after their abominable custom'.[118] Six months later the Danish fleet lay off Greenwich with Alphege still on board ship and in chains. They received £48,000 Danegeld as the price of their departure, but they also expected a separate ransom for the archbishop. Alphege refused to allow the ransom to be paid, he said the people had been taxed enough, and offered his own body as the only payment. The Danes brought him ashore to their drunken feast where they violently abused and eventually killed him. St Alphege's church in Greenwich is believed to have been built over the place of his martyrdom.

In 1014 Canute became leader of the Danish army and after many broken treaties and much warfare including a battle at Otford in 1016, he became the first Danish king of England. The agricultural communities of the Darent Valley, so close to the siege of London and the battle of Otford, would undoubtedly have been devastated. Taxes for Danegeld and repeated raids for food and livestock must have made life unendurable. The price of peace by subjugation to a Danish king might have been quite welcome.

The nineteen years of Canute's rule saw the strange translation of a barbaric young Viking into a Christian king and statesman. He strengthened an alliance with the Normans by marrying Ethelred's widow, Emma of Normandy, that powerful lady who was not only to be wife of two English kings but mother of two more, and was the pivotal point between Anglo-Saxon and Norman England.

Status

Anglo-Saxon society appears to have been fairly fluid. In 'a compilation on status' of about 1003-23, it was said that it was possible for a ceorl to prosper and become entitled to the rights of a thegn if he had enough land and had 'a belltower and a castlegate'.[119] Even slaves had upward mobility. King Canute's harsh laws of 1018-20, which included cutting off ears, noses and hands of felons, said that if a master forced his slave to work on a feast day then the slave could go free.

A text known as the *Rectitudines* or Rights and Ranks of People, gives the rights and dues of all sections of society on an agricultural estate such as might have existed in Farningham.[120] These ranged from the duties of the lord himself, for military service and hospitality to travellers, down through the various classes of peasant and the degrees of customary work and tributes they were expected to provide for their lord and he for them.[121]

Everyone is included, down through the sowers and reapers, herdsmen,

118-Thietmar of Mersberg, *Eng.Hist.Docs. Vol.1*
119-ibid.
120-D.C.Douglas & G.W.Greenaway eds. E.H.D. *Vol.2, (1953)*
121-H.R.Loyn, *Anglo-Saxon England, (1962)*

herdsmen, woodwards, shepherds, beekeepers, cheesemakers. Everyone paid their dues of rent or service and everyone received their dues such as the swineherd, who was owed six loaves from every member of his community when he set off for the swine denns. Dues of corn and beans, whey and buttermilk, shoes and gloves. Even the lowest female slave was to have corn and beans and a sheep for winter supplies.

All estate customs would differ but everyone would have the obligatory holidays and feasts at Christmas and Easter, ploughing, reaping and harvesting. It is not remotely likely that the four modest farms listed in Farningham at Domesday, would have employed more than a very few of these classes of peasant but some of the thirty or so peasant families living here at Domesday would have approximated to these descriptions.

A companion document was the *Gerefa*, or the duties of the Reeve, or manager, of the estate.[122] The reeve was chosen each year by the community and he was expected to know and be able to perform all the duties of the other peasants 'In the manor, on the downs, in the moors, in the water, in field and fold, indoors and out', and significantly, one of his tasks was to be able to construct a water-mill and a fish weir.[123] The fact that he was also expected to be able to make a vineyard indicates the continuing warmth of the climate.

The end of the era

In 1023 the bones of archbishop Alphege were ceremoniously removed from London to Canterbury in the presence of King Canute, the Archbishop, Queen Emma and the royal child Hardacnut. Alphege was later confirmed a saint of the church by the Norman Archbishop Lanfranc. When Canute's line of sons had died Emma's exiled son by Ethelred, Edward the Confessor, was brought back from Normandy as king, and married to the daughter of the dreadful Earl Godwin of Kent. While the devout Edward occupied himself with his new abbey at Westminster, Godwin and his sons, Harold and Tostig, virtually ruled the land.

The Bayeux Tapestry
Harold is crowned King

When Edward died in January 1066 Harold seized the throne. He is shown on the Bayeux Tapestry, orb and sceptre held high and surrounded by omens of ill luck, no doubt because it was known that he had sworn support to William of Normandy who had been

Edward's favoured successor. In April Halley's comet appeared in the sky for seven days, a sign interpreted as impending retribution. Sure enough Duke William was gathering his invasion forces across the channel, and on the morning of October 14th 1066 the Battle of Hastings took place. Harold was killed and on Christmas Day William was crowned king at Westminster Abbey.

122-Robert Lacey &
Danny Nanziger,
The Year 1000, (1999)
123-M.Swanton trans.
Anglo-Saxon Prose, (1993)

41

Chapter Three

The Normans and Domesday Book / The Four Domesday Manors in Farningham / Ernulf de Hesdin / Dering of Farningham Mill / Charton Manor / Wadard / Wadard's Mill / The Village Mill / FitzHelte and the de Cheritons / The Church / Tithe / Gavelkind or Partible Inheritance / The Village / William FitzHelte's Mill / John Scot.

Nearly twenty years later King William spent Christmas with his councillors and held exhaustive discussions. 'Then he sent his men all over England into every shire to ascertain.....what or how much each man who was a land-holder here in England had in land or in livestock, and how much money it was worth'[124]

The commissioners were to ask the name of the place, the past and present landholders, the acreage, the ploughs of both lords and men, the amount of woodland, meadow, pasture, mills and fishponds, and the total value both in 1066 in the time of King Edward and now, in 1085. The indignant chronicler adds 'so very thoroughly did he have the inquiry carried out...it is shameful to record it...not even one ox, nor cow, nor one pig...escaped notice'. The result of the enquiry was the Domesday Book.

The commissioners took evidence first from the county Sheriffs, or the Shire Reeves. The Sheriff was the direct agent of the king, responsible to him alone for the financial and judicial government of the county. The Sheriff would preside over the shire courts which were held twice a year. The Normans were preserving much of the Saxon organization of the county and the shires as administrative districts had come into being before the Conquest. In Kent the shire was sub-divided into lathes and the lathes into hundreds. The lathes, as already seen, were the primary administrative divisions of local government.

The hundreds appear to have been created by the Anglo-Saxons in the 10th century and were the smaller units of secular administration. They may have originated as a gathering from every hundred sulungs and are believed to have developed from the earlier assemblies known as folk-moots. The smallest official group was the 'tithing'. From the time of Canute every free male over the age of 12 was supposed to belong to a tithing, a group of 12 men with one senior tithing man, although in Kent these were called borghs and the senior man a borghsaldre or borsholder. The Hundred courts were held every four weeks and provided a link between the shire court and the village tithing. In the early days the meeting places were often in the open 'under the Hundred Tree', or 'at the Hundred Stone'. Domesday Farningham was described as being in the half-lathe of Sutton and the hundred of Axstane.

To visualise Farningham at the time of the Norman Conquest it is necessary to think of four small hamlets, each described as 'Farningham' in

124–*Anglo-Saxon Chronicle.* EHD *Vol.1*
125 J.E.A.Joliffe,
Pre-Feudal England, the Jutes, (1933)

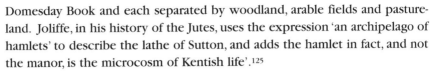

The Domesday Manors

1. Pedham Place?
2. Farningham, in
   market meadow.
3. Franks (Wadard)?
4. Charton
5. Chimhams

● *General location of
Charton Manor Chapel
(later text refers)*

Domesday Book and each separated by woodland, arable fields and pasture-land. Joliffe, in his history of the Jutes, uses the expression 'an archipelago of hamlets' to describe the lathe of Sutton, and adds the hamlet in fact, and not the manor, is the microcosm of Kentish life'.[125]

The north-west downland of the parish was undoubtedly still heavily wooded. Farningham Woods, Birchwood and Joydens Wood were probably continuous woodland, broken only by small pioneer settlements with clearings for animal pasture. It must be remembered that this was 'managed woodland', not primeval forest, meaning that it had been used for many centuries for timber, coppice, firewood and charcoal. Even so, this part of Farningham was still dense woodland and, as late as the 18th century, was haunted by robbers and highwaymen. Many small woods in the parish such as Swanton, Brushes, Oat-Ash, Wested, Longlands, Alchin's, Gabriellspring and Ram's Wood, all relics of this greater woodland, were still here in the 20th century.

The road through the village was still only a road in the sense of a 'ride' linking one settlement with another. The King's Highway already existed, but only as a right of way.[126] Although this route was later a road to Folkestone and the Continent, the Dover Road was always the important artery through Kent. Maidstone was not yet a town of any great significance and, even in the 18th century, it was quite usual to make the journey there from London by way of Rochester.

The four Domesday 'Manors' in Farningham

One of the four Farningham hamlets or farms was probably in the wooded north-west outpost of the parish, but its exact location is not known for certain. This Domesday farm was very small, with just one family, and was held in 1085 by a Norman known as Malgar of Ruxley who also held land at Ruxley and Lullingstone. The abrieviated Domesday entry reads 'Malgar holds half a yoke of land in Ferlingeham. Land for 3 oxen. 2 oxen with 1 bordar (or smallholder). Meadow 2 acres. Value 15s. Brown's son held it and could go where he would with his land'.[127] The last expression meant that Brown had been a freeman, tied to no overlord, and had been able to give away or sell his land and go to whichever overlord he chose for allegiance and protection. (These rough translations have been adapted from John Morris's *Domesday Book, Kent*).

The two most likely places for Malgar's farm are Pedham Place and Pedham Court, both still situated near today's Swanley roundabout. Pedham was the name of a later medieval manor, inhabited by a family called de Pethim. 'Court' being the usual name of a place where a manor court was held makes this the more probable original site, especially as it is the nearer to Ruxley where Malger held another manor. The Saxon called Brown's son, who had held the farm before the Conquest, may indeed have been the one recorded

126–S.& B.Webb,
*The Story of the King's
Highway*, (1913)
127–John Morris, ed.
The Domesday Book, Kent,
(1983)

43

smallholder now working for Malgar. Integration of the native population was considered important.[128]

Malgar's overlord, the tenant-in-chief, was Odo, Bishop of Bayeux, a great landholder who had been created Earl of Kent by his half-brother the King. Odo in fact was in disgrace and in exile but Domesday Book still credited him with lands in 16 counties.

Domesday is a notoriously difficult text to understand. The tenants-in-chief are given, and the sub-tenants past and present, but there is often no indication of whether the landlord lived on his property, or whether there was a church and a priest, let alone a miller. The number of villagers are given, but perhaps as a commodity like the oxen. They are categorised according to their value, villeins, bordars, cottars and slaves. Only the working men are listed, no women and children, so all villagers except slaves are assumed to have had families. All that really mattered to the commissioners was the value of the property, past, present and potential.

In theory only the king owned land, everybody else 'held' their property in return for certain obligations. Norman England was a military society, a chessboard of knights and bishops and castles, all geared for war, and the tenants-in-chief held by military duties or 'knight's service'[129]. This was the new feudalism. The actual word 'feudum' had not been used in England before 1066 and meant land held in feud, fee or fief under specific conditions. Knight's service would later be commuted to payments of 'scutage', or shield money.

Knights were the county aristocracy. They were created with ceremony and had ceremonial rights such as the heraldic devices by which they could be identified in battle or in tournaments. They also had the right to an equestrian seal to authenticate their documents. But holders of knight's fees were not neccessarily knights. Smaller tenants could hold fees and owed taxes and services to their overlords.

The chief landholders in Kent were the king himself, with large estates including Dartford; the tenants-in-chief, who included the Archbishop of Canterbury, his monks and his own men-at-arms; Odo, the Bishop of Bayeux; the Bishop of Rochester; the great abbeys, and a few Norman lords. Holdings were described by the Norman term 'manerium', or manor, and 'dominium' or demesne, meaning the lord's inland or home-farm.

Land in Kent was still measured in sulungs and yokes, a sulung still being roughly equivalent to between 160 and 200 acres, and a yoke being quarter of a sulung. These, as before, were nominal measurements for the purpose of taxation and could range in size according to the quality of the land.

Another of the Domesday settlements in Farningham was undoubtedly on the site of the present day village. A church is not recorded here in Domesday Book, but churches often failed to be entered and, as we have seen, a church had been listed here in the earlier Textus Roffensis. The mill however was certainly entered in Domesday Book, as was another half-mill, most probably

128–R. Weldon Finn, *Domesday Book, a Guide* *(1973)*
129–F. Stenton, *Anglo-Saxon England, op.cit.*

shared down at the parish border with the half-mill of Horton Kirby.

This village hamlet, with church and mill probably sited where they are today, supported at least five families. The tenant-in-chief also was Odo, Bishop of Bayeux and his sub-tenant was Ernulf of Hesdin. The abbreviated text reads 'Ernulf of Hesdin holds Ferningeham. There are 3 yokes. Land for 2 ploughs. Now 6 oxen, with 2 villagers and 3 smallholders. A mill at 10s; meadow 8 acres; pasture, 100 sheep; woodland 10 pigs. The value of the whole manor was £3 and is now 40s. Dering held it and could go where he would'.

The expressions 'villagers' and 'smallholders' and 'cottagers' have been chosen by John Morris, editor of the 1983 Phillimore edition of the Domesday Book for Kent, as the 'nearest ordinary modern English' equivalents of the earlier translations of 'villeins, bordars and cottars'. A villager, (villein or member of a ville), usually had more land than a bordarius, or smallholder, and a cottager, would usually only have a garden plot.

So here were 2 villagers that we can assume to have been fairly well to do free men, and three smallholders. None of them were as well off now as they had been before the Conquest and they only had 6 oxen, or one and a half plough teams to cultivate 3 yokes of land. Pigs were valued for tax at one in ten so there were at least 100 pigs up in the woods. The 100 sheep are interesting because sheep are only listed four times in the Kent Domesday Book; another flock was also held by Ernulf of Hesdin in Cliffe. It is surprising that so few are listed because we know that sheep were a great commodity in Saxon England, kept on the marshes at such places as Sheppey, 'Island of Sheep'. A hundred sheep were said to add £1 p.a. to the profit of a farm and English woollen cloth had been valued in Europe for centuries. Sheep must have been found everywhere because the list of a reeve's duties in the *Gerefa* included sheep-shearing.

Ernulf de Hesdin

Ernulf, the Domesday landlord of Farningham village Mill, came from Hesdin in the Pas de Calais. One of his larger Kentish estates was at Chelsfield, and Hasted even called him Ernulf of Chelsfield and believed that the medieval Chelsfield family descended from him. Hasted is not often wrong but this has not been confirmed. In Oxfordshire he is known as Ernulf de Hesdin of Chipping Norton. According to R. Lennard, Ernulf was tenant-in-chief in ten counties but his main residence was at Chipping Norton where the remains of his castle can be seen behind the church.[130] He was reputed to have been a caring landlord whose estates flourished under his personal management.

William of Malmesbury, a contemporary historian, said that he was 'remarkable alike for his skill in agriculture and his bounty to the church and to the poor'. There is a story that if a barn was filled with corn that had not been tithed, he would order it to be turned out and tithed without delay. Of course, a third of the tithe went to the landlord, and Lennard adds the

130-R.Lennard, *Rural England 1086-1183*, (1959)

45

suggestion that the gains in value of some of Ernulf's properties, such as Chelsfield, ('worth £16 before 1066'... and now £35), were the fruits of extortion rather than prudent husbandry. Lennard goes on to say that Ernulf was wrongly accused in the rebellion of 1095 and was so mortified that he abandoned his English estates and went on Crusade, where he died at Antioch. The *Calendar of Documents in France* says tantalisingly that Ernulf 'remains one of the most mysterious personages in Domesday', and that his heirs were his son William and daughter Avelina.

In Farningham we can afford to think the best of Ernulf. There is no sign of extortion in a manor which was worth £3 in Dering's time but by Domesday had dwindled to 40s. even with the valuable sheep. The description of his Farningham estate holds few clues to the site. No demesne, or home farm, is mentioned which makes one wonder whether the five families who had probably held their land first from Dering and then from Ernulf, were left much to their own devices by the absentee landlord.

Dering of Farningham Mill

Ernulf of Hesdin was a great Norman landholder, tenant-in-chief in ten counties, but the disposessed Saxon owner of this manor, Dering, is of greater interest to this history because he is the first named owner of Farningham Mill. One other Dering, 'son of Sired' is mentioned in Domesday, with a small holding of land at Deal. We do not know whether they were both the same man.

A Sired is listed as a canon of St Martin's of Dover and a Sired, possibly the same man, was a witness in about 1020 to a charter of land at Surrenden, the later home of the Derings. A 'Sired the Old' is also reported at the ceremonies held when St Alphege's body was removed to Canterbury in 1023. Robert Furley, in 1871, said that the Dering family of Surrenden Dering 'claim to be the only one in England...who have retained their unbroken descent in the male line from the time of Harold to the present day'.[131] Unfortunately this claim was said by Philip Blake in 1993 to be 'self deception' by the 17th century family historian Sir Edward Dering.[132] Other Derings existed in Kent in Saxon times according to Furley who gives two examples. A.J. Robertson in *Anglo-Saxon Charters* claims that Dering, son of Sired, was slain at the Battle of Hastings but gives no source for this information.

Hasted, some of whose information came from the suspect historian Sir Edward Dering, says that a Norman FitzDering was Sheriff of Kent after William of Eynsford, in about 1130-40 and that his wife was Matilda, sister of William de Ypres who founded Boxley Abbey. This is interesting in the light of later connections between Farningham and Boxley Abbey.

1158-1180
Henry II penny - Cross and Croslet coinage often referred to as the 'Tealby' coinage - King holding sceptre. Badly bent when found.

Courtesy of Geoff Burr

131-R.Furley, *History of the Weald of Kent*, (1871)
132-Philip Blake, *The Early Derings, Arch Cant CXII (1993)*

Furley reports a slightly different story in which Norman FitzDering was married to Blithildis, daughter and heir of William de Ypres, and he adds that their son, Dering FitzNorman saved the life of King Stephen at Lincoln for which he augmented his coat of arms with three drops of blood. Unfortunately Furley gives no source for his information. Hasted also says that 'Wimond FitzDering and his wife Levote gave 25 acres of land and wood and 3 houses in Farningham to Boxley Abbey in about the year 1200'. He gives as reference a text by Sir Edward Dering in the British Museum.[133]

Without more evidence it seems safe to say that Dering was a small Anglo-Saxon thegn, probably from an East Kent family and possibly connected with Canterbury, who may have built the first recorded church and mill here. It seems probable that he was killed at the time of the Conquest and it is more than possible that his wife and children kept a foothold here. Women, who had enjoyed a certain amount of freedom and power in Anglo-Saxon England, were now in the king's gift for remarriage and their under-age children were sold into wardship, but a son's property should have eventually come back to him. All we can say for certain is that a Saxon called Dering held Farningham Mill in 1066 and a Norman called Ernulf of Hesdin held it in 1085.

Charton Manor

There was a third, much larger, hamlet at Charton as it came to be called, on the downland to the east of the village towards Brands Hatch. The Charton Manor Nursing Home now occupies this site. Here, the tenant-in-chief was Lanfranc, the new Norman Archbishop of Canterbury, and this manor is most likely to have been the one associated earlier with St Alphege. The property is clearly documented in the archives of Canterbury Cathedral and Lambeth Palace.

It is described in Domesday Book as the holding of one of the archbishop's knights, Ansgot of Rochester. No previous Saxon tenant of this large farm is mentioned so it can be assumed that it had belonged to the Canterbury archbishops in the past. The settlement supported 18 families, 13 villagers and 5 smallholders. An abbreviated translation of the Domesday entry reads 'Ansgot holds Forningeham from the Archbishop. There is one sulung. In demesne 2 ploughs, and 13 villagers with 5 smallholders who have three and a half ploughs. Meadow, 6 acres; woodland, 20 pigs. Richard of Tonbridge has as much of the same woodland in his territory. Value of the manor before 1066, £7; now £11; of these the monks of Canterbury have £4 for their clothing'.

The demesne would be Ansgot's own inland, farmed for him by his five tied peasants. It is unlikely that this was his main residence, he held several other

133-BM. add mss 5481 larger estates including Aldington in Thurnham. The 13 free villagers possibly

The 13 free villagers possibly held their gavellands, or lands held by the Kentish system of gavelkind, on the poorer land to the east near Gabrielspring Wood, or Gavill-Land-Spring as it was called in the 18th century ('spring' being coppiced woodland). The manor was near the site of the early pagan Saxon cemetery. The woodland of Gabrielspring may have extended to Boxwood in Horton Kirby, and the woodland of Richard of Tonbridge would have been the swine denns of the Hollanden common near Leigh.

The final clause of the Domesday entry makes it easy to trace the later history of this manor and to identify at as Charton because the records of Canterbury Priory show that the monks continued to receive their rent for clothes from the lords of Charton until the dissolution of the monasteries. Monks needed a lot of clothing. In one year in the 13th century the monks of Canterbury Cathedral Priory puchased 250 ells of black cloth for £30, also grey cloth for drawers and linen cloth for undershirts.[134] The monk wardens visited their farms twice yearly to check efficiency and to collect their rents. In *The Lordship of Canterbury* F. R. H. Du Boulay traces the history of these manors of the monks.[135] He also identifies the Archbishop's knights such as Ansgot and says that these were sixty knights enfeoffed by Archbishop Lanfranc for the king out of the Canterbury estates, although it would soon be considered more suitable for the church to pay the crown nominal 'knight's fees'.

Bayeux Tapestry "Here is Wadard"

Wadard

The fourth Farningham farm was held by Wadard, a Norman knight who is actually named and depicted on the Bayeux Tapestry. He has been adopted as the patron of Farningham and copies of his portrait in wrought iron have been made for the village sign and the Village Hall weathervane. His holding was half a sulung of arable land. There was 'land for 3 ploughs in demesne, with one villager, 2 cottagers and 5 slaves. Half a mill at 5s. 4 acres meadow; woodland for 5 pigs'. He also held half a sulung in Maplescombe and had many other properties in Kent and in other counties. The value of the manor had been £4 and was now £6. The Saxon owner had been Alstan who also held land in Maplescombe.

134-R.A.L.Smith, *Canterbury Cathedral Priory,* (1943)
135-F.R.H.Du Boulay, *The Lordship of Canterbury,* (1966)

48

These were the only slaves recorded in Farningham, possibly prisoners of war. Wadard had played an active part in the Battle of Hastings, commandeering food for the troops so maybe he helped himself to some slave labour at the same time. Slaves would mostly be freed during the next century, only to become tied servants or serfs in the next.

Several half-mills are recorded in Domesday Book. They are thought to have been one mill shared by two owners, often at a parish border, or possibly two sets of mill stones, or maybe, as was the case with the Saxon mill at Chart, the mill profits were shared between two tenants. In this case it seems most likely that Wadard shared a mill at the parish border with Ansketel of Ros, another large landholder, who had a half mill at Horton Kirby.

Wadard's Mill

There have been many discussions about the location of Wadard's demesne farm. A later medieval manor at Chimhams, on the downland near Charton, would also have been associated with Wadard's neighbouring holding at Maplescombe, so that is a possibility, but it is not near the river. A stronger possibility is a farm on the river at the Horton Kirby border which later became the manor of Franks. In the middle ages this manor was known as 'Little Farningham'.

The river once divided here, suggesting a lost mill leat very close to the site of the earlier Franks Roman villa. Calfstock Lane, which is the traditional parish boundary between Farningham and Horton Kirby, would have run down to a river crossing at this spot before the lane was diverted to skirt the later site of Franks Hall. It does not seem too far fetched to suggest that the Roman villa once had a watermill here and that Wadard and de Ros shared a mill at the same site.

The annual value of Ernulf de Hesdin's mill was 10s. and Wadard's half mill 5s. There were about thirty Domesday mills along the Darent and their annual values ranged from 5s. to 25s. Lullingstone had a mill worth 15s. which also gave a rent of 150 eels. Eynsford had two mills valued together at 40s, but this may have meant two sets of millstones under one roof. From their valuation it would appear that all these were vertical waterwheels. Horizontal mills or animal or slave mills would have had a lower value, and windmills were not recorded in England until a century later.

The tenant-in-chief of three of these Farningham manors was Odo, Bishop of Bayeux. Wadard had fought at his side at the Battle of Hastings and had been rewarded by his mentor with lands in several counties, many of them in Oxfordshire. Odo himself had been rewarded by his half brother, the king, with many rich Kentish estates. His stronghold was Dover Castle, known Hasted says, as 'the lock and key of the kingdom'. Bishop Odo is believed to have commissioned the Bayeux Tapestry, which was most probably worked by the sewing women of Canterbury where there was a famous school for decorative embroidery. Odo himself, a warrior bishop, is depicted in the heat of battle, wielding a club and 'encouraging his boys'.

Although in fact Odo was in prison in 1086, Domesday Book still treats him as a tenant-in-chief even though his lands had reverted to the crown. He had been arrested and imprisoned in 1082 on suspicion of having organized a private army for an expedition to Rome in an attempt to obtain the papacy. He was only released at William's death in 1087 and restored to his Earldom of Kent, when he almost immediately raised an unsuccessful rebellion after which he was banished for ever in 1089.

Wadard appears on the Tapestry simply labelled 'here is Wadard', so perhaps he was too well known to need explanation. He is shown

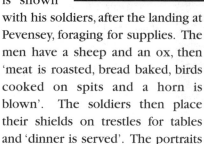

with his soldiers, after the landing at Pevensey, foraging for supplies. The men have a sheep and an ox, then 'meat is roasted, bread baked, birds cooked on spits and a horn is blown'. The soldiers then place their shields on trestles for tables and 'dinner is served'. The portraits are stereotyped although Wadard's face is surpri-singly realistic with hooded eyes and plump cheeks. Like all the Normans he is bullet headed and clean shaven while the Englishmen all have long hair and drooping moustaches. He is wearing a chain mail suit and, as befits a quartermaster, is very stout.

Wadard featured on the Farningham Millenium Village Sign, and on the weather-vane to the Village Hall, 1938

FitzHelte and the de Cheritons

To return to Ansgot's large manor at Charton. DuBoulay and others have followed the descent of Ansgot's estates to the family of FitzHelte, who were in turn succeeded by the family of de Cheriton, from Cheriton near Folkestone and gave the Farningham manor their name in the late 12th century. This manor had no mill at Domesday but had acquired one by 1143 when Ansgot's successor William FitzHelte gave a mill in Farningham to Bermondsey Abbey. William, at the same time, gave the Abbey 'Monkyn Lands' in Horton Kirby. This makes one think that the mill given to the Abbey was perhaps Wadard's half-mill at the Horton Kirby, Franks site. It is unlikely to have been a wind-mill as the first in Kent date from the 1190s and none are recorded in Farningham until the 19th century.[136] On the other hand of course it is

136–R. Holt *op.cit.*

Extract from a 19th facsimile edition of Domesday Book. Note Wadard and Enulf de Hesdin.

uertere cu tra sua quo uoluit.

Wadard ten de epo dimid solin in ferningeha. tra e iii car. In dnio sunt ii car. cu uno uillo 7 ii cot. 7 v seruis. Ibi dimid molds de v solins. 7 iiii ac pa. Silua v porc. Excepto q dim solin ten Wadard dimid uirg in ead uilla. qd nunq se quietaut apud rege. Int totu ualuit iii lib 7 m vi lib. E Stan tenuit T.R.E. 7 potuit se uertere quo uoluit.

Ips Wadard ten de epo Malplescap. p dim solin se defd. Tra e ii car. Ibi sunt cu i uillo 7 iiii bord 7 v seruis. 7 una ac 7 dim pa. Silua viii porc 7 xvi denar. Valuit iii lib 7 m vi lib. Vltan tenuit sub heraldo.

Ernulf de Hesding ten traningeha p iii uirg se defd. Tra e ii car. Ibi sunt m vi boues cu ii uillis 7 iii bord. Ibi un molds de x sol. 7 viii ac pa. pastura c ouibz. Silua x porc 7 xiii den. Rex hz de silua hui m. qd uat viii sol. Totu m ualuit iii lib 7 m xl sold. Dering tenuit 7 potuit se uertere quo uoluit.

Anschitillus de ros ten Tarent de epo. p dim solin se defd. Tra e i car 7 dim. In dnio e una 7 iiii uilli cu iiii bord hnt i car. Ibi iii ac pa. 7 ii molini de xvii sol. Silua iii porc. Rex hz de isto m p nouo dono epi qd ual x denar. Totu m ualuit 7 ual c sol. Aluric tenuit de rege E.

In ead uilla ht isde A i maneriu de epo. p dim solin se defd. Tra e i car 7 dimid. Ibi v uilli 7 v bord 7 un molds de xx solds. Ibi iiii ac pa. 7 i seru. Totu m ualuit lx sol. 7 modo lxx solid. O fuero tenuit de rege E.

Isde Anschitill ten de epo hortone p uno solin se defd.

possible that FitzHelte had acquired Ernulf de Hesdin's mill after Ernulf's death.

Although Ansgot was a knight of the Archbishop, he also held lands from Bishop Odo, as did Wadard. In fact Ansgot and Wadard seem closely connected, both holding adjoining lands in Maplescombe and Farningham. Many of Wadard's lands later became part of the barony of the Arsic family who were also closely connected to FitzHelte and the de Cheritons, especially in castle-guard service at Dover Castle where the Arsic tower was supported by both FitzHelte and de Cheriton. The de Ros family, who held the other half-mill in Horton Kirby, later also held land from the Arsics, although in time they had their own large barony. These great baronies of FitzHelte, de Ros, the arch-bishopric and the Eynsford family all interconnect like sections of a jig-saw puzzle. To make matters even more confusing there are also links between Wadard's heirs and the heirs of Ernulf de Hesdin.

The Village Mill

The Farningham village miller had paid a rent of 10s, presumably first to Dering and then to Ernulf. This was in addition to the stated value of the manor and so was a considerable revenue for the landlord who would also have taken a proportion of the toll corn. In earlier centuries the first water-mills were worked by tied servants or slaves for the owners who had built them, but by Domesday the majority of mills in Kent were farmed out at rent to millers.[137] The miller was probably one of the two Domesday villeins. His status as a skilled workmen would have been quite high. He paid a hefty rent and would have been responsible for the upkeep of his mill. Millers were often the village capitalists, and this miller might be seen as a descendant of those prosperous Anglo-Saxon Kentish ceorls and ancestor of the later rich Kentish yeoman.

With only two villeins and three smallholders, making five families in all of, say, six people in each family to include non-working old and young, the population was possibly thirty people, although it is possible that there was an unseen population of people too poor to be of interest to the commissioners.[138] This was a small hamlet, and it is difficult to assign the workload. There was surely a ploughman on a manor which 'answered for 3 yokes with land for 2 ploughs'. There should also have been a shepherd for the sheep and a swineherd for the pigs, though the care of the stock animals may of course have doubled with other work on the farm. Much may have been done by women and children. There should also have been a smith. Maybe there was one at the larger and more prosperous Charton farm.

The Church

No church or parson is recorded in Domesday book. We know that a church existed, but maybe only a very small one served by a visiting priest. The Canterbury archives frequently refer to Farningham as a chapel and perhaps,

137–R.Holt *op.cit.*
138–R.Bartlett,
England under the Norman and Angevin Kings, (2000)

if Everitt's theory is correct and the parish was carved out of the Eynsford estate, and the boundaries certainly suggest this, then maybe Farningham church started as a chapel of Eynsford. There is also the later confusion over the manorial chapel at Charton. A church could also be demoted to a chapel for a period as happened in Otford in the 13th century.

The Normans were great builders in stone. 'I hate small buildings' said Goscelin of St Bertin, 'Frankly I would not allow buildings to stand unless they were glorious, magnificent, big. He destroys well who builds something better'.[139] And by 1200 almost every Anglo-Saxon cathedral and abbey had been destroyed. Farningham church was probably not rebuilt until about 1225.

The first confirmation of both a church in Farningham and a chapel at Charton manor is given in 1225.[140] The earliest part of the church is usually dated to that period, so the first stone church is likely to have been built at this time. The dedication to St Peter and St Paul probably belongs to the earlier church. It is one of the most frequent in Kent, owing its popularity to the dedication of Augustine's first monastery in Canterbury. It is often an early dedication, but not the earliest which are usually made to local Kentish saints.

It is apparent that the village hamlet at Domesday was small and run down. A resident Saxon priest, if he existed, might have been one of the two villeins. Although he would probably have been the only literate member of the community and as such would have given evidence to the Domesday commissioners, he would not have been of great interest to the Normans.

Farningham would never be a rich living. The priest would have farmed his own small amount of glebe land himself. He would also have had the right to graze his animals in the graveyard. It is strange to think that, apart from the woods, this churchyard must be the oldest uncultivated land in the parish,

139-M.Wood,
Domesday, a Search for the
Roots of England, (1986)
140-Canterbury Cathedral
Library, *Register B.*

53

only disturbed by unnumbered burials.

In the records Farningham has always been a vicarage. However, the vicarage system appears to have been very much a creation of the 12th and 13th centuries so before that time the priest is an unknown quantity. Probably the church was served by a priest from the mother church at Eynsford. By 1225 Farningham church had been appropriated to the Prior and monks of Christ Church Canterbury. It might of course have belonged to them since the time of Alphege, or it might have been donated to them by Ralph of Eynsford in the early 12th century, or by his grandson William who gave 18 of his properties in Farningham to Christ Church in about 1150-80. There are records of several other gifts to Christ Church at this time from other Farningham residents. One, Walter son of Peter Bell, gave several lands, a dwelling and half an acre in 'a field called Stone' and another half acre 'next to the cemetery'.

Tithe

To begin with, the lay lords who had built churches on their lands, claimed a 'dominium' over the parish priests that they had appointed. They had authority over their churches and usually took the tithes, or conferred them where they pleased. It was much the same authority that they claimed over their demesne miller and their mill. By 1165 the Pope said that all tithes must go to the church. The parish priest who received the full income of the church would later be called the Rector, he was also known as the person or Parson of the church. If he could not minister personally he appointed a vicar, or vice, to act vicariously.[141]

The tithe system can be traced back to the Jewish mosaic laws which gave the tenth part of the produce of the land. In Leviticus the custom was a three-fold division of the tenths of corn, fruit, herd, flock etc. between the priests, the temple and the poor. In England, by the 12th century, the tithes were divided between the mother church, the clergy and the poor. Tithes in Farningham were to become a major dispute over the centuries.

According to R.A.R. Hartridge 'appropriation' of churches by monasteries meant the formal acquisition by them of the income of the church. The appropriating monastery acquired for itself the rectory and was henceforth the 'Rector Appropriate'. The bishop then ordained a vicarage which was to be a 'perpetual' or life-long benefice. This would be the position in Farningham by the 13th century. The general, but by no means invariable, custom would be that the rector, in this case Christ Church Priory, took the 'great' tithe of corn, hay and wood, and the vicar took the 'small' tithes of minor produce and labour such as wool, milk, eggs, honey and sometimes lambs and calves. This was always a very unsatisfactory tithe, being difficult to collect and leading to endless contention.

The possible, but maybe not very likely, Farningham priest at Domesday might have come from a villein family, a clever boy sent to the monks for an

141-R.A.R.Hartridge,
A History of Vicarages in the Middle Ages, (1930)

54

education. He would probably have a wife and family, celibacy was not popular among the minor clergy. Monks were celibate but it was their business to pray for men's souls, not minister to their needs. A hundred years later there is quite a lot of information about the Farningham priest, but not yet. As for their language, English would sometimes be used in sermons and homilies, but now Latin was to be the language of the church and French the language of the upper classes. On the whole only the peasants would speak English. Millers undoubtedly spoke English, but not as we would understand it today.

To turn from the church to the source of the greater tithes, the landlord's and the miller's income and the villager's staff of life, the arable fields. Much of Kent is thought to have had an enclosed field system from early times. Having said that, it should be added that there is evidence of some large open fields in Farningham which appear to have been sub-divided, such as Walter Bell's half acre in the field called Stone. This seems to indicate the presence of some large unenclosed fields with strip cultivation as in other parts of England, but there is no evidence of communally held arable fields. The open fields of Kent could be described more accurately as enclosed fields sub-divided into unenclosed or enclosed parcels, and may have resulted from co-operative ploughing and from the custom of partible inheritance.[142]

Gavelkind or partible inheritance

A major factor encouraging dispersal of settlement, and possibly of sub-divided fields, is the gavelkind system of land tenure and its associated laws of partible inheritance which often led to the division of farms. When a tenant in gavelkind died his lands could only be left to his sons in equal shares. The youngest son was entitled to the hearth or family home, and the widow to a half share of the estate for life. Failing sons, daughters could inherit.

William Lambarde gives a description of gavelkind, this legal system peculiar to Kent, in 1576,[143] and he translates a 13th century treatise describing these ancient customs or laws. The treatise is called the *Custumale of Kent*. Tradition says that it was handed to the Sheriff, Sir John de Northwood and endorsed by the Justices in Eyre at Canterbury on St Alphege day, 19th April 1293.

There are a number of curious Kentish sayings in the custumal, such as 'the father to the bough (gallows), the son to the plough', which derives from a clause allowing children of convicted felons to inherit land. (This much disputed text has now been corrected to the 'logh' or homestead instead of the plough). Another couplet says 'she that is a widow, she is the lady' meaning the rich widow with her half share in her late husband's estate. F. Hull in his discussion of gavelkind, says that these couplets 'have the very ring of early dooms' and may be part of an oral tradition of laws handed down by generations of illiterate people.[144] He adds that 'they could almost be said to be the Magna Carta of the Kingdom of Kent'.

142-H.E.Hallam,
Rural England, 1066-1348
(1981)
A Baker *'Some Fields & Farms'*
Arch Cant. LXXX (1965)
143-William Lambarde,
A Perambulation of Kent, 1570
(1970ed)
144-F.Hull, *'John de Berewyke*
& Consuetudines Cancie'
Arch Cant XCVI (1980)

55

It is believed that partible inheritance, a feature of Celtic society, was widespread in England before the Normans introduced primogeniture. Kent was always famous as the home of a free peasantry. The 'Invicta Legend', or 'Legend of the Green Boughs' was a tradition kept alive by the folk memory of a bargain supposedly struck with William I in 1066. According to the story, William was waylaid at Swanscombe by a rustic Kentish army camouflaged as trees, demanding recognition of their ancient rights. Ever since his supposed acquiescence, the people of Kent have claimed that they alone were invincible and never conquered, having made peace on their own terms.

The Village

The Farningham Domesday hamlets would have been little muddy settlements, full of peasants and animals. The houses were probably thatched huts like the little houses on the Bayeux Tapestry, there were no bricks and no local stone, although flint may have been used for partial walling. Excavated houses of this period show two small rooms, one with a hearth and one a byre for animals. Floors were of trodden clay and any timber wall supports rested on or in the ground and would not be likely to last more than a generation.[145]

The Norman landlords probably only occasionally visited their farms which would have been worked for them by their tied labourers, probably under the supervision of a reeve chosen annually by the community. If the farm was one of a large lordship dispersed in other counties then a peripatetic bailiff or steward might supervise the estates. The two larger hamlets would surely have halls, or larger barn type houses for accommodation of visiting landlords, stewards or ecclesiastics as well as the storage of grain. One barn could have many functions.

It is generally believed that the coming of feudalism created a social rift between the upper classes and the peasants. Ceorls might have become thegns in Saxon England, but villeins were not likely to become knights under the Normans. Sir Frank Stenton says 'the general drift of English peasant life...was undoubtedly from freedom towards servitude', and this was probably as true of Farningham as elsewhere. Centuries of war and privation, tax and tithe must have left the village sadly impoverished.

William FitzHelte's Mill

The history of the four Farningham farms is a web of family connections. The successors of Ansgot and Wadard, FitzHelte and Arsic, criss-cross and interchange, possibly through marriage, possibly through land acquisition by neighbours as family fortunes rose and fell. The history of the two mills is naturally even harder to follow than the families who owned them.

William FitzHelte, who inherited Ansgot's estates, was a great landholder in Buckingham as well as Kent. According to duBoulay his barony was centred on Aldington in Kent, although this was not the great manor of Aldington near

145-R.Bartlett, *op.cit.*

*William FitzHelte's seal
(Arch Cant.II 1859)
An equestrian seal
indicated knightly status.*

Vniuersis sce matris ecclie filiis Witt fili betronis salt. Rerum gestarum memoria
icirco inscripturam redigitur ne pcessu tempor in obliuione labat. Ideo notu fieri desido
ta plentab; q tutis qd ego Witt fili betronis dedi 7 concessi do 7 ecclie Sce ma
rie magdalene de cubwelle 7 fribz ibide do seruientibz in ptuua elemosina
eccliam beati petri de alduntunia 7 hoc feci p salute ame henrici regis 7
ame mee 7 antcessor meor his testibz. Witto de ainesfordia 7 Rad fre ei hug
de arruntinia Custacio de dikesmue Ioh de berhes. Gilebto capetto Barchot ca
petto helmulfo saluage 7 Thoma fit suo. Iacobo tunc diacono Walto d chanei
7 ajutis alii

Folkstone but the much smaller Aldington in Thurnham near
Detling. The estates appear to have descended from Ansgot
to Helto, who was possibly the steward of Odo of Bayeux,
to Helto's son William 'filius Helto' or FitzHelte.
Fitzhelte appears to have had no children and his
barony was divided between his three sisters
in 1179.

The sisters were Emma Septvans, who inherited
Aldington in Thurnham and Maplescombe, Alice
Canci and Sibil de Cheriton whose husband William de
Cheriton was lord of the manor of Cheriton near Folkstone.
The Cheritons inherited the Farningham manor and later
inherited Maplescombe from the Septvans. They were to hold
the Farningham manor, which now took their name, later cor-
rupted to Charton, from 1179 until at least 1258.

The first mention of a mill in Farningham, after the mills mentioned
in Domesday, came when William FitzHelte had gave 'a mill and lands called
Monkyn Lands' to Bermondsey Abbey in 1143. The original charter has not
survived, but the *Curia Regis Roll* for 1203 gives William de Cheriton's confirmation of this gift by his wife's uncle.

William was summoned to the King's Court to guarantee his charter, and
this is what he said.

I, William of Cirinton, for the salvation of my soul and that of my uncle William son of Helto
and of all my ancestors....by my sealed testament confirm to the church of St Saviour,
Bermondsey and the monks of that place....the gift of the entire mill of Fremingham, which
my uncle William, son of Helto, gave them in free and perpetual alms, with all its appurte-
nances namely in the highways, in the paths, in the lands, in the waters, in the meadows, in
the pastures and in all other privileges, especially in the path which runs from my courtyard
all the way to the aforesaid mill across the middle of my demesne, and in the path which runs
from the mill into Chimbeham and in the one which extends along the way to Boxerse as far

as my land reaches....and they may be able to proceed along customary paths in peace and without hindrance. I yield and confirm to the said monks the milling of my men of Fremingham and of Chimbeham and of Boxerse....that the said monks may freely and peacefully possess that mill just as my uncle held it in demesne....especially that they may be free and undisturbed by all worldly customs and taxes....as far as it extends to the 10 acres of Scot and except the milling for the house....'[146]

It was a popular pious gesture of the time to make gifts such as FitzHelte's. He had already given other lands in Farningham to the newly founded St Bartholomew's Hospital, and had given his church in Aldington to Cumbwell Priory.[147] This custom of making charitable donations to religious foundations, often with the clause 'for the good of my soul and those of my parents and grandparents' went on until the Reformation when it began to be seen as an attempt to bargain with the Almighty for a place in heaven and was banned as 'superstitious uses'.

In their *History of Corn Milling* Bennett and Elton quote from a charter of 1160 in which the lady of a manor in Yorkshire made a similar gift to the local monks. This charter adds expressly that no other local mill may be used, nor may the townspeople use handmills. This is given as an example of the monopoly of medieval landlords sometimes known as 'milling soke', which prohibited tenants from using any mills other than the demesne mill, or even keeping hand-mills or querns, on pain of heavy fines and confiscation of their corn. The excavation of an abbey in St Albans revealed a floor made of broken quernstones which conjures up an unpleasant picture of vindictive monks and downtrodden peasants. No wonder there was said to be great bitterness among the peasantry about this custom.

William de Cheriton's charter promises the monks the profits from 'the milling of my men of Farningham, Chimhams and Boxerse'; Chimhams being a farm beyond Charton to the east and Boxerse being possibly a lost farm site near Boxwood beyond Brands Hatch. A John and Thomas of Box were among the witnesses to one of William FitzHelte's charters of land in Farningham.

This promise that all the milling of the men of the estate would go to the monks shows that FitzHelte and his nephew Cheriton had manorial rights over the mill and so were able to force their tenants to relinquish their querns and go to the mill. The clause in the charter 'save for the milling of the house', meant that the domestic demesne household could use querns which explains the presence of several found in an outbuilding when the 13th century Charton manor chapel was excavated in 1939.[148]

Among the many other fascinating features of the charter is the freedom of the monks to go 'as far as (the land) extends to the 10 acres of Scot'. The *Curia Regis Roll* is written in Latin so Scot is 'Scotis' but it seems clear from later evidence that this refers to the miller whose name was John Scot. Very few records remain of Bermondsey Abbey, but the *Annales Monastici* confirm that the mill in Farningham, given to Bermondsey Abbey by FitzHelte

146–Roger Cockett trans, *Curia Regis Roll 30, 1203*
147–Arch Cant. *V&VI, 1866, Charters of Cumbwell Priory*
148–Dartford Ref. Library, *1939 report on excavation* by E.Greenfield & S.Priest

in 1143, was sold by the prior of the abbey, 'after the dimissum', to a John Scot, 'in perpetuity' for 11s per annum in the year 1211.

In this instance 'the dimissum' refers to the interdict and excommuniation of King John, a drama which lasted from 1208 to 1213. The king had refused to accept the pope's choice of Stephen Langton as archbishop and an interdict had been placed by Rome on all ecclesiastical rites in England. No burials, baptisms or marriages could take place and King John was excommuniated. In retaliation he seized much church property and many abbeys and priories were forced to sell their assets.

John Scot

The *Kent Feet of Fines* for 1221 confirms the sale, or lease, of the mill by the Prior of Bermondsey who claimed 'the services and customs' of one mill and ten acres of land in Farningham from one John Scot who was to pay a new rent of 40s 6d, and the Prior conceded to him and his heirs the right to the mill and land.[149] So, in John Scot we have the first named miller of Farningham, although perhaps, as a smallholder with ten acres of land and the ability to pay a high increase in rent as well as the upkeep of the mill, he may have paid a miller to do the work for him. Richard Holt, in *Mills of Medieval England*, says that the 12th century was a time when many mills were sold 'in perpetuity' with rents to be paid every year 'for ever'. The miller and his heirs, who had the right to succeed to the mill at the accustomed rent, were responsible for its upkeep.

John Scot was lucky. A tied demesne miller would have been the property of his lord. In a gift of a mill to the canons of Missenden in Buckinghamshire, Wulfric the miller was thrown in for 5s with the words 'I grant this man to them...so that they may do what they please with him as with their own man...if he shall wish to go away and desert at any time...I shall take and seize him wherever I shall find him'[150].

Again, there is no way of knowing for sure which of the mills was John Scot's. Was it Ernulf's or Wadard's, or had FitzHelte built a third mill? There is the curious coincidence of a ten acre field called Scot's Meadow at the very place near Frank's Hall where Wadard's mill might have stood. A medieval horseshoe and nails have been found here, suggesting an extension of Calfstock Lane down to the river. But one must beware of coincidences and, unless fresh evidence turns up to say that FitzHelte had indeed acquired Wadard's mill, we must assume that he is equally likely to have acquired Ernulf's.

To return to William FitzHelte's gifts to religious foundations. *Archaeologia Cantiana* vol.II, gives an account of his donation of the church at his principal manor of Aldington in Thurnham to Cumbwell Priory.[151] It also gives a facsimile of his seal which shows him as a knight on horseback. St Bartholomew's Hospital archive also has grants from William with the same seals.[152] A Thomas son of Scotland witnessed one of these grants.

149–Calendar of Kent Feet of Fines, Kent Archaelogical Society Records Vol.IXV (1956)
150–D.M.Stenton, English Society in the Early Middle Ages, (1962)
151–Arch Cant. 1859 Geneological Roll of Northwoods.
152–Nellie Kerling, Cartulary of St.Bartholomew's Hospital, (1973)

According to the *Kent Feet of Fines* Thomas, known as Escotland or Escolland, held sixty acres of land in Farningham and Horton Kirby in 1198 and 1206. So Scot and Escotland are probably another coincidence, unless of course John Scot the miller was a member of the same family.

The *Feet of Fines* are among the earliest records after Domesday in which to search for the history of the manors and their owners. A 'fine' being a formal, final agreement between parties at law, usually about the ownership of property. The top half of the document was divided among the parties for the defence and the prosecution, and the foot would be retained by the Treasury. The *Feet of Fines* for Kent began to be kept in the 1190s. They are often concluded in a friendly fashion with the donation of a nominal fine, payment or rent; in many cases a hawk, a pair of spurs or gloves, spices such as cumin or pepper, or even a rose or a gillyflower.

Thomas Scotland, or Escolland, was possibly a forbear of the family called Scoland who later held the manor of Frank's. He was married to Alice, daughter of Simon of Chelsfield and, to complicate matters, Hasted believed the Chelsfields to have been the heirs of Ernulf of Hesdin, which of course is the wrong family in the wrong place. Ernulf's heirs should have been in Farningham village. Local history is never tidy. All these paths have so many crossroads, leading sometimes to blind alleys.

The two fines brought by Thomas Escotland in 1197 and 1206 against his Chelsfield uncle and aunt relate to the 60 acres of land in Farningham and Horton Kirby on which Wadard's mill might have stood. There is no mention of a mill, but if it belonged to Bermondsey Abbey this is not surprising. My own theory remains that William Fitzhelte had bought Wadard's mill at, or near, Frank's Hall, which he then gave to Bermondsey. It was then tenanted by John Scot and his heirs for the next 50 years or so after which it maybe fell into disuse and vanishes from the story.

It has to be said that it is equally possible that Fitzhelte had acquired Ernulf's village mill. There is the third possibility that Fitzhelte had built a third mill closer to his manor of Charton. This might explain why the fields named on the earliest maps as Great Mill Field, Further Mill Field and Ware (weir) Mead and Lower Ware Field, are all so far down the river away from the village mill site. All these possible mill sites have vanished. Even the dry river bed of 1990 failed to yield any secrets.

The Scolands became an important local family. When the Cheritons died out for want of male heirs in about 1260 Charton manor was divided into two halves. One of these, 'Farningham Parva', or 'Charton Scodland' as they were known in turn, went to the Scolands and became the manor of Franks. C.Hart, in an essay on 'Shoelands' for the Place Name Society, discusses the possible origins of the name 'Scoland' and comes up with the interesting suggestion of the Old English word 'scrudland' or 'shroudland' or land provided for the endowment of clothing for religious community.[153] So was the Scoland's 'moiety of Charton' the land reserved for the monks of Canterbury?

153–*Article kindly brought to my notice by* Z&F Bamping

Chapter Four

13th Century Farningham / Odo de Cheriton / The de Freminghams /
Farningham Castle / Farningham's Jews / Farningham Market and Fair /
Statute Pistoribus / Feast Days / The Fair / The Assize of Bread and Ale /
The Market / John de Fremingham / Ralph's Tomb /
The Manor of Franks or Little Farningham / Mills as prisons.

There is a sad lack of evidence about what happened to Ernulf of Hesdin's hamlet during the century and a half after Domesday. All the documentation for this period concerns Charton manor and one must conclude that perhaps the de Cheriton family had acquired the village manor as well as Chimbehams, Boxerse and Franks.

William de Cheriton, inherited the estate from his wife's uncle FitzHelte in about 1180. The de Cheritons were a wealthy Norman family in their own right, although without such a great barony as FitzHelte. William's grandfather, Odo of Cheriton, held a knight's fee from Manasses Arsic in Cheriton near Folkestone. This was the estate from which they took their name. It seems that there were ecclesiastical connections and Odo was said to be a nephew of the Archbishop of Canterbury, Ralph d'Escures.[154]

By the time Odo died in 1166 the inquest says that his son William held six knight's fees in Kent and two in Buckinghamshire. This William and his wife Sibil FitzHelte had died by 1180 when the FitzHelte barony was divided and it was his son, the second William who inherited the Farningham manor as well as the Folkestone estates. He and his wife Matilda had seven children and appear to have spent a large part of their time in Farningham where they built a manor house with its own chapel.

Odo de Cheriton

Their eldest son, Odo, became one of the few internationally famous people to have lived in Farningham. He was a popular preacher and writer, best known for his animal fables which can be found in manuscript collections all over Europe. He appears in the *Dictionary of National Biography* and is described by one historian as 'a shrewd and humorous observer of the life of his time'.[155]

His father William's career can be followed in the public records. In 1190 he went on a Crusade for three years, leaving his brothers Helto and Hugh to manage the estate. The parson of Maplescombe in 1198 was called Helto, possibly this same brother. By 1210 young Odo had graduated from the University of Paris where he possibly studied under the exiled archbishop of Canterbury, Stephen Langton. This same year William paid the fine of 'one good haltein falcon' for Odo to have custody of the parish church at Cheriton.[156]

154–Albert Friend, *Speculum 23, (1948)* '*Master Odo of Cheriton*'.
155–ibid
156–*Calendar of Kent Feet of Fines, KAS Records VolXV (1956)*

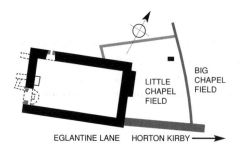

LITTLE CHAPEL FIELD

BIG CHAPEL FIELD

EGLANTINE LANE   HORTON KIRBY ⟶

The Charton Manor Chapel, the internal dimensions of which measure 20ft x 50ft. For general location see Page 43

Presumably he was also at liberty to preach freely in his father's manor chapel in Farningham, where perhaps he polished his style on his young brothers and sisters.

In 1213 William paid to have free warren, or hunting rights, over his lands at Cheriton. A warren was unenclosed land. Fowl of warren included pheasant and partridge and beasts of warren were the fox, rabbit, hare, cat and roe deer. Red and fallow deer belonged to the king. From these documents it would appear that the Cheritons behaved like most other medieval landlords, spending some part of the year on their estates in turn, keeping an eye on their tenants and living off the produce of different farms. Their manor court was held at Farningham every three weeks, the 'hall moot' of Farningham. Unfortunately the manor court rolls have either not survived or have so far failed to appear.

The Canterbury archives indicate that the de Cheriton's main residence was now in Farningham. Odo returned to Paris to continue his theological studies. It was another seven years before he could call himself 'Ego Odo de Ciritunia, doctor ecclesie minimus', or 'smallest doctor of the church', a title he modestly retained throughout his later life. It is a possibility that he was very small physically which might explain his choice of the academic life of the church rather than his father's field of active public service, also his sympathetic treatment of small animals in his fables.

Odo was to spend most of his life travelling; teaching and preaching in France and Spain. Like the Anglo-Saxon Aelfric much of his work was teaching preachers by means of homilies and fables.[157] In turn the preachers would be aided in their sermons to illiterate congregations by the colourful scenes painted on the walls of the churches. Farningham's last surviving wall painting, of Moses and Aaron, was to be whitewashed by a Victorian vicar in 1872.

William de Cheriton was often abroad on public affairs, and Matilda and the younger children, William, Robert, Lucy, Isabel, Margaret and Waleran appear to have stayed in Farningham where they had their own private chaplain, no doubt doubling as tutor, and where there must have been a large household of servants. No trace of the Cheriton's family house remains, but the excavation of their chapel in 1939 revealed a flint structure, about 50 feet long by 20 feet wide, with 30 inch thick walls, roofed with red tiles. There were a number of hewn corner-stones, the walls were roughly plastered and the floor was of stamped clay and chalk. The archaeologists thought they identified the site of the earlier manor in a field 50 yards away. There was also an outhouse with the remains of a fire and the household quern stones.

The Canterbury archives say that the chaplain celebrated mass every day.[158] He and the master both had a key to the chapel, and the vessels used for the

157–H.Harding, 'Odo de Cheriton' Dartford Historical & Antiquarian Society Newsletter (TDASN) No.28 (1991)
158–C.C.Library, Cartae Antiquae, F5-11

mass were kept in the manor house. All sacraments for the members of the household were to take place in the chapel except for the baptism of children which was to take place in Farningham parish church. The chaplain was supported by the family but appointed by the rector of Eynsford and the chapel was called a chapel of Eynsford.

According to his biographer, Albert Friend, Odo's sermons often shed an unappealing light on life in the countryside in his youth. There were fears of robbers and marauders, wolves and plagues, treacherous servants and filthy peasants. Unfortunately Odo never recorded a stroll down to the mill 'in the path across the demesne' and a chat with the miller John Scot.

The years 950 to 1300 had experienced the global warming known as the Little Optimum. The climate was amazingly mild and life was not so harsh for the peasants as might be imagined. The two south-facing fields near Charton manor called Hither and Nether Vineyard may easily date from this time. There were several vineyards in Kent and one as far north as Ely.

William died in 1232 and Odo was his heir. It is not possible to claim Odo as a lifelong resident of Farningham, although after his father's death he was the owner of the mill. He was occasionally in England to deal with his estates and is recorded as leasing some of his property, including a shop in London, to the London mayor, Andrew Bukarel. He died in 1246 and his brother Waleran, also childless, became his heir. With no surviving family males, their sisters, Margaret de Mereworth, Isabel des Arches and Lucy de Insula eventually inherited the Cheriton estates.

London has only come into the story once or twice since Domesday. It was now a great city, described by William FitzStephen in about 1180 as 'joined from the Palace of Westminster to the City by a populous suburb of houses with spacious gardens' and beyond, to the north, pastures and meadowlands 'through which flow streams wherein the turning of mills makes a cheerful sound'.[159] The Turnmill brook was one of these. There were also the wells with 'sweet, wholesome, clear water' such as Clerkenwell, much visited by students and young clerks of the city for fresh air on summer evenings. Also the river bank with its wharves and cookshops; Smith, or Smooth Fields Market and the horse fairs, ice games on the frozen marshes and sports such as bull and bear baiting and hunting with dogs and falcons.

The de Freminghams

The history of Farningham and its mill from the early 13th century for the next 150 years is tied to an important new family who took their name from the village, the de Freminghams. These people may have been smallholders in the time of the de Cheritons. William FitzHelte gave land here that was tenanted by Reynold, son of Ranulf de Fremingham to St Bartholomew's Hospital in about 1180 and the hospital rented it back to the tenants at 3s a year. The charter was witnessed by William de Cheriton and Thomas Scotland among others.[160]

159–D.C.Douglas, ed. *English Historical Documents Vol.2*
160–Nellie Kerling, *op.cit.*

The St Bartholomew's and the Canterbury charters give the names of quite a few of the FitzHelte and Cheriton tenants. Several were simply known by their first names, such as James or Richard, some by family names like Stephen son of Thomas or Geoffrey brother of Lionel, some take their name from their land, even from quite small holdings such as William atte Crofte or Robert Broadfield, and some take a surname from an occupation such as Ralph le Draper, Gilbert Cordwainer, Roger the cleric, Ernest Tailor and John Smith. By this time, nearly all first names were Normanised, even if some families had Anglo-Saxon ancestors.

Among them were this family who took their name from the village. They may have started out as tailors, shepherds, millers or shoemakers but, perhaps by long establishment, or by prosperity, or maybe to conceal some shameful earlier Saxon name, had simply become known by the name of the village. It is even possible that they were Dering's descendants. Land formerly tenanted by Reynold was confirmed to St Bartholomew's by William de Cheriton in 1205, and in 1215 Reynold himself gave land of his own to the hospital.

Seal of John de Fremingham (Arch Cant.III. 1860)

One of the charters is witnessed by the 'Hall Moot', or manor court, of Freningham, which included Reynold and his brother Thomas de Fremingham and Hugh and William de Cheriton. The court at this date was, we believe, held at Charton. Members signed the documents with their personal seals, and the device on Reynold's seal was a fleur de lys and an eagle. Other members of the family included a Richard and Geoffrey de Fremingham who are recorded in the *Pipe Rolls*, when they gave land in Farningham to Bermondsey Priory.

By the mid-century a Ralph de Fremingham had become a man of such importance that his name appears again and again in the public records. It seems very likely that he was a protege of the Cheritons. Like Odo he had a university master's degree and is always referred to as Master Ralf. His career was no doubt advanced by his marriage to Elizabeth, the daughter of Sir Henry Apulderfield, member of an influential family of Kentish landowners.[161]

Ralph first appears in the *Patent Rolls* for 1259 under 'protection, until his return, for Master Ralf de Fremingham, gone to the court of Rome on the King's affairs'. By 1265 he had become a King's Clerk, one of the elite band of legal clerics described by Sir Maurice Powicke as 'the nucleus of a Foreign Office'.[162]

A strange story is recorded about Ralph in the *Miscellaneous Inquisitions*

161-*The Topographer & Genealogist Vol.3 (1858)*, G.Steinman Steinman, 'Some account of the Manor of Apulderfield'.
162-M.Powicke, *The Thirteenth Century*, Oxford History of England, (1962ed)

de Fremingham

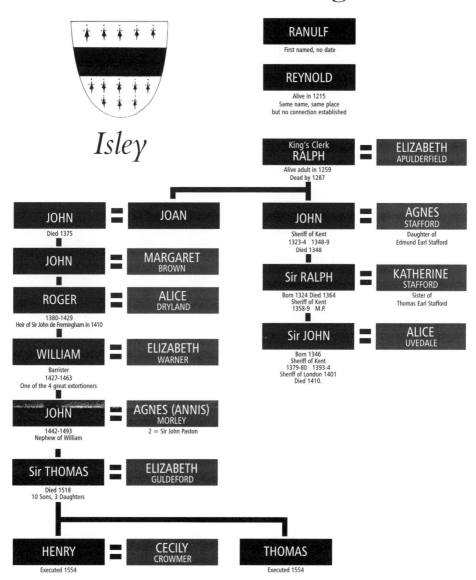

Isley

RANULF
First named, no date

REYNOLD
Alive in 1215
Same name, same place
but no connection established

King's Clerk
RALPH = **ELIZABETH** APULDERFIELD
Alive adult in 1259
Dead by 1287

JOHN = **JOAN**
Died 1375

JOHN = **MARGARET** BROWN

ROGER = **ALICE** DRYLAND
1380-1429
Heir of Sir John de Fremingham in 1410

WILLIAM = **ELIZABETH** WARNER
Barrister
1427-1463
One of the 4 great extortioners

JOHN = **AGNES (ANNIS)** MORLEY
1442-1493
Nephew of William
2 = Sir John Paston

Sir THOMAS = **ELIZABETH** GULDEFORD
Died 1518
10 Sons, 3 Daughters

JOHN = **AGNES** STAFFORD
Sheriff of Kent
1323-4   1348-9
Died 1348
Daughter of
Edmund Earl Stafford

Sir RALPH = **KATHERINE** STAFFORD
Born 1324 Died 1364
Sheriff of Kent
1358-9   M.P.
Sister of
Thomas Earl Stafford

Sir JOHN = **ALICE** UVEDALE
Born 1346
Sheriff of Kent
1379-80   1393-4
Sheriff of London 1401
Died 1410.

HENRY = **CECILY** CROWMER
Executed 1554

THOMAS
Executed 1554

of the same year, 1265.

The servants of Master Ralph de Fremingham, viz Master Robert de Cunebie, John the chaplain and others, seized the manor of Eynsford, late of William Heringod, worth £20...it was restored the Thursday before Michaelmas in the same year by Geoffrey de Marisco, the King's bailiff, and the same day came the said chaplain and Nicholas, brother of Ralph and seized the said manor...and overthrew the servant of the said William and still hold it. The servants of the said Master Ralf also seized the lands of John of Boxerse and caused the corn to be cut and carried, also a house which they restored with the land on the Sunday before the feast of St Mathew.[163]

The powerful house of Eynsford was in decline and their properties had been divided between William Heringod and Nicholas Criol who were engaged on the wrong side in the current Baron's War with Henry III, and this primitive show of strength by the bully boys of their neighbour, the new King's Clerk, was perhaps intended to establish the pecking order in the Darent Valley.

Ralph was obviously trusted by both King Henry and his son, Edward I; the former rewarded him with a prebend of St Paul's Cathedral and with other ecclesiastical positions which he twice resigned on account of his 'being continually attendant to the business of Edward the King's son'. Later, under Edward, he became a Judge of the Common Pleas.

In 1270 he obtained the ultimate reward as far as the village was concerned; the right to hold a weekly market and an annual fair in Farningham. He was also granted free warren on his estates, which now included lands in Eynsford, Chimhams, Biwimble (probably a lost part of Farningham parish), Loose near Maidstone, Swanton in Mereworth and the former Wealden swine pasture of Hollanden near Leigh. It appears from this list that he had now acquired many of the former Cheriton lands, although Roger de Mereworth, son of Odo's sister, still had rights of free warren in 'Cheryton Farningham' in 1290.[164] It is worth noting that the post-Domesday Dering family also held lands at Loose and East Farleigh (another de Fremingham property) a century earlier, suggesting again the possibility of a connection between the families.

Farningham Castle

Ralph was also, in 1272, given permission to 'stop up a lane under his court and house of Frinningham and enclose it for the enlargement of his house and court and turn it into his own soil, so that he will make another lane there'. This is about the only evidence, so far, of a claim by the historian John Philipot that the de Fremingham's property in Farningham was 'fortified and fenced in'.[165]

However, to substantiate this claim, the archaeological excavations on the site of Farningham manor by Brian Philp in 1972 revealed 'a major flint and masonry wall, 14 ft thick....defensive in character...fronted by a broad, deep ditch some 40 ft wide and nearly 10 ft deep'. The wall, appeared 'to be a curtain wall fronting the mound and the great ditch a defensive moat, all features

163–Calendar of Miscellaneous Inquisitions, HMSO
164–Calendar of Patent Rolls, HMSO
165–John Phillipot, Villare Cantium (1776)

66

common to a defended castle. A broadly similar castle still survives at nearby Eynsford'.[166]

Ralph's journeys abroad for the king included diplomatic missions to King Louis of France, and journeys to Rome to borrow money for the King from Luke of Lucca, one of the Italian financiers who were to replace the early Jewish money lenders in the 1260s. Jews had first settled in England after the Conquest. There had been a massacre of Jews in Rouen in 1096 by crusading knights and Henry I had issued them a charter of protection. They were encouraged as financiers by Henry II and set up enclaves, or Jewries, in several cities including London and Canterbury.

The first stone houses were often built by Jews. Henry III borrowed heavily from 'the King's Jews'.[167] The great majority of Jews lived in cities where they had synagogues and 'archas' or chyrograph chests for their deeds and documents. There were often pogroms and periods of violent anti-semitism. Enthusiasm for the Crusades hit the Jews hard, and during the Baron's civil war there was a massacre of Jews in Canterbury.[168]

Farningham's Jews

There were also times when they prospered peacefully and were even allowed, on payment of a fee, to live outside the Jewries. This would depend on the protection of the local landowner which must explain why there was a small settlement in Farningham, no doubt sponsored by Ralph de Fremingham whose market and fair would profit from their presence. As elsewhere, it was probably possible for the Jews to shelter in his castle in times of trouble. Winchester castle had a 'Jews Tower'.

We only know about the Farningham Jewish settlement from the *Plea Rolls of the Exchequer of the Jews* for 1273 when 'Sampson, son of Meyr and Cresse, his son, resident at Farningham, were there slain'...and an inquiry was requested 'in full County Court' in presence of the Sheriff and coroners...as to 'who the malefactors were that slew the said Jews'.[169] In this case it appears that the local villagers were innocent of the murder, because another Jew, Abraham Mutun, was later arrested for the crime. Nor did it lead to a break up of the settlement immediately. An entry five years later in 1278 shows that another Jew died in Farningham when 'Sampson of Norwich was killed by thieves and his goods carried off from his house in Farningham'.

This probably came at the end of the Jewish villagers usefulness to Master Ralph because the Statute of Jewry of 1275 said that in future no Jews were to lend money at usury and all those owing debts to Jews were to pay or be forfeit. All Jews were to live in the cities or towns which had Jewries and an earlier order for all Jews over the age of seven to wear a yellow badge on their outer garments was restored. They could now only gain their living by lawful merchandise, or hard labour.

The better-off Jews survived a little longer, but many were forced to convert to Christianity or were transported, and in 1290 all Jews were ordered to

166–Brian & Edna Philp, *Archaeological Excavations in the Darent Valley*, KARU, (1973)
167–Cecil Roth, *A History of the Jews in England*, (1964)
168–M.Adler, *The Jews of Medieval England* (1939)
169–With thanks to Z.Bamping for bringing this to my attention

leave England under pain of death. Although they were assured safe passage a shameful episode took place at Queenborough in Kent when the master of a transport ship put his passengers ashore to drown on a sand bank, reputedly saying 'Moses will look after you'. It is good to know that the captain later spent two years in prison.[170]

There is no evidence today of the houses of the Farningham Jews. One remote possibility could lie in the name of a field above Charton called Star Field. Jewish land transactions were called Starrs, from the Hebrew 'shetar'. It might have been hard for them to live in the village centre alongside the rural villagers so maybe they lived in the outskirts. But more probably they chose to live near their protector and near the market. Jews would only look different to their neighbours if they chose to wear the traditional spiked hat, otherwise they wore the universal hooded cloak and this was said to be the reason for the 'necessary' badge of identity.

Farningham Market and Fair

The advantages of the concession of a market and fair were of great consequence to the village and the mill. Markets and fairs were tremendously important in the middle ages as they provided the best means of trading for local people and attracted travelling merchants from the towns and from London. Local people usually had the first right of trading at the market, and the annual fair must have brought a great deal of pleasure as well as prosperity to the village. It would be wrong however to think of Farningham as on any kind of major trading route; travellers to the continent used the Thames or the Dover road; the usual route to Maidstone was by way of Rochester, and the roads that crossed the village were no more than dusty or muddy lanes until the late 18th century.

It is possible that a market had already existed in Farningham for many years, but it was in Ralph's interest to acquire the charter of 1270 because this brought him the right of levying tolls and rents from the traders. The Fair was to be held on 'the Vigil, the Feast and the two following days of the Festival of Saints Peter and Paul' to whom the church was dedicated. The day of the patronal saint's festival is still held on the 29th of June.

It seems safe to assume now that the mill in the village centre was in commission again, if indeed it had ever been out of use. All the evidence indicates that Ralph's dwelling was on the site of the later manor and the records of the vicars of Farningham always included the tithes of the mill of the de Freminghams. In 1271, when Master Ralph was again in Rome on the King's business, in addition to his £50 expenses, he was granted '40 quarters of barley of the King's gift to sow his land of Farningham'. This is a first detail of a crop actually to be ground in Farningham mill. Barley was not only needed for malting ale but was also traditionally grown to pay and feed the demesne labourers.

We have not seen much of the labourers, or the miller lately. It is very sad

170–Robin R.Mundill, *Englands Jewish Solution, (1998)*

that no manor court rolls appear to have survived for Farningham, but it can be imagined that Ralph kept his estate on much the same lines as his father-in-law Henry Apulderfield in Sundridge where the obligatory services of the inland and outland tenants, were listed in 1258.[171]   Herbert Knocker of Sevenoaks transcribed some of this *Custumale*, or customs of the community. The tenures were held by the Inmen, or demesne tenants, and the Yokemen, or gavelkind tenants.

The explanation of 'yokemen' has been discussed by K.P.Witney who points out that the rapidly growing population and free land market during the 12th and 13th centuries, coupled with the obligations of gavelkind, or partible inheritance, led to diminishing husbandmen's holdings.[172] The old sulungs were being replaced by yokes, or quarter sulungs. By the 13th and 14th centuries the yokes themselves were often divided into quarter fractions, or virgates.

The Yokemen, or gavelmen, held their land 'by deed' as free tenants and paid rents but they still owed light services and payments to the lord of their manor. The Inmen, the lord's 'famulus' or farm servants, 'infeoffed of demesne of the Lord without deeds', owed much heavier services. However, by the 13th century, even the Inmen were wage labourers, paid in terms of an annual 'stipend' of cash and a 'livery' of food, mainly barley, peas and 'oats for the pottage'. All tenants in Sundridge owed suit to the lord's court every 3 weeks and also suit to the lord's mill.

Although Ralph's miller could have been a free tenant like John Scot before him, he is more likely to have been a farm servant. A free tenant miller would have kept his own profits but demesne millers in the 13th century were paid a wage of no more than a ploughmen, about 5s. to 6s. a year and an equal value of grain. The contents of the miller's toll dish with which he took 'multure' out of the client's sack of grain would have gone to the lord as would all profits of the mill.[173] Ralph would have had the expensive upkeep of the mill but, against that, he would have kept not only the profits from all the tenants 'owing suit', but also the milling profits from the market and fair, which would have been considerable.

Statute Pistoribus

The Statute Pistoribus of 1270 said that the miller's dish should hold 1/20th or 1/24th, although 1/16 was quite common. Sometimes the demesne miller was allowed to keep a small proportion of this toll. At Sundridge he was allowed no more than 1/32 of the malt. Most mills had separate stones for the barley malt for ale. The miller also, if he was lucky, enjoyed a few perks such as fishing, but again, eels would go to the lord, and there was usually a limit to the amount of smallholding in land and livestock allowed to a miller.

The Sundridge yokemen owed their landlord a little ploughing and reaping (gavelerth and gavelrip), the use of their carts and horses for carriage (averagium), and the 'boon', or so called favour, of their services at harvest.

171-H.W.Knocker, 'The Manor of Sundrish' Arch.Cant.XLIV (1932)
172-K.P.Witney, Kentish Land Measurements, Arch.Cant.CIX (1991)
173-R.Holt, (1988) op.cit.

A typical custumal of the time said 'Every tenant of the said yokes...who has a horse must harrow for 13 days for the lord's corn... and call for seed at the lord's granary door...and he should receive one meal a day, namely barley bread, broth, one dish and cheese...and every tenant of the...yokes having a horse and cart must carry in the lord's corn for 3 days...and those who do not have them must come with forks to stook and lift the sheaves in the fields'.[174]

The Men of the Manor, or inlanders, held cotlands for which they paid rent each quarter day, unless they paid in kind such as in ploughshares, horse-shoes, pepper or cumin. They worked for a wage and also owed heavier oblig-atory services than the outmen. Everyone owed payments such as hens at Christmas and eggs at Easter, also a 'merchet' or marriage licence of 2s. to marry their daughters, and at a tenant's death the lord was owed the 'heriot' of the man's best beast.

A 13th century Rochester document, the *Custumale Roffense* [175] gives details of the customary services of the demesne tenants of Southfleet manor, a few miles away from Farningham, and says that the customary services included ploughing, sowing and harrowing 25 acres, and 'they will bring seed into the fields at the summons of the reeve at the time when wheat is sown, so that if anyone is found who has not accomplished this, so much as pertains to his land, before St Martin's Eve, he will be in the lord's mercy'.[176]

The reeve was one of the community chosen as leader, usually at the Michaelmas hall moot, for the following year. He would have to call out the demesne labourers to perform their 'boon'works, and take the blame for any shortcomings. In a comparable estate at Meopham in the early 14th century, the permanent agricultural staff included a reeve, or sergeant, a ploughman, carter, shepherd, cowman, pigman and dairymaid, although of course some family members would as usual have doubled up on the duties.[177] When not required, labourers at Meopham were laid off and their cash and food reduced.

Feast days

The ancient feast days and holidays were still the high lights of the labourer's year. All Saints, or Hallowmass, on November 1st when the animals were brought in from the summer pastures, and Halloween with the bonfires of the night before. The twelve days of Christmas with a feast in the lord's hall to which they were expected to bring their presents of hens and eggs, ale and bread. Plow Monday after the Christmas holiday with processions and dress-ing-up of men and beasts. Candlemas on February 2nd, the ancient heathen quarter-day now known as the 'feast of the purification of the Virgin Mary', and then Lady Day, or annunciation day, on March 25th. Mayday and the beasts out to pasture again with more processions. Shrove Tuesday, before Lent began, despite the shriving or penance, was generally a sports day.

Easter, with a week's holiday; Hocktide, when money for the church was col-lected; Rogation Days for beating the bounds; St John's Day in June for sheep

174-Witney *op.cit.*
Arch.Cant. (1991)
175-John Thorpe, ed.
Custumale Roffense, (1769)
176-George C.Homans,
English Villagers of the 13th century, (2nd ed.1975)
177-N.Goose,
'*Wage Labour Meopham 1307-75*'
Arch.Cant. (1976)

shearing; Midsummer's Day on June 24th with bonfires and revels and maybe a wheel on fire rolled downhill to signify the sun's full circle; Lammas, the old loaf mass, on August 1st and the bread from the first new wheat brought to church to be blessed. The reapers would work in teams with others behind to bind and stook the sheaves and, after harvest, the reeve would ring the bell for the gleaners to go into the fields.

The Fair

The night before the patronal festival, known as the Wake, was when people stayed up all night and then had mass the following day, and of course Farningham Fair, which began on the 28th of June, and continued over the feast day of Saints Peter and Paul on the 29th and the two following days, was the high light of the year.

Fairs were large scale markets, not fun fairs. They were comparable in many ways to present-day County Shows. Village markets dealt with small scale local business from maybe a ten mile radius, but traders came from far afield to fairs. A special court was held to oversee fair trading, the Court of Pie Powder, or pieds poudreux, the dusty feet people. There was a great deal of fun at a fair, but the main purpose was merchandise.

The Lord of the Manor, or most probably his steward, would open the proceedings, usually with trumpet fanfares and pealing church bells. He would then declare the days of fair and hours and conditions of trading, and would supervise the court of pie-powder which was usually held in a temporary toll-booth. J.J.Jusserand's marvellous book *English Wayfaring Life in the Middle Ages*, Langland's *Piers Plowman*, and Chaucer's *Canterbury Tales* and the illustrations to the *Luttrell Psalter* all give a good picture of life on the road and at the fairs and markets.[179] [180] [181] The entertainment part of a fair was provided by the minstrels and jugglers, performing bears and dogs and monkeys. There were gingerbread sellers and the Plowman's 'Pies, hot pies, good pork, good goose, come and dine'. Ale would flow freely, and 'small' or weak barley ale would be brewed by many cottagers.

The Assize of Bread and Ale of 1266 set up aletasters to check on the price and quality of both, but it was a law that was hard to enforce and frequently abused. Alehouses were advertised by a pole with a bush on the end. In the same way an inn with a connection to a religious foundation had a bull, or bulla, outside as a licence, making 'the old bull and bush'. The Farningham Bull Inn may possibly have started this way. From the time of the Cheritons travelling ecclesiastics, monk wardens and government officials would have needed somewhere to stay.

178-Hubert Hall, ed. *'Select Cases of the Law Merchant'*, Seldon Society Vol.46, (1929)
179-J.J.Jusserand, *Wayfaring Life in the Middle Ages*, (1889)
180-B.M.*The Luttrell Psalter*
181-A.Burrell,trans. *The Vision of Piers Ploughman*, William Langland, Everyman ed. (1912)

Cottagers with a temporary ale licence for a market or fair hung up a bough and were called bough or bower houses.

The not so attractive and romantic aspect of a fair would be the many hangers-on, the cut-purses and beggars, lepers and mutilated cripples, Langland's 'lollers and loafers and latch-lifters', quacks with cures, herbalists, tooth-drawers, palmers with holy relics and pardoners with pardons, all out to make money from gullible villagers. There are many familiar scenes in street markets and fairs in poor parts of the world today.

The main business of the fair would be the merchandise, often spread out on the road; cloth and lace, knives, shoes, spices, pottery and metalware, fruit and poultry, honey and eggs and vegetables. In a hot summer the atmosphere by the fourth day of fair must have been terrible. Perhaps under-

standably, horses and cattle were usually sold on the last day. Maybe people who were used to sharing their homes with their livestock, drawing their water from the river, and with little or no sanitation, found the whole four days totally profitable and pleasurable.

A famous fair associated with mills and millers was the Charlton Horn Fair. The story traditionally attached to its origin was that King John once seduced the wife of a miller of Charlton and, being caught by the husband, compensated the miller by giving him all the land visible from Charlton to Rotherhithe, and the right to hold an annual fair on his land. The fair became known as Horn Fair because of the cuckolded miller and it was the custom for many centuries for people to come there dressed as kings and queens and millers and wearing horns on their heads.

The Market

The linear shape of Farningham village, strung along the main road, suggests a street market. Maybe the first markets and fairs were held in churchyards, but a statute of 1285 put an end to that practice. The forerunners of village shops, the wooden market stalls and booths, would have been set up on either side of the road. From the illustrations in medieval manuscripts these would have looked like small, collapsible beach huts with folding flaps for counters. Stallholders would have wheeled them on barrows from some distance and then slept inside for security and comfort.

The weekly market would have brought many changes to the village. Quite a few of the residents would now be craftsmen as well as agricultural labourers. There would have been work for smiths, carpenters, harness makers, and possibly weavers, tailors, butchers and bakers. The families of the farm servants would also have the opportunity to sell and exchange their surplus eggs, fowl, fruit and honey, and no doubt some fast food was made and sold at cottage doors.

If the pattern of the year was dictated by the agricultural seasons and the church festivals, the high days of the week were market days and Sundays. Since the late 12th century markets were no longer allowed to be held on Sundays which were now supposed to be strictly observed as days free from manual labour and buying and selling. From now on mills would be expected to cease from grinding on Sundays. Robert Bartlett describes a miracle of punishment inflicted on a miller of Wakefield who found blood flowing from his millstones instead of flour when he ground on a Sunday.[182]

John de Fremingham

By 1287 Ralph was dead and his manor of Farningham and his other lands had been 'taken into the king's hands...for certain reasons'. A great commission of enquiry into official corruption during the king's two year absence in Gascony was held in 1289 and ten judges ended up in prison. Perhaps Ralph was lucky to have escaped the fate of a fellow judge, Thomas Wayland, the Chief Justice of the Common Pleas, who was forced to 'abjure the realm', barefoot, holding a cross and penniless, by way of Dover.[183] Edward I is sometimes known as 'the English Justinian' after the emperor who codified the Roman laws and this was a period of great legal reform.

There is no record, as yet, of exactly where and when and how Ralph died and whether he was in disgrace or not. He had gone 'on the king's business' the year before, to the Welsh Marches, the border country where a war was waging. Maybe he died there. His heirs are given in the *Close Rolls* as Ralph and John of Heyham who 'are to keep his lands tilled and sown until a month from Easter' (1288) 'until they shall restore them to the king'. The brothers Heyham do not appear again in connection with Ralph's estates. Ralph's son John is assumed to have been the next heir and was probably still under age at his father's death and, if so, was maybe in the Heyham's wardship. For a time John Aleyn of Ifield, who was married to Ralph's wife's sister, Margery Apulderfield, administered the de Fremingham estates, presumably during the minority of his nephew.

The marriage of widows and wardship of minors provided a lucrative income for their guardians, who sold them to the highest bidder. Widows could escape by paying a high fine, wards were less fortunate. An heir could not inherit his property until he was 21 and by that time his inheritance might have been squandered by his guardian. Both boys and girls were also sold in marriage in extreme youth, often to their guardian's son or daughter. This 'John son of Ralph de Fremingham' was married to Agnes Stafford, daughter of Edmund Lord Stafford but how he made this advantageous marriage is not known.[184] He does not appear in the public records for many years after

182-Robert Bartlett, *Norman and Angevin Kings* (2001)
183-M.Powicke, *The 13th Century, Oxford History of England,* (1962ed)
184-*Topog & Genealogist, Manor of Apulderfield op.cit.*

73

his father's death and can be seen for the first time in 1313 when a record of a complaint by Margaret the Queen Mother was filed in the *Patent Rolls* saying that he and others 'entered her park at Leeds, hunted therein and took deer and cut down trees'. Perhaps this was just a case of youthful high spirits because, four years later, he was appointed Sheriff of Kent, an Office he would hold for the next two years and again in 1322 and 1324.

Ralph's Tomb

It seems very likely that we owe much of Farningham parish church to Ralph. The chancel and nave are believed to date from the 13th and 14th century, as does part of the tower. Ralph, with his ecclesiastical background, his moated castle and his market and fair, no doubt would have wanted a more impressive church. In 1837 an Early English tomb containing a stone coffin, dated to the late 13th century, was discovered in the south-east corner of the church.[185] Such things were less precious in those days and the coffin was last seen acting as a horse trough in the Lion yard.[186] The coffin had been rifled and only contained a few bones, but a fragment of the lid with a carved device not unlike a fleur-de-lys is set into the south-east wall of the nave. Reynold, son of Ranulf de Fremingham,[187] used a fleur-de-lys on his seal so maybe this was Ralph's coffin, although the later Freminghams used a different emblem. The coffin was said by one writer to have had a 'Lombardic' inscription on the lid, which might have linked up with Ralph's journeys to North Italy, although the vicar of the time said that there was no such inscription.[188]

Carved fragment of coffin lid set into the wall in Farningham Church

The Manor of Franks or 'Little Farningham'

A scandal took place in Farningham in 1300 when Sir Richard Scoland, a Knight of the Shire in 1295/99, (one of 12 knights who represented their shire in parliament), and Henry Sheneholt, a cleric, who were both 'tenants of half the manor of Cheriton in Farningham', were accused, not only of having withheld payment of their tithes, but also of having 'violently ill-used the chaplain of the chapel of Cheriton'.[190] The official of the bishop of Rochester was required to proceed against both men and, in a short while, the official of Canterbury pronounced that the offenders had been excommunicated. In 1301 Richard Scoland, 'having died and still being unburied', the Dean of Shoreham was directed to enquire for any signs of penance which may enable him to absolve and bury the corpse.

This is presumably the same Richard Scoland who, a few years earlier, in 1293/4 is described with his wife Roesia as the defendants of 'a messuage, 2 carucates (yokes) of land, 6 acres of meadow, 60 acres of woods, 11 marks in rents, and the rent of 100 hens and 500 eggs, in Fawkham, Farningham, Hilles (St Margaret), Southfleet, Stone, the Holy Rood and Singlewell'.[191] Although not entirely certain, this would appear to include the moiety of Charton Manor later called Franks.

185–Rev.Snaith, *Farningham Church, a guidebook*, (1913)
186–Miss Edmond's *notes for F'ham local history,* F&ELHS
187–Norman Moore, *St.Bartholomew's Hospital,* Vol.1 (1918)
188–G.L.Gomme, *Topographical History of Kent, (1895)*
189–M.Powicke, *op.cit. (1962)*
190–Canterbury Cathedral Library *Cartae Antiquae* F13a,F14 & Register B
191–John Thorpe, *Registrum Roffense (1769)*

While this story has nothing to do with the Farningham village mill, the history of the Scoland family winds up the saga of Wadard's mill, or non-mill in Farningham parish. They are the family who may have been the same as the family seen earlier as Scotland or Escolland. No mill is mentioned in this, or any other documents relating to the Scoland property so it must be assumed that the mill, if mill there was, had fallen into disuse. It is interesting to see however that Charton chapel was still in use in 1300.

In 1280 Ralph de Fremingham had also been accused of witholding his tithes from the Charton chaplain. In 1285 Roger de Mereworth was the tenant of the Charton half of the manor, while the Scolands held the other, Franks half. It is hard to know who was actually living at Charton and paying the chaplain but the Canterbury documents indicate that Ralph most probably held the manor from Mereworth and no doubt he and the Scolands resented paying tithes to Farningham church as well as to Charton chapel. In time the de Freminghams would acquire the Charton half of the manor as part of their estate. The monks of Christ Church also still took their farm from the manor and would continue to do so until the dissolution of the monasteries.

A later Scoland, Frank or Franco, is interesting as the possible originator of the name of the later manor. The *Eyre of Kent* of 1313, which reported the proceedings of the circuit Justices, related a case in which Frank Scoland sued his cousin Richard, now deceased, and his wife Roesia for the return of Frank's rightful inheritance. Richard, excommunicated as we know, had died without an heir and Frank claimed that the property should have reverted to him. Frank must have had friends in high places because the king himself wrote a letter to the justices in which he said that he had Franco's interests much at heart and commanded them to make haste to see that he had his rights without delay.[192] It was apparently a great cause célèbre and, with the king's intervention, Frank won his case. In 1234 he and his wife Alice appear in the *Kent Feet of Fines* defending their right to the manor of 'Parva (little) Farningham' and winning rights to their heirs, who were still in situ in 1359.[193]

By 1407 a John Hamond, rector of Chelsfield, and others quitclaimed their rights to 'the manor of Horton Scodeland, alias Little Farningham'.[194] How they had come by the property is not clear and the first mention of the name 'Franks' comes nearly fifty years later in a deed of 1442. By this time the Martin family had acquired the title and the manor is described as 'Horton Scodland, otherwise called the manor of Little Farningham, otherwise called the manor of Frankes'.

Nowhere is there any mention of Hasted's 'family of Franks from Yorkshire' although of course they may have been there between 1360 and 1440. But, as a postscript, it appears from the *Inquisitions Post Mortem* 1300 that Frank Scoland had been baptised and born at Warle (or Warley) in Essex in 1280 and that Warle was known as 'Warle Scodland' and later as 'Warley Fraunkes', which maybe confirms the origin of the name 'Frank's Manor'.[195]

192-Seldon Society Year Books Series Vol.V 'Eyre of Kent 6&7 Edward 3, 1314/14
193-Calendar of Inquisitions Post Mortom, 1359, HMSO
194-S.Keyes, Further Historical Notes, (1938)
195-English Place Name Society, Vol4 'Shoelands' (1971-2)

This has been a long digression in memory of Farningham's second Domesday mill, which must now be laid to rest while we return to Farningham and its one remaining mill, in the 14th century.

Unfortunately John de Fremingham was not sheriff at the time of Franco Scoland's 1313 Eyre. The Eyre of Kent was a most extraordinary proceeding. It was the work of the Sheriff, every 20 years or so, to collect all the citizens of importance from each of the hundreds of Kent together in Canterbury. This assembly would include the five great Justices in Eyre, the former Sheriffs, the Knights of the Shire, the jurors, coroners, counsels, attorneys, bailiffs etc. The 1313 Eyre began in July 1313 and was still going in May 1314.

Mills as Prisons

Felons awaiting trial were kept in prisons, of which there were several in the county. Earlier, imprisonment meant simply to be kept in chains in a castle keep or donjon, but by 1165 the Sheriff of Kent had provided prisons at Canterbury and Rochester, and Maidstone had acquired a prison by 1279.[196] An interesting feature of the prison system in Kent, and possibly elsewhere, was the use of mills as prisons. 'As fast as a thief in a mill' is supposed to have been a proverbial saying. Millers even held their mills by sergeanty of guarding prisoners. Mills at Canterbury, Faversham, Chatham and Milton are recorded as prisons in the 13th and 14th centuries and the practice is believed to have been common all over Kent.[197] The maximum amount of time of imprisonment in a mill should have been three days but there were reports of millers keeping felons in fetters for eight weeks. The fetters were to be provided by the lord of the manor. With Ralph's connections as a Justice and John's duties as Sheriff we can imagine that Farningham mill may often have been put to this use.

Watermill from the Luttrell Psalter
By permission of the British Library

196-R.B.Pugh, *Imprisonment in Medieval England, (1970)*
197-F.R.H.DuBoulay *op.cit.*

Chapter Five

14th Century Farningham/ the Black Death /
Vicar Thomas and his Vicarage /
The Second Ralph and Second John de Fremingham / Chaucer's Mill /
The Peasant's Revolt.

During the next hundred years the de Freminghams became part of the inner circle of Kentish families who ran much of the business of the county. They were Sheriffs of Kent in three successive generations, also Knights of the Shire, or MPs, and Justices of the Peace. They were neither aristocracy nor high court officials, although John had made powerful connections by his marriage with Agnes Stafford.

There is nothing much on record of the de Fremingham's demesne farm during the 14th century. The records of a comparable manor farm at Meopham from 1307 to 1375 are discussed by Nigel Goose in *Arch. Cant.*[198] This manor belonged to Christ Church, Canterbury but the composition of the permanent agricultural staff, the famulus, is likely to have been similar all over Kent.

Presumably there was a reeve, or overseer, who would be answerable to the lord's steward, who would supervise all the family manors, paying wages, collecting rents and holding courts. The de Freminghams now had several manors in Kent so they would be likely to have employed a steward. Farm work was now nearly all for wages, customary servile labour had almost come to an end apart from seasonal 'boon' works such as carrying and harvesting. At Meopham the farm servant's wages were partly paid in food, usually grain, and partly in cash as an annual stipend.

The reeve was, as before, elected annually by his fellow labourers and was at the top of the pyramid of wages and status. Below him came the ploughmen and carters, probably two of each to manage the teams of oxen. Then came the cowman, shepherd, pigman and dairymaid. There would also have been temporary seasonal labourers for hedging, ditching and harvest time.

Somewhere in the hierarchy of labourers came the miller, not too high up if he was a demesne servant, but comparatively well off if he was an independent tenant who rented the concession from the manor. We can assume that if the mill was held by the de Freminghams it was a demesne mill; that the miller worked for a wage, and that his status was probably just below the head ploughman. The lord's farm servants would all have had to use the mill and pay the fee of a proportion of the grain to the miller which would go into the lord's coffer, although the miller would always be suspected of fiddling the quantity for himself.

Millers were also frequently elected as reeve and that was another unpopular job, being the petty taskmaster of the village, taking the blame from the steward for everything that went wrong on the farm and collecting the court

198-N.Goose, *Arch Cant XCII, 'Wage Labour on a Kent Manor, Meopham' (1976)*

fines. The position improved during the century and a capable reeve might be retained for many years.

Roughly speaking a reeve's annual cash stipend before the Black Death in mid-century would not have been more that about 10s. By 1368 the Meopham reeve was getting 20s. the ploughman and carter 9s.6d, the shepherd 7s.6d. and the pigman 6s. So a demesne miller's wages were likely to have been in the same range. In a demesne mill the miller's tollcorn went into the lord's locked 'multure ark'. An independent tenant miller of course kept his own toll. An early measure of toll-corn was two handfuls from each sack. Later, as has been seen, a statutory toll-dish was used and this would vary from one 16th to one 25th. The Statute Pistoribus of 1270 stated one 20th but it was quite usual for tenants who owed suit of mill to pay a 16th. Free tenants paid less.

The food stipends for labourers at Meopham were the equivalent of 25 pounds of grain every eight weeks. Grain for the peasants was usually of poor quality, often barley. William Langland, writing *Piers Ploughman* in 1362, says that bread with beans was for the poor, fine wheaten 'stamped' bread for the landlords. (Bakers were required by statute to put a stamp on their quality bread). Piers himself had loaves of beans and bran, but he also had parsley, cabbage and leeks, onions and baked apples, halfpenny ale and salt bacon.[199]

There was possibly a decline in the prosperity of the village after Ralph's death. Although there might have been some reflected glory in having the Sheriff of the county as your landlord it was not a popular office and John's duties would have increasingly meant his absence in his London house or on his other Kent manors. There was a song in the previous century about unpopular sheriffs which went

> 'Who can tell truly
> How cruel sheriffs are
> Of their hardness to poor people
> No tale can go too far.'

Many manors had a constable, or borsholder, who was also elected by his fellow villagers each year. All villages would have a pound for stray animals, and the constable would be responsible for impounding them. He would also keep the peace on market days, supervise the aletasters, collect the fines for misdemeanours, call up the jury for felonies and supervise the provision of watch and ward and hue and cry and civil defence training. Law and order was kept by 'Watch' at night and 'Ward' during the day. If evil doings were detected someone would raise the 'Hue and Cry' and everyone would down tools to chase the criminal, who would be arrested by the borsholder and locked up, probably in the mill or one of the few other buildings with a lock and key, until a court was held and sentence pronounced. Punishment was usually by fine or a session in the stocks, imprisonment in a county gaol to await trial was only for very serious crimes.[200]

Every male between the ages of sixteen and sixty was also trained in the

199-W.Langland,
Piers Ploughman op.cit.
200-Rowland Parker,
The Common Stream, (1974)

78

use of arms. For poor men this meant the bow and arrow and the knife and possibly a small sword. Sports other than the practice of archery at the butts was frowned on. Commissions were sent out to survey the talent and recruit, or conscript, foot-soldiers. The King wrote to the Sheriff of Kent in 1363 that he was 'not to allow the common people to play worthless games such as football, handball, stickball or hockey or cock-fighting, but to teach archery with bows, arrows or crossbolts'.[201]

The Black Death

By the 14th century the climate of the Little Optimum was over, and the century would be remembered for terrible weather, plague and famine. There were disastrous harvests and famines in England culminating in the arrival of the Great Pestilence, as it was then called, in 1348.[202] John de Fremingham was Sheriff of Kent that year, but died in July, too early in the epidemic, which had only just arrived in the West country, for his death to have been from plague. His heir was his son Ralph. The *Inquests Post Mortem* show that the family now had properties at West Barming, Loose, East Farleigh and Sundridge, as well as Farningham.

Farningham is not likely to have escaped the Black Death. The rats which carried the disease would have followed the main arteries of roads and rivers, and the market and fair would have attracted hordes of rats. The wooden buildings of water corn mills have always been notorious breeding sites for rats so one might imagine that the miller and his family were early victims.

Plague arrived in England in the spring of 1348 and spread to London by the autumn. It died down again in the winter months, but peaked in the summer of 1349. It subsided in 1350 but in 1360 another outbreak, possibly not plague, occurred. Smallpox, measles, typhus and dysentery were all killer diseases in 14th century Europe. The plague reappeared during the 16th century and culminated in the Great Plague of London in 1665.[203]

The Farningham vicar, Thomas of Huntingdon, unlike so many of his fellow clergy, managed to survive the plague years. Plague was a disease of the poor. People in better, cleaner houses would be more likely to escape, and maybe Thomas was not very diligent about visiting the sick.

Vicar Thomas and his Vicarage

Thomas is an interesting figure. We know quite a lot about him because he was involved in a lengthy dispute with Christ Church, Canterbury Priory who were the rectors of the church, over what he saw as an inadequate stipend.[204] It is not clear when exactly he was appointed, but probably he had not been long in post before 1340 when he made his first request for an increase in his annual wage. The argument appears to have continued until 1348 when a long document, signed with the great seal of the Archbishop of Canterbury, sets out the 'advice of law, by way of sentence', of the sufficiency of the portion of 'Lord' Thomas (the courtesy title of a cleric without a degree),

201-C.H.Williams, ed. EHD4, 1327-1485
202-J.F.D.Shrrewsbury, A History of Bubonic Plague in the British Iskes, (1969)
203-ibid
204-Canterbury Cathedral Archives, Cart.Ant. F16,17,18,19

'perpetual vicar of the church of Farningham', and discharges the 'religious men' of Christ Church from any further claim by this vicar who has 'harrassed them wrongly'.

The vicar's entitlement is listed in the same document and it seems more than adequate. 'First, (in primis) he has a suitable and decent dwelling house with a hall, rooms, kitchen, bakehouse, barn, stable, garden, and with all suitable demesne lands, one with a pretty and decent orchard. Also he has a dovecote of his own in the said orchard, value 6s. 8d. p.a. Then he has 12 acres of arable land. Then he has the offerings of 225 souls of the parishioners at Christmas, Easter and the festival of Saints Peter and Paul which amount to 32s. 6d. Also he has and collects mortuary and anniversary offerings, 5s.p.a., and marriage and purification dues of 7s. 4d. p.a.'[205]

In addition to these fees Thomas also had the so-called small tithes of wool, to the value of 40s.; 30 lambs, valued at 4d. a head; 8 piglets at 4d.; 6 geese at 3d.; calves to the value of 4s.; tithes of hemp and flax worth 6s.8d.; apples and pears from orchards in the parish worth 15s.; cheese at 3s.4d.; beans in courtyards worth 2s.; 2 Dovecots in the parish worth 2s.4d.; 400 eggs at Easter worth 16d. and, lastly, a tithe of 2 quarters of corn p.a. worth 6s. 4d. from the mill of John of Farningham. As well as the above items, which Thomas no doubt found extremely difficult to collect from his reluctant parishioners, he had his stipend (called the alms, or eleemosynary) from the Canterbury priory of 5 marks per annum, which, valued at 13s. 4d. per mark made 66s. 8d. He also had grain worth 5s., and a quarter of palm barley, presumably for ale. The total was reckoned by the officials in Canterbury to be 75s. p.a.

However adequate Thomas' living might seem in comparison to the majority of his 225 parishioners, it seems possible that he was a poor relation of a grand family and had hoped for better things. He signed his documents with a most elegant little seal, showing a pair of gloved hands with some coins either falling in or out of them, a suitable device in the light of his troubles. He was possibly a relative of Juliana de Leybourne, the great Kentish heiress, who had married the Earl of Huntingdon and had a large estate at Wingham.[206] Another possible member of the same family was a John of Huntingdon who shared a knight's fee at Barming with John de Fremingham in 1346.[207]

These details of Thomas the vicar's living give quite a lot of clues to the kind of lives led by his parishioners, and the food they ate, also the fact that this is the first full description of a house in Farningham with its hall and rooms, kitchen and bakehouse, orchards and garden and, most of all for this history, the mention of the tithe of John of Freningham's mill, the sum of which was meant to be one tenth of the profits, presumably one tenth of the miller's multure ark. Two quarters of corn worth 6s 4d does not sound like a very rich mill.

To examine Thomas the vicar's position in Farningham it is necessary to go back to 1222 and the so-called 'Magna Carta' of parish priests upheld by

205-Zena Bamping, translation for HH of Canterbury Library doc no. F15

206-Arch Cant. Vol.1 'Juliana de Leybourne, (1858)

207-William Farrer, Honors and Knight's Fees, Vol.3 !1925)

Archbishop Stephen Langton at the Council of Oxford. This reorganisation of the parochial system was intended to 'regularise the vicious custom' of monasteries claiming parish profits and leaving priests with 'scanty portions'.[208] In the past, monasteries such as Christ Church Canterbury had accepted gifts of churches and had appropriated the rectories with the rectorial tithes, appointing their own inferior lay priests to perform the parochial duties. Now it was decided that if the rector of a church was unable to reside in post they must appoint in their place a perpetual, or life-long, vicar. These were no longer to be lay clergy but priests in holy orders who must be given at least 5 marks stipend and a proper house with sufficient glebe land to support them.

As has been seen, Archbishop Stephen had presided over an enquiry into the status of Farningham church in 1225 by which it had appeared that the monks of Christ Church Priory claimed it as a chapel of their church at Eynsford. It seems likely that this had enabled them to appoint lay chaplains and to claim most of the tithes. In future it was agreed that the monks, by virtue of their earlier claim, should have 'to their almoner' the great tithes of corn and 'the messuage in the east part of the garden' which contained six and a half days-work of land. A 'daywork' was a recognised small measure of less than an acre of land. The growth of population in the 12th and 13th centuries had led to many sub-divisions of the earlier land measurements and the sulung had more or less vanished in favour of the yoke and virgate, a daywork being about one tenth of a virgate.[209]

The vicar, by this agreement was to have the small tithes and oblations and Christ Church, as rector, had the great tithes and 'for the time being', the rector of Eynsford was, 'on a vacancy, to present to this vicarage'. This was how the two 'messuages' came into being, the rector's parsonage and the vicar's vicarage, which appear to have existed ever since on either side of the church, and are there to this day although both now are private houses.

There does not seem to have been any noticeable change for many years. The first vicar recorded in Farningham was Roger, chaplain of Otford, who was not appointed until 1284. This was during the time of Archbishop John Pecham's reforms of 1279-92. Otford was by then a seat of the archbishop and the headquarters of a bailiwick which included Farningham.[210] It may be that the monks of Canterbury had continued to keep a lay priest in office in Farningham until that time, and the church may still only have been recognised as a chapelry of Eynsford. In about 1290 the church at Otford itself was demoted to a chapelry of Shoreham, so the status of churches appears to have fluctuated.

The same Archbishop Pecham laid down the rules that a vicar must preach four times a year 'in the vulgar tongue', making sure that his parishioners understood the fourteen articles of faith, the ten commandments, the seven deadly sins and the seven sacraments. He must say mass every day and observe all the festivals of the church as well as performing burials, last rites,

208-R.A.R.Hartridge, A History of Vicarages in the Middle Ages, (1930)
209-CKS P 145/3/1 Tithe dispute papers
210-D.Clarke & A .Stoyel, Otford in Kent, a History (1975)

baptisms and marriages. Communion only took place three times a year, at Christmas, Easter and Whitsun. A famous 14th century preacher in the vulgar tongue was the neighbouring William of Shoreham. Farningham's Odo de Cheriton appears to have only preached in Latin, but we can assume that vicar Thomas used the Early English Kentish dialect with its use of z for s, a feature of local speech still in use by Dicken's Sam Weller in the 19th century.

To go back to the Black Death.[211] It is hard to contemplate such an enormous and terrible disaster. One third of the population of England is believed to have been wiped out. How many of vicar Thomas's 225 souls survived? Since no records have survived for Farningham it is no use speculating, but the Black Death is generally regarded as a major watershed, after which feudal society would never be the same again.

The Statute of Labourers of 1351 was an attempt to freeze wages to pre-plague levels, but the loss of maybe a third of the labour force strengthened the bargaining power of those remaining. There was a sharp rise in wages which did not necessarily last long, but the new spirit of independence did. All over England labourers were in flight from their oppressive employers. The days were passing when a miller could be sold as his master's chattel for five shillings.

In the towns craftsmen began to organise themselves into fraternities, mysteries and gilds. The roaming building masons had lodges or workshops where they could hope to find employment. Even the parishes had gilds, usually attached to the church, with the offerings of altar lights and the provision of an alms box for poor members. There had been gilds in England, in the sense of local, voluntary self-help organisations, since Anglo-Saxon times.[212] The gilds, or guilds, of the London merchants would all come to form the great city Livery companies. Several people with local connections were part of this world of sheriffs, mayors, aldermen and rich merchants. The Bukerels, friends of the de Cheritons and mayors of London, were Vintners; the Peches, later of Lullingstone, were Fishmongers as were the Sibills of Eynsford, and the Rokesleys or Ruxleys were Goldsmiths.[213][214]

The smaller craftsmen and tradesmen such as the bakers and millers would maybe join the lesser gilds. Bakers had been organised for a long time, and millers would often join them in their proceedings, but millers never had a great city guild, and village millers would work alone with a boy, probably a son, as an unofficial apprentice. Entry to a gild was by apprenticeship, sometimes taking as long as seven years, at the end of which, if they passed their tests, the apprentice became a journeymen and, if successful, might become a master.[215] In later centuries this became the way to enter the trade, the 19th century census has apprentice and journeyman millers. In the 14th century millers were still individual craftsmen, handing on their trade by word of mouth.

The Lay Subsidy of 1334/5 has a few references to the millers of the

211-Phillip Zeigler, *The Black Death*, (1969)
212-H.F.Westlake, *The Parish Guilds of Medieval England*, (1919)
213-Sylvia Thrupp, *The Merchant Class of Medieval London 1300-1500*, (1948)
214-George Unwin, *Guilds and Companies of London*, (1908)
215-M.M.Postan, *The Medieval Economy and Society*, (1972)

Hundred of Axstane. Lay subsidies were replacing knights fees and were a tax levied on moveable goods.[216] Many surnames still appear to be occupational, but this is now misleading. John Baker, although his father or grandfather may have been a baker, is now a leather worker. However, it seems pretty clear that William atte Melle senior, who pays 2s.4d. and John le Mellere junior the same amount, are both millers. There are also several miller's widows, Agnes atte Melle, widow of William, and Matilda, Celestria and Godelfa, who were all apparently left in charge of mills. It seems more than possible that many millers often had their lives cut short by lung disease.

A large proportion of the population were so poor they paid no tax. The highest tax in the hundred was paid by Isabel de Horton at £2. The Master of St John's Jerusalem paid £1.13s. It is not easy to pick out Farningham residents but Lawrence, John and William de Chimbham paid 10s., 8s. and 2s. 4d. each and Frank Scoland paid 15s.8d. John de Fremingham paid his tax of 10s. at Maidstone, presumably for his manor of Loose, where there were two millers, John de Pettemelle, 1s 6d; and Roger at Melle, 1s.

The 13th and 14th centuries were the golden age of milling. England would never have so many corn mills again. Richard Holt puts an estimate of maybe 12,000 mills, including windmills which had flourished in England since their arrival in the 1180s.[217] Another type of watermill developed in the 14th century was the fulling mill. Fulling, or the thickening and felting of cloth with fuller's earth, had always been performed by foot. The cloth industry, having declined for many years, would now, with the invention of fulling stocks, or wooden hammers driven by waterwheels, expand enormously. There is no evidence that Farningham mill ever became a fulling mill, but there were many in Kent, especially on the Medway and its tributaries.

The labourers of Kent had probably enjoyed much greater freedom than the rest of England. Gavelkind was the custom of Kent tenantry and would remain so until the 20th century. A statute of 1439 says that 'within the county of Kent there be but thirty or forty persons, at the most, which have any lands or tenements out of the tenure of gavelkind'.[218] The farm servants and casual labourers without land were obviously still tied to their employers who were in many cases the free tenant smallholders as well as the lords of the manors.

216-KAS, Records VolXVIII, 'Documents illustrative of Medieval Kentish Society', (1964)
217-Richard Holt, op.cit. (1988)
218-C.L.Sinclair Williams, Arch Cant XCV, 'Codification of Customs of Kent', (1979)
219-Arch Cant XXI, (1895) 'Knights of the Shire'.
220-Topographer and Genealogist, 'Manor of Apulderfield'. op,cit.

The second Ralph and second John de Fremingham

Sir Ralph de Fremingham, knight, aged 25, was his father's heir in 1349. He was sheriff in 1358, and an MP or Knight of the Shire, also 'one of the 3 or 4 men, learned in the law, assigned for the keeping of the peace in the county', in other words an early JP, [219] and was married to Katherine, sister of Thomas Earl Stafford,[220] presumably a cousin on his mother's side. By this time the de Freminghams were living mainly on their estates near Maidstone at Loose, West Barming, Half Yoke and East and West Farleigh.

Sir Ralph also paid aid for one knight's fee in Sundridge in 1346 as well as

The stone bridge at Rochester, completed in 1392 as depicted in 'Rochester Bridge in Three Epoches' by H.G.Adams published in 1856. Being a memorial of the opening of the new bridge and the taking down of the old.

one knight's fee in Farningham.[221] The Sundridge manor had formerly been held by his uncle Henry of Apulderfield. The other Sundridge, or Brasted, manor belonged to his father's sister Joane de Fremingham who had married John de Isley, so the Isley and Fremingham manors ran side by side.

Sir Ralph appears frequently in the public records on county business connected with his official duties. One of his commissions was to 'survey Rochester Bridge over the water of Medewaye' which was reported to be in a dangerous state. There were few bridges in Kent at this date. Farningham most probably only had a ford, although several stone bridges were being built in the 14th century. The old wooden bridge at Rochester on the London to Dover road was considered the most important in the country and was to be replaced in 1391 by a stone bridge of nine arches, each arch to be maintained by different individuals, the Bishop of Rochester for the first, the Archbishop of Canterbury the 5th and 9th, the King the 4th, and various lords of manors, including the de Freminghams, for the others.[222]

Sir Ralph died, aged forty, in 1364. His heir was his son John who, aged only 18, was committed to Thomas de Uvedale of Titsey, Surrey for wardship and marriage at a price of 200 marks. Thomas Uvedale wisely kept this young man with great expectations in the family by marrying him to his own daughter Alice. John came into his inheritance at the age of 21 and, in the inquest into proof of his age, witnesses, probably godparents, William Apulderfield and Joan de Cobham said that he had been born at East Farleigh on St Stephen's day, 1346, and that they themselves had 'lifted him from the sacred font'. Another witness, John Baker, said that he remembered he had built a

221-*Calendar of Inquisitions Post Mortem*, HMSO
222-S&B Webb, *The Story of the King's Highway, (1913)*

mill in East Farleigh called Pattenmill in the year the heir was born. This may have been one of the Loose watermills discussed by R.J. Spain.[223]

There were several inquests with jurors into the legitimacy of his inheritance. One, at Dartford, shows that the de Freminghams held land on Dartford marshes with a wharf and meadows and pasture. There were also 180 acres of arable land held in 'gavelkindes' in Farningham from William Souche of Eynsford, who was owed a pound of pepper and a pair of gilt spurs each year.[224] There were also 246 acres of arable land held from the lady of Horton Kirby which included 10 acres of 'meadow that can only be reaped in wet weather' and 46 acres of pasture.

These sound like the meadows between Farningham and Horton Kirby and were probably part of Charton manor as they included the ancient payment to the ward of Dover Castle. Other rents from tenements held in gavelkind from John de Mereworth of Charton were to be paid to Ralph's widow and John's mother, Katherine. The de Chimbhams, who had apparently risen to the most important family in the village in the Freminghams frequent absence, now held the three weekly manor courts in the village.[225]

John and Alice had no children, and so he was the last of the Farningham branch of the de Freminghams. After his death in 1410 the estate would go to his heirs on the female side, the Islays of Sundridge. This John, the last of the de Freminghams, now belonged to one of the leading families in Kent and was one of the most active public servants of the day. He was Sheriff of Kent in 1378 and 1393 and Sheriff of London in 1401, and also had some minor position at court, receiving occasional fees for robes.[226] An interesting speculation about his life is his possible relationship with the poet Geoffrey Chaucer. They were both MPs for Kent during the reign of Richard II, although in different years. They were also on circuit as JPs for Kent during the years 1385 to 1389. The JPs met at four sessions a year in different towns.

Chaucer's Mill

Chaucer is believed to have started writing *The Canterbury Tales* in the late 1380s, and it is nice to think that perhaps he saw Farningham mill during those years on circuit. One medieval mill was surely much like another, and most of them probably looked similar to the one illustrated in the British Museum's 14th century *Luttrel Psalter*;[227] small thatched buildings like the one where Chaucer's miller Simkins and his family and their two mischievous guests spent their riotous night in one room 'twenty feet broad'. Of course not all mills were so primitive by this date, and it is thought that Chaucer exaggerated for the purpose of his satire. Salzman describes many much more elaborate mill buildings by the later 14th century.[228] Weatherboarding, sometimes called waterboarding, was already used on mills by this date and large mills were being built on expensive constructions. A notable feature of the Luttrel Psalter mill is the enormous strong lock on the door. Mills were still often the only places in a village, apart from the manor house and the church, to have a lock.

223-R.J.Spain, *Arch Cant.* *(1972), op.cit.*
224–*Inq Post Mort, 1364*
225–ibid
226–B.Webster, *'The community of Kent in the reign of Richard II', Arch Cant. VolC, (1984)*
227–Janet Backhouse, *The Luttrell Psaler, BM. (1989)*
228–L.F.Salzman, *Building in England down to 1540, (1952)*

Left–16th century
horizontally driven
mill.
Courtesy Science
Museum Library.
Above–16th century
overshot mill.
Courtesy of Library
of Rare Books
University of
Wisconsin

In 1384 the grant of Farningham's weekly market and annual fair was confirmed to John de Fremingham, which must indicate that the family had a continuous presence here and that this most important aspect of village life had now been taking place for more than a hundred years. The annual midsummer fair on the 29th of June, the patronal festival of Saints Peter and Paul, would continue until the 20th century and, according to the Government publication *Market Rights and Tolls* there was still some kind of a market here in 1792 and 1888. Even in the first half of the 20th century there was still a monthly market for cattle and horses.

There are several descriptions of 14th century markets in a collection of texts from the Pie Poudre Court Records.[229] They describe the clerk of the market with his palfrey and attendant packhorse to carry his official standard balances and weights, the extortions of middlemen and purveyors, the forestallers, engrossers and regrators, and the Plea and Account rolls recording the hundreds of convictions for false weights and measures for bread and ale of inadequate quantity or quality.

There are also many descriptions of European merchants coming to English fairs and of the fortunes of their merchant ships such as the St Dominic of Piacenza which carried 62 tons of white wine and was attacked by Bristol pirates; and the goods from Padua stolen by the men of Sheppey from a ship that had been wrecked in the Thames. Certainly the fairs, especially those close to London and on main routes to the Continent, would have attracted foreign merchants.

229-Hubert Hall ed.
'Select Cases of the Law
Merchant AD 1239-1633',
Vol.II, Seldon Society
publications, (1929)

A 'typical case' is quoted between a miller, the plaintiff, who sued a husband-man, the defendant, for defamation 'inasmuch as, at the instigation of the devil the latter had uttered aloud these false, odious and scandalous words, "I sent to thy mill, in a bagg, to be grounde, good, sweet and sufficient corne to make bread, and thou, falsely, hast changed my corne and bagg and hast sent me home badd and worse corne, which would make noe bread". For how many hundreds of years had these accusations been made ?

There are cases of millers being pilloried, fined and even dragged through the streets on a hurdle. A miller was a skilled craftsman, he was expected to dress his own stones and perform running repairs. Machinery and new stones appear on manorial reeve's accounts but if a wage-earning demesne miller only earned the same as a ploughman, it is not surprising that they earned a reputation for sharp practice. Tenant millers were another matter, but even they had an unfortunate reputation for greed and social climbing.

Chaucer's foolish and corrupt miller was one of many such folk stories. He was clearly one of the rich tenant millers using rule of thumb, miller's thumb, to fill his toll vats. It would not be until the 19th century that millers began to be seen in a romantic light by writers such as Thomas Hardy and George Eliot.

In 1369 the wheat harvest failed and prices reached famine levels. A harsh series of taxes followed during the next ten years, culminating in the infamous Poll Taxes. The Black Prince, that great hope of the people, died in 1376. His father, Edward III died next year leaving as heir the child, Richard II, son of the Black Prince by Joan, the Fair Maid of Kent. Edward's second son, the Earl of Lancaster or John of Gaunt, became the unpopular eminence grise behind the throne. All these stories are very local and close to home.

The first Poll Tax was called in 1376, and was for 4d. a head on all adults aged over 14. This was the equivalent of a labourer's daily wage. The third Poll Tax of 1381 called for 1s. per head. Only beggars were excluded. The next story, also local and close to home, is of Wat Tyler, supposedly of Dartford, and the tax-collectors and the Peasant's Revolt

The Peasant's Revolt

John Ball, the popular preacher who played a leading role in the Peasant's Revolt of 1381, also belongs to the history of milling. He often referred to himself, allegorically, as 'John the Miller' and liked to use the old saying about 'the Mills of God grind slow and small', meaning that retribution would come to all in the end. One of his favourite rhyming texts was 'John the miller has yground small, small, small, the King's son of Heaven shall pay for all, be ye ware or ye be woe, know your friend from your foe'.

These were the very early years of the English Reformation. The ideas that would culminate in Wycliffe and the Lollards were slowly spreading and Langland's political and ecclesiastical satires in Piers Plowman would by now be well known. John Ball had been excommunicated and imprisoned on three occasions by the Archbishop of Canterbury during the last twenty years but he still roamed the country preaching in churchyards and marketplaces. The popular appeal of his preaching was his call for social equality. He denounced the church and the law and called for a levelling of the social order by violent means. When the Peasant's Revolt began in June 1381 he was in Maidstone jail and one of the first actions in the uprising was to set him free.

The rising started in Essex then spread to Kent and the whole of South East England. 'Riotous assemblies' had taken place in Kent as early as April but the main events happened in June.[230] Several large companies appear to have roamed the countryside gathering followers as they went. The main leaders, Wat Tyler and John Rakestraw, or Jack Straw, marched their men on Maidstone, Rochester and Canterbury where they freed the prisons and then, on June 12th they assembled a huge multitude at Blackheath, where John Ball delivered his famous address on the text of 'When Adam Delved and Eve span, Who then was the Gentleman?'.

Very few gentry took part in the revolt, but many of the so-called peasants were small landholders, often the elite of the villages such as the reeves, constables, aletasters and craftsmen and artisans.[231] They were independent people whose resentment of the social order would have been fermenting for some time, and they would now lead the peasantry in this massive revolt against the ruling classes.

A surprising aspect of the rebellion was its organization and co-ordination in an age of general illiteracy and slow communications but, as has been pointed out by Hilton and others, the villages were in fact already used to organization by their parish and estate officers and by their parish gilds, and weekly market-places would be obvious communication points, so Farningham market may easily have been a meeting place for dissidents.[232]

The 'commons', as the peasants were called, crossed London Bridge on June 13th and, with the support of the London poor, proceeded to burn down John of Gaunt's great palace of the Savoy, to set free the prisons and to mur-

The Savoy as it existed in 1650.
Fired, pillaged, and almost demolished by gunpowder by a mob led by Wat Tyler, in 1381, John of Gaunt's palace reverted to the crown. It was later restored by Henry VII. The Savoy Hotel now occupies the same site off the Strand.

230-W.E.Flaherty, *The Great Rebellion in Kent, Arch Cant. III (1860)*
231-Christopher Dyer, *Everyday Life in Medieval England, (1994)*
232-R.H.Hilton, *Bondmen Made Free, (1973)*

der several eminent men including the Archbishop of Canterbury. In all about 160 people were decapitated and day and night passed 'with hideous cries and horrid tumult'.[233] The end came at Smithfield with the famous appeasement and false promises by the boy king, Richard II and the death of Wat Tyler.

Sir John de Fremingham was in the thick of these affairs. He had been a Knight of the Shire, or MP, in the parliament of 1377 and Sheriff of Kent in 1378 and, as a large landholder with many tenants, was an obvious target for the rebels. He and three other prominent men including William Septvans the then Sheriff of Kent, were seized and were lucky to escape with their lives. Later, in July after most disturbances had died down, he would be one of the commissioners to try the captured rebels who would include several of his own tenants. John Cote, a mason of Loose, was a ringleader of one of the assemblies. The renewal of a 'grant of special grace to John de Fremingham and his heirs of a weekly market on Tuesday at their town of Frenningham and of a yearly fair there' may have been by way of thanks from the king for John's part in putting down the rebellion.

It would be interesting to know how many millers took part in the insurrection. On the whole only non-agricultural occupations are named, the insurgents without an occupation after their name were presumed to be peasants. Several millers appear in the East Kent indictments and there are a number of Melleres among the North Kent lists.

The Great Revolt took nearly a month to be finally put down. 'Riotous assemblies' continued for several weeks. On the 15th of June, the day of Wat Tyler's death in London, insurgents came through Farningham where they 'feloniously broke into the house of Edmund Chimbeham and the house of Richard Simond, called the Brotherrede and feloniously burnt the fences of the said Richard'.[234] Looting was a very small feature of the rebellion. One of the great aims of the insurgents was to break into the manor houses and burn the court rolls and the tax returns. Another frequent action was the destruction of the hedges and fences which had been set up to enclose the common land. The Chimbeham family lived in the manor house near Brands Hatch from the 12th century to the 14th, first as tenants of the Cheritons and then of the Freninghams, and the three-weekly manor court was held at their house. Richard Simond, 'the Brotherrede' is a mystery. Brotherrede usually means brotherhood but he was obviously no brother to the rebels.

From the evidence of the public records the de Freminghams had built up their Farningham estate by the end of the fourteenth century by leasing from various neighbours and the manor farm now extended into Eynsford and Horton Kirby.

Medieval land tenure is a very complicated story. Everyone held land from someone else, and the someone else often held from an overlord. It all seems like the story of big fleas with little fleas to prey on them. But as feudal tenure weakened, the free gavelkind tenants of Kent strengthened and the new century would see the birth of that phenomenon, the Kentish Yeoman.

233-C.Oman, *The Great Revolt*, *(1906)*
234-W.E.Flaherty, *op.cit.* *(1860)*

Chapter Six

15th Century Farningham / The Farningham Font / Roger Isley's Mill /
Jack Cade's Rebellion / The Pastons / The Farningham Landscape /
John Isley / Gilbert Carleton.

John de Fremingham was Sheriff of Kent again in 1389 and Sheriff of London
in 1400. He died in 1410 at his Brasted manor, which in fact belonged to his
uncle the Earl of Stafford, and he was buried at Boxley Abbey where memorial stones for his family can be seen today. His will directed 'a chaplain to be
found to celebrate divine service in the chapel of the Virgin in the church of
East Farleigh for the space of 24 years for the souls of him, John, and Alice his
wife and of Sir Ralph and the Lady Katherine, his father and mother, and John,
father of Sir Ralph, and Agnes his wife, and for Hugh and Thomas, Earls of
Stafford'. He and his wife Alice were also named in the chantry chapel on
Rochester Bridge.

The Loose property went to his cousin John Pympe of Pympe's Court in
West Farleigh and the Farningham properties to another cousin, Roger Isley
of Sundridge.[235] Although there is no mention of the mill in the inheritance
records its history can now only be followed through the Isley family.

The middle ages were coming to an end. Not that the Farningham villagers
knew that. Their years followed one another, generation after generation,
with the regularity of the agricultural seasons, punctuated by storms and
droughts, famines and floods, pestilences and pleasures. The great pagan festivals of the year, adopted by the church and given the names of saints and
the Holy Family, still lightened the monotony.

The end of the year, the autumn equinox, was marked by Michaelmas on
September 23rd. It was a quarter day when the rents were due so was probably not a time for rejoicing. Then All Saints and Halloween; Christmas, Plough
Monday, Candlemas, and Lady Day which was another rent quarter day, on
March 25th. Then Easter and Mayday and Whitsun, preceded by the Rogation
days when the villagers followed the parson, with his cross and banners and
bells, to beat the bounds of the parish, stopping at landmarks to beat the
young boys so they would remember the extent of their territory. Farningham
and Eynsford are incredibly lucky to have a description of the boundaries of
the villages taken in 1431 and translated from the Latin by W.G.Duncombe.[236]
Some of the names of fields and farms were still the same in the nineteenth
century, other names have changed, but it is still possible to follow the
bounds roughly on the 1840-42 tithe maps.

Midsummer of course was a great holiday, translated to the feast of St John
the Baptist. This must have run into Fair Week in Farningham from 28th to
31st June. Then came Lammas on August 1st, the old loaf mass which was
surely the miller's favourite feast. Then of course there was another great

235-Arch Cant 'The
Descent of the Manor of
Evegate' (1960)
236-W.G.Duncombe,
'The Boundaries of the
parishes of Eynsford and
Farningham',
F&E Local Hist Soc.
publication No14 (1995)

rejoicing when the harvest was brought home and a good time for the poorer villagers, when they were allowed into the fields to glean the fallen grains by hand and take them to the mill in little bags.

Everybody, high and low, observed the feast days. The Norfolk Paston family of 15th century letter writers often finish their correspondence with dates such as 'The Wednesday before St George's Day, Monday after Hallowmass Day, Tuesday before Candlemas, St Luke's Eve', and such things as 'written in haste St Peter's day by candlelight', and 'written on the Tuesday after St Simon and Jude'[237].

The Farningham Font

Family births and marriages and deaths, then as now, were rites of passage for all villagers. The marvellous Farningham seven-sacrament font shows ordinary people celebrating these occasions. The font is believed to date from the mid-fifteenth century, making it difficult to attribute a donor, perhaps an Islay of Sundridge, but that seems unlikely as they probably hardly ever lived here.

William Gysborne was vicar from 1434 to 1456 and as he was rich enough to leave a brass for himself in the chancel floor, perhaps he was responsible for the commission.

The font was originally painted with bright colours like the rest of the church. It is one of only 30 seven-sacrament fonts in England, all dating from the fifteenth century and believed to have belonged to a Flemish tradition. There are only two outside East Anglia, one in Nettlecombe, Somerset and one in Farningham.[238] Some are very fine, elaborate sculptures but it is easy to imagine that this one was made by local craftsmen and that these crude, squat rustic figures were typical Farningham villagers. There is a font at Southfleet parish church which is very similar in style.

In the panel showing Baptism the child is being dipped in the font. The godmother, with a bun headdress, waits with the white chrisom cloth to wrap the child. This was always given to the priest later for church ablutions, unless the child died, in which case it was used as a shroud. In Holy Matrimony the bride wears an amazing folded headdress, said to be typical of the early 15th century, which would perhaps allow time for London fashions to reach the country, and the groom wears a kind of bowler hat.[239] The wed, or pledge, would have taken place at the church door with gifts of dower; money, land and ring. The marriage, or nuptial mass would take place at the altar.

In Extreme Unction the dying person lies in bed with, possibly, a chamber pot underneath, and is anointed with holy oil by the priest, while an acolyte holds the oil chrysmatory. Children were confirmed young and in the

237-Richard Barber ed. *The Pastons, a family in the Wars of the Roses, (1981)*
238-J.Charles Wall, *Porches and Fonts (1919)*
239-Rev.F.W.Snaith, *op.cit. (1913)*

Left - Baptism
Right - Holy Matrimony

Left - Extreme Unction
Right - Confirmation

Left - Confession
Right - Mass

Left - Ordination
*Right - Administration of
the Holy Sacrament*

Confirmation panel a godmother holds an infant sideways. She looks a bit like Tenniel's Duchess with the pig child in *Alice in Wonderland*. The Confession panel has an evil demon standing behind the penitent, holding him in its claws. In the Mass the priest holds the Host in the air. It looks like a large round loaf; perhaps the first depiction of Farningham bread.

In Ordination the bishop, in alb, chasuble and mitre, holds a large cross in one hand and lays the other on the head of the small priest, or candidate. The eighth or Extra Subject is peculiar to Farningham and appears to show the administration of the holy sacrament to a dying or dead person, but this is open to other interpretations.

The churchwarden's accounts for a seven-sacrament font in East Dereham, Norfolk have survived from 1468.[240] This is a much more elaborate and elegant piece of sculpture than Farningham so perhaps the costs cannot be compared, but it is a fascinating document. It starts 'Imprimis, payd to the mason quan he toke the said funte in arnest...4d.', and continues with the costs of carrying the stone, chalders of lime and tile, iron and lead work and a number of expenses. The mason was eventually paid £10 'for workmanship of the seyd funte' and £1 for his reward.

Archbishop Peckham had said that parish priests need only preach four times a year, in the vulgar tongue and with proper attention to the seven sacraments of grace. Communion for parishioners was only neccessary three times a year, at Christmas, Easter and Whitsun, but everyone must go to church each Sunday to witness the mass. Preaching in the vulgar tongue had become a fierce subject of debate in the late 14th century. Wyclyffe and his followers, the Lollards, had pressed for reform of the church and he and the the Oxford scholars had produced an English translation of the Bible. By the early 15th century Wyclyffe's ideas had permeated a new class of literate artisans and craftsmen. A miller of Norwich was sent to prison for seven years for heresy. Among other things he had said 'Holy water is no more holy than that of a river or well because God has blessed all things'.[241]

Roger Isley's Mill

There is a superb inlaid brass in memory of Roger Isley on the floor near the chancel steps in Sundridge church. It shows him in full armour with a lion at his feet and is dated 1429, eighteen years after he inherited the de Fremingham lands. In 1433, four years after his death, a Roger Burys, miller of Farningham, was pardoned in court for not appearing to answer a debt of £40 to Roger Isley of Sundridge. Roger's heir was his son William who was to become one of the infamous 'extortioners of Kent' in the second peasant's revolt of 1450, and it might appear that William had tried to call in a debt that had already been paid.

The only reason that seems possible for Roger Isley to have lent Roger Burys £40 would be to have built a new mill in Farningham.[242] £40 would have been a lot of money for a mill. According to a contract between the prior of

240-J.C.Wall *op.cit.*
241-A.R.Myers ed. EHD *VolIV, 1327-1485*
241-A.R.Myers ed. EHD *VolIV, 1327-1485*
242-Gordon Ward *notebooks, Sevenoaks Ref.Lib.* Calendar of Patent Rolls, *HenryVI, 1433*, HMSO

Christ Church, Canterbury and two millwrights, a fulling mill to be built at Chartham in 1437 was to cost 22 marks or £14.13s.4d.[243] Another fulling mill made by two brothers of Pluckley cost of 23 marks and included 'bays, wheels, fulling stock, tail of the middle water through the mill and all manner of timber work'.

R.Holt in *Mills of Medieval England* says that the golden age of milling was over by the 15th century. Low prices of grain, shortage of labour and higher wages had made demesne agriculture increasingly unprofitable. It seems most likely that Isley had sold the lease of the demesne mill to Roger Burys and loaned him the money to set him up in business, maybe to build a new mill or maybe to include a lease of land. Maybe of course the debt of £40 was part of the widespread extortion that was taking place ten years later.

Jack Cade's Rebellion

In January 1450 there were mass demonstrations in South East Kent. Several ringleaders, who gave themselves names such as 'King of the Fairies, Robin Hood and the Hermit Bluebeard' were executed.[244] Tensions built up and in February and March an embargo on carrying arms was placed on Kent, Middlesex, Surrey and Sussex. In May the Duke of Suffolk was murdered at sea off Dover and by the second half of May a great Kentish rebellion was under way.

The dissidents later said that it had been rumoured that the king intended to devastate Kent to avenge Suffolk's murder. They said in their bill of complaint 'it is openly noysed that Kent should be destroyed with royall power, and made a wylde forest...' By the 8th of June an estimated crowd of 4000 insurgents had gathered at Canterbury. They had elected a leader, 'Captain' Jack Cade, and marched to London where they encamped at Blackheath. Unlike the 1381 rebellion, this was no longer a working class revolt against the established order of church and law, serfdom and the demesne system, which had already begun to lose its hold over the labourers. This appears to have been a rebellion against corrupt government, abuse of power, extortion, oppression and violence on the part of those who held high office.

It was not a rebellion of labourers; a large proportion of the dissidents were from a new middle class of small gentry, yeoman farmers and husbandmen as well as artisans and craftsmen who had gained the franchise by a statute of 1429-30 which gave the vote at elections of Knights of the Shire to all 40s. freeholders. By comparison, in the reckoning of status, an esquire's annual landed income was estimated to be from £20 to £40 and a gentleman's at £10 to £20.

The rebel's most detested official had been the murdered Duke of Suffolk, next was Lord Saye and Sele, Lord Treasurer and proprietor of Knole and the manors of Seal and Kemsing. Another, to a lesser extent, was William Isley, son of Roger of Sundridge, a lawyer and Sheriff of Kent in 1446. There were three other officials, William Crowmer, the present Sheriff of Kent, Robert Est,

243-L.F.Salzman, *op.cit.*
244-W.D.Cooper, *Jack Cade's followers in Kent, Arch Cant.VII, (1868)*

Keeper of Maidstone jail and Stephen Slegge, a previous Sheriff. These four, Isley, Crowmer, Est and Slegge were named by the rebels as 'the Four Great Extortioners of Kent'.[245]

Isley, Crowmer and Slegge had held all the offices of power in the county turn and turn about, Sheriff, Justice of Peace and Knight of the Shire. Later indictments show them as a kind of Mafia at work in the county. They and their underlings were accused of demanding and obtaining money and goods by menaces and acts of violence. Their bailiffs had taken possessions, crops, animals and even houses by extortion.

The 'dissidents' were chased by the king's men into Kent and down the Darent Valley where the king's army intimidated the population with unnecessary violence. This seems to have led to greater sympathy for the uprising which was now joined by men from other counties and Cade's men reassembled at Blackheath and Southwark. The king escaped with his court into the country, leaving the citizens of London to look out for themselves and on July 3rd the rebels flooded into the city. Lord Saye and Sele and William Crowmer were murdered and their heads set up on London Bridge. Cade was eventually persuaded to withdraw under terms of a general pardon and retreated to Kent where he was declared a traitor and was hunted down and executed in Sussex on the 12th July, 1450.

There is a long list of over 3000 names and occupations of people who received a pardon. Participants on both sides, including William Isley and Robert Est put in claims for pardon so it is not easy to see exactly who Cade's men were. Among them were one knight, eighteen Esquires and seventy four gentlemen including Richard Lovelace of West Kingsdown. The constables of several hundreds and the bailiffs and mayors of several towns claimed pardons for their whole populations. There were tailors, clothmakers, weavers, bakers, coopers, tilers, drapers, masons, mercers, grocers, chandlers brewers, innholders, vintners, taverners, butchers, thatchers, tanners, glovers, doublet makers, barbers, chapmen, mariners, shipmen, watermen, saddlers, grooms, poulterers, spicers, hackneymen, fish rippiers, sawyers, carpenters and haberdashers and, of course, millers.

Cade's rebellion rumbled on for several years after his death until popular revolt spilled over into the Wars of the Roses. Robert Poynings, younger son of Lord Poynings of Sussex, a landowner in Sussex and Kent, who had called himself Cade's 'Carver and Swordbearer' and had taken a leading part in the insurrection, canvassed in Kent for a fresh rebellion in 1453 and next year rode with a cavalcade 'in riotouswise and arraied in manor of warre' with 'sackes, hauberks, cuirasses, coats of mail and sallettes' through North Cray and Farningham. Nothing much came of this picturesque revolt and Poynings was later pardoned and lived to marry Elizabeth Paston of Norfolk in 1458.

245-I.M.W.Harvey, *Jack Cade's Rebellion of 1450*, (1991)

The Pastons

The Paston family of letter writers into which Poynings had married spent much of their time defending their Norfolk manors against other local families and their overlords. These were the savage years of the Wars of the Roses and faction against faction, family against family fought bitterly to keep their properties. Margaret Paston, Elizabeth's sister-in-law, was forcibly evicted from her home in 1448 by 'riotous people to the number of a thousand...arrayed in manner of war with cuirasses, body armour, leather jackets, headpieces, knives, bows and arrows, shields, guns, pans with fire and burning tinder in them, long crowbars for pulling down houses, ladders, pickaxes...and long trees with which they broke up gates and doors'. They cut through the posts supporting the house and let it fall down and carried away all her goods and money. [246]

Like Robert Poynings, William Isley was also pardoned and lived on through the 1450s and was again employed as a JP. There were several commissions of inquiry into the complaints of the people of Kent, and in 1461 inquiries were made into the charges of extortion and oppression by Isley and others at Sundridge. Isley's enemies, local yeomen, husbandmen and labourers, presumably his tenants and servants, rose up against him, resisting arrest by a posse led by Sir William Peche of Lullingstone. They hunted Isley down at Farningham where he was apparently being hidden by the vicar and, as he lay asleep in the vicarage, they broke in and murdered him.

Looking back on his career it seems clear that he was clever, politically ambitious and unscrupulous. He was a barrister-at-law, Steward to the Inner Inn, MP in 1441-42 and 1449-50, Sheriff of Kent in 1446-7 and JP on many commissions. His reputation makes it fairly certain that he was not a good or kind landlord and that the Farningham villagers suffered in the same way as his Sundridge tenants, and were no doubt jubilant at his fate. His brass monument on the floor of Sundrige church shows him in his legal gown. His wife, Elizabeth Warner of Foots Cray, was the daughter of John Warner, Sheriff of Kent in 1441 and another of the detested inner circle of influential people in the county. They, perhaps fortunately, had no children and he was succeeded by his nephew John.

The Farningham landscape

If, in the mid-fifteenth century, you were to stand at the top of Farningham hill and look down on the village you would see a fairly enclosed landscape, not so completely different to the present day, bar the motorways. The woods, though far more extensive than today, probably gave way to an open field between wood and village. This land had been cleared since early times so would have been good arable land and unlikely to have reverted to woodland. We know that some villagers owned parcels of land in some open fields and it seems likely that the large fields would have been divided with hurdles

246–Richard Barber ed. *The Pastons*, (1981)

or ditches to mark the boundaries. While there was no culture of open field agriculture in Kent, many large fields were subdivided. However, on the whole it was a patchwork landscape of enclosed fields and hedges.

Farningham Woods too would have been divided in parcels between different owners, the banks and ditches are still there. John de Fremingham's '25 acres of wood in parcels to be cut every 8 years' was one of many such copicelands. Down along the river was a long meadow stretching into Eynsford and known as Scheplonde in 1431 when the bounds of the two villages were written, or as Sheeplands on the 1841 tithe map. Sheep were a valuable commodity, not only for wool but for manure and would have been taken up and enclosed in the arable fields when there were no crops. They were of course also eaten for 'moton'. The Canterbury document giving the boundaries of the two villages is very rare and precious and gives many details, not only of the fields and woods but also of the inhabitants of the villages. Unfortunately, as it says, the information is restricted to the land on each side of the Farningham and Eynsford boundary.[247]

Brass in Farningham Church. The cross plate at the bottom (not shown here) reads 'Pray for the soules of William Pethim & Alys his wife which William died the 26th day of January Anno 1515'

Across from the woods one would have seen Petham Place farm, 'a certain house of John de Pethim' in 1431, and a brass in the church asks us to pray for the souls of William and Alys de Pethim who died in 1517. Then there were fields called 'Bennetsland' in both 1431 and 1841, now buried under the Swanley motorway interchange. A 'certain quarry' by Petham Place in 1431 had become 'Little Dark Holes' by 1841; possibly deneholes which were still quarried for chalk and flint in the middle ages. The best flints for building were found in the deep seams and the chalk was for liming the fields.

Other fields in 1431 such as Buddsdean, Claytons, Colescroft and Broadfield were still there in 1841. The field called Stone, or Stene, part of which was given to the Christ Church Priory in the 14th century by Walter Bell, is still there in the 15th and in the 19th centuries and some of the hedges described in the boundaries can still be traced. Several outlying small farms, now lost, have the names of their owners, William atte Moor, William atte Lofte, Richard Broadfield, William Bykyndle, Walter atte Hoke, John Melchaker, some of these are described as messuages or houses, others as closes or gardens. A close seems to have been about two acres, a garden would presumably be smaller. None of the names, apart from Bykindle or Bywindle appear in later documents.

On the hill opposite was Charton manor, which remained occupied as a private house until the 1980s when it was demolished. Its chapel, still there in 1450, continued to collect small tithes for the chaplain according to the Canterbury Priory documents. Although the Isleys had now inherited Charton there was presumably still a large farm there on lease to tenants and the Chimbeham family of the farm beyond with their tenants and servants would surely all go to Charton chapel rather than walk to the village.

The lanes linking the villages today are still much as they were in 1431. 'Scherlonde's Lane' (Scoland's?) is now Priory Lane which is now only linked

247-W.Duncombe, Bounderies of E&F op.cit.

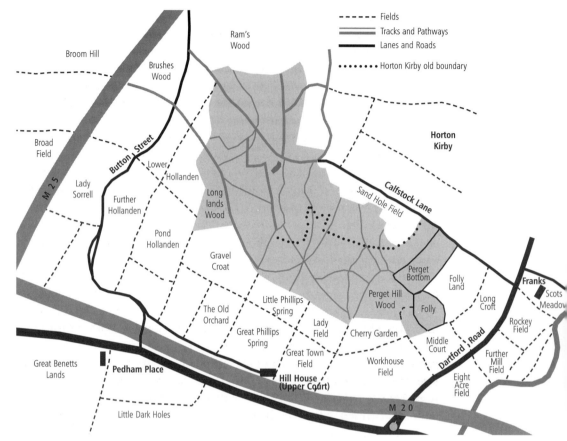

Farningham Woods and surrounds

by footpath to the Charton lands via Donkey Lane. 'Pethimlane' in 1431 is now Wested Lane and Crockenhill Lane was then called 'The King's Highway to Cray'. The 'King's Highway between Eynsford and Dartford' became 'Sparepenny Lane' in the age of turnpikes, and the 'King's Highway from Farningham to Maplescombe' has become Beesfield Lane. The King's Highway from London to Maidstone is not mentioned in 1431, but it would have been there, a wide dirt track below the woods. The expression King's Highway simply meant a right of way, it was not a 'made' road although 200 feet on either side were supposed to be kept clear to protect travellers from highway robbery.

The few small houses in the village would probably be hidden from sight by trees but one might see the remains of Ralph de Fremingham's castle, perhaps with a farmhouse inside the walls. The only house in the village which might have existed at this time is Lion Cottage which has been identified as a medieval yeoman's hall house.[248] Only a wealthy yeoman could afford such a well built house with its heavy cruck timbers and king post roof. Most of the village houses would have been as easily knocked down with crowbars as the Paston's house had been.

There would certainly have been alehouses in a village with a market and

248–P. Tester, personal communication

98

fair, and it is possible that the Bull Inn already existed because the name often derives from a bulla or seal of a monastery and the Bull Inns of Dartford, Wrotham, Otford and Maidstone are all thought to have the same origins and to date from the middle ages. The monk wardens of Canterbury would have needed to visit their farms and collect their rents and were surprisingly keen on commerce and providing hospitality for travellers. The Farningham Bull has records going back to 1587.[249]

The new class of yeoman came from the better-off free tenants. A forty shilling freeholder could usually be called a yeoman while the lesser farmers would be known as husbandmen.[250] The gavelkind yeomen of Kent became a byword for wealth and lavish living. There is an old country rhyme 'A Knight of Wales / A Gentleman of Cales / A Laird of the North Countree / A Yeoman of Kent / On his Yearly Rent / Can buy them out all three'.[251] Much later it was said that 'when hospitality died in England, she gave her last groan amongst the yeomen of Kent'.

Most of the other houses in the village would probably still be made of wattle and daub with thatched roofs. The tilers of Crockenhill were already at work in the 15th century so maybe the church and the better houses were tiled. The church itself of course was there, with a much shorter tower and without the porch but with the vicars 'good small house' next door and its garden for peas and herbs and the pigeonhouse. The rectory on the other side of the church must have been one of the better houses, it was rented from 1418 for £13.6s.8d. 'with all the profits thereof'. It was described as 'a house and garden with an orchard, two closes and 7 acres of land, and a barn to store all the great tithes of corn from the parish and the small tithes from Charton chapel. By 1450 a John Boteler, 'gent'. was the tenant at the same rent with all the tithes of corn in the village but the obligation to pay the vicar his salary of 5 marks.[252]

The village would be full of the sounds of chickens and geese and pigeons, horses and cows and oxen, sounds of the sawyer and the smith and cobblers mending shoes, men working in the fields and women in their houses and gardens and, at the heart of it all, the click-clack of the mill wheel turning, the sound of countless folk songs in so very many countries.

John Isley

There is not much evidence of what was happening in Farningham during the hundred years between 1450 and 1550. The Sundridge manor court records unfortunately have little to say about the Isleys possessions here. It seems from the Isley wills that they rented the manors to tenants but as yet the tenants names have not surfaced. The Farningham mill does not appear on the Sundridge accounts so that it too seems almost certainly to have been leased to independent millers such as Roger Burys. The weekly market may have continued, but probably on a smaller scale, and the annual fair certainly never seems to have stopped until the 20th century, but it looks as if the lord

249-H&W Harding, *The Pubs of Farningham*, F&ELHS No.19 (1996)
250-Mildred Campbell, *The English Yeoman* (1942)
251- Arch.Cant. Vol.9 1874, from Dr Pegges *MS of Kentish Sayings*
252-Canterbury Cathedral Library, *schedule C, Vol3*

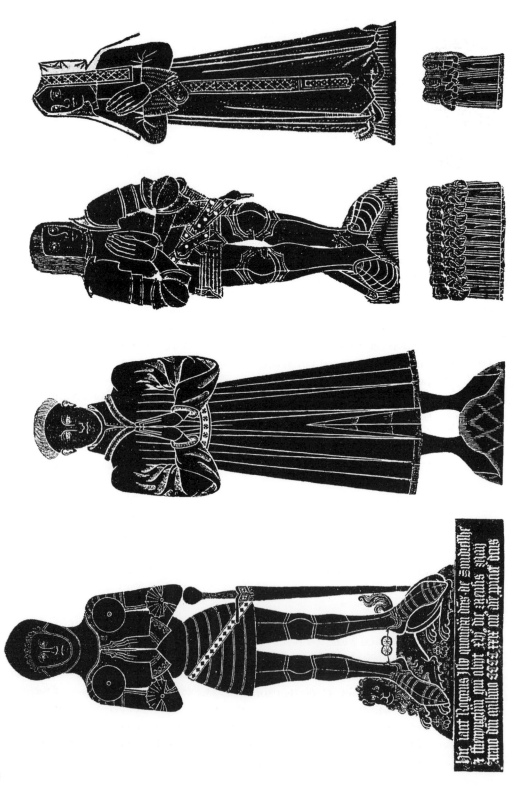

of the manor left his tenants pretty much to their own devices and desires so long as they paid the rents.

John Isley himself seems to have lived a fairly quiet life until his last years. He was Sheriff of Kent in 1474-5, but he became involved in Buckingham's rebellion against Richard III of 1483.[253] Buckingham was beheaded later that year and large rewards were offered for the capture of the Kentish rebels, including Isley who was later pardoned. He died in 1484, a year before the Battle of Bosworth decided the fate of Richard and the succession of the Tudors. The Isleys seem to have had an unfortunate penchant for choosing the wrong political side.

John had married Annis Morley of Glynde, Sussex and they had three sons, Thomas, William and Edward. His will, which was not proved until ten years after his death, left all the Farningham lands including Upper Court and Nether Court to his wife for her life and then to his son Thomas 'according to the tail (male) of cozen John of Freningham', there were also 'lands, tenements and houses purchased in Farningham' to go first to Annis and then to Thomas.

There are nice touches in the will such as the furnishings at Sundridge with 'tappets' in the parlour, bed hangings of silk and cloth of gold (bawdekyn), fustians, pillows and counterpoint, 'my grete chayne of gold', silver salts and pots down to 'three pissing basons'. He also left bequests to several churches including £26 to Farningham church and £6 to buy an antiphonar, or psalm song book, for the church. The feoffees, or tenants, of Farningham Upper and Nether Court and half the manor of Charton were to 'make estate' to Annis during her life and then to Thomas, and the feoffees of Bradbourne and Timberden mill to make estate to his son Edward. But no mention of Farningham mill.

Thomas was still a minor and the 'Overseer' of the will, Sir John Guldeforde, another high political figure in Kent and presumably Thomas's guardian, appears to have later organised his ward's marriage to his daughter Elizabeth Guldeforde. Thomas's mother Annis made two more marriages, the first to a John Harvey and the last to Sir John Paston of Norfolk. Unlike the other Pastons she left no letters, but her will is interesting even if it does not mention Farningham.

It is dated 1510 and says, 'If I die in London...to be buried in Blackfriars by my husband John Harvey lying there'... and if in Kent, in Sundridge. Son Thomas is to have the bedding 'in the chamber where I do lie when I come and am lodged in Sundridge', and her youngest son George was to have one pair of large sheets 'of my own spinning'. Other bequests went to daughter Isabel, wife of William Hatclyffe, and 'my cosen Alice Petham' who was to have her 'new black gowne furred with mynkes' and her husband 'a gowne cloth of russett'. Perhaps these are the clothes the Pethams are wearing on their brass in the chancel of Farningham church.

Clothes were a very important part of bequests, the best clothes went to friends and everyday clothes to servants. There were strict rules on clothing at that time. Only the royal family could wear purple or gold; no one under the status of knight could wear wool made outside England or velvet of crimson or blue, and no-one under the degree of gentleman could wear furs of animals grown outside England, so the mink fur was a status symbol. Annis also left 10 marks yearly to pay for a chaplain to pray for the souls of herself and her three husbands.

Her son Thomas Isley only outlived her by eight years. He seems to have managed to keep free from political troubles and he and his wife Elizabeth Guldeford had ten sons and three daughters, all of whom are depicted on his brass in Sundridge church. Thomas died in 1518 and left his estates in 'Frennyngham, Kyngesdowns, Charton, Maplescombe, Fawkeham, Eynesford and Horton' to his wife and his executors for the minority of his surviving young sons Henry, Anthony, Thomas and James.

Gilbert Carleton

One of the most interesting documents belonging to the late middle ages in Farningham is the last will and testament of the vicar Gilbert Carleton. It is dated 'the sonday on the next morowe after the fest of lammas called the old vincle of Seynt Peter the apostyll'. The year was 1500 and Gilbert had only been in Farningham for two years. It gives the impression of being made by someone old and 'seke in body' even if 'of goode mynde and hole memory'.

First he bequeathes his soul 'to almighty god and to our lady seynt mary ...and to all the saints and hallows of heven'. His body is to buried in the parish church of Farningham 'in oon of two places as can be thought most conveneyent by my frendes, other before the high awter in the chancell ther so that my feet may be under the preestes feete standyng atte masse, or elles under the steppe comyng yn at the church dore so that eny creature comyng yn att the same dore may trede upon my buriall'.

He then charges his executor to

New peynte and burnyshe with golde in such places as can be thought moost convenyent the ymage of our lady standing att the high awter ther and the ymages of peter and poule standing above the same awater...in lyke maner and forme as of late the ymages...in the psshe churche of Swanscombe be paynted and gilted. And also I will that every preest beying at my burying have in his hande burning a tap (taper) of three quarterns weight of waxe and the same to remayne to my moneth`s day...Also I bequeth to evry preest being at my dirige...say masse and be at my buryinge on the morowe have 12d for his labour, and every clerke being in lyke some 4d. And to every other child saying his de profundis have 2d. And to every preeste being att my burying and say masse and not being at my dirige 8d And whete to be baken in brede and malt to be browyn in ale and spende att my dirige and burying'[254]

And at his 'month's day' it was all to happen again, for priests, clerks and poor people to the sum of 2 quarts malt with wheat according and 'with vittall as beffe and moton accordying'. Also there were to be provided five priests to sing and say dirige in the quire of Farningham church for the space of a month, 'havyng at my charge mete and drynke convenyent and takyng for their salary 10d.' There were other bequests, such as to Lady Peche (of Lullingstone) 'my booke of legenda aurea' (the Golden Legend, one of 254-PRO,Prob11, 1500

Caxton's first printed books). Thomas, his servant was to have Gilbert's 'hole arrayment', short doublet, hose, shoon, gown, bonnet, hat, horse, saddle, bridle and 20s money. Yet another servant, Henry Godfrey, was left his whole wages and a gown. Charles Carleton 'preest and brother to me' was executor and was to dispose of remaining goods in the most charitable manner possible.

The village cannot often have seen such a splendid, lavish and generous funeral, and what an extraordinary change in the circumstances of the vicar since poor clerk Thomas tried to persuade the prior of Canterbury to raise his salary from five marks. It is also a wonderful picture of the interior of the church, with the carved and gilded statues above the rood screen and beyond. We can imagine too that the walls were still covered with their medieval paintings and that there were lights in front of all the images and small and large candles burning and the smell of incense. It is a last glimpse of the middle ages.

By 1552 the Farningham churchwardens, Leonard Taylor and John Everest, had taken 'into safe keeping' the plate, vestments and valuables of the church in accordance with the new, Protestant guidelines.[255] Medieval vestments were forbidden, and only a surplice allowed. The chalice of silver with the cloth of gold vestment and the albe went, along with lesser vestments and albes of velvet, tawney and blue crewel work. Only a vestment of cloth of gold remained in the posession of Richard Goodhew, yeoman, whose sister had apparently hidden it.

Also confiscated were three bells 'situated in the steeple', which maybe means the tower or perhaps the tower then had a small steeple on top. The gilded statues are not mentioned so had presumably already been demolished by an act of 1548 for the abolition of images in churches and chapels.

The office of churchwarden was already quite old. They were sometimes called church reeves and were responsible for maintaining the fabric of the church and for fund raising by means of church-ales or hiring out church property.[256] From 1538 they were, with the vicar, to become registrars of baptisms, marriages and burials. They would later 'meet in Vestry assembled with the principal inhabitants', or higher ratepayers of the village. The vestry being the little room in the church where ecclesiastical vestments were kept. The officers of the Vestry would be the Constables, Highway Wardens or Surveyors and, after the Elizabethan poor laws, the Overseers of the Poor. The Vestry would continue as the instrument of local government until the establishment of Parish Councils in the late 19th century.

The English Protestant Reformation was a long time in the making. At the beginning of the sixteenth century dissent and heresy only existed in isolated pockets. Some Lollard communities in East Kent were denounced in 1511-12 and several heretics burned at the stake.[257] Most Lollards were small tradespeople and artisans. Lutheran ideas only started to filter through to the gentry from the late 1520s.

255-*Arch. Cant VIII* (1872) Inventories of church goods 1552.
256-W.E.Tate, *The Parish Chest,* (1946)
257-A.G.Dickens, *The English Reformation,* (1964)

Chapter Seven

*Sixteenth Century Farningham / the Ropers / Wyat's Rebellion /
Anthony Roper / the Theewes Claviorgan / Law and Order /
Assizes / Murder / the Poor Laws / the Inns / Titles /
The Roper's Manor House.*

The lands of the de Freminghams at Maidstone which had gone by marriage
to the Pympe family, came back to the Isleys on the death of Reynold Pympe,
the last of his line, in 1530. These high Kentish families intermarried
throughout the centuries and it is difficult to keep track of them. Sir Henry,
or Harry Isley, Thomas Isley's son, had married Cecily Crowmer from the family of the infamous extortioner. The Apulderfields, last seen in the time of
Ralph de Fremingham, owned Badmangore near Lynsted, and now come back
into the picture with an Apulderfield daughter whose marriage to Sir John
Fyneaux produced a daughter, Elizabeth Fyneaux who married John Roper of
Well Hall, Eltham. The Ropers, who were on the opposite side to the Isleys in
the troubles of the mid-century, were about to take over the history of
Farningham.

The Ropers

John and Elizabeth Roper had two sons, William, the elder, who inherited the
family's Eltham and Canterbury properties and Christopher who inherited
the Lynsted property. William, a lawyer, became the protégé, and biographer,
of Sir Thomas More. He lived in More's house and married his daughter
Margaret in 1521 when she was fifteen and he twenty three. Margaret, as a
highly educated young woman, presumably had some choice in the matter
but a story, probably apocryphal, told by John Aubrey in *Brief Lives* says that
More took Roper to the room where his daughters lay asleep and told him to
choose one of them. More then whipped off the sheets, exposing both girls
'on their Backs and their smocks up as high as their armepitts. This awakened
them and immediately they turned on their bellies. Quoth Roper "I have seen
both sides", and so gave a patt on the buttock he made choice of, sayeing
"Thou art mine."'[258]

William Roper dabbled with Lutheranism to his father-in-law's distress. More
apparently once said to his daughter 'Meg, I have borne a long time with thy
husband; I have reasoned and argued with him in those points of religion...but I perceive none of this able to call him home; and therefore...I will
clean give him over, and get me another while to God and pray for him'.[259]
Time answered More's prayers; Roper returned to the old religion and
remained a staunch defender of More throughout his trials and execution.
Thomas More had foreseen his fate early on, when he was at the height of
King Henry's favour; 'Son Roper' he said '...if my head could win him a castle
in France, it should not fail to go'. He went to the scaffold in 1535 and his

258-R. Lawson Dick,
Aubrey's Brief Lives,
Peregrin ed. (1962)
259-R. W. Chambers,
Thomas More, (1935)

104

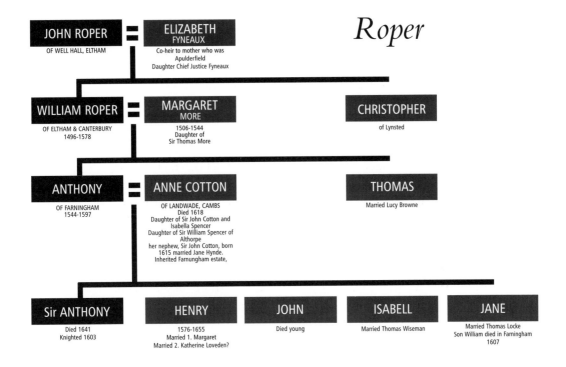

Roper

JOHN ROPER
OF WELL HALL, ELTHAM

= **ELIZABETH FYNEAUX**
Co-heir to mother who was
Apulderfield
Daughter Chief Justice Fyneaux

WILLIAM ROPER
OF ELTHAM & CANTERBURY
1496-1578

= **MARGARET MORE**
1506-1544
Daughter of
Sir Thomas More

CHRISTOPHER
of Lynsted

ANTHONY
OF FARNINGHAM
1544-1597

= **ANNE COTTON**
OF LANDWADE, CAMBS
Died 1618
Daughter of Sir John Cotton and
Isabella Spencer
Daughter of Sir William Spencer of
Althorpe
her nephew, Sir John Cotton, born
1615 married Jane Hynde.
Inherited Farnungham estate,

THOMAS
Married Lucy Browne

Sir ANTHONY
Died 1641
Knighted 1603

HENRY
1576-1655
Married 1. Margaret
Married 2. Katherine Loveden?

JOHN
Died young

ISABELL
Married Thomas Wiseman

JANE
Married Thomas Locke
Son William died in Farningham
1607

head is buried in the Roper family vault in St Dunstan's Canterbury.

William Roper was imprisoned in the Tower at various times but released on payment of a fine of £100 in 1543. This was the year of Queen Mary's accession and, in the change of religious climate, William was made Sheriff of Kent and was later an MP in Mary's parliaments of 1554, 56 and 57. It is sad, but probably true, to think that he must have condoned some of Mary's persecutions of Protestant heretics.

Fortunately perhaps, Margaret Roper died in 1544 at the age of forty, before the burnings began, and shortly after giving birth to her youngest surviving son, Anthony. Fifty eight Protestants were burned at the stake in Kent; Edmund Allen, a miller from Frittenden and his wife Katherine were burned at Maidstone in June 1557, his crime having been that he was 'given to reading the Bible to his neighbours'.[260]

The vicissitudes of religious belief that took place after Henry had made the severance from Rome meant that the first vigorous swing towards Protestantism under Edward VI gave way to a violent swing back to Catholicism under Mary. However, Sir Thomas Wyatt's Kentish rebellion of 1554 against Mary's Spanish marriage appears to have been motivated more by xenophobia than religious fervour. A foreign king was considered 'the undoing of this realm'.[261] Young Sir Harry Isley and his brother Thomas probably joined the insurgents from the same motives. There must also have been an element of the prominent Kentish families sticking together. Thomas Wyatt of Allington and Boxley, Henry Isley of Sundridge, Farningham and

260-Ed. Michael Zell, *Early Modern Kent*, 1540-1640, (2000)
261-Robert Furley, *History of the Weald*, op.cit.

Maidstone and Thomas Culpeper of Begbury had all been Sheriffs of Kent under Edward VI. No doubt too there was a higher political Protestant influence making the most of the divisions in Kentish society.[262]

Wyatt's Rebellion

Wyatt raised a large army of Kentish rebels from his friends and neighbours and their tenants. The Isleys raised another band from the Weald and marched to meet Wyatt at Rochester but were intercepted by the Sheriff and his men, who remained loyal to the Queen and who engaged them in battle at Wrotham where they were defeated. Wyatt's men marched on to Blackheath and into London but his followers suddenly melted away in the face of the Queen's army of opposition. Wyatt was declared a traitor and beheaded in the Tower. The Isley brothers were taken prisoner at Maidstone and were both executed there for treason.

The Royal marriage went ahead and in 1555 Henry Isley's lands were sequestered by the crown although his son, William Isley, 'from pity of the king and queen for him and in consideration of £1000 paid by him', was granted restoration of his father's properties. However he was eventually forced by debt to sell them back to the crown. The Farningham lands were all listed in the public records in 1555 at the time of their seizure and it seems worth while to quote the full description.

'Henry Isley knight, lately attainted of high treason, was seized of various lands including the following, all in Farningham. viz a yearly rent of eleven and a half pence and service from lands of Edward Marten at Calvestoke, lands in the several tenures of the heir of Lancelot Sibbell, gentle-

262-Peter Clark, *English Provincial Society from the Reformation to the Revolution,* (1977)

man, and of John Everhurste (Everest) and Richard Goodhew, alias Goodeawe, a messuage called 'Uppercourte' with lands (242 ac) belonging thereto in the tenure of Leonard Taylour, alias Gibson, woods and woodlands called 'Fernyngham wood' and 'Frith wood' lying on the north of the high road leading from Fernyngham to Fotescraye in the said Tailour's tenure, the site of the manor of Farnyngham called 'Nethercourte' with barns, gardens etc belonging thereto in Tailour's tenure, demesne lands (15ac 1r) belonging to the same manor in certain places called 'le eight acres, 'le great meadowe' and 'Foxhill', a cottage and lands (30ac) called 'Charton felde', a meadow called Charton meade' (7 ac) in Tailour's tenure, all lands (230 ac) parcel of the said moiety of the manor of Charton on the east side of the way leading from Farnyngham to Horton and on the east side of the way leading from Farnyngham to Maplescombe in the tenure of Alan Best, a parcel of land (2 ac) with all coneys in the same adjacent to the chapel called 'Charton chapppell' in the said Best's tenure, a cornmill, a messuage and a stable and divers arable lands called 'le Myl Crofte' (5 ac), certain other lands called 'le Myl Hope (4 ac meadow) in the tenure of Lawrence Jackson, and all lands (80 ac) in the tenure of John Notte the younger.......[263]

So there is the mill, tenanted by Lawrence Jackson about whom we unfortunately know nothing as yet. The Farningham parish records only start in 1589-90 and, although there are Jacksons living in the village in the early 17th century they are not necessarily the same family. The first miller mentioned in the records is not even given a full name, simply the date of the death in 1593 of 'Matthew a myllar'. He probably worked for William Stransham who appears as the Farningham miller in the 1593 Quarter Sessions records, standing surety for John Miller, the Farningham baker.[264] The Millers were a great Farningham family for several generations and may well have been the descendants of actual earlier millers.

Richard Goodhewe and John Everest have already appeared at the Protestant confiscation of the church property. The Everests were one of the oldest recorded Farningham families and were still represented in the village in the year 2000. Another of the Farningham families mentioned above were the Sibills who acquired the manor of Chimbhams in the late 15th century.[265] John Sibill, citizen of London, who died in 1401 apparently bought lands in Kent which were inherited by his sons and grandsons. An Alderman Sibbil, Fishmonger, was among those who opened the gates of London Bridge to the Kentish rebels in the Peasant's Revolt of 1381. There is a brass dated 1519 in memory of Thomas Sibil of Chimhams and his wife Agnes in Farningham church. The Sibils bought up a number of Farningham lands including Shepelands, Buddsdean, several crofts and Bywymble from Richard Goodhewe and later aquired several lands from the Isleys. Their main residence became Little Mote in Eynsford. They were connected, perhaps by marriage with a family called Gibson, alias Tailor, who are also mentioned above, and were yeomen of Eynsford who owned or leased several lands in Farningham including an inn called the Swan and another called the George,[266] the last being remembered today in the name of the cricket field or George Meadow. Leonard Tailor, the churchwarden in 1552 may have been a member of this family, as may Alice Taillor who has a brass in the church chancel.

263-Calendar of Patent Rolls, 8 March 1555, from a translation by Roger Cockett
264-Calendar of Quarter Session Records 1574-1622
265-Arch. Cant Vol XXVI, 'Little Mote, Eynsford' (1904)
266-Probate 26 June 1528 transcribed by L.L.Duncan c. 1900. courtesy Zena Bamping

Women in Farningham

Meanwhile, what of women in the sixteenth century? Anthony Fitzherbert wrote *The Boke of Husbandry* in 1523 which tells a housewife how to spend her day. First she gets up, makes the sign of the cross and says her Paternoster, Ave and Credo. Then she must sweep the house, get dressed, milk the cows, suckle the calves and strain the milk and then dress the children. Then she must see that breakfast, dinner and supper were arranged for the day. She must send corn and malt to the mill so that she can bake and brew when it is needed, 'and meete it to the mill and from the mill and see that thou have thy measure again beside the toll or else the miller deal not truly with thee'.

Then she must make butter and cheese when she may, serve her swine morning and evening, give the poultry their meat in the morning and take heed how hens, ducks and geese do lay and gather the eggs, and when they wax broody to set them where no beasts will harm them and look after them when hatched. March is the time for the wife to make her garden and get good seeds and herbs for the pot and to sow hemp and flax so she can spin, wind, wrap and weave for sheets, broad cloths, towels, shirts, smocks, and if there are sheep then there is wool to spin. 'And let thy distaff be always ready for a pastime that thou be not idle'. It is also a wife's occupation to winnow corn, make malt, wash and wring, make hay, shear corn and, in time of need, to help her husband fill the muckwain or dung cart, to drive the plough, load the hay, and go to market to sell butter, eggs, cheese, milk, chickens, capons, hens, pigs, geese and corn. Also to buy all necessary things for the household and to make a true reckoning.

These instructions were undoubtedly intended for a rich yeoman's household. Very few women in Farningham would have had the chance to look after so much livestock and prepare so many meals although most would surely have worked from dawn to dusk and even the poorest would have taken gleanings to the mill. There were many years of famine during the century and probably half the rural population lived in poverty. Harvest failures, rapacious landlords and endemic disease made life for the poor very hard. Plague returned every few years and there were many other killer diseases for the weak and underfed. Farningham market seems to have disappeared for a while during the sixteenth century so it is unlikely that the village was still such a prosperous place as before. William Roper, the new owner of the manor was to be an absentee landlord, as the Isleys had been, so there was still no resident proprietor to oversee the running of the estate and the welfare of the inhabitants.

William's brother, Christopher, had been on the commision of conservative Catholic gentry appointed to try Wyatt's rebels, and William himself was MP for Rochester in 1554 and for Canterbury in 1555-7. These Catholic gentry and, in William's case, high powered lawyers for the Crown, were in a position to benefit from the redistribution of rebel property and, some time during the next few years of Queen Mary's reign, William acquired the Isley's estates in Farningham. He continued his work in London as Protonotary (first clerk) of the Queen's Bench and presumably lived mainly on his London property or at Eltham. Records of Lincoln's Inn show that in July 1565 he obtained admission to his own chamber for his two sons, Thomas and Anthony. Anthony would by then be twenty years old.

Anthony Roper

The Roper's London residence had been the house built in the grounds of Thomas More's house in Chelsea, right on the river next to the old church. They also had Well Hall in Eltham and the Roper house in Canterbury of which the gateway, dated to William's time, still remains.[267] Where Anthony was brought up is not known, but Well Hall is assumed to have been the main family house with a large staff of servants and relations. The Ropers were a large family and Anthony had three elder sisters as well as his older brother and many aunts and uncles to assist with the motherless child.

William Roper died in 1578 at the age of 82 having been a widower for 34 years. He had remained a Catholic to the last, although he had been summoned several times to keep the peace for failing to go to church, for refusing to sign the Act of Uniformity and, by Queen Elizabeth's Privy Council, for helping Catholics with funds and for publishing subversive books.[268] By his will he asked to be buried in Chelsea parish church 'with the bodie of my dearlie beloved wief... and where my father-in-lawe Sir Thomas More did mynd to be buried'. He was however buried in the Roper vault in Canterbury. His will left property in Kent, Middlesex, Staffordshire, Oxfordshire and the City of London.[269]

His house at Eltham was to be maintained for two years with wages, meat and drink for his servants so 'that every one of them may have more time to provide for themselves'. Also his clerks were to be provided for. His younger son Anthony was to inherit 'all my landes, tenements and hereditaments in ffarningham, Horton Kirby, Kingsdowne, Mayplescombe, ffawkham, Eynsford, Sutton-at-Hone, Cherendge and Estgrenewich'. Anthony was also to have other properties in Middlesex, Oxford and the City of London. His elder son Thomas inherited the Eltham and Canterbury estates.

Anthony continued his practice as Clerk of the Papers of the Queen's Bench. His brother Thomas had followed his father as one of the two Protonotaries of the same court. Catholics and non-conformists were now known as recusants and both Ropers were still on the recusant lists of Lincoln's Inn in 1577 although in 1575 Anthony had been warned that he was 'spared from the expulsion of the Fellowship of this House until the end of Hilary Term next so that (he) in the mean time receive the communion'. He must have found some way of avoiding expulsion, probably with a fine.

The anti-Catholic climate hardened in the 1570s and by 1582 it became treasonable to be a Jesuit or missionary priest, or to harbour them.[270]

267-T.P.Smith 'The Roper Gateway, Canterbury', *Arch. Cant.* CVIII, (1990)
268-E.E.Reynolds, *Margaret More*, (1960)
269-*Dictionary of National Biography*, (compact ed. 1975)
270-P.Clark op.cit.

Any 'images of idolatry' and 'papist toys' remaining were to be removed, a fine of 1s for non-attendance at church on Sundays was imposed and rood screens were pulled down. The only remaining vaulted screens in Kent are at Shoreham and Lullingstone.[271] In 1581 'A Masse Priest and certen Popish trash for massing' were found at Well Hall and Thomas Roper was committed to the Fleet prison for 'Papistry'.[272] This may have been the time Anthony decided to leave London for a quiet life in the country. There is no record of when he first came to live in Farningham. The parish registers do not start until 1588/9 and the first Roper entry is for Anthony's death and burial in 1597 at the age of 53.

Anthony had married Anne Cotton of Landwade, Cambridgeshire in about 1570. The Cottons were another old recusant family and Anne was the daughter of Sir John Cotton and Isabella, daughter of Sir William Spencer of Althorpe, (so she was an ancestor of Princess Diana). The Roper's wall memorial in Farningham church shows Anthony and Anne with their three sons, Anthony, John and Henry, and two daughters, Isabella and Jane. The younger Anthony was probably still a minor at his father's death and Jane the youngest, was only nine.[273]

The left-hand shield in Anthony Roper's memorial. The crescent moon which can be seen in the centre of the shield has special significance. The heraldic rule of 'cadancy' is that the first son may take over the father's arms, but younger sons have to make a slight change, known as a 'difference'. Second sons have to add a crescent. It is this crescent, present on both the memorial and organ case, which links Anthony Roper, a second son, directly with the claviorgan.

It must have been hard for a successful young lawyer to leave London, the city described by John Lyly in 1579 as 'A place both for the beauty of building, infinite riches, variety of all things, that excelleth all the cities in the world, insomuch that it may be called the storehouse and mart of all Europe'[274] To leave the crowded streets and river, the palaces and inns, the new theatres and the masques and pageants and plays, the bookshops and the company of his intellectual equals, for what must have been little more than a dilapidated farmhouse in a one-horse village was surely cruel. However, we now believe that he took his music with him.

In 1579, a year after he inherited the Farningham manor from his father, Anthony commissioned a magnificent claviorgan, or combined organ and harpsichord from an immigrant Dutch harpsichord maker, Ludowick Theewes. Theewes was, ironically, a Protestant who had fled to London from Catholic persecution in Antwerp. The claviorgan, signed by Theewes and painted with the coat of arms of a Roper younger son is now in the Victoria and Albert Museum and has been extensively researched by Malcolm Rose.[275] It seems likely that the organ, an instrument proscribed as Catholic, was combined with a harpsichord to disguise its identity.

The Thweewes Claviorgan

Music was very important to the Elizabethans. Most gentry families would have a few musical instruments and all classes of people would sing the popular songs of the day. Elizabeth herself not only loved dancing and secular

271-Pat Morlock, 'The Elizabethan Religious settlement', *KASN winter (2002/3)*

272-John Bennett, A Tallis Patron, *Proceedings of the Royal Musical Association*, & Victoria County History

273-PRO, Prob 11, 15 March 1594

274-M.St Clare Byrne, *Elizabethan Life in Town and Country*, (1961 ed.)

275-Malcolm Rose, 'Further on the Lodewijl Theewes Harpsichord'. *The Galpin Society Journal* LV, April (2002)

music but was an enthusiastic patron of church music and the music of the Chapel Royal was the finest in Europe. The great musicians Thomas Tallis and William Byrd shared the honorary position of organist to the Chapel Royal and, although Byrd was an acknowledged recusant and Tallis most probably had Catholic sympathies, the Queen was prepared to turn a blind eye to her musicians religious beliefs. In 1575 she gave them both a 21 year monopoly on music publishing which must have provided a welcome supplement to their seven and a half pence a day pay . Wages were low, labourers would get about two or three pence a day and master craftsmen maybe between four and eightpence a day.[276]

When Thomas Tallis's widow Joan died in 1587 she bequeathed 'to Anthony Roper esquier one guilte bowle with the cover thereunto belonging in respect of his good favours showed to my late husband and me'. It seems very probable that Anthony was not only a friend and patron of Tallis but that the Tallises, who lived in Greenwich, lived as 'grace and favour' in one of Anthony's properties. Curiously enough Byrd's house in Middlesex also belonged to Anthony Roper.[277]

The Theewes Claviorgan by permission of the Victoria & Albert Museum

We do not know how or when the organ was transported to Farningham. The days had not yet arrived when the miller's waggon, returning empty from a journey to the Corn Exchange, might have brought it here. Corn was purchased and stored by the city companies at Bridge House at the Southwark end of London Bridge, but it is not likely that the Farningham miller travelled so far afield. It is more likely that such a precious object, with its intricate workings and inlaid gilding and paintwork, had a specialist transporter.

All we know is that, over a hundred years later, a room in Farningham manor was still known as the Organ Room.[278] We must also guess that this was the Roper's private chapel where they and their friends and relations would not only celebrate the Catholic sacraments but where they also listened to glorious music performed by the great musicians of the day.

Law and order

The highway from London to Farningham was still a perilous journey. Roads were simply trodden tracks and people on horseback would ride into the fields alongside the highway to avoid the holes and ruts and mud. Coaches and waggons would have a hard time getting through. The 1555 Statute of Highways had passed the responsibility for roads to the parishes, and every parishioner had to perform a number of days 'statute labour' to keep the highways open. Each parish had to appoint an annual Surveyor of Highways

276-M.St Clare Byrne, op.cit
277-Malcolm Rose, pers com
278-PRO, Prob 4, 1684, Inventory Sir John Beale

111

whose duty was to round up the reluctant parishioners. The better off inhabitants, such as the miller, were expected to provide their waggons and labourers, the poorer people had to turn out in person. Work was unpaid and naturally unpopular and so the roads deteriorated more and more.

The possibility of getting bogged down in a ditch paled beside the danger of being waylaid by highwaymen. These were less likely to be the cloaked and masked 'gentlemen of the road' of popular fiction than members of the lawless underclass of rogues and vagabonds who might easily be known to their victims and who would lie in wait for them in the woods. The Assize records for Queen Elizabeth, 1559-1603, give details of several highway robberies in the road from Birchwood to Farningham. In one case in May 1587, two men and a woman spent the night at the house of John Miller in Farningham, before setting off for London and 'at Byrchen Wood' one man attacked the other with a staff, stunned him and cut his throat.

This may of course have been a crime of passion rather than robbery, but there were plenty more cases of 'assaults on citizens in the highway at Birchwood in Farningham', and it seems clear that the highway went through more or less continuous woodland from Farningham Woods to Joydens Wood and Foots Cray. Felons were usually hanged at Penenden Heath near Maidstone but there was also a gibbet at Birchwood where local criminals would be left to hang as a warning to others.

The Parish Register

When vicar Henry Farbrace came to Farningham in 1589 he noted that 'Ther was no register book extant yt ever I could fynde'. The parish registers began under his supervision with baptisms and burials starting in 1589 and marriages in 1590. Henry Farbrace had resigned as Rector of Ightham in 1586, which is surprising as Farningham would have been a downgrading for him. Since the dissolution of Canterbury Priory the Dean and Chapter of Canterbury had the advowson and perhaps he asked for the transfer. It could be that he was prepared to not only condone, but to participate in, the Roper family's adherence to the old religion. When Anthony died he left Henry Farebrace and his wife each 'a peece of gold conteyninge twentye shillings', which certainly indicates a degree of friendship.

The parish registers give us the names of many of the inhabitants of the village in the Roper's time and sometimes their occupation or their cause of death. The first entry in the book is for the baptism of a daughter of William Stransom, the miller. The first burial is Robert Miller, a baker, followed by Arthur Pound, a 'shoomaker'. An early entry is for the death of 'a mayd a waygoer her name unknown'. In some years the burial entries indicate an outbreak of plague or smallpox, such as the Gylbart family and their servants who all died in March/April 1594. Sometimes the vicar allows himself an observation such as on the death of Roger White, 'an honest man'.

Assizes

Another place to find details of villagers is in the Assize Records which of course deal with citizens who fell foul of the law. Roughly speaking, crimes fell into two categories. Felonies, or serious crimes such as murder, the theft of goods worth more than one shilling, violent assault, treason, arson, rape, witchcraft, highway robbery and burglary; and misdemeanours, or minor crimes, which covered the theft of goods worth less than one shilling, drunkenness, selling short measure, dumping rubbish and disturbing the peace. Felonies were punishable by death, usually by hanging. Penalties for misdemeanours were likely to be 'whipping until the body be bloodied', either at a whipping post or tied behind a moving cart. Fining was fairly frequent, but rarely for large sums of money for fear of filling the prisons with debtors. The most usual sentence for a misdemanour was an ignominious punishment such as sitting in the stocks or standing in the pillory or being ducked in a river or pond in a ducking stool.

When a crime was discovered to have been committed in a village it was still the custom to call out the Hue and Cry. Everyone was obliged to lay down their work and follow the hue, and cry out to attract attention. Two thieves in Sutton at Hone were pursued as far as Crayford in 1596. Failure to respond to the cry was a misdemeanour. Once caught, the parish borseholder would have to take the accused to the village lock-up or 'cage' to await transfer to gaol.[279]

Although the death sentence was statutory for felony, there were several loopholes. Escape from gaol was surprisingly frequent, thanks to corrupt gaolers. Pregnant women could not be hanged and sometimes gaolers would help them achieve this status. While women could plead 'benefit of womb', men could claim 'benefit of clergy' in which they had to pass a literacy test. This privilege could only be claimed once and the accused would then be branded in the hand to make sure they did not claim twice.

One of the first trials of Farningham people during the Elizabethan period was that of Stephen Watts, a tailor who was indicted for grand larceny, or theft of goods worth over a shilling. He was accused in 1572 of breaking in to William Browne's house in Horton Kirby, and stealing sheets, a coverlet and 14s in money. He was tried at the Assizes, successfully claimed clergy and was branded in the hand after which he had to 'purge' himself on the Bible in public. But benefit of clergy did not always succeed. Two men who broke into a mill at Lullingstone and stole a flitch of bacon claimed clergy but proved unable to read and were sentenced to hang.

Several Farningham tailors appeared at the Assizes. The village was on the clothiers route to London from the weaving centres in the Weald, and Beesfield Lane was known as the Clothier's Lane. Perhaps there was a good living here for tailors who could undercut London prices. There was a case in 1573 when two Farningham labourers broke into the close of Thomas

279-Elizabeth Melling, *Crime and Punishment in Kent.* Louis Knafla, *Kent at Law, 1602,* (1994)

Foster and stole 30 yards of 'turkey coloured broadcloth' belonging to John Cowchman. Presumably Foster was a tailor and Cowchman his customer.

Murder

Two cases of attempted murder were reported in Farningham in the Elizabethan Assize records. One concerned two brothers called Alcherne from a large family of local husbandmen whose name lives on in Alchin's Wood. The brothers were working for the vicar in a field called Pyecroft when 'John, without provocation, suddenly struck William on the head with a mattock and killed him'. An inquest, under the coroner and a jury of thirteen local men, was held over William's body and John was comitted to Maidstone gaol, but he was found not guilty at the Assizes where it was decided that 'William Death', a fictional name for an unknown assailant, had killed his brother. The parish register shows that John married seven years later, had six children and died a natural death in 1605.[280]

The next Farningham murder suspect was William Smaleman, another tailor, who was indicted for the murder of his wife in 1589. At an inquest held over the body of Jane Smaleman, a jury which included Hugh Alcherne, father of John and William, heard that 'on the night of August 1st William Smaleman was lying in bed in his house in Farningham, arguing with his wife who was sitting on the bed. In the course of their quarrel William suddenly leapt from the bed intending to slap his wife but instead, by misfortune, kicked her in the back and killed her. Myldred Taylor, who was in the room at the time of the accident, and Thomas Gyles of Farningham, butcher, have testified to the couple's honesty and good conversation'.

The verdict is not given but William must have been acquitted because he reappeared in the church register when an unbaptised infant of William Smaleman died in 1591. The mother's name was not registered. The story looks like another crime of passion in the small, overcrowded dwelling houses of the time. Probably the Smaleman's bed was just a curtained alcove in the one living room. Even so, one is left wondering about how a husband's slap turns to a kick which actually kills his wife.

Most of the crimes committed in the villages at this time were attributed to local labourers and artisans, and were either domestic incidents or thefts from local houses or farms. When Londoners or people from other counties appear as accused criminals they are usually connected with highway robbery or horse, cattle and sheep stealing. London, as all the literature of the time testifies, was a capital of crime with an army of vagabonds and thieves with their own language in which a 'prigger of prancers' was a horsethief and a 'bawdy basket' a woman with a basket who stole linen off clotheslines.

The Poor Laws

After the Reformation responsibility for the poor had passed from the monasteries and the church to the lay community. The succession of Elizabethan

280–*Calendar of Assize Records, Kent Indictments, Elizabeth 1*

Poor Laws made it the responsibility of each parish to appoint two Overseers of the Poor who would sit on the Vestry and collect a poor rate from the parishioners to assist the aged, impotent and sick. To refuse to work for lawful wages became a punishable offence and the Vagrancy Act of 1597 said that all Rogues, Vagabonds and Sturdy Beggars over the age of fourteen found begging were to be stripped naked from the middle upward and openly whipped until their body be bloodied and then passed back to their birthplace, and if that was not known then to be sent to the House of Correction for a year.[281]   One of the last named reformatory prisons had opened in Maidstone in 1593.

The list of those named as rogues and vagabonds covers many colourful wayfarers such as 'wandering scholars seeking alms, idle persons using subtle craft such as fortune telling, Egyptians or gypsies, common players, bearwards, minstrels, jugglers, tinkers, pedlars, shipwrecked mariners, discharged prisoners and all those able bodied wandering persons and labourers without means refusing to work for current rates of wages'.

A number of Farningham people who appeared at the assises were not committed for crimes, but were there to answer charges for small matters of negligence such as failing to collect taxes or for failing to keep the peace. Two very old Farningham families, the Everests and the Bests, who both had yeomen, husbandmen and labourers as family members, and who were often selected as churchwardens, attended to pay the parish assessments for contributions to various taxes such as the county stock, 'the relief of poor prisoners languishing in Maidstone gaol', contributions to maimed soldiers and the House of Corrections. The Bests have left their name in Bestfield, or Beesfield Lane, and many Everests are buried in the three churchyards of Farningham, Horton Kirby and Eynsford.

The Inns

Other villagers to appear at the Assizes were the inn and alehouse keepers whose licenses or Victualer's Recognisances had to be kept up to date, and again there was frequently a Best or an Everest in attendance. Farningham, on the Folkestone Hythe road, the third major route through Kent from London to the Channel, has always had a number of inns and alehouses.[282] The inns were primarily for travellers and the alehouses for local people. At a time when twenty miles a day was considered a reasonable journey, the village made a good stopping place for travellers from London. The Bull is probably the oldest inn and belonged to the Sibbils of Chimhams in 1587, the innholder was a John Hinton. The Black Lyon inn belonged to the manor in the mid-17th century so may have belonged earlier to the Ropers. The remains of the Tudor inn building can be seen behind the present-day hotel.

Other Tudor inns or alehouses included the George, which probably stood on the George Meadow behind the manor; and the Swan.[283] Both the last named also belonged to the Sibbils, so it seems that all the Farningham inns

281-S&B Webb, *English Poor Law History,* (1927)
282-H&W Harding, *F&ELHS No.19 'Pubs of E&F'* (1996)
283-Zena Bamping, from L.L.Duncan's notebooks in KAS library Maidstone

belonged to gentry families who leased them to innholders. Gentry neighbours of the Ropers would have included Robert Bosville of Eynsford, who was married to Elizabeth Sibbil, and was the local JP to whom Anthony would have had to report for any breaches in the recusancy laws; Percyval Hart of Lullingstone who was another JP; Lancelot Bathurst, a London Alderman and member of the Grocer's Company, who had built a fine new house at Franks Hall in 1591; and Leonard Lovelace of Kingsdown, who had inherited his property in 1578 on his father Thomas's death.[284]

Title

John Hope of Kingsdown and Eynsford, who had married Anne Sibbil, a Sibbil heiress, is singled out in the Farningham parish records as 'Mr'. Titles are an important symbol of status, and 'Mr' indicates someone of some standing, such as a higher yeoman, slightly lower than 'Gentleman' which indicated someone of an old family with an entitlement to bear arms. An 'Esquire' came just below a knight and was a title which might be given to a JP, a barrister or someone with a very large estate. The title. 'Sir' of course means a knight or baronet, and 'Dame' his wife. Higher titles than these are very rare in the parish records.[285]

One gets the impression that Anthony kept a low profile as a recusant exiled from London, and maybe did not mix much with his neighbours. He does not appear in any of the parish records nor, thanks perhaps to Mr Farebrace, does he appear on the recusancy records. His will and that of his widow, indicates that they were closely involved with their farms and kept their own animals and farming equipment.

The Roper's Manor House

If, as we believe to be the case, the Roper's manor house was the one sold by their heirs to Sir John Beale in about 1660, and which is depicted on Beale's estate map of 1665 and described in the inventory made at his death in 1684, then it was a low, two story building with a courtyard in the middle set back from the road in a walled enclosure of orchards and gardens. The great barn, today converted into four houses, was off to one side and there was a gatehouse set in the wall on the road with a drive leading to the gabled front door.

The front wing of the house would have had the best family rooms, the Long Hall, the Great Parlour and the Little Parlour and the best bedchambers above them. The famous Organ room or chapel was probably hidden away upstairs. Then, round the courtyard, would be the kitchen, the buttery, the brewhouse and cellars, the bakehouse, larders, dairy, the servant's rooms, the well yard, coach house and stables, granary and hay house.[286]

Anthony Roper made his will in 1594 aged 50.[287] Although he says he is in 'perfecte health and of good and sounde memorie' maybe he had some intimation that he would not live much longer. His younger daughter Jane was only six and Isabel, the elder, had married Sir Thomas Wiseman of Rivenhall

284-Zena Bamping, *West Kingsdown,* (1983/91)
285-Peter Laslett, *The World we have Lost,* (1971)
286-B.M.Beale map ref.op.cit
287-PRO. Prob 11

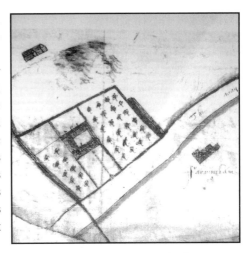

Essex, in 1588. The third son John is not mentioned and so must be assumed to have died. Although it seems a perfectly fair disposal of his property, the will does seem to dwell a long time on his second son Henry and very little on Anthony the younger. It also seems curious that the younger Anthony was not to be an executor of his father's will, but perhaps he was still under 21. The only executrix was Anne, his mother.

Anne was to receive the profits of all the properties bequeathed to Henry for his 'bringinge upp' until the age of 21. She was also to deal with the conveyance of the houses and lands in East Greenwich 'to some charitable uses with as much speede as convenience may be'. This clause in the will became the origin of the Roper Charity which would benefit the villages of Farningham, Eynsford and Horton Kirby for the next four hundred years.

Anthony the younger was to inherit all the heirlooms such as 'the greate peece of unicorne horne with the gold which is the case to yt', the gold ring and chain and the silver, including the two silver bowls called the 'Sir Thomas Moores Boules'. (The horn of the Narwal whale was known as 'unicorn' horn). All the 'household stuffe' in Farningham was to be divided between Anthony and his mother, and the residue of money, plate, jewels, corn, horses, kine, steers and sheep were bequeathed to Anne. The Farningham manor and the other properties which were not left to Henry went to Anthony.

Anthony the elder died in January 1597. The cause of his early death is not given in the register and there were no other deaths that month to suggest an epidemic. His wall monument in Farningham church shows him and his wife, in their Tudor robes with ruffs at the neck, kneeling at prayer with the three sons behind Anthony and the two daughters behind Anne.

The inscription below says 'Here lyeth buried the bodies of Anthony Rooper Esquier younger sonne of Willis Rooper of Eltham Esqr. He lyved 53 years and dyed the 21 of Jnvye Anno Dni 1597. Also of Anne Rooper his wyef....' This is followed by a latin verse which translates 'R.S. ON THE DEATH OF ANTHONY ROOPER HIS MASTER. Prayers ascend to God, I have left worldly things in the world and fame to my family. My body lies in the dust. After death the only virtue remaining to me is to be able to lead a blessed life in the presence of Eternal God'. (trans. Z.Bamping)

A few things remain unexplained. The identity of R.S. is still not solved. Also, why if Anthony died on the 21st of January, did Mr Farbrace enter the date of his funeral in the register as the 8th of August ? Did he die in London, or was

117

a funeral ceremony held for the village much later than the burial which, as for the later Ropers, took place privately in the chancel at night. Another mystery is the claviorgan. Why was it not mentioned in the will? It was surely as precious an heirloom as the 'unicorn' horn.

When the organ was discovered many years later at Ightham Mote, the Roper arms on the instrument had been overpainted with the arms of the Hoby/Carey families, and these have been traced to between the dates of the marriage of Sir Edward Hoby with his wife Elizabeth Carey in 1582 and her death in 1605. Sir Edward was Constable of Queenborough Castle in Sheppey and entertained Queen Elizabeth there in 1582 so was it possible that Anthony sold or gave him the organ for that occasion? But why? Or is it more likely that the second Anthony had no interest in music and sold it to Hoby after his father's death.

William Stransom, the miller, died in 1600, a week before his third daughter was born. His wife remarried in 1601. Mr Farbrace died in 1601 and his widow remarried in 1602. No doubt these widows were lucky to find second husbands to support them and their children. There is a brass in the church to say that Mr Farebrace left a charity of £15 to the poor of Farningham. He also left a similar bequest to the poor of his other parish of Ightham, where it is known as the Charity of Henry Firebrass.[288] He was replaced later that year by a new vicar, William Perneby who would stay in the village for the next 35 years.

The Anthony Roper memorial in Farningham Parish Church

288-H&W Harding
Charities op.cit

Chapter Eight

Seventeenth Century Farningham / The 1616 Terrier /
The Case against Sir Anthony Roper / Civil War / The Bull Inn /
John Kemp, Miller / The Hearth Tax and the Inventories /
John Kemp's Mill / The Poor / Sir John Beale /
Early 18th Century Farningham / the Woods /
The Craykers of Charton Manor / William Ebbutt.

Anne Roper did not remarry, and it was not until 1614 that she put into effect the transfer of the Greenwich properties to a trust to bring in an annual income for the poor of Farningham, Eynsford and Horton Kirby. This was made possible by the 1601 Act of Charitable Uses by which a testator could convey in trust property to be used for charitable purposes.[289] W K Jordan estimates that the capital value of the Greenwich properties in 1614 was £400. The investment flourished and by 1885 when the properties were sold, they fetched £11,829 for the Roper Charity which continues to this day and, by the year 2000 the capital value of the charity's holdings was £150,000.

So at the beginning of the 17th century Anne Roper and her son Anthony lived at the manor house with daughter Jane and occasionally son Henry, and their servants. Henry's education is well documented. He went to school at Westminster and in 1594, at the age of 18, he went to Caius College Cambridge, and was admitted to Lincoln's Inn in 1597. Unfortunately, there are no such records for Anthony the younger who seems to have devoted himself, with his mother, to the home farm. Jane had married Thomas Locke of Marton by 1607 when the first of her sons was baptised in Farningham church. Maybe the Lockes lived here for some years, because two more sons were baptised in the parish church, which indicates perhaps that their private chapel was no longer in use. The Queen died in 1603 and for a time, when King James first arrived, there was a short swing in favour of the Catholics. Anthony and his uncle John Cotton of Landwade, among many others, were both knighted at his coronation. It was not a very great honour and they would have had to pay for the privilege.

By 1606, after the 1605 Gunpowder Plot, severe penalties had been reimposed on Catholics and recusants were told to live a 10 mile distance from London. Probably this was when Henry, who married at about this time, came to live in Farningham again. By 1611 Sir Anthony, as he must now be known, had the first of many indictments for recusancy. This was the year that his troubles began in earnest. He was called before the Grand Jury at the Assizes to answer charges that he had, during the last two years, diverted the road from Farningham to London 'against a farme house... called Petham Place and hath set up a great barne upon the higheway' and 'laid out another road very foule and offensive to the passengers'.

He had also 'blocked and enclosed the road from Fawkham to Farningham

289-W.K.Jordan, Social Institutions in Kent, *Arch. Cant* LXXV (1961). & *The Charities of Rural England* (1959)
290-Calendar of Assize Records,
Kent Indictments, James 1, 1603-1625
291-W.G.Duncombe, 'Sir Anthony Roper and some 17th century Road Closures' F&ELHS No.32 (2002)

and Eynsford near a wood called Gavill land Spring and that from Farningham to Horton Kirby'.[290] These roads have been fully discussed by W.G.Duncombe.[291] One was the footpath known today as Horton Way, and the other was the footpath from Priory Lane in Eynsford to Donkey Lane in Farningham which ends in Gabrielspring Wood.

It appears from the indictment that Anthony was already enclosing his arable lands for sheep pasture, a practice which had become increasingly popular since the enormous growth of wool production during the previous century. Anthony's great grandfather, Sir Thomas More, had said some harsh things about this in his *Utopia* ....

'Sheep...these placid creatures which used to require so little food...have now apparently developed a raging appetite and turned into man eaters. Fields, houses... everything goes down their throats. To put it more plainly...gentlemen have grown dissatisfied with the income their predecessors got out of their estates. ...they must actively do harm by enclosing all the land they can for pasture, and leaving none for cultivation...They're even tearing down houses and turning every scrap of farmland into a wilderness. So what happens? Each greedy individual preys on his native land like a malignant growth...Result, hundreds of farmers are evicted...men and women...and tiny children, together with their employees...nobody will give them a job...for farm work is what they are used to. Get rid of these pernicious practices. Make a law that anyone responsible for demolishing a farm...must either rebuild it himself or else hand over the land to someone who's willing to do so.'[292]

An early depiction of Farningham Bridge. It is interesting to note the background which shows the medieval appearance of the Black Lion, prior to the Georgian facade that we know today.
By permission
British Library

Another indictment in 1613 said that Farningham Bridge is 'utterly defective' and the highway near it 'much annoyed' by water overflowing from a mill erected a short time ago by Sir Anthony Roper.[293] Good as it is to hear about the mill again after so long, it is very curious that Anthony should have built a new mill just at the time he was getting rid of his arable lands, but perhaps he only started his new agricultural practices after his mother's death in 1618. By 1634 his farm houses had been deserted and his 'Water-Grist-Mill gone to decay and ruin'.

Obviously much happened during the course of the next twenty years.

292-Sir Thomas More, *Utopia*, trans. Paul Turner (1965)
293-Calendar of Assize Records, *Kent Indictments James 1 CKS*

William Perneby seems to have been a good hard working vicar, and not unsympathetic to the Catholic Ropers if the nocturnal burials in the chancel are anything to go by, and the fact that in his will he left his son-in-law a 'Rhemist Testament' or a translation of the Bible from the Catholic college at Rheims. But even the good Mr Perneby seems to have fallen foul of Sir Anthony and his mother. He added a note to Mr Farbrace's entry of Anthony the elder's funeral in the register that 'With him died much goodness to ye churche, for his succeeding sonne withdrewe from the Churche the tythe of all the woode his mother and he burned, they burninge each year 100, or 120, 130 or 140 loades'. So perhaps Anne was as ruthless a landlady as her son.

Mr Perneby was a poor man. He and his wife Sybil had five daughters and a son to support and he had a hard time collecting his tithes. The arguments with Canterbury over the vicar's tithes had continued since the time vicar Thomas was rebuffed by the Prior of Christ Church. In 1616 Perneby made the following 'Terrier' or account of his territory for the Dean and Chapter. It can be found, upside down, at the end of the first book of church registers. Neither Mr Farbrace nor Mr Perneby were very tidy in their entries, and the handwriting is very scribbled and jumbled. However, the little remarks in the margins make it clear that these were the vicar's entries and not the Parish Clerk's.

The 1616 Terrier

The title is
'The True Note of the gleabe lands, meadowes, gardens, orchards, houses and portions of tithes belonging to ye vicarage of ffarningham...had made & taken & exhibited into ye office of the most reverend father in God George Archbishop of Canterbury.. then called Mr Weston his office neare Paules Chaine in London by William Pernebye the vicar of ffarningham and John Best and Thomas Adgore then churchwardens of the said pshe Anno Domini 1616'.

1. In primis. A mansion house and a Barne wth a fore Yarde whereon the same barne and 2 hoggestyes doe stand

2. Item 2 gardens 1 for herbes the other for pease or beanes, on the North and Easte side of the House

3. Item an orchyarde on ye South side of the Mansion house.

4. Item 1 meadowe conteyning 3 roodes of grounde or thereabouts on the East side of the House abutting North upon the Kings Hyghe waie leading towards London: East upon the Landes of the Hides and Thom.Miller, South upon the glebe landes of the said vicarage and West upon the barne garden and orch yarde of the same vicarage.

5. Item 1 ffielde conteyning 4 acres & or thereabouts abutting East upon the landes of Thomas Miller aforesaid & ye landes of John Miller, West upon the landes of Sir Anthonie Rooper knight, South upon ye landes of the same John Miller and Sir Anthonie Roop; North upon the orchyarde and Meadowe appertayning to ye vicarage aforesaid.

6. Item 1 other ffielde called Perresks /Pecrofte ? (pyecroft, the vicar's field where Alchin's death took place), lying in the parish of Eynsforde, conteyning by estimation 2 acres or thereabouts, Abutting East upon the landes of Sr Percyvall Hart knight, & West upon the kings highe waie leading from Eynsforde aforesaid towards ffarningham aforesaid, South and North upon the landes of Sr Robert Bosseville knight, all wch premises are in the occupation of the vicar himself..

121

7. Item One other ffielde called the upper Ende of Ambrye landes conteyning 1 acres abutting East and North upon a little ffielde of Sr Anthonie Rooper knight, West upon the Landes of the Rectorie of ffarningham called Ambrye Landes and South upon the highewaie leading from Kingesdown to ffarningham nowe in the occupation of William Marshall senior or his assignes.

8. Item One other acre called Lockscroft which abutteth North upon the Clothiers Lane. from the upper ende of ffigges Crofte to a certain hawthorne and lieth open and unclosed toye landes of John Beste called Bestfielde in the occupation of John Best. South (Notes added ' nowe 1626 Sr Anthonie Roop hath bought this ffielde and doth deteine this acre from the vicar...the paiment of rent for the same though from 1574 till 1626 there hath been rente pd for it, in 1574 3s p annu in Mr ffarbraces tyme, 3s all my tyme till Sr Anthonie came to have it'.)

9. Item All the small tythes of and in the pshe of ffarningham aforesaid (except the Tithe Haye of 2 meads there the one called Charton Meade, the other John Bestes Mead wch the Rectorie of ffarningham, the memorie of man not to ye contrarie ever had) as woode, haye, hempe, flaxe, pease, Beanes in gardens, hoppes and wool, lambe, lactage of kine, calves, coltes, pigges, pidgeons, ducks, geese, Barren cattel, fruites in gardens orchyardes or other places, conies &c, egges at Easter, the tithe of the mill...there or composition for them to ye vicars content and liking and so have been tyme out of mynde.

10. Item All the churche duties for Churching of women, Cresoms or offsprings (offerings ?) (more or lesse for Marriages and Burials and oblations and for burying of anye Corpses in ye Chancel.

Willmus Pernebejus vicarius, Johannes Best & Thomas Adgore guardians.

There seems to have been little change in the two hundred years since vicar Thomas's time. The Pernebys no longer have a dovecote, but they do have two hogstyes instead. It is to be hoped that the vicar's salary has increased. He should have been paid out of the profits of the Rectory but by 1575 was still only receiving 5 marks. By the time of Thomas Browne, the vicar from 1646 to 1678, the vicarage was said to be worth £40 pa which was such an enormous increase one wonders whether it was a mistake.[294]

The Parish Clerk at this date was William Reynolds. His could be a very important office, a superior clerk might even act as a surrogate clergyman and assist with services, but most usually he was a sort of dogsbody, washing the surplices, digging the graves, cleaning the church and tolling the bell. He or the vicar would be expected to keep notes at the quarterly parish meetings with the Churchwardens. After the Elizabethan Poor Laws of 1563 and 1601 and the establishment of Overseers of the Poor these became Vestry meetings, usually taking place in the vicar's robing room where he kept his vestments.

The vicar would lead the meeting, with the two Churchwardens, the two Overseers of the Poor, the Surveyor of Highways (a post created by the Highway Act of 1555) and the Constable or Borsholder. Senior residents, 'the Principal Inhabitants in Vestry assembled', would attend, such as the yeoman farmers and the higher husbandmen, the innkeepers and probably the miller and maybe some senior artisans. The manor court had probably lapsed during the time of the absentee Isleys, and there is no evidence that it ever revived under the Ropers. It seems likely that Anthony the elder, with his good relationship with the vicar and the village in general, attended the Vestry

294-Lambeth Palace Library, Survey of Church Lands 1649

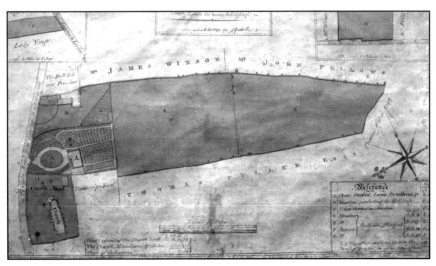

meetings, and equally likely that Anthony the younger did not.

In 1618 Mrs Anne Roper died and was buried in the night in the chancel. Her will indicates that she had kept a tight reign on the running of the estate and on her unmarried son Anthony. She left 'the hangings in the chamber where I now lodge at ffarningham' to her second son Henry. Presumably as the married son he was to have the best bedroom. All her cattle, wheat and farming equipment went to Anthony, her 'son and heir'. There were also bequests of silver and jewellry to her daughters and granddaughters, to Henry's wife Margaret and to her brother John Cotton. This brother died in 1620 and his heir was his son, a third John Cotton, aged five.

Plague

In 1625 plague struck Farningham again. This time it was the Newingtons who succumbed; a family of well-to-do yeomen of Pedham Court. 1624 had been a terrible plague year for London with up to 4000 people a week dying in August, lessening in September. The next year John Donne, the poet and Dean of St Pauls wrote that he believed up to 1000 a day were dying around London, 'The citizens fled away as out of a house on fire and threw themselves into highways and were not received so much as into barns and perished so, some of them with more money about them than would have bought the village where they died'.[295]

No wonder people locked their doors and barns against the unwelcome refugees, but it appears that the Newingtons locked themselves in with the disease. Thomas Newington was a Yeoman of the Guard and so had maybe come home from London on 20th June 1625, and knowing himself to be ill, made his will.[296] Of course, the fact that he had time to make his will might mean that this was not plague but possibly one of the other deadly diseases prevalent at the time, such as smallpox and typhus. Whatever the cause, by the 28th June he and his servant Thomas Peryall, his ostler John and another

295-J.F.D.Shrewsbury, *A History of Bubonic Plague in the British Isles,* (1970)
296-PRO, Prob11, June 1625

servant Richard Fielder, who had witnessed his will had all been buried. On the 2nd July his brother Robert Newington and on the 10th July his wife Elizabeth and daughters Jane and Elizabeth followed them. Twenty people were buried in Farningham that year as opposed to the usual five or six.

In 1624 Sir Anthony, Henry and Margaret Roper were indicted again for recusancy. In 1629 Margaret Roper died, leaving the two brothers alone. Mr Perneby gave her the usual nocturnal burial in the chancel, for which her mother-in-law Anne had left 18s. It seems that Anne was still organising everything from beyond the grave. However, even she could not protect Sir Anthony from the trouble that was to descend on him in 1634.

The case against Sir Anthony Roper

Even in the context of the last decade of King Charles I and his anxiety to raise money by increasing taxes and fines, it is hard to understand the incredibly punitive fine of £4000 set against Sir Anthony for the crimes of enclosure and depopulation, by the Court of Star Chamber. The Court was the King's own, and the judgement was surely endorsed by him. The Queen was Catholic and, although recusants were fined, the laws were not vigorously enforced, and on the whole the Catholic gentry supported the King, so religious persecution is not likely to have been the reason, and Anthony was only, as we have seen, following the fashion for sheep farming so much deplored by his great grandfather. However, as one historian says, malicious prosecutions by the Court were not unknown.[297] Star Chamber Court was to be abolished by Parliament in 1641.

The informant against Sir Anthony was John Philipot Esq, Somerset Herald and author of *Villare Cantium,* who held several public offices in Kent such as Bailiff of Sandwich and Steward of the Royal Manors of Gillingham and Grain. In the collected letters of the Oxinden family of Barham he is referred to mockingly as 'The Maltman Viceroy of Sandwich', and it was indicated that in their opinion he was an interfering, jumped-up busybody.[298]

Philipot appears to have had a dislike of 'English Catholikes' and 'Papistical Speeches', but it is to be feared that maybe Mr Perneby also contributed to the indictment against Sir Anthony, he certainly received the benefit of '£100 each to the Minister of Farningham and to the Poore of the said Parish'. John Philpot, (the i was his own addition to his surname) the 'Relator' or Informer was to receive the same amount.

The Prosecution against Sir Anthony declared that he had converted great quantities of land into pasture 'which formerly had been arable and used to tillage', and suffered five ancient farmhouses, as well as one water-corn-mill 'which heretofore ground good store of corn weekly', to go to ruin and become uninhabited. Two of the farms were Pedham Place and Pedham Court, both formerly inhabited by the Newington family, where depopulation may have had natural causes, and two other farms were occupied by the Best family of Beesfield. Pedham Place is described as 'a great defence and succour

297-C.V.Wedgewood, *The Kings Peace* (1955)
298-Dorothy Gardiner ed. *The Oxinden Letters 1604-1642* (1933)

to Travellers who passed that way and the same, since the depopulation thereof, hath been a harbour for Thieves and many Robberies have been thereabouts committed'. This indicates that Pedham Place had been an unofficial inn, another source of infectious disease.

Sir Anthony was not only committed to the Fleet prison until he paid the £4000 fine, but was to appear at the Assizes to acknowledge his offences 'to the end others seeing his punishment, may thereby hereafter be warned to forbear to commit the like Offences'. And further, having paid the Relator his costs and the £100 each to the Relator, the Minister and the poor he was within the next two years to repair and build again all the farmhouses with their outhouses, and the corn-mill, and restore the lands formerly used, with the farmhouses which were to be let again to tenants 'for reasonable rents', and all the said lands to be again ploughed up and used for tillage once more.

One is left feeling more than a little sorry for Sir Anthony who, after all, was only following a farming trend which so many of his contemporaries had got away with. One wonders too whether perhaps there was not something amiss with someone from such a highly educated family, who appears not to have gone to a London school or one of the two universities like his younger brother, (although of course there were several good grammar schools now in Kent); who never married, and at that date this was unusual for an elder son; who allowed his mother to dominate his household and who was also so insensitive to the hardship he had created for the small community where he had lived for most of his life.

Mr Perneby probably never saw his £100. He died in 1636 having made his will that year, commending his soul to 'the Companie of the Heavenly Angells' and 'the Holie Saints', another indication of his Catholic sympathies. It is curious that his burial is not recorded, because in February 1636 the first surviving assessment for rates had been made during his illness by the 'Clarke of ffarningham', so there was now someone other than the vicar to keep the books. The new rate book assesses Sir Anthony for all his houses including Petham Place farm, Charton farm and John Best's farm at 12s. There are 23 other ratepayers, the highest being Mr Thomas Smith, Thomas Adgoe and Virgil Blunt who are rated at at 2s 8d, 1s 6d and 1s 4d respectively. The other rates charged range from 1s to 4d. Villagers with property assessed at less than 4d a year did not pay rates.

In 1636 Sir Anthony and Henry took a mortgage from Sir David Polhill of Otford for £1,700 on Charton farm and its estate which included 200 acres of fields 'about or near a chapel there called the Charton Chapell'.[299] The chapel itself had probably been closed since the Reformation, although the Ropers still had to pay the £6 a year out of Charton farm to Canterbury. The fields included 'Gavellands, a messuage and lands now divided called Bystfield, Lorkscroft, Holmford, Shortgoss, Callow Downs and a piece with

299-Cambridge County Record Office, Shire Hall, Ref 588/T121

appurts called Hanging Bank and Great Bank and the appurts of Eglantine'.

Sir Anthony did not survive his disgrace for very long and he died on

January 27th 1641, having made his will a fortnight earlier. He indicated his disenchantment with Farningham by asking to be buried in his mother's family church at Landwade in Cambridgeshire, and he left £10 to the poor of that parish and £10 to his sister Jane. He gave his three maidservants a quarter's wages each and bequeathed all the rest of his goods, lands, tenements whatsoever, 'when my debts, legacies, funeral expenses are discharged, to my loving cousin John Cotton of Landwade Esq whom I make my heir and sole executor...desiring my said cousin John Cotton to maintain my brother Henry like a gentleman'[300].

In January 1641 the Long Parliament which would pave the way for the Civil War, was still sitting. In January the next year, King Charles I left London for the last time before his trial and execution in 1649. John Cotton, Sir Anthony's young cousin and heir, was Sheriff of Cambridge in 1641 and was made a baronet that year. He was a loyal supporter of the King and would play a part in the Royalist cause by attempting to escort the Cambridge College silver to Oxford for the King, pursued by Cromwell's horsemen.[301] After that contribution to the war effort he is said to have left England and lived mostly abroad during the Interregnum.

Civil War

Henry seems to have decided to maintain himself like a gentleman without his cousin's help. Anthony was declared to have died intestate and was buried quickly in Farningham, not Landwade. Henry was, after all, a lawyer and knew what he could get away with. The newly enobled Sir John Cotton, if he had any doubts, may have said that, what with his Shrievalty of Cambridge and his exciting involvement with the Civil War, he could not spare the time to come and investigate his cousin's affairs. Whatever happened, or did not happen, Henry appears to have lived on in Farningham for the next fourteen years, until Sir John came to claim his inheritance and get the will proved by his oath in London in June 1657.

We know that Henry was still living here in 1652 when a 'Richard Fuller gent, servant of Henry Rooper esq' was buried in the churchyard, but that is the last we hear of the Roper family in Farningham, except for a 'Katherine Roper, widow', who may possibly have been Henry's second wife. She made a will in 1676, leaving her house in the parish of Farningham to her sister Frances Loveden and Frances's son Walter.[302]

A Walter Loveden, Gent. had died in Farningham in 1658 and a second Mr Walter Loveden paid rates for a small house here in 1695. We do not know when or where Henry died, but it seems likely that Anthony's will was only 'discovered' at Henry's death which may have been in about 1655, because in the next year a John Bentley of Newmarket was buried here who is described as 'servant to Sir John Cotton Knight & Baronet who then lived at ffarningham'.

The Civil War years in Kent have been described elsewhere.[303] Henry does

300-PRO, Prob 6/18 (admins 1642), & Prob 11, 1657 (will)
301-Cambridge County Record Office, Handwritten account of the Cotton family 'Gens Cottonia Cambridgensis' by W.Cole & W.M.Palmer Landwade and the Cotton Family
302CKS. Kath Roper, ref PRS/W/14/82. 1676
303-A.M.Everitt, The Community of Kent and the Great Rebellion, 1640-1660 (1969)

not appear in any of the action which smouldered rather than raged round Farningham. He no doubt felt it wise to lie low. The gentry of the Darent Valley were mostly Royalists and were involved in the two Kent uprisings of 1643 and 1647/8. Tenants of the Harts of Lullingstone, Bathursts of Horton Kirby and Bosvilles of Eynsford would have been drawn into the skirmishing, but the dearth of gentry families in Farningham maybe left the villagers here in comparative peace. They would have seen plenty of action on the road, and the inns and alehouses would have benefitted from all the travelling horsemen, as would the blacksmiths, saddlers, small craftsmen, traders and cottagers.

The Bull Inn

The Bull Inn in the 1650s to 70s became especially prosperous. The innkeeper, Thomas Astwood and his wife Mary Magdalene had at least seven children, five of them baptised in Farningham, and the inventory attached to his will at his death in 1677 and the Hearth Tax returns of the 1660s show that this was

The Pied Bull as it is today, and good to see it prosperous once again under family management in the early 21st century

now the second largest house in the village. The Astwoods now owned the inn themselves. Thomas left it to his wife, and after her death their daughter and her husband lived there until they sold it 1713. The Hearth Tax reckoning of 1662 says that there were 10 fireplaces and the inventory gives the names of the main bedchambers as the Sun, the Bull, the Star, the King's Head and the Parlour Chamber which would all have had fireplaces, as well as the reception rooms, the Hall, the Dining Chamber and the Kitchen. By comparison, the Manor House had 13 hearths, the Red Lion 4, and the White Hart which was a small alehouse, had 3.[304]

The majority of houses paying tax had two hearths, and about ten houses only had one. Those living in houses valued at less than 20s pa or those on poor relief were exempt from paying tax. Dr Duncombe assesses the total population of Farningham parish at this date as about 148.[305]

Sir John Cotton lived here on and off during the time it took to sell up his cousin's estate. His absence was not noted in the Landwade records, although he appears in several Farningham records when he paid rates and taxes on the manor estate. He had married a Jane Hynde during the Civil War and lived mainly at her home, Madingley Hall near Cambridge. He sold Farningham Manor to Sir John Beale, a London merchant who had been living in Chillington House in Maidstone, the present day Museum. Then he sold Charton Manor to Charles Crayker, a London wool merchant of St Olave's, Southwark,[306] and lastly Sir John sold Farningham Mill in about 1675 to another yeoman William Ebbutt, of Pedham Court Eynsford.[307]

304–Lambeth Palace Library, VH 96
305–W.G.Duncombe, 'The Hearth Tax Returns for Eynsford, Lullingstone and Farningham' 1662-1671, F&ELHS paper No.1 (1990)
306–CKS Maidstone, handwritten account of Crayker family by Mrs Beryl Watson (1982)
307–CKS ref U30 T10

John Kemp, Miller

The mill was then in the occupation of John Kempe, miller, who had been living in Farningham since at least 1658 when he and a Mary Browne were married in Farningham church by the minister of Chevening. During the Interegnum only civil marriages were permitted and most were performed by local JPs but the vicar, Thomas Browne, sometimes also perfomed a ceremony in the church. Mr Browne had been the acting vicar since 1646 but was not inducted until 1660 and why he did not perform the Kemp's marriage is not clear. He was also Rector of Halstead and he entered the date of his arrival in Farningham as 'The Feast of St Michael the Archangel' and the date of his son's birth as 'Saint Valentine's Day', so he was no Puritan. If he had Royalist, recusant sympathies that might explain the postponement of his induction.

The Hearth Tax and the Inventories

The Hearth Tax of 1662 says that Mr Browne had 4 fireplaces in his house, Thomas Carpenter, who had taken the lease of Pedham Place, had 6 and John Kempe the miller had 2. It is interesting to compare the tax returns with the Farningham inventories for the late 17th, early 18th century at Lambeth Palace Library. They vary from the long lists of the property of the yeoman farmers such as Thomas Carpenter with his 70 acres of wheat on the ground, 2 waggons and 4 dung carts, 8 horses, 38 ewes, 8 cattle and 17 pigs and a large simply furnished house with chests full of linen, to the small craftsmen and traders such as Richard Smith, a blacksmith, who had a one hearth house with the 'Shop', or workshop, containing several hundred pounds of iron, bushells of coals, a cask of nails, his bellows and anvil, and a bedchamber with one bed and one sheet, adjoining. His inventory, 'taken, valued and appraised' by his neighbours John Moreby and Mathew Saxton, valued his belongings at £52.

Houses with one fire in the middle of the room and an outlet for smoke in the roof, were now unusual; most would have brick fireplaces and chimneys and a ladder staircase to a loft or bedchamber above. The upper floor in the roof space meant a loss of height below, leading to the familiar low ceilings of houses of this period. As a picture of the interiors of houses in Farningham the inventories are invaluable, but as a record of their monetary worth they are probably fallible, depending as they do on the arbitrary estimates of neighbours.

Henry Pound, tailor, John Pound, mercer and John Sibley, weaver, all had two hearths which gave them a 'Fireroom', or room with the fire for living and cooking, and a 'Shop' or workshop, each with a bedroom above. Henry Pound had a lot of valuable cloth, serges, cotton, wool, dimity and linen, he also had grocery and butcher's ware and, most surprisingly, a clock and a gun, all bringing the total estimated value of his posessions in 1669 to £113. His brother, John Pound, also had valuable cloth, haberdashery and another clock, all valued at £250. John Sibley had a mercer's shop with wool and linen cloth as a weaver's shop with 'looms and other weaver's tackling'. Both workshops were probably outhouses because they had no rooms above them, his two firerooms were called the 'Parlour' and the 'Hall' and he also had a 'Brewhouse' with equipment for making beer.

Beer was the everyday drink and most of the people who were well off enough to make a will had brewing utensils. John Udall, 'Husbandman', had a 'Fireroom', a 'Back Room' and a 'Buttery' and two bedrooms above the fireroom and the back room. The back room appears to have been for baking and washing, the buttery was for brewing and was often an outhouse extension, probably under the traditional Kentish 'catslide' roof. Everything in Udall's house, the money in his purse, furniture, linen, pewter and brass and, out of doors, two hogs, added up to £24. It is a low valuation for such a well furnished house with linen which included 11 pairs of home made sheets, pillow cases and table cloths, rugs and cushions and blankets, and a lot of pewter such as plates and 'sawcers' for sauce, pottingers, salts and even three pewter chamber pots.

Adjustable pot-hanger, typical of the period

His will, which he signed with a shaky X, left £20 each to his 'loving sons' John and George, and £5 to his, maybe not so loving, son Thomas, and all his worldly goods to his wife Dorothy for her lifetime. Apart from his two hogs there is no mention of farm implements or other livestock, none of the yeomen's 'wheat or barley on the ground', or 'payres of plows', not even a shovel, all he had was 'one grindstone' worth 2s.6d. Presumably John rented his holding and was now too old and infirm to do any active farming. His sons may have worked for other farmers or perhaps had their own establishments. By the next two generations the Udalls had become prosperous enough to afford some of the finest gravestones in the churchyard.

The furniture in these houses, even those of the wealthiest yeomen, was very basic. There were tables, wooden chairs, 'joined' stools and forms (made by a joiner/carpenter), cupboards and chests and trunks. The most expensive article was always the best bed and, with the better off people, it would be a fourposter with its furnishings of curtains and valance, feather bed, feather pillows, bolster, blankets and coverlets. Linen and pewter were also of particular value.

A well equipped Fireroom would have not only a table and chairs and maybe some cushions but also brass kitchen utensils and pewter dishes, gridirons, smoothing irons, pot-hangers and a spit for the fire with bellows, andirons, fire-shovels and tongs, and maybe a warming pan or two. The occasional 'carpitt' would be for hanging on the wall or over a table. As yet there was no china and the everyday earthenware and wood platters and mugs were not considered worth mentioning.[308]

Mathew Sweetapple's inventory is particularly interesting, because it is one of the few houses in the village which can possibly be identified today. Lion Cottages is a late medieval hall house, so it was probably already nearly two hundred years old when the Sweetapples lived there in 1684. Mathew was a

308–Rowland Parker
The Common Stream (1975)

129

collar, or harness maker and also kept a small alehouse known as the White Hart. He was married to Lucy who was the executrix of his will and inventory. They had a 'Hall' with a table and '4 fine old chairs', cooking equipment and '5 or 6 pounds of pewter'; a 'Brewhouse' with a furnace, kettles, skillets, tubs, koolers and a kneading trough for making bread; a 'Cellar' with barrels and drink tubs; a 'Shop' with nine horse hides and 5 calf hides; four bed-chambers above the shop, the cellar, the hall and the brewhouse and there was also a 'Garrott' apparently used as a store room. Again the furniture is basic and the value of everything was put at £25. (Although there is no cellar any more the house has obviously sunk and a cellar would probably have flooded from the river and been filled in.)

Matthew Sweetapple's residence in 1684, now known as Lion Cottages. Reputed to be the oldest known domestic structure in Farningham still occupied.

John Kemp's Mill

The most interesting inventory of course is that of John Kemp or Kempe of Farningham Mill which was made on the 29th of December 1701 and deserves to be given in full. His wife, who was the executrix of his will, is called Dorothy which might mean that he had married again, or that the vicar or clerk had got his wife's name wrong at their marriage. John Kempe died on 12th December 1701 following both his son Thomas, also a miller, and his servant Tamaris Mills. All three died within the space of two weeks, probably as a result of some contagious illness such as smallpox or influenza; plague had subsided after the last great visitation in 1665.

True and Perfect Inventory of all and singular the goods and chattels debts and credits of John Kempe, late of ffarningham in the County of Kent, miller, taken and appraised the nine and twentieth day of December 1701 by Edward Chapman and William Draper as followeth

	£	s	d
Inprimis ...his wearing apparell and money in his purse	05	00	00

In the ffire Room

	£	s	d
Item.....one table and fourm all the pewter and all other furniture therein	03	00	00

In the Milkhouse

	£	s	d
Item.....2 Brass kettles, 2 iron potts, 5 kilderkins & other old lumber	03	05	00

In the [room] over the ffire Room

	£	s	d
Item.....2 ffeather bedds & 2 ffeather bolsters, Beddstedde & the furniturethereto belonging, 3 chairs, andiron, fireshovel & tongs & other things	06	19	00
Item...all the Linnon	05	00	00

In the Chamber over the Milkhouse

	£	s	d
tem....1 flock bedd & Bolster & other furniture thereto belonging	01	15	00

In the Millhouse

	£	s	d
Item....Oats thrashed	04	10	00
Item....Scales ,Beame and Weights	01	10	00
Item....Sacks & Bolling Mill & other things	03	00	00

In the Barne

	£	s	d
Item......Wheat unthrashed	05	00	00
Item......Barley and Oats unthrashed	09	00	00
Item......Seed Clovergrass	03	10	00
Item......One ...& Bushell & other thrashing implements	00	12	00

In the Stable

	£	s	d
Item.....Horses, ffodder, Pannel & other things	14	00	00
Item.....Cows & Calves & Hoggs & sheep	15	13	00
Item.....Wheat on the ground	19	10	00
Item.....Wheat & Milling thrashed	12	00	00
Item....Things out of sight and forgott			
Summa Totalis	113	07	10

Appraised by Edward Chapman, his mark EC
William Draper.

Courtesy of Lambeth Palace Library Ref VH96 4961

There, for the first time, we see the interior of the millhouse, the mill and the outbuildings. It is not a very fine or valuable set of buildings, nor is it poor, and John Kempe is comfortably off and is one of the middle class of villagers. The parish registers show that the Kemps were highly respected citizens, frequently chosen as churchwardens, and that they farmed some land, 'Kemp's farm', in addition to keeping the mill. John Kemp the younger would take over from his widowed mother Dorothy in 1708. The inventory shows that the house still only had two hearths as recorded in the Hearth tax of 1664, one in the Fireroom or kitchen, which had a cold milkhouse or pantry adjoining, and one in the warm family bedroom above the fireroom. The bedroom over the milkhouse was presumably for the servant.

Most of these inventories are of people of the 'middling sort' and 'working trades' according to Daniel Defoe's six famous categories, '1, the great, who live profusely; 2, the rich, who live very plentifully; 3, the middle sort who feel no want; 4, the working trades who labour hard but feel no want; 5, the poor that fare hard; 6, the miserable that really pinch and suffer'.[309]

The Poor

The poor in Farningham fell into several groups. First, the farm servants or agricultural labourers who lived 'as family' with the farmer and most of these were single men and women, usually employed by the year and paid a quarterly wage. This ranged from £2 10s. to £6 p.a. and included food and lodging. Second were the agricultural labourers, mostly married men and women, who lived in rented cottages and worked for a daily or weekly wage and 1s to 1s 8d a day was usual, with from £1 to £2 p.a. rent for a one roomed cottage.[310] This work of course depended greatly on the seasons, and women as well as men could earn well at harvest time but the family would feel the pinch in winter.

Others among the poor would be the boys apprenticed to a craftsman or tradesman, although these would often be their own sons or relations, and girls sent out into service, such as Tamaris Mills who was John Kemp's family servant. The miserable that really pinched and suffered in Farningham would have been the aged and disabled, the widows and single mothers who would all get a barely adequate poor relief sum from the vestry and be boarded by the parish with any parishioners who could take them. The poorest of all were the 'vagabonds' who would be moved on from the parish as quickly as possible unless they fell sick and had to be housed in someone's barn.

An indication of the sort of arrangement for boarding a poor person was given by the vicar Thomas Browne in a note of an agreement in the parish book of 1668 which said that 'Soe long as Elizabeth Reynolds of the said parish shall dwell and abide in the west part of the house of Mr Thomas Browne...being the part that the widdow Joane Benge did inhabit in, that the Overseer for the Poore for the time being...shall pay or cause to be payed to the said Mr Browne...the summe of twentie shillings by the yeare'.

Thomas Browne died in 1678 after a series of the usual arguments over his tithes in which he was assisted by his son Samuel who had by then become a lawyer. His successor, John Pendlebury continued the appeal in the Court of Exchequer in 1686 under Justice Christopher Milton, brother of the poet. Mr Pendlebury's wife is believed to have been one of Sir Christopher's daughters, so maybe he had high hopes of a little family influence. Her maiden name was certainly Milton and her two sisters, Mary and Catherine (from Highgate) both came to live with her and died in Farningham.[311] Sir Christopher lost his position next year so was probably no great help to his son-in-law.

Sir John Beale

Sir John Beale, the new squire or Lord of the Manor, was one of the influx of London merchants buying up country seats. He had already retired to

THE TWENTIE ACRES

309-Roy Porter
English Society in the Eighteenth Century (1982)
310-C.W.Chalklin, *Seventeenth Century Kent*, (1965)
311-CKS P145/1. D of NB

Maidstone where he lived in the very grand Chillington House, now Maidstone Museum. He had married Anne Colepeper of Aylesford in 1655 and no doubt such a wife from one of the oldest Kent families helped his career. He was made a baronet in 1660 and after Anne's death he married for the second time in 1662, a Jane Duke of Maidstone. He was appointed Sheriff of Kent in 1664 and by then had moved to Farningham.[312] He and Jane had five daughters, all baptised in Farningham but only three survived. There had been no children from his first marriage and he must have been disappointed to have had no son to inherit his title. Lady Jane Beale died in 1676 and Sir John in 1684.

Sir John's estate map, made in 1665, shows that he had not bought all the manor lands from Sir John Cotton, although he later aquired many of them.[313] The map shows 56 acres in one plot at the back of the manor house, divided into fields called the Twenty Acres, Coblands, Court Gardens and The Walled Peece together with a two acre plot laid out to orchard and garden which surrounds the site of 'The Place' or the manor house itself.

Below.
After the Beale estate
map of 1665.
The Manor and orchards
covered the area now
occupied by Market
Meadow and the Village
Hall.
For detail from the
original map see page
117.

The inventory made at his death in 1684 has already been discussed because it is assumed that it describes the Roper's old house. It seems, from the inventory and from the small picture on the map, to have been a fairly typical late Tudor manor house, built round a central courtyard and is part grand house, part farmhouse. Sir John left his property to his three surviving daughters, Mary, Jane, and Anne, the last of whom with her husband Sir George Hanger of Driffield, Gloucestershire inherited the Farningham manor.

At his death Anne became his executrix. Possibly on her father's instructions she disregarded the new Burial in Wool Act which was intended to protect the wool trade, and had her father buried in a linen shroud. An informant told the local JP and 'fifty shillings was paid to the church wardens and distributed (as a forfeiture) to the poor of ffarningham'. The informant, John Peak, does not appear in any village records and was maybe a resentful servant. It was a most unpopular law with the upper classes who tried to cheat if they could, and on several future occasions in Farningham when the necessary affidavit was not brought to the vicar, the poor always gained by fifty shillings.

Anne Hanger and her husband also inherited Reynolds Place in Horton Kirby which Sir John Beale had purchased from the Grimstone family. Reynolds Place was reputed to have been an even finer and larger house than the Bathurst's Frank's Hall and Sir John is reputed to have planted an avenue of lime trees between Farningham manor and Reynold's Place.[314] This house and many of the lime trees were destroyed in the terrible hurricane of 1703. These were not the native English lime trees, but the imported ornamental variety believed to have been introduced to England by Sir John Spielman the famous paper-maker of Dartford. The few remaining trees came down in the great storm of 1987, but one or two large limes still stand outside the present-day manor house.

312-*The Complete Baronetage.HMSO*
313–British Museum Add.Ms.23 196,c
314–Edward Cresey, *Horton Kirby*, (1857)

133

Early 18th Century Farningham

The 1676 *Compton Census* had instructed every parish priest to return a census of parishioners with details of their church-going habits and in 1717 Mr Pendlebury had sent a report on Farningham to the Archbishop. He said that he had no curate and lived in the vicarage. The number of families was 'about 36'. 'Sarah Swan, widow is an Anabaptist but there are no other dissenters, no meeting houses, no public school endowed but a private one for parish children to be taught to read and write, no almshouse, Anthony Roper left £6 p.a .to the poor out of lands in Greenwich but no money recived for 10 years. Public service 2 times every Lord's Day, catechism in Lent, Sacrament of Lord's Supper 5 times p.a. Circa 40 communicants'. He adds that no public penance has been performed in his time. Mr Pendlebury died in 1720 and was succeeded by William Fuller, vicar until 1738.

The seventeenth century had been a time of great change in the rural community. Although there had been plenty of writers of books on husbandry and surveying, there had been very little scientific theory applied to agriculture until the end of the century, and very little change in methods of farming since medieval times. The changes affected Farningham in several ways. Probably the most noticeable were the new apple and cherry orchards. Farningham Woods lost many acres to plantations of cherry gardens for the London markets, where Kentish cherries were in great demand.

The Woods

The woods had suffered during the 17th century. The timber was needed increasingly for house and ship-building and the underwood for bricks and glass and household fires. Defoe commented on 'the vast quantities' of faggots and bavins from North Kent sent to light the London tavern fires.[315] John Evelyn, one of the new scientific writers, in his *Silva, or a Discourse of Forest Trees,* tried to draw attention to the despoiling of the woodlands.

The Roper's half of Farningham Woods had been sold by Sir John Cotton, but unfortunately the ownership of the different parts of the woods has been difficult to trace. The other half of the woods still belonged to the Bathursts of Frank's Hall. Vicar Thomas Browne, who was interested in the vicar's tithe of tenths of the underwood as opposed to the rectory's tithe of timber, noted in 1675 that Mathew Hills had been appointed to fell Longland's Wood but he does not say by whom. By the 18th century a large part of the woods had been acquired by Lord Romney of Maidstone and were tenanted by Mathew Hills who appears to have lived at the top of Calfstock Lane, but does not feature in the Farningham parish register so was probably either a Horton Kirby

Illustration left: 'Charcoal burners in a wood, from John Evelyn's Silva'

315-C.Chalklin op cit (1965)

or Sutton at Hone parishioner.

The Horton Kirby parish bounds with Farningham were taken in 1684 and this partial transcription gives some idea of the Farningham half of the woods as they were then.

'The Bounds of Horton on the Farningham side...the old mark when you come out of the wood on Farningham parish was an old remarkable tree called Mark Beech and Oak, one tree growing out of the top of another but since grubbed up. A cross was made in the hollow place where it grew formerly, a little distance from the ditch and bank that surrounds Old Franks Park Wood which are the true bounds.

Thence, keeping the wood on the left hand, viz Old Franks Park, the bounds goe at the woods, and the left hand hedge to Longland's Field is the bounds to the very bottom of that field on the lane that goes up from Matt Hill's house to Farningham Woods...the lane up towards Calverstock is the bounds till you come to the great hanging gate in the hollow way (Memo, added in 1734, the great hanging gate mentioned is not now remaining). The bounds goe down the lane into the road from Farningham to Sutton, thence cross Culvercroft field to the Cherry Orchard of Franks'[316]

Another great local change was the increase in hop production. Hops had been added to ale to improve the flavour and keeping quality since the 15th century and the resulting beer had become enormously popular. Hops were expensive to grow in terms of time and labour but the profits were high. It was said that in a good year an acre of hops could be worth more than 50 acres of arable land.[317] One of the Farningham vicar's most precious tithes was that of hops. The attendant woodland industry of coppicing for hop-poles and charcoal for drying the hops had a negative effect on Farningham Woods where sweet chestnut coppice became over abundant.

Other local agricultural changes included the introduction of clovergrass, sainfoin and turnips for winter feed. Also the use of leys, lays or temporary pasture among the arable fields, to allow two or three years for livestock to feed and manure the fields. Another introduction was the use of water meadows along the rivers where a network of channels and drains with hatches brought a shallow sheet of water over the pasture fields in winter, providing nutrients and stimulating early growths of hay.[318] Although there is no proof that this was practiced in Farningham, there are some traces of what may have been these channels in the early maps.

The Craykers of Charton Manor

Another important family in the village during Sir John Beale's occupancy of Farningham manor was that of the Craykers of Charton manor. Charles Crayker, wool merchant of St Olave's Southwark, bought the manor from Sir John Cotton in about 1665. He had married a Huguenot heiress, Anne Delanny and they had three surviving sons, Samuel, Benjamin and Joseph. The Craykers kept a London house, and when Charles died in 1686, although he was buried in Farningham, he is described as 'of the parish of St Stephens Coleman Street in the city of London'.[319] After Charles Crayker's death, his Farningham property was divided between the two younger sons 'share and share alike'. Samuel the eldest had been disinherited. According to Hasted, Benjamin, born in 1659, built himself a new house on his inherited land

316-CKS Maidstone ref P193/28/1&2
317-Richard Filmer, *Hops and Hop Picking* (1982)
318-Joan Thirsk, ed. *The English Rural Landscape*, Joseph Bettey, 'Downlands'
319-Mrs Beryl Watson, op.cit. CKS Maidstone

adjoining the bridge. This is now the present-day manor house. He married three times and had 8 children by his second wife, all baptised in Southwark, but no sons survived. He had taken over his father's wool business in Southwark and became a member of the Staplers Company. He died in 1731 and was buried in Farningham.

Charles Crayker's will names several of the fields belonging to Charton such as 'Chappel Fields', although the chapel itself is not mentioned and must have fallen, not surprisingly, into disrepair. He also mentions a 'piece of Bushey lands or pasture grounds called Millbank adjoining to the...Hopes ...together with the river thereunto belonging', and this was presumably the land on which Benjamin built his house. This land, which had probably always belonged to the Charton manor estate, is an argument in favour of the earlier de Cheriton's mill being the one in the village and not the one at Franks.

Joseph Crayker, born in 1661, appears to have had Charton Manor as his country home. He married Ann Dunkin of Canterbury in 1688 and is described as a Linen Mercer, and became a member of the Mercer's Company. His London residence and business premises were in Gracechurch Street and his children were baptised at St Benet's, Gracechurch. Both he and his wife were buried in Farningham, and after his death in 1732 his elder son, Joseph, curate of Wilmington, inherited Charton. Joseph died young and the property went in 1738 to the younger son, another Benjamin, a lawyer, who lived in Farningham until his death in 1773.

William Ebbutt

William Ebbutt, the new owner of Farningham Mill, was a wealthy yeoman, owning and leasing extensive properties in Kent as well as his home, Pedham Court in Eynsford. It seems strange today, in a more literate age, that all his surviving papers, title deeds and his will, are signed with an X. The actual document of sale of the mill between Sir John Cotton and William Ebbutt is missing, but there is a title deed of 1677 which gives a clear description of the property. It is a settlement 'in consideration of a marriage by God's grace shortly to be solemnised' between William Ebbutt and Mary Miller, widow of Tonbridge.[320] In it Ebbutt makes over the mill and other properties in Farningham including a small alehouse called the White Hart, two houses, a forge and a shop, all near the river, also land and houses in neighbouring villages, to his future wife Mary and her two trustees, George Castle and William Waller. We now believe that the White Hart, the houses and shop correspond to today's Lion Cottages, Cherry Tree Cottage and the butcher's shop. The forge, as it included river access or a 'watering place', may have been today's Vanity Box hairdressers. After a legal preamble the deed describes

'All that Mill house, water mill, 2 acres land, half an acre pasture and a nine acre field, and all millstones, wheels, fludd gates, coggs, dams and bankes, waters, watercourses and throoways, situated, standing and being in ffarningham, now or late in the tenure or occupation of one John Kempe miller, and all other messuages etc in the tenure of the said John Kempe, late of Sir John Cotton of Landwade.'

320-CKS Maidstone, ref U30 T10

The measurements of the fields correspond to the Isley's 1554 'Le Myll Crofte and Le Myll Hope'. William Ebbutt died in 1690 and, in about 1720 his son, Castell Ebbutt, a London wool draper, sold the mill to Thomas Colyer of Southfleet whose family were to own it for the next 280 years.

Sir John Beale's daughter Anne and her husband Sir George Hanger, the new owners of Farningham manor, lived on the Hanger's estate in Gloucestershire and leased the manor house in Farningham to tenants. A title deed of 1690 lists their Farningham estate as follows

The Black Lyon in Farningham & 3 pieces of land called the 2 crofts & the Millfield adjoining containing 20 acres then or late in the occupation of Robert Smith ,AND all that messuage or farm commonly called Upper Court farm together with barns, stables and gardens, & all that close called Pond Hollandens of 18 ac. & close of Further Hollandens of 15 ac. & close of Great Hollandens of 30 ac., & close Gravel Croft of 16 ac., & a close adjoining the said farmhouse containing 11 ac., & all those pieces of land Philip Spring of 9 ac., & 2 fields the 18 Acres, & 2 closes Ludsfield of 18 ac. & a close Upper Cherry Garden & a close Puckards Hill excepting one acre at the top, & a piece of land Puckards Bottom of 10 ac.& a piece of wood, Hawkenest Wood of 8 ac., which last named farmhouse and lands in Farningham...in occupation of Thomas Harman. AND 4 pieces of meadow land containing 21 ac. one called 12 Acres & other 3 pieces of 11 ac. of last mentioned in occupation of John Moyes & a parcel the Court Gearne of 12 ac. in tenure John Kemp & an arable field called Whithills of 6 ac. in tenure Thomas Stedalp, AND a parcel of land Millfield of 2 ac. in occ.John Ludlow, & 4 pieces of land & one barn late John Moyes. 2 closes called Courts of 58 ac. & a close Cherry Garden of 4 ac. and land by said Barn cont. 10 ac. then occupied by Robert Smith. 2 pieces called Coblands of 12 ac. & Stanells of 15 ac. in occ.Thomas Miller.Also...a messuage or tenement in Farningham with garden and 2 pieces of land belonging, one piece lying in front and the other leading up to the stables in occ. Mrs Ann Crayker,...& 2 fields called George Yard and Pale Plot of 8 ac. in occ Mrs Crayker and all appurtenants'.[321] (this deed transcribed, probably with some inaccuracies, from copies of indentures dated 1690,1710, 1726, 1730, 1771).

In 1693 George Hanger commissioned an estate map from Joseph Duke of Cranbrook which shows not only all these fields and their occupiers but also gives a list of all the trees on the property. There are many 'great elms', also 249 'elms of all sorts' along 'The Old Lane' as Button Street was then known. Not many of the famous limes are mentioned but there are '15 young lime tree pollards against the House in London Road', and 13 pollards against the George Yard. Puckards Hill has 'one good oak' against a mysterious Dr Bright who is given as the occupier of the woods. (His identity remains unknown.) It is a very fine map, with ornamental borders and the different occupier's lands picked out in yellow, dark and light brown, dark and light blue, pink, red and green.[322]

The occupiers listed are Robert Childemaide who is not in the parish registers so was probably a farmer from a neighbouring village who leased 25 acres of Hanger lands behind the manor house until 1707. Thomas Stedalp was probably Stiddolph, a blacksmith who leased a 6 acre croft at White Hill. Thomas Harman was a yeoman from a large Wilmington family who occupied

321-CKS ref U36 T30
322-B.M. Add Ms 23, 196 B Whitehill, or Farningham Hill farm which, with 174 acres, was a major part of

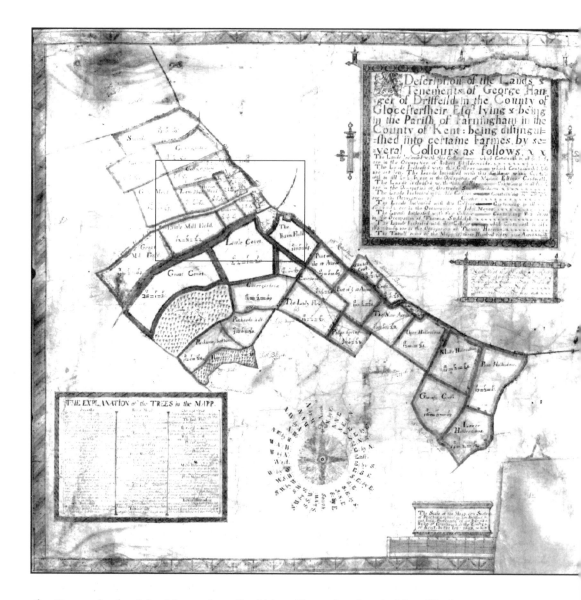

the Hanger lands. John Moyce described himself as a butcher in his will of 1711 and owned six houses in Farningham as well as farming 65 acres behind the London Road. Gertrude Smith was the widow of Robert Smith, the innholder of the Black Lion who had died in 1690 and had kept the fields along the river beyond the inn. 'Cocks' was probably Thomas Cox of Downe, another butcher who farmed the 19 acre Great Mill Field beyond the Lion. The manor house, George Yard and Pale Plot had been let to an unknown lady, Madam Elinor Cordwell, and John Kemp, the miller, was farming 12 acres opposite the church.

The map has a very small, fine drawing of the centre of the village which shows the manor house and barn, the Bull Inn, the new Crayker house with

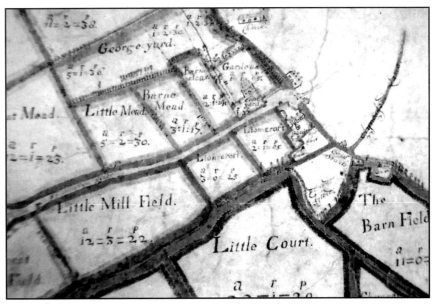

The Hanger map 1693 is the most important early map of Farningham. Regretably it is so faded that it is difficult to reproduce. The whole map left, is a one off, hand produced map in colour by Joseph Duke of Cranbrook and whilst there is no reason to doubt its accuracy Mr Dukes sense of direction leaves something to be desired, the legend being 180 degrees out. In the detail right, the old Manor in Market Meadow and the new Manor House opposite can just be discerned. Map BMAdd.Ms. 23,196B(1693) By permission British Library.

the lime trees outside, the church, the little White Hart and the old buildings of the Lion. There are two curious features, one is the smallness of the bridge and the large space in front of it, suggesting a wide ford, the other is the manor house itself which is no longer Beale's low courtyard building, but a fine tall William and Mary type house.

If the drawing is correct then the Hangers had built a new house which seems most surprising as they do not feature in any parish records and were, almost certainly, not living here. There is now no way of knowing about this house. Fifty years later the Hanger's son, William, came to live here and is said to have built yet another new house which burnt down before it was finished. Since then the site of the early manor houses has remained an empty field which, after the market began to be held there, came to be called Market Meadow.

The bridge, such an important feature of Farningham life, was one of 15 'County Bridges' considered important enough to be maintained by the county rather than by private landlords. It was first recorded in 1613 when it was already described as 'decayed' so was presumably a 16th century or earlier bridge.[323] It was described in 1701 as 'The ancient bridge of Farningham, 28 foot in length, 8 foot in breadth from outside to outside, with the water (under it) running 1 foot deep in August'.[324] By 1733 the bridge was described as 'ruinous and dangerous with walls on either side, little of which was standing, must be pulled down and new built'.

There is an undated drawing of a very decayed stone bridge with gothic arches in the British Museum which is labelled on the back 'Farningham Kent, Black Lion Yard'. (see page 120) It is possible, with some imagination, to see the rounded arches of the county bridge behind it. So maybe, if the

323-W.G.Duncombe, 'The bridges of Eynsford and Farningham' F&ELHS pub 33, (2003)
324-CKS Q/CSU 3/42

bridge was demolished and new built between 1701 and 1733, the old stone bridge was left to decay beside it. It is a very beautiful, detailed water colour drawing and hard to believe that it is a fantasy. The buildings in the background could easily be the former, probably Tudor, Lion Inn and the old Lion Cottages.

The 'cattle screen' bridge beside the main bridge is an abiding mystery and the cause of much comment and speculation. It exists in a drawing of 1790 where it is apparently already quite old with bushes growing out of the top and is described as 'having been erected long since'.[325] This would date it perhaps to the 1740s, in which case it might well have been built as a decorative 'folly' by the Hanger's son William at the time he built his new house. He would have owned the land on either side and so he is the most likely creator of the bridge and the small Tudor bricks may be from the Roper's old manor house.

George Hanger died in 1726 leaving his Gloucestershire estate to his elder son Gabriel. The Kent properties were to go to the younger son William, 'now residing in Constantinople', after his mother's death. Dame Anne died in 1740 and William immediately appears in the parish books paying the rates for his houses and lands. He remains as enigmatic a figure as his incendiarised house and his folly bridge. He apparently came to live in Farningham to build his new house in 1740 but, according to Hasted who knew the village well, it burnt down before it was finished. He then went to live in the Crayker's house on the opposite side of the road until his early death in 1750 aged 48. This was when the Crayker house first became known as the Manor House. He was unmarried and appears to have played no part in the village life of church and vestry. His memorial stone is on the south wall of the chancel in the church.

The 'cattle screen' bridge
Photograph by
Jennifer Gough-Cooper

325–John Byng,
The Torington Diaries 1781-94,
1934 ed.

140

Part Two Modern

But the sound of water escaping from mill dams...willows, old rotten planks, slimy posts and brickwork, I love such things, as long as I do paint I shall never cease to paint such places`.
John Constable

141

Chapter Nine

The Colyers of Farningham Mill / Charles Colyer, miller /
The Colyer's first Mill House / The Willow Orchard Deed /
Charles Colyer and the Vestry / The Hamptons and the Pawleys /
The Principal Inhabitants / The Nash Family /
The Middling sort of Ratepayers / The Poor / Dr Harris.

Farningham Mill was sold by William Ebbutt to Thomas Colyer, a yeoman farmer from Southfleet, shortly before the latter's death in 1722. The actual sale document is lost, but a demand for the surrender of John Kemp's lease was made in 1725 by the new owner 'Elizabeth Collier widow' in which she refers to 'the recent purchase to himself and his heirs' by her deceased husband.[1]

Thomas was a prosperous yeoman farmer, as his will and the inventory of his possessions show. The will, made a week before his death of smallpox at the age of 41, 'sick of body but of sound mind and memory' left all his property in Kent to his seven sons when they became 21, 'share and share alike as tenants in common' according to Kentish custom.[2] His widow Elizabeth and brother-in-law, William Turkey, were to use 'the shares and profits to (the children's) education and bringing up'.

Although Thomas was a farmer, milling may have been a family occupation, there was a James Colyer, miller of Horton Kirby in 1689, perhaps an uncle. With seven sons to provide for he had probably seen Farningham Mill both as an investment and a future career for one of them. He may also have been a bit of a speculator and entrepreneur, having acquired a wharf with houses and a creek in Greenhythe 'commonly called the Callis Sands...and since known by the sign of the Swan' in 1716.[3] This was occupied by his brother-in-law William Turkey who is described as a wharfinger, or wharf manager. Grain production and export were big business in the early 18th century and rewarded with government bounties; so farming, milling and wharfing were naturally related.

Thomas's seventh son, Samuel, died of smallpox a few days after his father. The rest of the family survived, although two more children died young, William, the second son at eighteen and Mary, the younger of the two daughters, at ten. The four elder sons remained on different Southfleet farms for most of their lives; the youngest surviving son, Charles, was to come to Farningham Mill. Thomas's father, also Thomas, came from Stone near Dartford and, according to a 1706 map, probably lived at a farm called Beene-in-Stone.[4] He died in 1710, having apparently already set up his only son at the neighbouring Mates Farm in Southfleet at the time of the younger Thomas's marriage to Elizabeth Phillips, herself an only child and heiress.

Although the present-day branch of the family have arms granted in 1558, it is not possible at present to connect the original owners of the arms, a

1-CKS ref U 306
2-CKS, Southfleet parish registers, PRO. Prob 11, 1772
3-CKS ref U219 T1-5
4-CKS ref U 146 P2

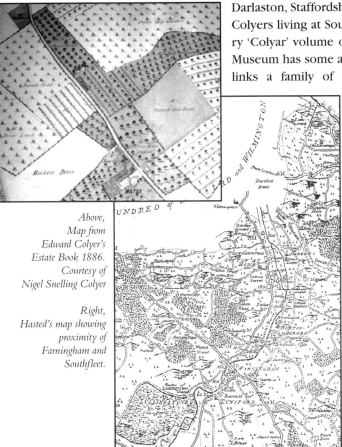

Above,
Map from
Edward Colyer's
Estate Book 1886.
Courtesy of
Nigel Snelling Colyer

Right,
Hasted's map showing
proximity of
Farningham and
Southfleet.

Darlaston, Staffordshire Colyer family, with the Kentish Colyers living at Southfleet and Stone. The 12th century 'Colyar' volume of the Lambeth Bible in Maidstone Museum has some added genealogical information that links a family of Colyers, Colyars or Colliers (the spelling varies) of Lenham near Maidstone with the well known Hales family of Canterbury.

There were also Colyers in Cranbrook in the 15th century and a ship-owning family of Colyers in Maidstone in the 17th century.[5] There is also a possible connection with the London merchant Richard Collyer who founded Collyer's School in Horsham, Sussex by his will of 1522.[6] Until more information turns up the origins of the Southfleet family remain obscure.

Thomas himself used the title of 'yeoman' in his will which, at that date, would mean a farmer cultivating his own, or leasehold lands. A yeoman's place in society still came between the husbandmen or small farmers and the gentry, who were in theory from old families entitled to bear arms. But rank and status were no longer so rigidly defined, and the criterion was rapidly becoming one of personal wealth.[7]

Kentish yeomen had a particularly proud history and presumably the elder Thomas was content to live within that tradition but, from the younger Thomas's expanding interests, it might be assumed that he had higher ambitions, frustrated by his early death. The Colyers were obviously an important local family, and the younger Thomas quickly became established in his new community of Southfleet, being appointed Overseer of the Poor at the age of 22 in 1704, and Surveyor of Roads, a position which required financial backing, in 1708. The inventory of his possessions made after his death in 1722 gives a good picture of family life at Mates Farm, the scene of the childhood of the future Farningham miller, Charles Colyer.[8]

The main room, the 'Hall', was clearly a large farmhouse kitchen where the three women, Elizabeth, her elder daughter and the maid would have prepared and cooked meals and where the family of eleven and their farm servants sat to eat. There was an iron crane in the chimney from which cooking

5-Seldon Society Vol 46, *Select Cases of the Law Merchant.* op cit
6-A.N.Wilson, *A History of Collyer's School* (1965)
7-Peter Earle, *The Making of the English Middle Class, 1660-1730* (1987)
8-PRO Prob 11.

143

pots would hang over the open fire, and a jack with two spits for roasting meat. There were tables, chairs, forms, a dresser with drawers, a clock with weights, a bird cage, an old cradle, a small looking glass, box irons and a number of brass and iron utensils and pewter dishes, plates and porringers.

There was one other living room, the 'Parlour', with oak furniture, a writing desk, a press cupboard, a child's chair, pewter flagons and tankards, tables, chairs and stools and a fireplace. This was obviously the room where Thomas wrote his accounts, where visitors were entertained and where the children did their lessons. Upstairs, the parent's bedroom, the 'Best Chamber', had a fourposter bed with feather overlay, feather pillows and bolster, blankets and quilt, curtains round the bed as well as window curtains, a looking glass, tables and chairs, fireplace and 'severall other things' including a pewter chamber pot. There was also a closet with more stored pewter and brass.

The furnishings of the other rooms indicate that most probably Elizabeth, the elder daughter, slept in one with the smaller children Mary, Samuel and Charles. This room had two beds with comfortable furnishings, a looking glass, a close stool or commode and a chest of drawers. The bedroom most probably shared by the elder boys, Thomas, William, John, James and Edward was more sparsely furnished with only three beds; a fourposter, a half header and a string bed. There was also a 'Cloath Press' where the family linen was stored; 56 pairs of sheets, 2 dozen napkins and 6 tablecloths. The value of the linen was £57, more than the total value of all the furniture and pewter in the house.

There was a maid's room, a men's chamber, a granary, bakehouse, brewhouse, milkhouse and strong beer cellar. The farm implements and stock were listed outside in the stable, the barn, the storehouses, suckling house, hop kilns and farmyards. There were 17 cows and a bull and 7 fatting calves, a boar, 8 hogs, 22 pigs, 81 sheep and 10 horses. Arable land included at least 75 acres of wheat, peas, beans and barley and there were 80,000 hop poles.

No Farningham yeoman's farm inventory of this period, except that of the rich Chapman family of Maplescombe Farm, compares in wealth and comfort with this. A second farm, 'Beene-in-Stone', probably Thomas's father's farm, just across the Southfleet parish boundary, is also listed in the inventory with £250 of property including arable, fruit and woodland.

The total assets of the two farms came in the will to just under £1000. There were also 'Debts owing to Debtors at time of death' of £1400, a mortgage 'Esteemed Desperate' of £50 and 'Due upon Bonds and Notes in Hand £520'. Farningham Mill is not mentioned, nor are the other properties such as the Callis Sands wharf, but a third farm, 'Betsham in Southfleet' was left specifically to Thomas, the eldest son. The hamlet of Betsham was next door to Mates Farm, as was the hamlet of Beane, indicating that Thomas had been building up his estate from neighbouring farms. Presumably there were no financial problems at his death, because there is no evidence of a sale and all the properties remained in the family, including the rented Mates Farm which, as 'Part of the Ancient Manor of Poole' was sold by Lord Romney to Thomas's grandson in 1803 and is now known as Manor House Farm.[9]

The first document linking the Colyer family with Farningham Mill is very similarly worded to the Ebbutt's deed of 1677. It is the negotiation for the surrender of John Kemp's lease in 1725 and describes the property as follows: 'All that messuage wherein John Kemp then dwelt with the millhouse, water corn mill, barn, stable, buildings, yards and gardens, 2 acres meadowland and 4 acre Westfield, together with millstones, wheels, cogs, floodgates, weirs, dams, banks, watercourses, tolls, privileges...to hold at a yearly rent of £25'. The deed goes on to say that since Thomas Colyer purchased the same, there had been 'several disputes and differences concerning the breach of some covenants in the lease by John Kemp, who now therefore surrenders the same'.[10]

Perhaps John Kemp's farming activities had competed with his milling and the mill buildings had been allowed to deteriorate. A John Snelling, the name of a family later related to the Colyers by marriage, appeared on the rate books paying for the mill, presumably as a caretaker miller, and John Kemp retired to his farm until, in 1733, 'Mrs Kemp widow' paid his rates.

Charles Colyer, Miller 1716-1778

No Colyer name appears on the parish rate books until Charles Colyer arrived in 1735.[11] This Charles Colyer, miller of Farningham from 1735 to his death in 1778, seems to represent all the best aspects of English 18th century rural life. He was a mainstay of village society, serving voluntarily year after year as Churchwarden, Overseer of the Poor and Surveyor of Roads. He was a working miller all his life, employing and housing workmen and building up a model estate. Much of his work on the mill buildings and waterways can still be seen, and his scrupulously clear accounts in the Vestry books list his activities and give valuable details of the life of the Farningham community.

It is only possible to guess the circumstances of his upbringing between the ages of eight at his father's death and nineteen at his arrival in Farningham, but it seems likely that he first went to school in Southfleet and later was aprenticed to a miller in Horton Kirby.

In 1637 Sir John Sedley of Scadbury in Southfleet left £400 by will for the purchase of lands 'To the end that the profit thereof shall be imployed for the maintenance of a schoolmaster for the teaching of the children there'.[12] His daughter left a further £400 to augment the schoolmaster's salary and maintain the schoolhouse. 'Every scholar of the parish of Southfleet shall be taught freely, only at his first admission he shall pay the schoolmaster one shilling, and one shilling yearly. Those who cannot read have no right of admission and will be required to pay 2 pence a week'.

The school still exists, with the Sedley coat of arms embedded in the Jacobean brickwork of the entrance porch, and is a short walk across the fields from Mates Farm. It is now a primary school for 35 children, and

9-CKS ref U1644 T184
10-CKS ref U306
11-CKS ref P145/5/1
12-PRO, Prob 11, CKS ref P343/8/9 Southfleet Vestry

Assembly is held in the Hall of the 17th century building. Perhaps it is too easy to imagine the seven young Colyers coming to school here nearly three hundred years ago. Maybe they were sent as boarders to one of the large grammar schools in the county, or to London, or maybe they had a private tutor. But this was a well endowed school with a qualified schoolmaster, as well endowed as some of the famous grammar schools and a great cut above a village dame school or a church charity and, at a time when even the aristocracy made use of the free schools, it would be surprising for a yeoman to spurn one so close to home.

The fact that the school never became better known is perhaps explained by its location. Edward Hasted, writing about Southfleet at the end of the 18th century, says 'This parish is rather an unfrequented place, nor is it much known, there being no public thoroughfare through it; and the gentleman's seats, of which there were several, having been greatly neglected and suffered to run to ruin'. The average age of admission for a boy to grammar school was between 7 and 9, he would be expected to be able to read already, and boys going on to an apprenticeship would leave between 12 and 13. Boys who went on to university stayed until 15 to 18 but, as Charles appears as miller of Farningham at

Southfleet School

the age of 19, he is most likely to have been serving an apprenticeship.

The only clue to this stage of his life is given by his marriage in 1737 to Elizabeth Knight, eldest daughter of Henry Knight, miller of Horton Kirby. Unfortunately Henry Knight died in 1724 which rules him out as Charles's apprentice master, but the Horton Kirby registers show an earlier miller called James Colyer, indicating a long standing family connection with this mill, so the strong likelihood is that Charles served his apprenticeship in Horton Kirby where he met his future wife.

The next question is how did Charles live on his arrival in Farningham in 1735, what sort of a mill and mill house did he find and were they at all as they are now? It is usually accepted that a water mill is likely to remain on the same site for its working life, being restored or rebuilt as necessary and leaving little trace of previous buildings behind. So it is not surprising that there is no evidence of any building earlier than the 18th century on the present site. Unfortunately however the first clear description of a mill on this particular piece of land was not made until 1743.[13] So although it seems clear that the de Fremingham/Isley/Roper/Ebbutt mill stood on this site we cannot be entirely certain. There is still the curiosity of two field names, Great and Little Mill Fields some way down the river beyond the Lion on the 1693 map that make one wonder whether an earlier mill existed below the medieval manor east of the High Street.

13-CKS ref U219 T 1-5

146

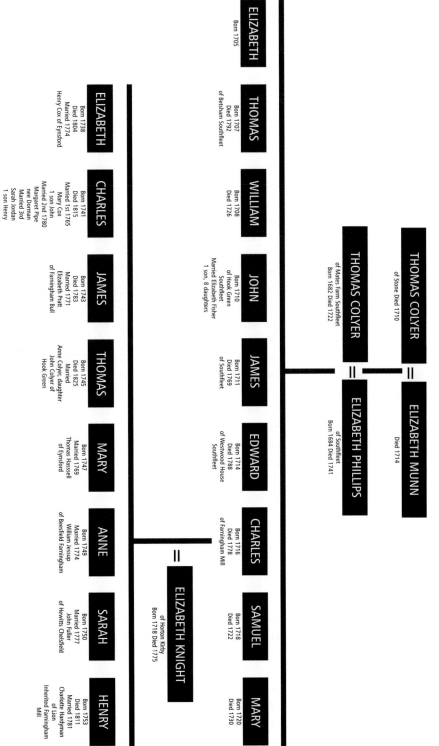

THOMAS COLYER
of Stone Died 1710

ELIZABETH MUNN
Died 1714

THOMAS COLYER
of Mates Farm Southfleet
Born 1682 Died 1722

ELIZABETH PHILLIPS
of Southfleet
Born 1684 Died 1741

ELIZABETH
Born 1705

THOMAS
Born 1707
Died 1792
of Betsham Southfleet

WILLIAM
Born 1708
Died 1726

JOHN
Born 1710
of Hook Green
Southfleet
Married Elizabeth Fisher
1 son, 8 daughters

JAMES
Born 1711
Died 1769
of Southfleet

EDWARD
Born 1714
Died 1788
of Westwood House
Southfleet

CHARLES
Born 1716
Died 1778
of Farningham Mill

SAMUEL
Born 1718
Died 1722

MARY
Born 1720
Died 1730

ELIZABETH KNIGHT
of Horton Kirby
Born 1718 Died 1775

ELIZABETH
Born 1738
Died 1804
Married 1774
Henry Cox of Eynsford

CHARLES
Born 1741
Died 1815
Married 1st 1765
Mary Cox
1 son John
Married 2nd 1780
Margaret Pipe
nee Dorman
Married 3rd
Sarah Jordan
1 son Henry

JAMES
Born 1743
Died 1783
Married 1771
Elizabeth Pratt
of Farningham Bull

THOMAS
Born 1745
Died 1825
Married
Anne Colyer, daughter
John Colyer of
Hook Green

MARY
Born 1747
Married 1769
Thomas Hassell
of Eynsford

ANNE
Born 1749
Married 1774
William Jessup
of Beesfield Farningham

SARAH
Born 1750
Married 1777
John Fuller
of Hewitts Chelsfield

HENRY
Born 1753
Died 1811
Married 1781
Charlotte Hardyman
of Lion
Inherited Farningham
Mill

Unfortunately the early maps of Farningham are not much help with this problem. Sir John Beale's map of 1665 only shows his 50 acre 'Walled peece' east of the High Street and nothing to the north. By this time of course the mill had been sold to Ebbutt and no longer belonged to the manor. The very detailed Hanger estate map of 1693 shows all the manor lands east of the High Street, so at least by elimination, Ebbut's mill was to the west where the mill is today and there is even a small unmarked lane where the present day mill drive leads into the High Street.

One of the most useful ways of tracing the history of a house is through the parish rate books. The earliest Farningham rates appear in a Churchwarden's book of 1707. This gives 'An assessment made by the Minister, Churchwardens and other principal Inhabitants of the parish for ye necessary reparacions of the Church and Churchyard. Assessed at every man at 6d in the pound according to his rent. On one page is a list of the ratepaying inhabitants, and on the opposite page is the 'Disbursments of the Churchwardens'.[14]

Apart from the upkeep of the church the rates paid for such things as the Clerk's wages, the year's supply of communion bread and wine, the bell-ringer's wages and upkeep of the bells, and the expences of the twice yearly visitation by the representative of the Deanery of Shoreham, to which Farningham belonged, and his dinner with the vicar. The Deanery was one of eight 'Peculiars' of the Archbishop of Canterbury which had been founded in the 13th century and were exempt from the 'Ordinary' or Archbishop of the diocese in which they lay. The Shoreham Deanery was only transferred to Rochester in 1902.[15]

The rates also paid for the many small disbursements to the travelling poor to encourage them to go on their way and not to dally through sickness or exhaustion and become a charge to the parish. Other small payments were for vermin, one shilling for the head of a fox or badger and sixpence for a hedgehog. The disbursements give a fascinating picture of life in the village, and the assessed rents give useful clues to the size and nature of different properties.

For instance, in 1707 Dorothy Kemp, widow, paid 18s. 'For Ye Mill' which assesses her yearly rent at £36. By comparison, Mr Thomas Polhill, Under-Sheriff of Kent and tenant of the old manor house, paid 10s., assessing his rent at £20 p.a.. Mr Benjamin Crayker, son of Charles Crayker of Charton Manor, paid a £1 rate or £40 p.a. for the fine new house he had built by the river which later became the present day manor house. Edward Chapman of Maplescombe Farm paid the highest rate of £2.2s. The rating was linked to the amount of land held, and for size and content this was the only farm that could be compared to Mates Farm in Southfleet. Mathew Sweetapple, saddler, and keeper of the White Hart, and George Udall, husbandman, both typical small ratepayers, each paid 2s..

The next year Dorothy Kemp's son John had negotiated a new lease with the Ebbutts at a yearly rent of £27. The sixpenny rate fluctuates each year it

14-CKS ref P145/5/1
15-Lambeth Palace Library. Inventories

is called, presumably according to the amount of land held, with John Kemp paying 15s. in 1716 and 19s. in 1720. In 1724 John Snelling, the caretaker miller, paid 14s., and in 1735 Charles Colyer paid his first rate of 10s., a sum which remained constant until he expanded his property in 1757. From this evidence, although the assessed rent of the mill dropped from 1707 to 1735, and this could have been due to a number of factors such as the deterioration of the property, the price of corn or the rental of fields, the rates indicate without doubt that Charles Colyer's mill of 1735 was the same as John Kemp's mill of 1707.

Although so little is known of the Ebbutts' 60 years of ownership, they appear to have been speculative mill owners rather than operative millers, content to allow the Kemps to keep the wheels turning while they reaped the rewards and managed their other properties in Kent. It is most unlikely that they built a new mill during those years and so it seems more than probable that Charles Colyer's mill of 1735 was the same as that bought by William Ebbutt from Sir John Cotton in about 1665 and that in turn was likely to have been the same mill forcibly rebuilt by Sir Anthony Roper in 1635.

The Colyer's first Mill House

The Hearth Tax of 1664 and the inventory of John Kemp's mill and mill house have already been examined, and although the inventory is very sparse compared to that of Thomas Colyer at Mates Farm, it suggests a perfectly comfortable small house for a young newly married couple.

Charles Colyer's first house of the 1730s can be seen behind his son Henry's house of the 1790s. John Kemp's earlier house may lie underneath.

It was a basic two rooms down and two up, with the adjoining watermill most probably standing directly on the river. Whether there was a mill leat leading from a weir cannot be determined; if so then the mill and mill house may have stood where they are today. It seems quite possible though that the mill stood directly on the main river with either an undershot wheel in the river itself or with a short leat to an overshot or breast wheel. This would mean that the house adjoining may have been on the site of the present day line of stables and cottages.

There is a small mid-18th century weather boarded house with a mansard roof, joined to the back of the present day Mill House. It seems fairly certain that this is the house in which Charles and his wife Elizabeth brought up their eight children, born between 1739 and 1753. Other houses in Kent of this period sometimes had the new French mansard roof added to older houses to make more space. If this was the case, then the mansard roof was simply added to the Kemp's house, and the present day Mill House kitchen would have been John Kemp's Fireroom, the two rooms above his bedrooms and the two large attic rooms in the mansard roof added by the Colyers for their growing family.

The Willow Orchard Deed

No brick or wood work survive from an earlier period. There is a document of 1743, 'The Willow Orchard Deed', in which John Fullerton, who had bought Benjamin Crayker's new house in 1735, sold a willow orchard to Charles Colyer. The document is fragile and some words are torn and rubbed but the description is mainly as follows; 'All that small piece of common ground called the Willow Orchard situated in Farningham near or adjoining the County or Stone Bridge...also an Oast, Hop or Kiln house lately erected...on part of the same ground'. The length on the south-east side 'next the Bank or Wastewater or river running under the Stone Bridge' was 140 feet. The north-west side 'next the Roadway leading from Farningham Street along the main or mill river towards the house and mill of Charles Colyer' was 144 feet. The north-east side 'near or adjoining the Stone Bridge' was 22 feet, and the south-west side 'to the yard or ground of said Charles Colyer' was 26 feet.[16]

If these measurements are correct, and they are repeated twice, they must describe the piece of ground on which Charles would shortly build his workmen's cottages, the present day terrace of Bridge and Mill Cottages. The distance from the High Street falls short of today's mill buildings, stopping at the present day Gardener's Cottage. This can simply mean that the mill yard began there. Also, as the document mentions the main river', this can be read to mean that there was already an alternative river or mill stream.

All in all it seems that the site of the mill and mill house were where they are today, and any earlier water mill, built directly on the main river, no longer existed. In fact the long mill-leat, or head-race, from the weir to the mill and the tail-race from the mill to the road may have been there for many centuries; the technology had been known to the Romans. Any early wood and brick work would have long vanished. The very pretty blue and red striped brickwork of part of the tail-race has the same 18th century appearance as the brickwork under the 18th century main road bridge, so was probably the work of Charles Colyer's bricklayers.

On whichever site Charles and Elizabeth first lived when they came to Farningham in 1735 there is little doubt that they occupied a small mill house with a water corn mill, barn and stable adjoining with two and a half acres of meadow and a 4 acre field. That they were comfortable and well fed is proved by the fact that their eight children not only survived infancy but all outlived their parents, a remarkable feat in the 18th century. The children were Elizabeth, born in 1739, Charles in 1741, James in 1743, Thomas in 1745, Mary in 1747, Anne in 1749, Sarah in 1750 and Henry in 1752.

All eight grew up to be interesting people but, apart from their baptismal dates, little is known about their early years. Their childhood must have been fairly happy and healthy. They lived in idyllic surroundings and, although their father had not yet made his fortune, they belonged to a small minority of 16-CKS U 219 T1-5

'Principal Inhabitants' or elite of the village. Even for 18th century children, treated as small adults from the moment they were out of petticoats, there were surely all the pleasures of a childhood spent living beside a river in an agricultural village.

They were surrounded by open fields and a profusion of wild life far richer than today. There must have been boating, fishing and eel trapping and no doubt there were dogs and cats kept to protect the family from human and animal marauders. The Colyers also had their own small farm and there would have been poultry, cows and horses. All this would have meant hard work from an early age for the children, as well as the schooling they undoubtedly all received.

The presence of the mill itself must have been all-important, but probably as little regarded as a familiar ticking clock. There are many technical descriptions of working watermills in numerous books, but few people today know the experience of being inside one at first hand, so this eye-witness account, written by Gertrude Jekyll at the turn of the 20th century, seems worth quoting.[17]

'The constant vibration as of something alive, some sort of plodding lumbering, good-natured, meal-producing monster, fed and guided by the careful miller. The mill is in three floors, the sacks of grain are hoisted to the top floor where the corn is cleaned. It then descends by a hopper and shoot to the middle floor, and here are the millstones, enclosed in a wooden casing. The lower stone is fixed, the upper rotates upon it, not quite touching, but near enough to grind the corn which gradually passes along the grooves that lead to its outer edge. From there it passes by another shoot to a bin on the ground floor. The wheel is just outside the lower floor of the mill; its ponderous axle is prolonged and passes through the wall, ending in a powerful cogwheel which engages with a smaller horizontal wheel to turn the spindle that passes up through all the floors, and communicates the power to the stones on the middle floor and the cleaning machine at the top. The power is produced by the weight of water falling on the floats of the wheel. To go into one of these old mills gives one a sense of being in close touch with a thing that has gone on unchanged throughout the centuries, for a water flour mill three or four hundred years ago would have presented the same general features, the same sound, the same good smell, the same mealy coating. The harmonious colouring of everything, lightly coated in mealy dust'

This was the background to the Colyer's life and no doubt they were all lightly coated in mealy dust much of the time. Charles Colyer, like his father before him, was quickly integrated with the village society. Even at the age of nineteen when he arrived, the miller was a man of importance. He became a Churchwarden in 1737 and Overseer of the Poor in 1740 and from then until his death in 1778, aged 62, it is possible to trace many of his activities through the Vestry books.

Charles Colyer and the Vestry

If the magistrates, as was said, ruled the county, the Vestry ruled the village. Thomas Pearce in *The Compleat Justice of the Peace and Parish Officer* of 1756 defined the Vestry as 'The assembly of the whole parish met together in some convenient place for the dispatch of the business of the parish...this meeting being commonly held in the place for keeping the priest's vestments

17-Gertrude Jekyll,
Old West Surrey(1904)

151

adjoining or belonging to the church'. The Vestry officers were the Churchwardens. the Overseers of the Poor, the Surveyors of Roads, the Constable and the Parish Clerk. The Vestry met in the church once a year at Easter to elect new officers. Other occasional meetings often took place in one of the inns.

The Parish had gradually taken over the functions of the church and the manor. The vicar naturally still had care of the souls and morals of his congregation, he also acted as chairman of the vestry, and he appointed one of the two churchwardens; the other was chosen by the inhabitants. Some parishes had a 'select' or 'closed vestry', restricted to a few landowners but the Farningham vestry appears to have been open and attended by the principal ratepayers as well as the officers.

The Churchwardens were custodians of the church and churchyard and, to a certain extent, looked after the social welfare of the village. They kept the church accounts and called the church rates. The Overseers had been created by the Elizabethan Poor Laws 'to maintain and set to work the poor and raise the necessary funds by levying Poor Rates'. They were supposed to be 'substantial householders' and two were nominated by the vestry and appointed by the magistrates each year. The late 17th century laws of Settlement and Removal had extended the overseer's duties. Before 1662 the poor had some right to go where they chose to find work, but after that date the Overseers had the power to remove strangers who could not prove settlement either by birth in the parish or by producing a certificate from their native parish guaranteeing to take them back if they became a charge on the poor rates. A great deal of the Farningham Overseers' time and budget was spent removing people without certificates or contesting their settlement claims.

The Poor Laws grew harsher and more punitive during the Age of Enlightenment. More Poorhouses were built for the incapable poor and Workhouses for the capable and vagrants. Farningham had a small poorhouse and also, as has been seen, boarded out poor people. In the mid-century able bodied paupers were also sent to Shoreham Workhouse. Paupers were made to wear badges with the letter P on their shoulder. There were rewards for arresting vagrants and fines for sheltering them, and vagrant men and women could be whipped before being sent home to their native parish.

There is no evidence of really inhuman treatment in Farningham, but the Constable's records, which listed punishments, only date from the 19th century. The stocks were mended in 1727, so presumably some punishments were carried out in the village, and there must have been a lock-up or cage.

A stream of vagrants trudged through the village during the 18th century, as might be expected from the siting on two crossroads, one of which roads was the second or third busiest in Kent. Most were helped on their way with a few pence, and those who lingered, either sick, or in childbirth or dying in the barns or on the roadside, were usually fed for a while before being dispatched again, either to the next parish or to the churchyard.

It is a pathetic procession of 'passingers, travellers, strangers, big-bellied and liening women, people burned out of house and home, maimed soldiers, shipwrecked sailors, Turkey slaves', (the last being seamen rescued from the Barbary pirates). They go on through the century, soldiers filtering home from Marlborough's wars to Napoleon's, women widowed and abandoned, labourers without settlements, sad little orphans such as 'a mayd a waygoer' who died by the road, the wretched of the earth, all seem to have come through Farningham.

The Surveyor of Roads was nominated by the Vestry and appointed by the magistrates. He was chosen from the higher ratepayers, a specific property qualification being required for the post so the wealthier farmers with access to waggons and labourers were usually chosen. The Surveyor had to inspect the roads three times a year and both organise and supervise the reluctant parishioner's annual six days compulsory 'statutory labour' of road repairing. It was not a popular post.

Once the Turnpike Roads were created the tolls raised were supposed to pay for road repairs which were meant to be supervised by the County Surveyor, but statutory labour was not abolished until 1835, and Farningham still had four surveyors of its own at the end of the 19th century.

Charles Colyer is quite often listed as Surveyor of Roads in the Vestry books but unfortunately the Surveyors accounts only date from the 19th century and so there is not much information about the actual work on the roads, apart from the paupers who were paid in pennies for breaking stones. Improvement came with the creation of the Foots Cray to Wrotham Turnpike in 1752 and the Dartford to Sevenoaks in 1766.

The Constable, still known in Farningham as the Borseholder, was the 'conservator of the peace'. Constables were descendants of the ancient tithing men, they carried a staff of office which was their badge of authority as well as a useful weapon and this sometimes hung outside the door of their house. There was plenty of work for a constable, supervising settlements and removals, billeting the poor, attending the sessions, dealing with the disorderly, rounding up the militia or their substitutes in times of war, and inspecting the alehouses. Two Borseholders were appointed by the Vestry each year in Farningham during the 18th century. The position was unpaid although they could, and did, claim expenses. They usually appear to have been chosen from the smaller ratepayers such as shopkeepers, small husbandmen or able bodied men on poor relief.[18]

The Parish Clerk was paid from the church rates and seems to have kept his job for life. Four members of the Monk family were Clerks for Farningham during the 18th century and three at least died in office, John Monk 'the Old Clerk of the Parish above 50 years' died in 1732; Robert Monk in 1756; Thomas Monk, in 1766; and 'John Monk Parish Clerk' in 1791. Their wages were about £3 a year at the beginning of the century and £4 at the end. They

18-W.E. Tate
The Parish Chest (1946)

153

called the courts held at the twice yearly church Visitations, arranged the baptisms, marriages and burials, acted as witnesses, collected and accounted for the church offerings or 'Briefs' and performed many other menial duties for which they were paid small sums or 'Dues'.

The Briefs would have been read by the vicar from the pulpit and collected by the Clerk as the congregation left. Records for Farningham start in 1681. The usual collection was only a few shillings, but at times of local disasters, such as the Great Hail Storm of 1763, £1 11s. 3d. was raised for sufferers in Kent. On a typical Briefing Sunday in 1695 Mathew Sweetapple, John Udall and Walter Loveden all gave 2d.; Samuel Browne, the lawyer, gave 2s.6d.; and Mr and Mrs Pendlebury, the vicar and his wife, set a good example by each giving 5s. and 3s.

Farningham does not seem to have had a paid sexton, and it looks as if the Clerk did much of his work. For instance, he was once paid 2s. 'for Ringing the Bell and digging the Grave'. He also acted as mortician and was paid 3s 'for sitting up 2 knights' with a parishioner and then 'laying him forth'. He often received a small sum for 'washing the linnen and altering the surplis' and also for 'pints of Oyle and Brushes and Brooms'.

The major part of Farningham parish in the mid-18th century was owned by landlords who did not live in the village, such as the Hangers of Gloucestershire, the Bunces of Kemsing, the Bosvilles of Eynsford, the Dykes of Lullingstone and the Bathursts of Horton Kirby; even the Craykers of Charton Manor also had homes in London. The only inhabitant resembling a village squire was usually the tenant of the Manor House.

In 1740 there were 35 rate-paying inhabitants. Almost everyone was engaged in some form of agriculture; even the vicar had a small farm. There were yeomen and husbandmen and labourers, and others closely connected with the land such as the blacksmith, the wheelwright, the carpenter and the harness maker. The two innkeepers and the butcher also had farms. In addition, a baker, tailor, bricklayer, shoemaker and grocer made it a self-sufficient community.

Both as the miller and as a frequently serving vestry officer Charles Colyer must have known his neighbours very well. The farmers from miles around would be his customers, and he theirs, and he must surely have made it his business to know all the local shopkeepers as well as the travelling traders and the townspeople of Dartford Corn Market. The other officers of the vestry and 'Principal Inhabitants' of the village would be his friends, so far as he had a social life. The parents of the children his own children would later marry were all local people. In 1740 he was one of only seven men given the title of 'Mr' in the rate books. Only two, William Hanger and John Fullerton had the title 'Esquire'.

The Principal Inhabitants

John Fullerton was not in the village for very long. He rented the Parsonage before buying Benjamin Crayker's riverside house after Crayker's death in 1731, but sold it again in 1740 to William Hanger who, as Lord of the Manor, called it the Manor House by which name it has remained ever since. The old manor house had always been known as 'ye Place' and the Crayker house, confusingly, was called 'ye Great House'. After 1740 when 'ye Place' burnt down it is no longer mentioned and the rates simply say 'ye Meadow`. (This is now Market Meadow). William died at ye Great House in 1750 and his brother Gabriel, who had inherited the family estate in Gloucestershire, became his heir.[20] Gabriel was created 1st Baron Coleraine in 1762 and appears in several Farningham deeds with his trustee, Lord Romney, on behalf of his younger son William who was heir to the Kent estate, but who died without heirs and the estate was sold in the 1770s.[21]

The vicar in 1740 was Mr John Andrews MA who applied for a licence to teach grammar in the village in 1749. Three vicars, of Orpington, Wrotham and Foots Cray bore witness that he was 'a person of sober, honest and virtuous life and conversation'.[22] He did not leave the village until 1754 and must have baptised all the Colyer children and possibly taught the elder ones.

The vicars still had constant disputes about their tithes.[23] In 1722 'an injured vicar', William Fuller, had sought 'redress' from the Dean and Chapter for the loss of the tithe of hops which which his predecessor had allowed to fall into the hands of the tenants of the Rectory at the Parsonage. The dispute was still continuing in 1840. It was not a rich living and no doubt Mr Andrews in 1740 was as glad of his 12 acres of glebe land as Fielding's Parson Trulliber who 'stript into his waistcoat to serve his hogs'.[24]

The Nash Family

Mr Edward Loxley, yeoman, was a Principal Inhabitant at this time, first renting the old manor house from the Hangers and later, after William Hanger's return, renting Pedham Place from Lord Romney. He had married Mrs Elizabeth Nash, widow of William Nash, another Farningham yeoman, whose two sons were making names for themselves outside the village, John Nash as a medical practitioner in Sevenoaks and Thomas as a calico printer in Lambeth. The whereabouts of William Nash's home remains unknown; the present day Social Club is a possibility.

When Thomas Nash died in 1778, the mausoleum in the churchyard was built in his memory. The assumption that John Nash, the famous Regency architect designed the tomb has yet to be proved. Sir John Summerson, the historian of 18th century architecture, agreed that the architect Nash came from a completely different family, but also thought that the style of the mausoleum made it more than possible that the design was his. Dr John Nash, Thomas's brother, who is also buried in the mausoleum, frequently came over

20-CKS U36 T449
21-Burke's Extinct Peerage
22-Lambeth Palace Library, Farningham file
23-CKS P145/3/1. & Canterbury Cathedral docs.
24-Henry Fielding, *Tom Jones* 1749

The Nash Mausoleum.

The faculty for building a mausoleum in the churchyard.
Courtesy of
Lambeth Palace Library.

to Farningham to attend patients. He was possibly the Colyer's family doctor, but the confinements were probably conducted by Mrs Pinden, the shoemaker's wife, who was the village midwife.

Edward and Elizabeth Loxley had one daughter, Sarah, who married Thomas Fuller of Lullingstone in 1751. The Fullers were to rent the Farningham manor estate from the Hangers in the 1770s and Thomas Fuller and his son would become the village squires for the last part of the century and the beginning of the next. He and the Colyer family would become the principal landowners in the village for many years to come.

When Edward Loxley died in 1751 he left everything to his granddaughter Elizabeth Fuller, who would later marry a Waring of Chelsfield and inherit the manor property. Everything, that is, except for his best perruke and hat and set of razors which he willed to Thomas Monk the Parish Clerk, and his 'tea equippage with cannisters, cups, sawcers, slopbasons, sugar dishes and silver teaspoons and tongs' which he left to the Gutsells of Eynsford who had nursed him in his last illness.[25] James Gutsell, or Gudsell, was the local surveyor and map-maker who made most of Charles Colyer's maps and plans. We can imagine the Colyers at the mid-century enjoying the new fashion for afternoon tea although, with such a large family, probably without such elegant 'equippage'

25-PRO Prob 11

The Hamptons and the Pawleys

Mr Edward Hampton, yeoman, had become another important resident. At first he had rented the Parsonage but by 1740 he had bought Brown's farm and John Kemp's lands, along what is now Sparepenny Lane but was then called Eynsford Lane. He built a house, later known as Hampton Court. Edward and Anne Hampton's two sons died young, and their property went to their daughters. Mary, the elder, married George Pawley, an Eynsford carpenter, who came to live in Busses Farm next door, in the house now known as Mount Pleasant.

Mount Pleasant,
Sparepenny Lane, the
Pawley family
farmhouse.

The Pawleys had a large family of five sons and two daughters, born between 1745 and 1757 who must have grown up with the Colyer children. Edward Hampton started a school in the village, or maybe took over the small private school noted by the vicar in 1717.[26] By 1758 the new vicar, Dr John Perry, reported that this had become 'a large private school in which Boys and Girls are taught Arithmetic and Reading and Writing'.

Dr Perry resided at Ash, where he was the rector, and paid Mr Thomas, a curate, to take the services in Farningham with 'Prayers and sermons every Lord's Day, Ash Wednesday and Good Friday and Sacrament of the Lord's Supper four times a year'. The Colyers, we know, were good churchgoers. The Hamptons paid rates for a school in 1759, and John Taylor, a writing master from Frittenden had settled in the village as early as 1752. The Hampton's second son-in-law, Richard Manning, a yeoman who farmed Charton manor, still paid rates for the school in 1769 and it seems more than probable that the Colyer children received at least part of their schooling here.

Another principal inhabitant in 1740 was the last member of the Crayker family of Charton, Benjamin Crayker the younger, 'Attorney of Dartford'. He inherited the property on his brother Joseph's death in 1738 and appears to have lived there until his death in 1773. His name often appears on local legal documents such as title deeds and wills, and he paid the rates for the house but not the farm. His bill to Edward Hampton for the purchase of Brown's Farm in 1736 lists their journey to London together by horse, searching a will and a fine, 'ingrossing skins parchments and duties', drawing an abstract of title deed, writing letters, porterage and postage. All this for £5 16s.[27] Benjamin was a bachelor and after his death his nephew Daniel Cabinel sold up the Charton estate.

The highest ratepayers in the village in 1740 were still the Chapman family. Thomas Chapman the elder rented at least 700 acres of land at Maplescombe from the Bunces of Kemsing. His son Thomas occupied Beesfield farm. Two other yeoman farmers were Mr Buss and Mr Burr. John Buss rented Busses farm, later the Pawley farm, from the Bosvilles of Eynsford,

26-Lambeth Palace Library MS
1115/9
27-CKS U36 T448

he also farmed land at Charton and Eglantine. Nicholas Burr rented different farms in turn. According to his granddaughter Elizabeth Burr, writing in 1822, he lived at Pedham Place. His son, her father William Burr, lived at Whitehill farm, now called Farningham Hill and formerly known as Upper Court. He was a frequent Vestry officer and is buried in the fine box grave by the church door.

In 1740 the two inns, the Bull and the Lion, were still owned by two of the large landowners. The Bull, then called the Pied Bull, belonged to the Bosvilles of Eynsford and the Black Lion, as it was known until the mid-19th century, belonged to the Hangers. The history of the tenants of both inns in the early19th century is confusing because so many of them were called Smith. In 1740 Mr Thomas Smith was innholder of the Bull and Mrs Jane Smith of the Lion. Both inns would later belong to the Colyer family.[28]

The Middling sort of Ratepayer

The second tier of villagers in the mid-18th century were the smaller ratepayers such as the husbandmen, craftsmen and shopkeepers. These were often people from old village families whose names recur again and again in the parish registers, such as John Moice, butcher; Thomas Stiddolph, blacksmith; John Udall, husbandman; Robert Nightingale, baker; Edward Loft, carpenter; Thomas Pinden, shoemaker; Henry Wallis, tailor; and Nicholas Sharp who kept a small alehouse and sold provisions. The Sharps were mostly bricklayers and would also serve as parish clerks after the long reign of the Monk family. None of these people served as Overseers or Surveyors, but several were Churchwardens and Borseholders. Charles would have known them all very well.

Farningham's Poor

Below them was a third tier of people, harder to trace because they paid no rates. They were the labourers and the poor. The Farningham parish register shows many marriages, baptisms and burials of non-ratepaying villagers. This is sometimes the only way of tracing the history of the labourers and the poor. Some farmers may have provided accommodation for labourers with families. Also some names indicate that some young married couples lived with ratepaying parents. There would also have been a large number of single labourers and servants who lived with their employers. It is also possible to follow a few of the labourers stories from the surviving Settlement and Removal certificates and from the charity accounts.[29]

The first Farningham book of the Overseers of the Poor starts in 1748, and records of gift money to the poor from the Anthony Roper Charity start in 1756. From then on it is easier to follow the fate of some of these families, and to see how few managed to move away, and how many died here, and how age, infirmity and widowhood sent some low-income families into poor relief. Old village families such as the Monks, Udalls, Stiddolphs and

28-H&W.Harding, *The Pubs of Eynsford & Farningham* F&ELHS. No19
29-CKS P145/13 &25

Nightingales all fell on hard times at various stages, and some poor families never knew anything else.

J.L. & B. Hammond's history of *The Village Labourer* gives the yearly wages appointed by the Kent Justices in 1732 as £8 a year for a head labourer, scaling down to £2 for the lowest paid woman.[30] Presumably these were farm servants who received bed and board. Seasonal day labourers received 1s. 2d. in summer and 1s. in winter. Arthur Young's estimates of labourer's wages, and the price of food were collected in the 1760s and are thought to have remained stable during the mid-century.[31] He estimated the annual labourer's income in the south of England at about £20 with £9 p.a. wages for servants boarded with a farmer. Bread in the mid-century would have cost about 4d. a four pound loaf, cheese 3d. a pound and meat 4d.

Poor widows could earn a little money by boarding orphans and aged or handicapped people, also by acting as 'gossips' or godparents at a pauper's baptism, and by nursing, washing and laying out the dead. There was also work for the poorest people collecting and breaking stones for the roads and the odd seasonal jobs on the farms. Unmarried mothers were a grave expense to the vestry. Every few years the baptism of a 'base born' child appears in the register, and usually every effort was made to get maintenance from the father or to arrange a shotgun wedding. In 1758 the parish paid £4 for 'expenses marrying Mary West', and on one occasion they even paid 9s. for a gold wedding ring.

Girls who were habitual offenders were treated with surprising patience. In 1761 Charles Colyer, as Overseer of the Poor, paid out 'to Mrs Pindin for deliveryng Mary Petman 5s; for beer when she was in labour 1s.; for sugar and spice 8d.; for the gossips that stood by her bastard child 3s.; for her examination and a warrent to apprehend John Whitnam on whom she swore a bastard 2s.; to laying her child for the affidavit 2s.; for coffin for said child 2s.; Minister and Clerk 4s.'. In 1763 it all started again with the feckless Mary Petman swearing a bastard on Thomas Lee, though this time the child, Thomas, survived.

Dr Harris

A series of extraordinary bastard maintenance proceedings involving Charles Colyer as Overseer took place in 1763 in 'the Case of the Parish of Farningham and William Harris, Surgeon and Apothecary'. William Harris was said by Edward Hasted to have built the large black and white house known as the White House on the corner of Dartford Road and the High Street. Certainly his granddaughter Camilla Harris owned it later in the century.

Dr Harris had lived in the village since at least 1750 and had taken over many of Dr John Nash's patients. The case concerned his servant, Mary Garrot, who had lived with his family in the 1750s. During that time she had born him two children 'to the great scandal and offence of the parish, his own wife being in the same house'. In 1759 Mary went to London as a servant and

30-J.L.&B. Hammond,
The Village Labourer 1760-1832
(1987, first pub 1911)
31–Aspinall & Smith eds.
English Historical Documents
1783-1832

was 'frequently visited by Harris, whose wife dieing he brought said Mary back, and declaring he had been married to her, co-habited publickly with her as his lawful wife'.

Mary had another child, whose baptism was registered as 'Sarah, daughter of William and Mary Harris', and Harris attended the baptism and churching as the father. Some time the following year Mary paid a visit to her family in Maidstone but on her return Harris refused to admit her 'alleging that he was not married to her nor the child begotten by him but by one Davison as she herself confessed, nor would he give her anything but one moidore which he sent her by his son'. (A moidore was a gold coin worth 27s.) .

Charles Colyer, William Burr and Mary Garrot set out for Maidstone Quarter Sessions in Mrs Pratt of the Bull's chaise. The bills incurred by the parish for solicitor's fees, counsel's advice and all the various expenses were large and the scandal enormous. Mary confessed before the Justices that she was not married to Harris 'but had been prevailed upon to come and live with him in that public manner by repeated and solemn promises of marriage, also

The White House

that Davison had carnal knowledge of her but once, by force and against her inclination and will'. The Justices were satisfied with the truth of her statement, and Harris was directed to pay 1s. 6d. a week for maintenance of the child which he refused to do. The case dragged on with 'the Parish highly scandalised and aggrieved as the said child is likely to be an heavy charge'. They added with piety that it was all a flagrant and barefaced violation of Decency and Virtue.

In the end the court ordered that William Harris should pay the Overseers 1s.6d. weekly for maintenance of the child and that Mary herself should similarly pay 6d. William Harris died next year, in 1764. His son James, also a surgeon, stayed on in the village, unabashed by the scandal, and took over the poor law practice, prescribing paregoric, anodyne pills and 'nervous drops' for the paupers well into the 19th century. The Overseers book shows that the maintenance was paid for several weeks but then Mary and her child disappeared, probably into the workhouse.

James Harris married an Elizabeth Andrus from Southfleet in 1774, and they appear to have continued living at the White House. Seven of their daughters and one son were baptised here, and Camilla, one of the daughters, was living in the White House in 1798.

A John Harris, whose relationship to William and James has not been established by the Harris family historian, lived at Farningham Hill House from at least 1790 to 1810.[32] His sister Elizabeth Harris married Thomas Fuller of Lullingstone in 1777 who was to become the owner of Farningham Manor. John and his wife Mary, nee Collins, had nine children who were baptised here. The Harrises were a large and very respectable North Kent family, many of them from Chelsfield. Several members of the family in a later generation were also surgeons.

In 1756 Charles Colyer took on the lease of the Lion farm, part of the Hanger estate which was managed for them by Lord Romney whose agent collected the rents. This commitment increased Charles's estimated rent from £20 to £82. During the 1760s and 1770s his vestry activities continued as before. There were no more great dramas, just a lot of hard work, unpaid and carefully accounted in the books in his distinctive copperplate handwriting. By 1760 his elder sons were 19, 17 and 15 and so were able to help him with parish affairs as well as with the mill and farm. He was more generous these days as Overseer than in the early years.

There are many small disbursments that give an impression of small kindnesses, such as 'a spelling book for Reynold's son, petticoats and strings for Reynold's daughter, a hat and stays for Hawley's girl', physic, milk and wine for the sick people in the poorhouse, sugar and spice for a travelling woman lying in at Mr Jessup's barn and the occasional leg of mutton for poor families. There are often entries where he charges the parish 'nil' for errands run by himself or his sons or workmen. One gets an impression of benevolence combined with strict correctness.

There was one labourer, Richard Allen, who seems to have actually beaten the Settlement and Removal system, possibly against Charles's better judgement.[33] Allen, a native of West Wickham, had been hired by Richard Manning of Charton, Edward Hampton's son-in-law, for a little less than a year. This was a trick played by some employers to avoid giving settlement certificates. After his discharge Allen went to Sevenoaks Hiring Fair where he met Manning who rehired him for another year at 7s. a week plus board. He was again discharged just short of the year and again rehired, but this time on an agreement by which he paid Manning 5s. a week and worked 'by the groat' or four penny piece. Presumably 'by the groat' was a saying which meant piece work.

Manning paid him by the year, as he did his other farm servants, but because Richard Allen had no contract he could not get a Farningham settlement. He married Charity Goodwin in 1761 and they are described in the register as 'both of Farningham'. Their daughter Sarah was baptised in October, the same month that Allen was called before the magistrates in Dartford for failing to have a settlement. Manning had probably sacked him when he married, and now the three Allens would be a charge on the parish. Manning was summoned and Allen examined but to no avail, and the family was removed

32-Geoffrey Copus, Chelsfield & Harris family historian, pers.comm.
33-CKS P145/13/1-7

to West Wickham by the Borseholder. Next month Allen was apprehended for returning to Farningham without a certificate. Perhaps it was now a question for him of the West Wickham workhouse or the possibility of a job in Farningham where he was known. Charles Colyer went to see the Justice at his house, then to Dartford and then back to the Justice, a day's work for which he actually charged 2s.

We don't know whether he wanted an injunction to keep Allen out of the parish or, more possibly, he pleaded on Allen's behalf because, next year, Allen appears as a Farningham ratepayer in a house worth £3 p.a. He also received a regular Roper pension and he and Charity stayed in the village until their deaths in 1773 and 1780. The villain of the piece was Richard Manning, and it is satisfying to see in his father-in-law Edward Hampton's will that none of the legacies going to his daughter Anne Manning are to fall into the hands of her husband Richard.

A sadder story came in 1763 when Charles Colyer worked from 10 in the morning till 8 at night with two men and a four horse waggon to clear the Horton Kirby house of a man with a Farningham settlement who had died of smallpox. William Smith was one of the poorer labourers in regular receipt of Roper Charity money. He, with his wife Ann and four children had apparently found work in Horton Kirby. He must have done well to acquire a houseful of possessions, but then he fell ill. A waggon was sent to collect Mrs Smith, who was pregnant, and her children and two beds, and take them to Farningham poorhouse, maybe to save them from infection. A man and a nurse were sent to look after William, but he died, and the usual melancholy expenses were paid, of coffin and shroud, bearers, Minister and Clerk, affidavit and beer all round.

Next came the full day's work clearing the house and nailing up the windows and doors. Henry Loft, the carpenter, put up the Smith's beds in the Poorhouse and Thomas Sharp was sent to collect William Smith's clock and bees which the family were apparently allowed to keep. But the family brought the smallpox with them, the baby died and soon five other people in the poorhouse were getting physic for the disease. The other children sur-

The dispersements of Mr Charles Colyer, Overseer of the Poor 1762-3.
May 8 - Order to remove Richard Allen, his wife and child from Farningham to West Wickham £5.2s.
Courtesy CKO Maidstone

vived and were later put out as apprentices by the parish. Dame Smith joined the ranks of poor widows who scraped a little money from washing, mending and nursing the sick. The only faintly cheerful thing about the story is the thought that the Smith's bees were maybe the first to live in the Farningham Bee Bole, an alcove made to house the straw bee-

hives known as skeps, which is now a listed structure set in the wall which joins Dartford Road with the entrance to the field once known as Workhouse Field.

Reading the stories of the Farningham poor it is sad to see how close to poverty even the successful families lived. One of the blacksmiths, Nathanial Stiddolph, belonged to an old village family and was a regular ratepayer for many years. Then, as he got old, he started to receive small weekly allowances from the overseers. Then his wife died and was given a good parish funeral with all the trimmings, but Nathanial went downhill and was soon being 'washed and mended' by one of the unmarried mothers. Among his expenses were a chamber pot costing two and a half pence and 'a pint of wine to take some doctors stough in'. Then Butcher Jack sat with him day and night for five weeks consuming 'Potts of Bear' and no doubt giving him comfort before the end when the blacksmith went to join his wife in an unmarked grave in the churchyard.

Some prosperous families had poor relations who were assisted by the parish. John Pratt, innholder of the Bull, had 'Widow Pratt', presumably his mother, who came from Eynsford with a settlement certificate witnessed by her son and received small parish allowances before she died. In the Jessop family, Joseph, a former Borseholder was given Roper Charity money as well as parish payments in his old age; young Jane Jessop was apprenticed by the parish to a husbandman to 'learn to be a housewife', and young Mary was sent away to 'learn the Art and Business of Mantua maker'. When William Jessop, the well to do farmer at Beesfield, was Overseer, he paid maintenance to his grandmother, 'Dame Jessup in distress', and the usual sums for her burial.

William Budgin, an orphan who was probably mentally handicapped, was a villager who became a constant charge for many years for care and clothes, washing, mending and lodging. He did not receive direct payments, apart from the occasional 'to Budgin in distress', but roamed the village, wearing out countless shoes which were never 'soaled and healed' like the shoes of the younger orphans, but 'specked and plated' with metal by the blacksmith. He had a year of glory under Charles Colyer's Overseership in 1761, when he was kitted out very splendidly, first with two shirts made by Mrs Dobbinson for 7s.6d., then the tailor Mr Wallis made him 'a pair of Russia Drab drawers, a pair of leathern breeches, a cloth waistcoat, bootlegs, stockings and a hat', but this seems to have been a one-off special occasion. He was never so well dressed again. Usually Mary Starling, one of the unmarried mothers, made him a couple of shirts for 2s.8d. Different women washed and mended him over the years, though he usually lodged with a man. Richard Allen had him as a lodger after his wife Charity died.

Budgin got smallpox in 1769. Dr Harris junior came and prescribed physic, and the widowed Dame Smith nursed him. He recovered and outlived Charles Colyer, making a surprise appearance later in the books as 'William Budgin, Flint Knapper'. Knapping flints for builders could be a skilled process, and it is possible that he had only been breaking stones for the roads, but was at last dignified with a profession. He died in 1784 and had the poorest of funerals for 5s 4d.

The worst poverty of all that was recorded in the books had been experienced by one of the parish widows, Elizabeth Rawlins, who had been apprehended in Southwark in 1771 with her three children as a 'Rogue and Vagabond'; in other words she was begging. Her late husband's last settlement had been in Farningham where he had worked for William Burr at Whitehill farm as a single man in the 1750s but had never gained a subsequent settlement. The widow and children were conveyed, by different Constables from parish to parish, all the way to Farningham, a place presumably completely unknown to them, with a pass that has amazingly survived for over 200 years. After a lengthy examination by the magistrates the Rawlins family were allowed to stay and Dame Rawlins took up her lowly place with the other village widows. Young Thomas Colyer, Overseer for the first time in 1774, gave her £1.11s.6d to 'get her cloaths out of pawn to go down to her brothers in Buckingham shire'. But the brother must have proved a disappointment to both his sister and the parish because she returned and remained on the parish books until 1790.

Chapter Ten

Charles Colyer, the Later Years / The Turnpikes/ John Byng /
The Cox Family / Charles Colyer the Younger /
James Colyer of Dartford Mill / William Hardyman of the Black Lion /
Farningham Bridge / Henry Colyer, Miller / The Fullers / The Folly.

The condition of the roads in Kent had been notoriously poor until the mid 18th century. Their only fame was for unpassability and highwaymen. The 17th century Assize records showed countless highway robberies along the 'narrow and dangerous' wooded road through Birchwood before you got to Farningham, and of course Blackheath and Gads Hill were famous black spots for armed robbers. Until the middle of the 18th century the roads would have mainly been trodden by human and animal feet. There would have been local wheeled agricultural carts and waggons, and the occasional heavy unsprung coach or hackney carriage would come from far afield. The trudging wayfarers would be light enough, but the constant stream of men on horseback, pack animals, droves of cattle, pigs, sheep and geese heading for the London markets, strings of packhorses, galloping post boys and messengers, fish rippiers with their express deliveries from Folkestone would all take their toll on the ruts and mud in winter and dust and pot holes in summer.

The parishioner's obligatory Statute Duty of six day's roadwork a year was generally inadequate, especially in villages on main highways such as Farningham. Charles Colyer, as the owner of a waggon and a team of horses would have been obliged to lend them for four days a year with two workmen, and when he was Surveyor it would have been his duty to put a notice on the church door to call up the workforce and then to supervise their labour. But the village Surveyors were not skilled road makers, nor were the reluctant parishioners.

Roads in general were in a poor way in England. A correspondent to the Gentleman's Magazine in 1753 asked how it was that 'A wretched trumpery despotic government like France has enchanting roads...smooth, wide and most judiciously laid out...from the capital to each remote part', whereas in England 'the respective parishes either can or will do nothing, nor have the inhabitants abilities to make or mend a road.'

The Turnpikes

The Turnpike Acts of the 18th century set up various Trusts which took on the upkeep and improvement of a stretch of main road, erected turnpike gates and houses and charged a toll for the use of their section. The Act to turnpike the first section of the London to Hythe road as far as New Cross was passed in 1718. The Act creating the Footscray to Wrotham Heath turnpike which passed through Farningham was passed in 1752 and the Dartford to Sevenoaks Trust in 1766. Turnpike Trustees were mainly local landowners

34–S.B.Black,
Farningham Crossroads
35–Geoffrey Hindley,
A History of Roads, 1971

165

with a property qualification of £50 p.a. income from their land. They employed surveyors, clerks, treasurers and toll collectors, and the surveyors had powers to take road building materials from unused land. The tolls charged were graded from 1s. for coaches and carts drawn by four horses, 6d. by two horses and 3d. by one. A man on horseback paid 1d. Droves of cattle were charged at 10d. for twenty and droves of sheep or pigs at 5d.[34]

Parishioners were still expected to perform their unpaid Statute Duty or to pay a fee for someone else to do it, and also to pay to use their own roads although many categories of local traffic were exempt from charge. Evasive action led to the use of byeways such as Farningham's Sparepenny, (or save-a-penny), Lane, and in many parishes the gates and toll houses were vandalised. Padlocks were issued to local farmers to prevent the illicit use of their fields as bypasses. The great days of road building were still to come. Thomas Telford, 'the Colossus of Roads', and John Macadam, 'the Macadamiser', were active in the late 18th and early 19th centuries, but there were many changes in the village generated by the creation of the two turnpike roads.[35]

The main highway, today's A20, which came through the village, was straightened and strengthened, and the gradient of Farningham Hill improved. Possibly the small gravel quarries, now ponds, in Farningham Woods were extracted at this time. Gravel and broken stones were needed for the hard new surfaces. Travel on the new roads grew fast. Formerly travellers from London to Maidstone tended to use the Rochester road by way of Watling Street but now they came through Farningham. Trade for the two inns and for Charles Colyer's mill must have vastly improved. By the 1760s and 70s lighter carriages with springs began to replace the old heavy coaches and tourism could be said to have begun, with pleasure seekers and boy racers in four-in-hands bowling along the new roads at speeds of up to ten miles an hour.

Sparepenny Lane in the early 20th century

John Byng

John Byng, later Lord Torrington and author of the Torrington Diaries, was a regular traveller through Farningham between his home in London and his family seat at Wrotham.[36] Writing in 1790 he remembers childhood journeys in the mid century and describes the changing scene. The family coach 'unassisted by springs', would arrive at Eltham 'where the road became so narrow that a servant was always sent half a mile ahead to remove obstructions. Instead of those cool overshaded lanes there now runs a wide exposed road over the Hill and Dale, which no doubt meets with universal approbation; but I look back with pleasure to the shaded lanes twining round the Cherry Orchards'.

They would arrive, 'after a long though pleasant crawl...to the top of Farningham Hill, where the road was then so narrow and steep that the Drag

36–John Byng, *The Torrington Diaries,* republished 1938

chain was fastened'. At two o'clock they would be at 'the Red Bull kept by Widow Prat...for a joyful regale of Beans and Bacon and Fowls...and a history of the county...related by Widow Prat'. John Byng is a delightful diarist. His travels are full of feasts of gooseberry fools and pigeon pies. 'I always think of dinner for half an hour before my arrival at the inn'. Sometimes he takes his little son Frederick, later to be the Prince Regent's friend, Poodle Byng; 'Frek blows the fire, he cuts the cucumber and then says "how comfortable we are, this is a good inn"'.

When he came through Farningham again in 1790 he stayed at the Black Lion, which he only rated a 'T' for tolerable, and paid 9s.3d. for the night's lodging and dinner, bed and breakfast. After 'breakfast and the hot rolls' he walked across the bridge and made a sketch of the so-called cattle-screen which, as an extension of the old Manor house wall may simply have marked the manor boundary. This mock-bridge continues to be a mystery. Probably, as has already been conjectured, it was built by William Hanger in about 1740 and intended as an ornamental Folly for his new house.

The Cox Family

In 1765 Charles Colyer's eldest son, Charles the younger, was married to Mary Cox of Eynsford. He was 24 and the first of the Colyer children to marry. Charles the elder now paid an estimated rent for rate purposes of £30 pa for the mill and £95 for the Lion Farm. He also took up the lease of Pedham Court farm, the Ebbutt's old home, for the young couple, who would live there until Mary's death in 1779. Charles and Mary had three children but only one, John, survived infancy.

Mary Cox's family were butchers and farmers in Downe, Chelsfield and Chiddingstone. A Joseph Cox son of a Chiddingstone butcher, had come to Eynsford in the early 18th century and built up a considerable property there. He owned seven houses 'abutting the Street and River' and also the butcher's shop with a granary, stables, slaughterhouse, cowhouse, garden and a house called 'Coffins'.[37] Joseph's son Henry carried on the family business and married a woman of property, Mary Penury of Ash. They had three children, Joseph, Henry and Mary. The family connection did not end with Charles the younger's marriage to Mary Cox; his sister Elizabeth married Henry Cox in 1774.

Butchers were often also farmers and men of property. In Farningham the Moice family of butchers, who had been in the village for several generations, left a series of deeds and wills in the 1760s and 70s which indicate that their property was based on the house in the High Street now known as the

37-Cox family papers, private property Goldsworthy family

167

Cottage. They farmed the Hanger fields between the High Street and the woods and they also owned neighbouring houses which they leased to other shopkeepers, and John Moice was able to set up his son and daughters handsomely when he died. [38]

Henry Cox the younger inherited the family business in Eynsford, where he and Elizabeth Colyer lived for the rest of their lives. They had no children and their share of the Cox family property went to the sons of Henry's elder brother

The Cottage is one of the older domestic dwellings in Farningham, belied by the early Victorian facade facing the High Street. This photograph circa 1936

Joseph. This Joseph Cox came to Farningham to farm at Chimhams in 1763. He became an important member of the village community, often serving with Charles Colyer on the vestry. He bought Charton Manor in 1789 and, by the time of his death in 1793, was able to style himself 'Gentleman'.

Charles Colyer the younger

Charles Colyer the younger married three times. His second wife, Margaret Dorman, was the sister of Edward Hasted's wife. Hasted lived at St John's, Sutton at Hone at this time and rented Mrs Pratt's house in Farningham for two years between 1763 and 1764. His sister-in-law Margaret Dorman was married for the first time in 1764 to John Pope of Darent as a Farningham resident and maybe he rented the house for her marriage. After her death Charles the younger married for a third time, Sarah Jordan, by whom he had a son, Henry who had been born 'out of wedlock' while he was still married to Margaret. They lived in Horton Kirby where Charles is described as 'Miller' in his brother James's will, so he had presumably taken up the family business there.

Charles the elder's will, made a year before his death in 1788, indicates that perhaps this Charles, his eldest son, was not his favourite child. He would be following a Royal fashion if this was the case. George II habitually referred to his eldest son as a 'villain, scoundrel, puppy or rascal', and George III was generally at odds with his heir, the Prince Regent. Charles Colyer treated his eldest son very fairly in his will, as he did all his children, but he did not make him an executor and he made sure that an earlier loan he had made to the younger Charles was to be repaid in full.

James Colyer of Dartford Mill

James, the second son, became the miller of the family mill in Dartford. This mill, known in their time as 'Colyer's Mill' and later as 'Keyes Mill' and 'Acacia 38-CKS ref.U1322 T1

Hall', must have been acquired by Charles in his later years. He refers to it in his will as 'My Dartford Mill' and leaves it to James who was already in residence there. James had married Elizabeth Pratt of the Bull, daughter of 'Widow Prat', in 1771. They had five daughters, four of whom died young, and one son. This son, James, and the surviving daughter Anne, came to live together in Farningham House, the house built by their grandfather, John Pratt, where they both died, unmarried, in the early 19th century.

By 1769 Charles the elder had taken the lease of Pedham Place Farm for his third son, Thomas, who went to live and farm there. Thomas later married his cousin Anne Colyer of Southfleet and they lived in Eynsford. They had no children and when he died in 1825 he is described in his will as 'Gentleman of Eynsford' although in his brother James's will of 1783, when Thomas was still living at Pedham Place he is described as 'Yeoman of Farningham'. Thomas and his younger brother Henry often served on the Vestry with their father as Overseers and Churchwardens.

Henry, the youngest of the Colyer children, was to inherit Farningham Mill and to live there with his family until his death in 1811. Two other Colyer daughters married local yeoman farmers, Mary married Thomas Hassell of Eynsford in 1769, a farmer who was also a butcher and who bought up Henry Cox's business after Henry's death. The Hassells had several children. Anne married the younger William Jessup of Beesfield farm in Farningham and they had one son, another William. The youngest daughter Sarah married John Fuller of Hewitts in Chelsfield in 1779, after her father's death. They too had several children.

In May 1770 Charles Colyer the elder, still very fit and active at only 54, walked the parish boundaries to celebrate the Rogation ceremony of Beating the Bounds. This was not a token ramble to bless the fields as it is today but the ancient and serious two day exercise to establish the exact limits of the parish.[39] The new vicar, the Revd. Saunders; Mr Hunter, the tenant of the Manor House; Mr Colyer; Mr Jessup senior and Mr Jessup junior; Henry Chapman of Maplescombe; John Atkins, publican and 'more than a dozen others', assembled at the new Chequers Inn to start their marathon walk.

They went from marker to marker, from Horn Beech to Elm Tree Pollard, to Crooked Willow to Maple Stump; across fields with names such as Grub Piece, Jack's Croft, Strawberry Hill and Little Dark Holes; across stiles and footbridges, through woods and hedges. In some parishes boys were still taken along to be beaten at strategic points to make sure they remembered the limits of their territory but there is no evidence of any boys that year and maybe the custom had died out. Curiously, some years later, in 1838, 'Boys' are listed along with the adults but their purpose is not given.

In 1775 Elizabeth Colyer died. She was 58 and had lived to see six of her eight children leave home and five of them married. She was buried in the vault under the fine box tomb in the churchyard, shared three years later by her husband. Also in 1775, the Hanger and Crayker estates were finally sold

39-W.G.Duncombe, The Boundaries of the Parishes of Farningham & Eynsford, F&ELHS, no14 (1995)

169

Thomas Fuller, who had moved from Pedham Place to the Crayker 'Great House', now bought up the manor from the Crayker heirs and the Lion and Lion farm from Lord Romney, the Hanger's trustee.[40]

The existing Manor House in an earlier manifestation. Originally known as 'Ye Great House' built by Benjamin Crayker in 1730.

William Hardyman of the Black Lion

William Hardyman, who had been the innholder of the Black Lion since 1759, was now able to buy the inn from Thomas Fuller, and as 'William Hardyman Gent' leased the inn to Martin Masters in 1777. Thanks to the Turnpike roads the Black Lion had risen from being a small wayside inn to a large coaching establishment, outclassing the Bull which now catered for the stage coach traffic. The Black Lion attracted the gentry and the carriage trade and from now on is often mentioned as a meeting place for formal occasions. William Hardyman and his family lived in the low ancient part of the inn known as the German End which can still be seen at the back of the Lion Hotel. The Hardyman's only son died in 1764, and their remaining child Charlotte, who would inherit the property, was to marry Henry Colyer in 1781.

A great reorganisation of the mill and its waterways took place in 1773, but unfortunately no documents survive to tell the story. It seems most likely however, from the brickwork, that the waterways of the mill race were built, or possibly rebuilt, in the late 18th century. There are two pairs of little plaques set into the brickwork of the small bridges above the exit of the tail-race that confirm this statement. One, on the side of the bridge next to the road, says 'This Bridge Built By' and its neighbour says 'Charles Colyer Miller   40-CKS U36 T448

170

1773'. The other pair of plaques on the side next to the mill say 'Thomas Sharp Bricklayer 1773' and 'George Pawley carpenter 1773'.

Farningham Bridge

Farningham Bridge itself was also rebuilt by order of the Quarter Sessions in 1773 and, although it was rebuilt again in the 1990s, it is still possible to see the 18th century red brickwork, with the small traditional blue glazed headers, so similar to the brickwork of the tail-race, underneath the arches where they meet the yellow stockbrick of an 1833 bridge extension.[41] The rebuilding in 1773 cost the County £499.2s. There were four County bridges across the Darent at Dartford, Eynsford, Farningham and Shoreham, all maintained by the West Kent JPs at the Quarter Sessions.[42]

Charles Colyer the elder died in October 1778, two weeks after the death of one of James Colyer's little daughters. Perhaps their deaths were caused by the same illness, there is no indication in the parish register, which seldom gives a cause of death. John Pratt was one exception with the word 'Dropsy' after his name. To die at the age of 62 would not cause much comment in 1778, but one might wonder whether the ingestion of much 'mealy dust' might not have contributed to Charles's death. Two of his sons, James and Henry, both millers, also died fairly young, at 40 and 58.

Charles had been active in the Vestry until that year when he and his son Thomas were both Churchwardens. He had served the village in many ways for over forty years and he had created a fine mill estate with new waterways and model cottages for his workmen and he had set up all his eight children for life in what was surely a most satisfactory manner.

In 1777 he had a plan made of his mill estate by the local surveyor, James Gudsell. At the top right hand corner is a drawing of the mill with the small, mansard roofed mill-house which is now behind the large grey house built by his son. On the left is a similar drawing of the mill 'tenements' or workman's cottages. There is a central cartouche with the title description, and below is a drawing of the waterways from the weir to the bridge with small decorative features of ducks, rabbits and a horse. It now belongs to the eighth generation of his family who still own the mill and is a beautiful and fitting memorial to the man and his work.

41- W.G.Duncombe, F&E Bridges.
42- Eds. A.Detsicas & N.Yates, Studies in Modern Kentish History, C.Chalklin, Bridge Building in Kent.

Henry Colyer, Miller, 1753–1811

Henry and his sister Sarah were the only members of the family left at home when their father died. Henry appears the most favoured of the children in his father's will. He not only inherited the family house and mill and the cottages and lands in Farningham, but also most of the contents and all the store of corn, flour and implements, and even the 'Ready Money and Debts due in the way of Business'.[43] Sarah was left a bequest of £700, to be paid by Henry 'out of the mill'. She was also to have any bed of her choice and board and maintenance for a year if she chose to remain at home and, although Henry was to have all the parlour furniture and the brewing equipment, he and she were to share the rest of the household goods.

Charles left bequests to all his children, but he made it clear that he had already distributed property and money among them, probably when they married. The younger Charles, described as 'yeoman' in the will and living at Pedham Court, was left 60 acres of woodland in the Dartford area, 'over and besides the moneys I have already advanced him', but he was to pay back into the estate the £300 he owed his father. The woodland was probably Darenth Woods, part of which is still owned by the family.

James, the second son, who was living and working at the Dartford Mill, was to inherit 'the mill and house and land in his occupation', but he was to pay a debt of £700 owed to his uncle Edward Colyer of Southfleet, and £900 to pay bequests to his sisters Elizabeth and Mary and brother Thomas.

Thomas, living and farming at Pedham Place, was to have £700 over and above the monies already advanced and over and above a debt of £300 he owed his father. The second daughter, Mary Hassell of Eynsford, inherited £100 and a house and land at Hodsoll Street, Ash, and the third daughter Anne Jessup, had £100 'over and beyond that which has already been given to her husband'.

43-PRO Prob 11

The Fuller family

It was sad, in such an age of competitive marriages, that Charles did not live to see his youngest daughter Sarah make a fine match with John Fuller of Chelsfield. It was a story of great social success for the miller's daughter. John Fuller was a cousin of the Farningham squire Thomas Fuller. He was an only child, and his parents, both of Orpington, had been married in Farningham in 1750. John bought Hewitts Manor, Chelsfield in 1781 where he and Sarah would spend their married life. Several of their children died young, but two daughters survived. One, Mary Fuller, lived at Woodlands, a house in Chelsfield built for her by her father in 1815. The other, Sarah, married Thomas Waring who later inherited the Farningham manor estate .

The first Farningham Thomas Fuller appears to have belonged to a Shoreham family, although he is described in the parish register as 'of Lullingstone'. He had married the heiress Sarah Loxley in 1751, half sister of the Nash brothers who built the mauseoleum in the churchyard. Thomas and Sarah Fuller lived as tenants in Farningham manor until Thomas bought the estate from the Hangers in 1775. They had two children, Thomas and Elizabeth. The younger Thomas became the village squire after his father's death in 1788. He married Elizabeth Harris, daughter of John Harris of Farningham Hill (or White Hill) farm, in 1777, and his sister Elizabeth married Dr Richard Waring of St Mary Cray in 1774.[44]

The younger Thomas Fuller had no children and so his inheritance eventually passed to his sister's son Thomas Waring who in turn, married his cousin Sarah Fuller daughter of John Fuller and Sarah Colyer, and so the Farningham manor estate would pass to Charles Colyer's granddaughter's family.

In March 1781 Henry Colyer married Charlotte Hardyman of the Black Lion. Their eldest child, a second Charlotte, was born in May the same year so perhaps it was a shot-gun marriage. The wedding took place discreetly in London, and it seems possible that the stress of the occasion caused William Hardyman's death, possibly that very day, because he was buried in Farningham four days later. William Hardyman had been an active vestry member, and must have been an old friend of the elder Charles Colyer, acting with Thomas Fuller as one of the witnesses to Charles's will. His widow Mary Hardyman remained living in the German End of the Lion until her death three years later.

Despite the unpromising start it seems to have been a successful marriage. Henry and Charlotte had nine children, Charlotte, William Hardyman, Charles, James, Mary-Ann, Thomas, Friend, Sarah and Elizabeth. They were not such healthy children as the previous generation of Colyers. Friend, Mary-Ann and Elizabeth all died as infants and Charlotte and Sarah died as young unmarried women. The four surviving sons all reached old age and Charles, the second son, was to succeed his father and become the third Colyer miller of Farningham.

44-Geoffrey Copus, Fuller, Harris & Waring family historian, pers. com.

Henry Colyer had a very different personality to his father. The elder Colyer seems to embody all the sterling qualities of an English 18th century countryman. The thought of him conjures up an old fashioned figure, perhaps looking like Thomas Coram the philanthropist whose statue, wearing wig, three-cornered hat, frock coat and knee breeches, stands outside the orphanage he founded in London. Charles Colyer belongs to the age of Hogarth and Handel, his son Henry moves forward into the age of the Prince Regent and his architect John Nash.

By 1785 Henry and Charlotte and their first two children were settled in to their inheritance. They now owned the Lion, still 'known by the sign of the Black Lyon' and rented to Martin Masters innholder at £65 a year. The 'German End' of the building, which was also rented out after Mary Hardyman's death, brought in £15.[45]

Henry had now become an important member of the Vestry, first serving as Overseer in 1781, and as Churchwarden in 1789. He continued to serve all his life, often alternating with his brother Thomas and brother-in-law William Jessup. If, as we assume, Henry was the creative force behind the mill buildings as we see them today, it would be interesting to know where he had been educated, but unfortunately we know nothing about the Colyer's choice of schools apart, that is, from the assumption that they made use of the Hampton's school in the village for the children's early years.

It seems extraordinary today that a country miller not only knew so much about the taste and fashion of the day, but was prepared to spend a great deal of money following it. Henry was 28 at the time of his marriage in 1781; the year he first appears in the vestry books. Such a late start might indicate a lengthy education. Even so, his father had considered him ready to take on the mill at the age of 25 which indicates that they had probably been working together for some time.

Henry's entries in the vestry books are always written in the finest, blackest Indian ink, in a large, flamboyant copperplate handwriting with lots of elegant twirls. He is very neat and each month is carefully accounted. There are little kindnesses such as 'Bottle of Port for Pierce while ill', but he does not come across as such a compassionate person as his father; people are called 'Objects in distress', and when he visits the poorhouse he finds it full of 'Capital Rugs, Decent Bedsteads and Good Blankets'. Maybe this is unfair, perhaps someone really had donated good new furniture to the poorhouse and perhaps 'Objects' was simply the accepted term for paupers. It is probably a reflection of the changing, harder attitude to the poor.

A sympathetic light on life in the mill at this time comes from a legal settlement claim in 1820 by a man called George Ambrose. In the words of his solicitor, Ambrose claimed that 'about 35 years ago, when he was a single man, he let himself to Mr Henry Colyer, miller, to serve him as Flour Dresser at 4s. per week and board and lodging in his master's house. He was also to have a shilling when he worked on Sundays, and another man and himself 45-CKS U36/T449 were to divide the Shooting Money, which is a perquisite given by the farmers to the millers for unloading and emptying the sacks of corn brought to the mill. He continued to serve Mr Colyer under such agreement for upwards of three years and, during that time, lodged and boarded in his house in Farningham, except for the time he was absent in the third year on account of illness'.46

'When he worked on Sundays... and when it was not his turn to work he used to go to church and take a walk for an hour or two without saying anything to his master, but he never went out on Sundays to spend the whole day without his master's permission. ... his master always paid him the Sunday money when he settled the Shooting money, and that during the first year of his living with Mr Colyer he received of him £5 in account of wages and when he had been there a year...the remainder of his wages'. The solicitor, continuing his statement, said that during the second year 'Ambrose received no wages till it was expired, when his master called him into the Counting House to settle and put ten guineas into his hand, which was 2s. more than his due but Mr Colyer refused to take the change, observing that he (Ambrose) was a pretty good fellow and desiring him to make good use of the money'.

Later, Ambose was taken ill and was unable to work and requested Mr Colyer to get another man in his stead. He said there was never any argument between him and his master and that Mr Colyer might have turned him away whenever he pleased. Since that time he had married but had done no work to gain a permanent settlement. The circumstances of work and wages were held to indicate that this had been a permanent job and Ambrose was given a Farningham certificate. Henry certainly comes out of the story as a fair and just employer.

The composition of the village in 1785, the year George Ambrose was living at the mill with Henry and his young family, was much the same as it had been in 1735 when the first Charles Colyer arrived in Farningham. The villagers fall into their usual three categories, high, medium and low. The high are still the 'Principal Inhabitants' of the vestry books, the people who fill the posts of Churchwarden, Overseer and Surveyor, and these are usually the landowners or the people who pay Land Tax and have the right to vote at parliamentary elections.

They are the occupants of the larger houses and farms; the squire of the manor, the yeoman farmers, the clergymen, the doctors and the innholders of the larger inns. The medium are the lower ratepayers; smallholders, tradesmen, craftsmen, shopkeepers, alehousekeepers and skilled labourers. The low are the agricultural labourers, domestic servants and the paupers. These categories fluctuate as usual, people's fortunes rise and fall, sometimes with startling suddeness. Unexpected early death often created a fall into poverty for the surviving family, as did its opposite, living too long.

46-CKS P 145/13/4   As usual in Farningham it is the solid yeoman farmers who form the back-

Hampton Court House, left and Mount Pleasant in Sparepenny Lane as they are today.

bone of the village. These would have been Henry's friends and work associates. The Pawleys of Sparepenny Lane are a good example. They were carpenters as well as farmers and a George Pawley is commemorated for his work on the mill on one of the plaques by the mill bridge. They appear to have acquired their farm from the Bosvilles of Eynsford in the 1750s. George Pawley the elder married his neighbour Edward Hampton's only surviving child, Mary, and they had five sons who inherited equal shares of the Hampton/Pawley farm. One might expect a decline in prosperity from this sub-division, but on the contrary all five brothers prospered.[47]

George Pawley the younger, and John Hampton Pawley, both described as carpenters, bought out their other brother's shares and lived side by side for a time in Hampton Court and Mount Pleasant. Both houses are still there. Later, George moved to Eynsford and another brother, Henry, moved back, often serving on the vestry with John. All three had become so well-to-do that they are described as 'Gent'. Titles such as 'Gent' and 'Esquire', 'Master' and 'Mistress' were still of great social importance, and usually a matter of money and property. Mobility up and down the social scale was very possible. The Pawley brothers were close contemporaries of Henry Colyer and his siblings, the Colyer and Pawley baptisms often side by side in the parish register. Some of the Pawleys became early members of the Eynsford Baptist church and the next generation of Pawleys are in the Baptist registers. Henry Pawley's daughter Mary would later marry Henry Colyer's son James.

The Jessups were a large local family whose elderly relatives often fell into poverty although William Jessup junior, who had married Henry's sister Anne, clearly prospered and was able to take on a great deal of land in the 1780s including the lease of the Parsonage farm and some of the Charton lands as well as his own Beesfield farm.

47-CKS U36 T450

The Folly

An interesting side-line on William's farm land is the story of the Folly. Hasted, who must have known the place well, described this as 'the estate known as the Folly', but as far as we know there was never a house there. In 1769 William Jessup paid rates on 'Beesfield farm, Charton Lands and the Wood'. There are similar entries in 1779 and 1789, although the wood is now called 'Fruit Wood'. In 1792 he paid exactly the same rates on all three properties, but now Fruit Wood has suddenly become 'The Folly'.

The Folly in the late 20th century was a plantation of ancient beeches, most of which fell in the great storm of 1989 and were estimated to have been about two hundred years old. Beech plantations were a fashionable passion in the 18th century, 'tall straight trunked, Palladian columns in wood', so perhaps it was simply considered a folly to dig up a good fruit wood and plant pretty beeches.[48] The use of the term is confirmed by Edward Thomas in his biography of Richard Jefferies of 1909, 'At the top and in the camp...and near by the "folly" of twenty-one lean beeches'.[49]

But who planted the Farningham beeches? The owner of Charton Lands, Eglantine Farm, the fruit wood and the lease of the parsonage in 1756 was Bourchier Cleeve who built the Palladian villa of Foots Cray Place. He would have been just the person to plant a folly of beeches but unfortunately he died in 1760, before the wood changed its name. His estates all went to his daughter Anne who married the politician Sir George Yonge in 1765. Her marriage settlement names all her Farningham lands which from this date were leased to William Jessop.[50] Although the Yonges continued to own these lands for about 50 years they never lived in Farningham and so, although of course they may have planted the beeches, it seems more likely that William Jessup, who paid for the land, planted them himself. He may have been influenced by his brother-in-law Henry Colyer's fashionable tastes.

Dame Anne Yonge's 1765 settlement gives the names of all the old Charton Lands fields, including many of those mentioned in Charles Crayker's will of 1686 and some of those detailed in the possessions of Harry Isley in 1555; she also owned Eglantine farm and a house and close called Tilmans. In none of these is a wood specified but it must be remembered that Isley's lands in 1555 included 'woods and woodland called Fernyngham wood and a wood called Frith Wood'. The curious thing about this is that in the 1840 tithe map the Folly which lies in the middle of Folly Lands, is called 'Frith Wood' again, so the name came full circle. Perhaps some of the old magic of Puckard's Hill remains attached to this place.

48-Richard Mabey,
In Pursuit of the Wild (1987)
49-Edward Thomas,
Richard Jefferies (1978 ed)
50-CKS U1283 T2

Chapter Eleven

Henry's Mill / The New House, Garden and Grove / Food Riots /
Wartime / The Yeomanry Cavalry / Henry's New Mill /
New Milling Technologies / The Search for a Poorhouse /
Imminent Invasion / The Farningham Riflemen /
The Second Charles Colyer, Miller / Wellington / The New Poorhouse /
William and the Baptists.

Henry's Mill

In 1790 Henry Colyer began his great rebuilding scheme. Most of the mill buildings we see today can surely be ascribed to him, although it must be added that Charles Colyer of Benenden always said that his great-great-uncle Thomas was responsible for the rebuilding and that it did not take place until 1804. At that date Henry's brother Thomas was over 60 and living and farming in Eynsford and his son Thomas was only 12. Henry was the owner of the mill and he made the payments of the rates and the insurance so it just does not make sense that either of these uncles was the creator of the new mill.[51]

The grey brick house with its double bay windows and splendid porch, the little gothick touches on the Counting House and the venetian arches over the stables and the pulley house, or 'locum', the eagle finials and the urns, the enormously enlarged weather boarded mill itself and, perhaps most interesting though now sadly decayed, the delightful 'Garden and Grove' for which Henry started to pay increased rates in 1794, all add up to work commissioned by the miller himself.

The new House and Garden and Grove

The Garden and Grove, although ostensibly a fashionable 'folly', actually hid a practical and secret storage place for grain at a time when poor harvests and wartime shortages were forcing up prices. The land behind the mill rises steeply in a chalk cliff into which were cut the storage caves for the wheat,

51–Colyer Family Tree, pers. com.

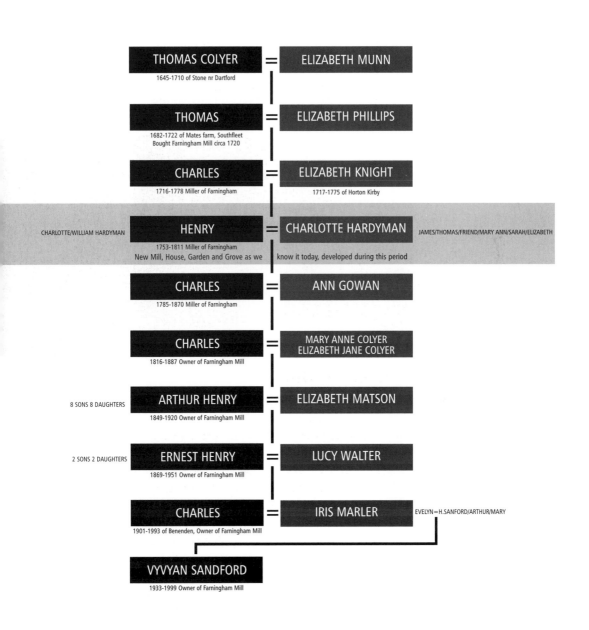

THOMAS COLYER = **ELIZABETH MUNN**
1645-1710 of Stone nr Dartford

THOMAS = **ELIZABETH PHILLIPS**
1682-1722 of Mates farm, Southfleet
Bought Farningham Mill circa 1720

CHARLES = **ELIZABETH KNIGHT**
1716-1778 Miller of Farningham   1717-1775 of Horton Kirby

CHARLOTTE/WILLIAM HARDYMAN   **HENRY** = **CHARLOTTE HARDYMAN**   JAMES/THOMAS/FRIEND/MARY ANN/SARAH/ELIZABETH
1753-1811 Miller of Farningham
New Mill, House, Garden and Grove as we   know it today, developed during this period

CHARLES = **ANN GOWAN**
1785-1870 Miller of Farningham

CHARLES = **MARY ANNE COLYER**
ELIZABETH JANE COLYER
1816-1887 Owner of Farningham Mill

8 SONS 8 DAUGHTERS   **ARTHUR HENRY** = **ELIZABETH MATSON**
1849-1920 Owner of Farningham Mill

2 SONS 2 DAUGHTERS   **ERNEST HENRY** = **LUCY WALTER**
1869-1951 Owner of Farningham Mill

CHARLES = **IRIS MARLER**   EVELYN=H.SANFORD/ARTHUR/MARY
1901-1993 of Benenden, Owner of Farningham Mill

VYVYAN SANDFORD
1933-1999 Owner of Farningham Mill

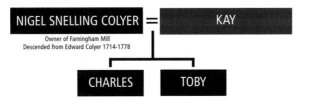

NIGEL SNELLING COLYER = **KAY**
Owner of Farningham Mill
Descended from Edward Colyer 1714-1778

CHARLES   **TOBY**

179

similar to the caves in France for storing wine. These cellars were ventilated by brick funnels or chimneys cut up through the chalk and topped by ornamental brick and flint turrets. Decorative 'hanging gardens' with flint walls were terraced on the side of the cliff with steps leading up to the turrets and to a grotto or gothick summer house lined with scallop shells. On the summit of the hill was a grove of trees with the statue of a wood nymph on a plinth in the middle. From a distance the whole thing looked like an interesting, possibly medieval, ruined castle. It is easy to imagine, at a time when tourism was becoming popular, all the curious people who would have come,

in their Jane Austen muslins and high collared suits to gaze at the novelty and wander up and down the little paths. Jane Austen herself was fond of a bit of sight-seeing.

This was Henry's legacy to posterity, a sublimely elegant and charming collection of buildings. He even signed it because, inside one of the caves or storage chambers, there is a lead pump with the initials HCC for Henry and Charlotte Colyer and the date 1790. It is possible that Henry took an architect's advice on his buildings. Unfortunately

Henry's garden and grove.

no Humphrey Repton style Red Book remains and most probably the Sharp brothers, the Farningham bricklayers, simply worked to Henry's instructions and from pattern books. We can assume that the building work took some time. The new grey brick house is really a front added to Charles Colyer's earlier house which remains clamped on behind. The new house was approached by a flight of steps leading up through the pillared porch and fan-lighted front door into a hall with two large new bow-windowed rooms on either side.

A flight of stairs leads down at the back into the old house. Each of the two new rooms has a fine marble fireplace fitted with steel baskets which were designed to allow the ash to fall through gratings to the basement. Henry was so proud of his 'Grates' that he mentioned them in his will, but the decorative inset marble panels were added at a later date, between 1804 and 1810.

180

52-R.J.Spain
'An 18th Century Corn
Watermill
Arch Cant LXXXV 1967)

There are two bay-windowed bedrooms above and two smaller rooms in the new, mansard roof. It was a grand new house and Henry and Charlotte soon filled it with their nine children born between 1781 and 1802.

No ledgers survive for Farningham Mill, unless they are hidden away in some dusty trunk, but it is possible to make a guess at the Colyer's business by comparison with the ledgers of an 18th century mill at Fairbourne near Harrietsham discussed by R J Spain in Archaeologia Cantiana in 1970.[52] We can only make a very rough comparison because we have no idea of the Farningham mill capacities. The two Fairbourne ledgers date from 1751 to 1760, Charles Colyer's mid-years, and from Henry's early years of 1782 to 1784.

The first surprise is that, in the earlier ledger a large percentage of the grain milled was bought by the miller from the farmers, very few farmers simply paid for their corn to be milled and took it away as flour. By the 1780s there was an almost equal proportion of grain bought by the miller from the farmers to be sold on by him as flour to bakers and domestic customers, and grain milled for the farmers and returned to them as flour. The Fairbourne miller does not appear to have used a corn market, but perhaps Maidstone corn exchange would have been less accessible for a mill at Harrietsham than Dartford may have been for Farningham mill.

About 132 farmers delivered grain to Fairbourne mill during the nine years of the ledgers, sometimes only a few sacks, each of which would hold 2cwt., and sometimes up to 50cwt. Sometimes the mill would hold a large store of grain, enough for two months' work, and sometimes stocks fell low but never low enough to cease production. On average about 20 sacks or one ton a week was ground. A 2 cwt sack of grain could be processed through the mill in one and half to two hours. Nearby farmers came many times a year but outlying farms only occasionally used the mill, probably finding other outlets for their grain.

Deliveries and collections and the work of milling itself appears to have been constant all the year round, which is another surprise taking into consideration seasonal demand. Prices rose and fell according to the harvests, but the mill-wheel seems to have turned steadily all the year round, sometimes through the night. The Sabbath was observed, presumably at all mills, and there must have been periods when the mill stopped working for maintenance and the dressing of the stones, usually by peripatetic stone dressers. Heavy frosts and hard droughts would surely have slowed and even stopped production at times.

In another article Mr Spain describes the proceedure of starting a mill up for work.[53] First 'the sluice gates at the waste (or head-race) would be closed to divert water over the wheel, the brake would be taken off and the stones lifted; then very slowly, with a noise like an express train, the gears would turn. When the stones were running - each weighed about a ton - the building had a definite movement, pronounced in the loft'. Maybe, to the miller's family these noises and that of the eternal click-clack of the mill-wheel, had no more significance than the ticking of a grandfather clock.

Some customers, such as the big bakers, would take large amounts of flour, other, domestic customers, would take a 2cwt.sack every week or fortnight, presumably on baking days. Flour was graded according to quality. The flour dresser, such as George Ambrose, would use a system of wire sieves to refine the flour. In the early ledger there were few grades, the largest amount of wheat was sold as 'middlings'. By the 1780s there was Fine flour for Wheaten bread and Coarse flour for wholemeal bread, also 'headers' and 'meal' and 'offal' such as pollard, bran and hulls.

The Fairbourne mill had two sets of stones, one for wheat and one for barley. The barley stones were not only used for brewer's barley, but also for the 'hog-milling' of beans and peas and oats. By the 1780s milling work had doubled at Fairbourne due, Mr Spain suggests, to an increase in domestic cus-

53-R.J.Spain, 'The Len Watermills' *Arch Cant LXXXII* (1967)

tomers and a great new demand for animal feeds. People were keeping more horses and hogs and feeding them better. Pigs were fed a meal of beans and peas and barley, as were sheep at lambing time. Horses were fed a supplement of bran and oats.

There was an enormous increase in production and profits during the mid-1750s at the time of the Seven Years War, when the Fairbourne miller was supplying flour to the naval victualling yards on the Thames. There were also the bounties paid by the government for grain exports. This is probably an explanation for Charles Colyer's great increase in prosperity at that time, especially in the light of the Colyer family's earlier connection with the wharfingers and their later ownership of land, and probably a wharf, on the Dartford marshes.

The wider historical world of wars and plagues and fires and famines continued to affect the village and the mill and no longer at such a distance; communications had changed with the new roads. Henry's father Charles had probably been little affected by the outside world, apart from the effect that world affairs had on the price of corn. Overproduction of British corn, much of it for distillation into 'Mother Gin' had forced down the price of grain for a while, making lower profits for millers. The wars in Europe naturally affected the fluctuating markets and no doubt Charles had followed the successes of local figures such as Amherst and Wolfe in Canada in the 1760s. There were scares of an invasion by the French during the Seven Years War and again when the French allied with the Americans in 1778, but probably there was little personal fear in village hearts in 1790, when Henry began his programme of rebuilding.

In 1788 the Revd.John Saunders MA, vicar of Farningham from 1768 to 1807, filled in his report on the village to his bishop 'There are about 50 houses' he said, 'but only one gentleman's family'. He, the vicar, 'resides constantly in the Vicarage House' having put a curate in his former parish of Newington. He says the church is generally well frequented and he preaches twice on the Lord's Day. 'There are no Papists, Dissenters or Quakers. No free school, hospital or alms-house. There is a good school but not a charity one, however some poor children are sent to it by some inhabitants'.[54]

Food Riots

In 1765 poor harvests had led to food riots and high bread prices. In 1768 troops were sent to Tenterden where there was a threat to destroy the premises of those millers who paid more than a certain amount for corn. Rioters attempted to regulate prices and to restrict millers from bulk buying and hoarding corn. The pattern of behaviour for the 'mobs', both then and later, was seldom violent, although several mills were burnt down.

54-Lambeth Palace Library. Miscellaneous papers, Farningham

The crowds, often women, demanded justice and offered to pay a reasonable price. The success or failure of the harvest was all-important to economic stability. Crops could fail at any time of year, from sowing to harvest. Usually one poor year was balanced by a better one, but now the war years of the 1790s and early 1800s were to see runs of bad harvests that threatened the whole structure of society.

The outbreak of war in 1793 was immediately followed by a series of poor harvests. The shortage of wheat led to a monopoly situation for farmers and millers. Speculators who were able to store grain sold it later at vast profit. It was a common occurance for millers to be accused of profiteering, and mills were a frequent target for rioters. Maybe it is unkind to suggest that Henry Colyer was one of these millers, but the records leave no doubt that his prosperity increased enormously at this time. After all, the old sins of regrating and forestalling, although censured and occasionally brought to court, were no longer generally considered a crime. Everbody else was doing it.

The price of wheat quickly doubled. George III was mobbed by crowds demanding bread. Emergency measures were taken for state-controlled granaries and some communities built their own subscription mills to grind corn at fair prices. One such mill was built in Chislehurst, presumably, from the location, a windmill. Bakers were urged to make mixed breads of barley and rye. A tax was levied on hair powder. The rich were exhorted to change their diet, to cut out pastry and cakes, and in turn the rich exhorted the poor to eat rye bread, oatmeal and potatoes.

Unfortunately the labourer's standard of living had been so reduced during the later 18th century that their diet, which had formerly included meat and cheese, was now mainly bread and weak tea. When Pitt complained about the 'groundless prejudices' of the poor to a mixed diet he made no allowance for a digestion no longer strong enough for coarse cereals, nor a morale high enough to experiment with new menus.[55]

Many circumstances had contributed to the falling standard of living for the poor. Among them were the pressures of a rising population and increasing unemployment. Then there were the settlement laws which meant that the labourers had lost much of their freedom of movement in the labour market. Another contribution was the new trend to employ labourers by the day or week, rather than as farm servants living in their employer's house, as was the case with George Ambrose. The Agricultural Revolution of the late 18th and 19th centuries meant that many of the new farmers were producing for the large city markets and were no longer interested in small sales to cottage buyers. All this added to a general sense of loss and deprivation.

A small but important additional freedom which had also been lost at this time was the right to glean in the fields after the harvest which, after 1788, depended on the individual farmer's discretion. Often the church bells would have rung out to call gleaning time and energetic women and children used to gather substantial bags of corn to take to the mill, enough to feed the family for several months. Gleaners were an ancient part of milling history. It was

55-J.I.&B.Hammond, *The Village Labourer* (1911)

184

said in Leviticus 'thou shalt not...gather any gleanings of thy harvest; thou shalt leave them unto the poor'. However, the good Farningham farmers appear to have continued the custom because it certainly still existed in 1900.

Another lost tradition at this time was the miller's 'toll vat' or right to be paid in kind, although this had already more or less become obsolete. In 1796 this system of toll was abolished; 'no miller shall take any part of the corn for toll but shall demand payment in money... where no money is available the miller may take corn equal to money price in payement'. A table of prices was to be put up in every mill and similarly a proper balance and weights displayed.[56]

Pastor Moritz from Berlin visited England in the 1780s.[57] The Thames was so crowded with boats that it took a long time to get to Dartford, where he landed and, because he was travelling on the cheap, he walked up the creek to get a shared stage coach to London. He was amazed by the large signs hanging across the entrances to the villages 'being fastened to large beams extended across the street from house to house'. It seems probable that Farningham had one of these, maybe stretching from the Lion across to Lion Cottages. A similar signboard still exists at Edenbridge. He was also struck by the way men's hair was dressed and curled with irons and powdered, and that it was not unusual for men 'to walk out in a sort of négligée your hair merely rolled in rollers'. He found the towns strangely free after the walled and garrisoned ones in Germany, but he found the food terrible, 'cold meat and sallad mostly', apart from toast which he loved. Poor Pastor Moritz was treated with derision for walking everywhere and often put to eat in the kitchen of the inns where he stayed.

Wartime

France declared war on Britain in February 1793 and the danger of invasion became imminent. The war was to last for twenty years. Henry's son Thomas, three months old at the beginning, would wear uniform before the end. Farningham would not have been affected by the war at once, and life probably continued normally for a while.

The British army was not exactly prepared for war. In 1792 there were only 13,000 regular soldiers. By 1794 there was a regular army of about 175,000, an embodied militia of about 52,000 and about 85,000 sailors.[58] The peacetime unembodied militia were recruited by ballot from about one in ten able-bodied civilians who received about a month's basic training a year. If they were rich enough they could always pay for a substitute, and this happened several times in Farningham. When embodied, in times of war, they served as regulars but could not be sent abroad.

Now, at the outbreak of war, two new types of soldier appeared, the Volunteers and the Fencibles, or Defensibles. The latter were recruited as paid voluntary regulars to serve on home soil. The Volunteers were a great

56-Bennett & Eltton, op.cit.
57-R.Nettel ed. Carl Phillip Moritz, *Journeys of a German through England 1782* (1965)
58-Clive Emsley, *British Society and the French Wars* (1987)

185

new patriotic movement drawn mainly from the gentry and yeomanry and small farmers. They were expected to put in a certain amount of drill and training and were not paid unless they were embodied into active service.[59] The largest group of Volunteers in West Kent were the Yeomanry Cavalry.[60] As early as February 1793 the London Chronicle reported that 'in all the counties fronting the French coast the gentlemen are now mounting themselves on horseback'.

In March 1794 Pitt called for the gentry to raise more Volunteer companies and in April that year the Lord Lieutenant of Kent, the Duke of Dorset, called a great meeting of the county at Maidstone to put this into action. Cavalry troops of fifty men were to be raised by subscription. Each man was to supply his own horse, stabling, food, lodging and clothing. The Government was to supply arms and accoutrements. As well as an anti-invasion force, volunteers could also be called out for the suppression of riots.

The Yeomanry Cavalry

Eight West Kent troops of Yeomanry Cavalry were formed; Sevenoaks, Cobham West and Cobham East, Tunbridge, Chislehurst, Tunbridge Wells, Coxheath and Farningham. The Farningham troop under Captain Dyke numbered 52 with a lieutenant, a cornet, a quarter-master, two sergeants and 46 rank and file. All the men had swords, pistols and horses. The Gravesend and Northfleet Volunteers were infantry troops and had no horses, swords or pistols but were issued with firelocks and pikes. There is a nice 'Dad's Army' touch in the Inspection Returns of 1797 which included 'three young boys of the Northfleet Volunteers who play on the triangles'.

Captain Dyke was probably Percival Hart-Dyke of Lullingstone, although the Army Museum records say his name was Henry Dyke. The date of his appointment was 1794 and so we can be reasonably sure that the Farningham troop was formed that year. The unnamed lieutenant may have been Charles Milner, the tenant of Farningham Manor House who had married a Dyke daughter in 1791. Thomas Fuller the elder had died in 1789 and Thomas junior had been 'drawn to serve in the militia' in 1793 so it was not him. Millers were usually exempt from army service but, in the light of his later participation in the volunteer movement Henry Colyer may very possibly have joined the troop at this early date.

There is also the aspect that the Yeomanry Cavalry, for all the jokes about stout farmers on fat horses, quickly became something of a social club. The uniforms alone must have been a great attraction. One London troop of Volunteers wore scarlet jackets with yellow lapels and gilt buttons, white breeches and bearskin helmets with white cockades, and the Farningham troop may not have been far behind.

Henry's brothers Charles and Thomas were also likely volunteers although they were getting a little old. Others to enlist in the village may have been John Harris and John Colyer, son of the second Charles, although as another

59-Peter Bloomfield, Kent and the Napoleonic Wars (1987)
60-Lt.Col. J.F.Edmeades, Some Historical records of the W. Kent Yeomanry 1794-1909 (1909)

A Cornet of the West Kent Yeomanry Cavalry, circa 1801

miller he was probably exempt, William Jessup and the Pawley brothers. There would surely have been several other able-bodied men in the parish who had their own horses, and of course the 46 rank and file of the troop would also have been drawn from neighbouring villages. By 1798 a William Colyer was named as a cornet in the Cobham West troop but this may have been a Northfleet Colyer as Henry's son William was still only 15.

The first surge of patriotism was not as great as had been expected. In 1797 Arthur Young, the agricultural writer, demanded 'You, gentlemen, the yeomen and farmers of England...what steps have you personally taken to add to the defence of the country? Have you enrolled yourself in a patriotic corps? Have you arms prepared for the hour when they may be neccessary? Or have you, in a contemptible sloth, rested in tranquil security and trusted all to Government ?'[61] It is good to think that Farningham had so quickly acted in a far from slothful manner.

The first hardship years of the war were cruelly felt by the labouring population. Many of the men had gone to war and these were the years of 'the petticoat harvests' when women and children went into field work. In January 1795 and again in July there were special meetings of the Farningham Vestry to collect money for the poor. In January at least 34 people, including Henry, Thomas and Charles Colyer, subscribed between 2 guineas and 5 shillings each. Generous Mrs Cox, widow of Joseph and mother-in-law of two Colyers, gave £4. These emergency collections were distributed in the form of bread, beef and coals.

It was not exactly a famine. The death rate that year was no higher than usual. Friend, the curiously named son of Henry and Charlotte, died in 1795 as did three other small children and five adults. In 1796 only two burials are recorded for the whole year, but in 1797 the burial rate rose to sixteen, including five children, a soldier and a wayfarer. No real significance can be read into these figures, a much more careful comparative study of the baptisms and burials in neighbouring villages would be needed before coming to any conclusion.

It is highly doubtful whether Henry Colyer echoed the egalitarian young Wordsworth's sentiment of 'Bliss was it in that dawn to be alive' in the early days of the French Revolution, and when heads began to roll in Paris Henry probably felt, with most Englishmen, some dread of similar happenings in Britain. Even in Farningham there might lurk some 'saucy objects' amongst the lower orders, reading clandestine copies of Tom Paine's *Rights of Man* and plotting sedition.

61-A.Aspinall ed *English Historical Documents VollXI 1783-1832*

In the early years of the war the plight of the agricultural labourers caused concern at every level, reformers, reactionaries, employers and employed alike. Labourer's wages had completely failed to keep pace with the soaring inflation. Whitbread's proposals for a minimum wage were put before Parliament in the winter of 1795 but defeated by Pitt's unadopted counter-proposals to reform the Poor Law. The answer to a hungry and potentially dangerous underclass was the 'Speenhamland System'.[62] This policy, drawn up by Berkshire JPs at Speenhamland near Newbury in May 1795, was a mis-guided attempt to regulate the wages of day labourers. The system meant that when the price of bread reached a certain sum the labourer's wages would be subsidised by the parish out of the poor rate. This allowance was to be regulated by a sliding scale depending on the price of bread and the size of family. Despite an easing of the settlement laws, these allowance systems which were adopted all over England after Speenhamland, meant that farmers could pay low wages and the labourers would become depend-ent on parish hand-outs.

Meanwhile, in Farningham, where Henry may or may not have joined his local patriotic volunteer corps, he was still busy with his renovations. He and Charlotte now had a free hand with the Lion Inn and in 1795 they leased it to William Wells who, with his son after him, would run the inn for the next fifty years.[63] Wells added a memo-randum to the lease by which he agreed to pay an extra £5 p.a. rent 'in view of Henry Colyer's considerable addi-tions to the premises... building coach-houses and altering and enlarging the Bar and removing the Granery and Barracks to the place whereon they now stand'.

Whether this meant that the inn had been completely rebuilt is not certain. Probably that came later. The late Regency features and the remarks by Dickens in the later 19th century suggest that the building we see today prob-ably dates from the early 19th century. Undoubtedly Henry was upgrading the premises for the new carriage trade along the Turnpike roads. Barracks were also necessary for the heavy troop movements along what was now a major artery through Kent, and it was quite usual to billet troops in local inns. Probably the Bull did the same; there is a local tradition that some of the cot-tages opposite the Bull were built as barracks at this time.

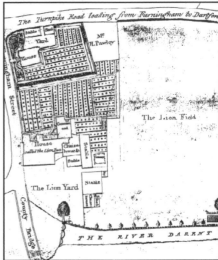

Gudsell's map of 1817 shows both the White House and the Lion Inn. It is interesting to note that the Lion Yard extends to the river and is bordered by a stable, chaise-house and shed. To the right of the land next to the large tree is a barrack building.
Colyer family map.

Henry's New Mill

Henry's building works can only be conjectured from a few incomplete ref-erences. One of course is the increase in the rates he paid. Another is Hasted's reference to a new mill, 'built on a most expensive construction'.[64] Another is the little drawing of a much smaller mill and millhouse in Charles Colyer's plan of 1777. Other sources of information are the insurance policy records which indicate an increase in the value of Henry's mill equipment.[65]

62–ibid
63–CKS U36 T449, 1795
64–E.H. Vol.2, 2nd edition op.cit.
65–Science Museum Library, refs Sun Fire Ins, 1782; & Royal Exchange Fire Ins. 1801

In 1782 the April Sun Fire Insurance record gives 'Henry Colyer Miller, on his dwelling house and water corn mill communicating, with the going geers belonging, £160', and in August the same year a second policy for the same gives a valuation of £800. So is it possible that he built the new mill that year ? We simply do not as yet know, but in the light of his recent inheritance and the traditonal view that the new mill was not built until 1790, perhaps this is not really a very likely conclusion.

In 1801 the Royal Exchange Fire Insurance Policy gives 'Henry Colyer miller and farmer, on the water corn millhouse, brick and timber built and tiled, adjoining his dwelling house at Farningham, having a party wall (except a doorway on the ground floor) £800; on the water wheels, standing and going geer, millstones, machines etc, £800; on stock in trade and utensils, £800'. It is quite an increase, probably partly owing to wartime inflation. Whatever the correct date may be, it seems certain that a new mill was built between 1782 and 1800.

New Milling Technologies

The late 18th century was a time of great innovations in milling technology. Several new treatises on millwrighting appeared, written by engineers such as Smeaton and Telford. Poor harvests and an increased population meant that even during the war years corn was imported, at high prices, from Ireland, Russia, Prussia and North America and even from France itself. Experiments in increasing milling capacity were being made all over Britain, and in America Oliver Evans introduced the first fully automated corn mill. Corn milling was the first industrial process to be power driven in Britain. In 1788 John Rennie built the famous steam driven Albion Mills at Blackfriars, just down the road from William Blake who must have been familiar with their satanic smoke.[66] Steam would soon become the most important prime-mover in British industry.[67]

Until now the art of milling had been a craft tradition handed down by word of mouth and practical example from father to son, master to apprentice. 'The trade is a branch of carpentry, with some assistance from the smith'.[68] Now it was becoming a science with iron replacing wood and engineering firms manufacturing metal parts. Rennie's engines for the Albion Mills were made of cast iron, the amazing new material which would transform later Victorian architecture. The cast iron breast-wheel was the key introduction in Smeaton's technology. Another important innovation was the sliding hatch to the overflow sluice gate introduced by John Rennie. Thomas Telford, that Colossus of Roads, wrote a treaty on Mills in 1796.[69]

We know that Smeaton was active in Kent during the 1770s, 80s and 90s. He worked on mills at Poll Mill and Loose near Maidstone between 1779 and 1789.[70] Maybe the old Fremingham and Isley mills. His work included the great new waterwheel at Deptford victualling yards. It is known that 'if a mill

66-Concise Dictionary of National Biography, John Smeaton; John Rennie; Thomas Telford.
67-Terry S.Reynolds, *Stronger than 100 Men,* (1983)
68-T.Reynolds, op.cit. (1983)
69-Science Museum mss.
70-R.Spain, op.cit.

had to be renovated Smeaton was called in as consultant engineer to measure and advise the owner'. What could be more likely than that he came to Farningham to advise Henry.

Meanwhile Henry's work as Churchwarden and Overseer continued and is well documented.[71] When it was his turn he collected the rates and paid out the doles. He paid the man who wound the church clock (Mr Butterly, a Dartford clockmaker), the man who made the bell ropes, the innkeepers who provided the communion bread and wine. He paid the little boys who killed the hedgehogs and sparrows. He sent off the list for the hair powder tax and, no doubt, the window tax and the horse and dog taxes too. He paid the bill for the archdeacon's annual visitation and the dinner at the Lion for the vicar Mr Saunders and the 'Apparitor' or archdeacon's clerk. Not out of his own pocket of course, but out of the rates.

He paid the bellringers for the six ringing days of the Restoration of Charles II, King George III's accession and birthday, the birthday of the Prince of Wales and the day of the Gunpowder Plot. He paid the carpenters, the bricklayers and the clerk, who still dug the graves and tolled the bell and washed the surplices as well as his usual clerkly duties. He distributed the charity moneys and the small payments to the poor travellers with passes who now included soldiers and sailors and their wives and families. He got one parishioner into hospital and another arrested for bigamy.

Smeaton's model for testing the comparartive efficiency of undershot and overshot water wheels.

He paid the doctors for their services to the poor; for bleeding, blistering, inoculating, extracting teeth, setting broken limbs and prescribing paregoric, anodyne pills and nervous drops. He was also responsible for setting out the apprentices; the orphans or poor children bought or sold into service such as young Ann Whale, hired into service by a family at Northfleet for £1.10s. a year, or 12 year old William Mace 'apprenticed to an Eynsford bricklayer till he be 21 years at 5 guineas consideration money'. He paid the County Stock rate, the money for substitutes for the Militia and the Constables wages plus an extra 3s. 6d. for handcuffs for a felon who had killed a man. All this in one year.

Inoculation was a great new discovery, or rather a very ancient folk medicine that had been brought to Britain by Lady Mary Wortley Montague in 1721 after she had seen its effects in Turkey. By the 1750s the Sutton family of surgeons were practicing as inoculators and in 1766 conducted a mass inoculation in Maidstone.[72] Edward Jenner and his cowpox vaccine came much later, at the end of the century. There is an unattractive contemporary description of the early method in a journal of 1758 which says 'it is no more than scrattin a bit of a haul in their yarm and a pushin in a peece of scraped rag dipt in sum of the pocky matter of a child under the distemper'.[73] In Farningham in 1780 an amateur inoculator, Thomas Swan, was paid between four and five shillings for each poor child he inoculated.

71-CKS Vestry docs. ref P145
72-Peter Razzell,
The Conquest of Smallpox, (1977)
73-Clifford Moseley,
*News from the English Countryside
1750-1850*

Presumably the better off villagers went to the doctor. The thought of Thomas Swan and his pocky rag must have been intimidating. A few years earlier Thomas Swan had been one of the local boys being paid a shilling a head each for a badger and a fox. The famous Dr Thomas Fuller of Sevenoaks spent much of his life researching the eruptive fevers and his protégé, Dr John Nash, of Farningham was no doubt also at the forefront of the inoculation movement.

The search for a Poorhouse

Henry and his fellow Overseers also continued the search for a better Poorhouse. In 1799 it was agreed by the Vestry to hire Mr Bryan the butcher's slaughterhouse for the use of the poor, but fortunately this ghoulish idea was scrapped when the squire, Mr Fuller, stepped in with the offer of his small house at the junction of Sparepenny Lane and the London Road, now called Laurel Cottage, for use as a Poorhouse at a rent of 3 guineas a year.

The Poorhouse was always overflowing, and a number of people still had to be boarded out in lodgings in the village. Many poor people, usually widows and widowers, gave lodgings to other poor people such as single mothers and their children, or the elderly and infirm. Old Mrs Jessop, on poor relief herself, boarded another old lady for 2s.6d. a week. The parish supplied bedding, clothing and furniture. Several paupers each year were also sent to the larger Poorhouses at Sutton and Shoreham.

It seems likely that Henry and his family now lived in some style. The days of farm and mill labourers living in with bed and board in their employer's house were coming to an end. Gillray amused himself with a popular cartoon of Farmer Giles showing off his daughter Betty as she played on the new piano in the family parlour. The 'lower orders' were considered to be aping their betters. No doubt Henry with his fashionable tastes, bought some fine furniture and probably a piano for his elegant new bow windowed drawing room and his family took afternoon tea with delicate china 'equippage'.

In the spring of 1797 the navy at Spithead mutinied and all the fears of a Revolution in Britain seemed confirmed. The sailors were protesting against poor food, low pay and refusal of shore leave. The mutineers moved to the Nore and attempted to blockade the Thames. The ships of the 'Floating Republic', as it was called, flew a red flag and the sailors, 'who were very violent in their proceedings', stopped all vessels going up and down. Armed forces were deployed along the river and the West Kent Yeomanry were embodied and camped out at Sheppey. The mutiny was over by June and the leaders hanged. Probably the nearest the Farningham Yeomanry Cavalry ever came to active warfare was careering across the Sheppey marshes in pursuit of escaping sailors.[74]

Between October 1797 and May 1798 Napoleon's soldiers were encamped on the French coast opposite Britain. It was possible to see their tents and troop formations through spyglasses and it became a popular day out to go and look at them. Alarm beacons were set up on all the hills, pikes were issued to villagers and the whole population was in a state of excited alarm.[75] In the spring of 1798 Napoleon decided that 'the pear is not yet ripe' and departed for Egypt. The Volunteers relaxed, and on August 1st 1799 King George III held a grand Review of their companies at Mote Park, Maidstone. There were 11 West Kent Yeomanry Cavalry troops, including the Farningham Troop under Captain Dyke. 'The corps were drawn up for inspection before marching smartly before His Majesty at the salute'. Manouvres followed and a sort of war game. Finally a dinner was provided for all ranks where, 'to prevent any chance of Inebriety', one bottle of wine was placed between every two soldiers. His Majesty was said to have expressed 'heartfelt satisfaction' at the military appearance of his loyal volunteers.

The harvests of 1799 and 1800 were again deficient and women and children were called into the fields to replace the men serving in the army. There were more food riots. One famous handbill said 'Peace and Large Bread or a King without a Head'.[76]

Imminent Invasion

In 1801 the Volunteers were again ordered to be in 'a state of the utmost readiness'. Napoleon had returned and had collected a fleet of boats and an army of about 100,000 men on the Channel coast. The hills above Dover were again full of sightseers hoping for the worst, but again Napoleon failed to invade. In March 1802 the Peace of Amiens was signed and everyone, more or less, went home. The peace lasted little more than a year. War was again declared in May 1803, and Napoleon yet again assembled a great invasion force, the Army of England, which could be seen massed on the French cliffs. His flotilla of invasion craft lay waiting. Rumours flew round that the

74-Lt.Col.J.F.Edmeades,
Some Historical Records of the W.Kent Yeomanry, (1909)
75-Clive Emsley,
British Society and the French Wars, (1979)

French had not only dug a Channel Tunnel but that they would also use a fleet of air balloons.[77]

Colonel George Hanger, a nephew of the late William Hanger of Farningham, devised an extraordinary defence against the air balloons, which were reputed each to carry 300 troops. He demonstrated his device, an 'Anti-Air-Invasion-Grapnel' in front of Pitt at East Cliff Lodge on the cliffs above Ramsgate. It consisted of a large kite from which dangled a barbed rope with a heavy clawed grapnel. Hanger, an eccentric friend of the Prince Regent, does not appear to have been taken very seriously.[78]

An 'Additional Military Force for the Better Defence and Security of the United Kingdom' had been formed, the 'Army of Reserve', and in July the Government called a Levy en Masse into home defence of all able-bodied men aged between 17 and 55. Volunteers were exempt and there was an unseemly rush to join their companies. Press gangs were out in the streets and the situation was one of dire anxiety. Pitt, in retirement at Walmer Castle as Lord Warden of the Cinque Ports, raised his own company of Volunteers. As Churchill later commented 'few things in England's history are more remarkable than this picture of an ex-Prime Minister, riding his horse at the head of a motley company of yokels, drilling on the fields of the South Coast, while a bare twenty miles away across the Channel the Grand Army of Napoleon waited only for a fair wind and a clear passage'.[79]

77–Peter Bloomfield, *Kent and the Napoleonic Wars* (1987)
78–*Concise Dictionary of National Biography* (1975)
79–Winston S. Churchill, *A History of the English Speaking Peoples Vol.3* (1957)

Perhaps Ann Pring, the cook, frightened the younger Colyers, Thomas and Sarah, aged 10 and 5, with the current stories of 'Boney is coming'. Sadly, their sisters Mary Ann, aged 13, and one year old Elizabeth had died earlier that year and they were the only young children left at home. Thomas Hardy gives a wonderful picture of life in a miller's family during the Napoleonic wars in his novel *The Trumpet Major*. Much of the action takes place in the floury interior of an old mill and mill house and one of the heroine's suitors is even a Yeomanry Cavalryman, unfortunately a figure of sinister fun rather than heroic gallantry. In the story the beacons are fired by mistake and the family flees in disarray from Boney's imagined invasion.

The winter of 1803 came and the immediate danger passed, to be renewed again in the spring of 1804. Napoleon, now Emperor, was more determined than ever to gobble up the glittering prize across the Channel. Cartoons showed him at supper preparing for the feast. Only the British fleet stood in his way. In 1804 there was another great recruitment of Volunteers. Kent was now considered the front line of defence and Wordsworth, no longer a revolutionary, expressed the nation's hopes, 'In Britain is one breath, We are with you now from shore to shore, Ye Men of Kent 'tis Victory or Death'

The Farningham Riflemen

Thomas Fuller, Henry Colyer and William Jessup had heard the call to arms the previous year and had formed a new group of Volunteers, 'The Farningham Riflemen'. Captain Fuller, who probably organized the group, joined in August 1803 and the others, Lieut.Colyer and 2nd Lieut.Jessup, in October.[80] Charles Milner, tenant of the Manor House, was less patriotic and paid 22 guineas for a substitute to take his place in the Royal Army of Reserve. The War Office records also show that the Farningham Yeomanry Cavalry under Captain Percival Hart Dyke were still active that year. By 1806 the Farningham Riflemen numbered 58 men with one captain, 2 subalterns, 3 sergeants and 2 trumpeters or drummers and 50 rank and file.

Riflemen were something new. In 1793 the British infantry had been armed with muskets; weapons which could only be fired accurately at 80 yards. The rifle, which had been known abroad for some time, could be accurately aimed up to 300 yards, but British tradition appears to have been that 'aimed fire was contrary to military etiquette'. In other words, to shoot your man as if he were a partridge was not sporting.[81]

Nevertheless the British had experimented with rifles as early as 1776 when a Major Fergusson, firing at the rate of 6 shots a minute, hit the bulls-eye most times while 'lying on his back on the ground'. In 1797 the successes of the French Tirailleur and Voltigeur riflemen prompted a change of heart among the generals and politicians and the first British rifle battalion was raised from two foreign regiments in British pay, Homptesch's Chasseurs and Lowenstein's Jègers, 'soldiers of fortune well aquainted with the rifle'. The riflemen were dressed in green because part of their performance in what was called 'la petite guerre' or 'skirmishing' was to hide in trees to surprise the enemy. In *The Recollections of Rifleman Harris* the author relates how, in 1802, he was 'so captivated by the smart, dashing, devil-may-care appearance' of the Greenjackets that he volunteered to join them on the spot.[82]

80–National Army Museum, A List of the Officers of the Gentlemen and Yeomanry Cavalry and Volunteer Infantry of the UK, War Office 1804
81–Lt.Col.Lewis Butler, *Annals of the King's Royal Rifle Corps* (1923)
82–Christopher Hibbert ed. *The Recollections of Rifleman Harris* (1970 ed)

Above top
The two plaques added
later to the Mill House
mantle-pieces.
For photographs of the
complete fire surrounds,
see page 181.

Above
At Astorga,
Tom Plunkett lay on his
back with deadly effect to
kill the French General
Colbert, allegedly on
being offered a bag of
money to try.

The experimental rifle corps were trained by Sir John Moore at Shorncliffe in Kent and perhaps the Farningham Riflemen picked up some of their training from him. The tactics learnt by Moore's men would be used to great effect in the coming Peninsular War. Part of their drill was the curious, even bizarre, method of firing their rifles from a recumbent position. Although this is still part of rifle shooting practice it hardly seems practical in the heat of battle. However, there is a famous story of a rifleman, Tom Plunkett, who, during General Moore's fatal retreat to Corunna in 1809, threw himself on his back in the snow and, with the sling of his rifle caught over his foot, took deliberate aim and shot the French General Colbert dead.

No wonder that Henry Colyer, who loved the fashionable and new, became a rifleman. Before his death he commissioned two sculptured marble insets to the chimney, or mantel-pieces, of his 'Grates' in the new Mill House front rooms to commemorate his years in the Volunteers. These decorative marble tablets are often a feature of late 18th century fireplaces. The artist Angelica Kauffman designed similar ones for Attingham Park in Shropshire. The Mill House plaques are not so elaborate as hers but they are very finely executed. Henry also left a record of the three officers of the 'Farningham Riflemen' inscribed in the brickwork above the front door.

One of the Mill House fireplaces shows a rifleman in exactly the same position as Tom Plunkett, lying on his back with his left toe through a loop in his rifle strap. The other panel shows a soldier either kneeling or lying prone on a grassy knoll and aiming his gun at some target beyond a little tree. There is a fallen standard in front of him and a line of soldiers with shouldered guns and two raised standards behind him. Both soldiers wear high rounded hats with cockade feathers, cross sash and belt over their jackets, pantaloons and buttoned puttees over their boots. The standards do not give many clues but one is probably the Great Union flag of St George and St Andrew, without St Patrick, and the other possibly a regimental badge on a plain ground.

Pictures of officers and men of the Rifle Brigade at this date show very similar uniforms. Officers wore voluminous bearskin helmets with rosettes and feathers, much like the hat on the kneeling soldier. Their uniform was a jacket, a barrel sash, a sword belt with pouch and whistle, pantaloons and boots.[83] Riflemen, or private soldiers, wore 'a plain jacket with short skirts looped up in front, pantaloons and half boots and a tall peakless cap, slightly belltopped, with a green feather' and were armed with 'a rifle-gun, a sword

83-National Army Museum,
The Navy and Army Illustrated,
March 11 1898

which may be used as a bayonet, a pouch for cartridges, and a powder horn suspended from a cord slung over the shoulder'. So, allowing for some artistic licence and the Volunteers adaptation of official dress, the uniforms of the chimney-piece soldiers correspond to those of an officer and a rifleman of the period.

A piece of family history should be added here. Charles Colyer of Benenden always said that Henry's eldest son 'Uncle Willy', went to fight in the Napoleonic wars with the Duke of Wellington who later came to visit the mill, dandled the miller's baby on his knee and saw the chimney-pieces which had been commissioned to celebrate Willy's safe return.[84] He added that William's brother Charles built the Mount house in Sparepenny Lane for the returning hero. Unfortunately William does not appear in the Army lists, but of course it is possible that he enlisted as a private soldier, in which case the chimney-pieces may well represent Henry as a Lieutenant in the Volunteers and William as a rifleman in the Rifle Brigade.

In 1798 a William Colyer was named as a cornet in the Cobham West troop of Yeomanry cavalry. This may have been one of the Southfleet Colyers or it may have

Riflemen of the period
Courtesy Army Museum

been Uncle Willy limbering up for the real war at the age of 15. By 1803, when Henry became a Farningham Riflemen, William was 20 and maybe feeling stifled by village life and left out of the war effort. Also, if he did not join the army where was he for the war years ? He does not appear on any Vestry or property records and, although the eldest son, he did not follow his father as miller of Farningham.

If William really did fight with Wellington as a rifleman in the Peninsular he was a very brave man. Life without a commission for someone from his sheltered background would have been very hard. Wellington himself described his soldiers as 'the scum of the earth', and Rifleman Harris's description of their return from Vigo, barefoot, with long straggling beards and rusted weapons, clad in blood-soaked rags and barely able to walk is a revelation of the horrors of war.

84–H.Harding, F&E Local History Soc. publication No.29, 1999

The second Charles Colyer of Farningham Mill

In Farningham, 1804 was a busy year. Henry's son, Charles aged 19, signed the Vestry book with his father for the first time although he was not yet a Vestry officer. Henry and Charles were in charge of the distribution of the desperately needed charity moneys. The Anthony Roper Charity was increased and there were gifts of quartern loaves at 1s. 4d. for the poor.

Thomas West, the Constable, still sometimes referred to as the Borseholder, had a very full notebook for the year. He billetted many hundreds of soldiers and 'pressed' waggons into service 'to carry ye King's Stores and Baggage' through the parish. He relieved countless soldiers and sailors and their wives and children with small sums of money or provisions as they trudged through the village on foot to destinations as far away as Liverpool or Cornwall. Officers wives were no exception; in October he gave 6d. to relieve 'Margaret Hachet, wife of Major Hachet of the 10th Royal Irish Regt. on foot to Liverpool and Ireland'. He also gave 2s. to a man with a wife and children, 'the youngest but 3 weeks, having a pass 'from Appledore to Lancaster in Scotland, 233 miles'. The village inns, alehouses and barns must have been filled to capacity with hungry and exhausted travellers.

In 1804 Lord Romney sold the last of his inherited 'Bosville Lands' in Farningham, Eynsford and Horton Kirby. This was Charles, 1st Earl Romney of the Mote, Maidstone, who had entertained George III at the great Review of Volunteers in 1799. The sale, which was in 20 lots, took place at Garraway's Coffee House in Cornhill on May 15th. Particulars were on show at the Black Lion in Farningham. It seems surprising that such everyday events took place in such times of crisis but no doubt ordinary life in the towns and villages continued much as usual.

A copy of the printed sale particulars has pencilled prices against each lot and these appear to have been the asking, not the sale price. The lots include the house which is now the village Social Club with the 5 acres of land on which the Croft house was later built and this has a pencilled price of £850. The 4 acre field on which Tilmans Mead now stands was £250. Pedham Court Farm, with the Lordship of the Manor and 303 acres, occupied by Mr John Colyer, had a price of £10,500, and Cold Harbour Farm, including fields in Farningham and part of Farningham Woods was £5,500, but Horace Balls says that it did not reach the asking price and remained unsold.[85]

A later deed in the Romney archive says that Cold Harbour was sold in 1806 for £5000 and that John Ebbutt, the occupier, bought a cottage and 9 acres of the estate for £650. Whether this Ebbutt was a direct descendant of the William Ebbutt who owned Farningham Mill in the early 18th century has not been established. We have no evidence that Henry Colyer bought any of the properties, but as his family later owned several of them, it seems quite probable. His friend Henry Pawley bought one of the lots, the 9 acre Barnfield for £808.

85-Horace Balls, History of Cold harbour Farm etc, typescript Dartford Museum.

197

It is a pleasant touch of normality in wartime to think of the two Henrys, dressed in their best, in the setting of Garraway's Coffee House in Exchange Alley, Cornhill. Garraway's was one of the oldest London auction houses, and Cornhill, where the medieval grain markets had been held, was a place to stir the blood of any miller. [86]

Their friend, and Henry's co-Rifleman, squire Thomas Fuller, was surely there because he also acquired some of the properties. He now lived at Farningham Hill House and rented the Manor House to tenants. He and his wife had no children, but he was guardian to the four orphaned Cox boys whose parents had died in 1793 and 1798. Their other guardian was John Colyer, son of Henry's elder brother Charles and the tenant of Pedham Court, who had three young children of his own. From the Cox family records Thomas Fuller was the guardian remembered with most affection.

John Colyer was the only surviving legitimate son of Charles and his wife Mary Cox and like his father before him was something of a black sheep in the family and was to die in penury in 1829, avoiding his creditors in Brussels. His relationship with his two sons was very strange, especially with George, who later emigrated and founded one of the Australian branches of the Colyer family. However, in 1804 John's fortunes were high, he had married an heiress, Sarah Godden, in 1799 and he is described in a deed of 1806 as 'Miller of Deptford'. It would be interesting to know more about this side of his career and whether this was the famous Smeaton mill at the Deptford Victualling Yards. After the sale of Pedham Court in 1804 John took a 22 year lease on Eglantine farmhouse and 340 acres of Charton lands from Sir George and Lady Anne Yonge who also owned William Jessup's farm at Beesfield. The Yonges never lived in Farningham but continued to own village properties until Lady Anne's death in 1833.

In 1805 came the last and greatest of Napoleon's hopes for a full scale invasion of Britain with the vast army now at his command. His only problem was the British navy. The French Admiral Villeneuve was despatched across the Atlantic to decoy Admiral Nelson to the West Indies but the plan failed and Nelson returned to his great victory and death at Cape Trafalgar on October 21st. There must have been scenes of mixed rejoicing and sorrow in Farningham as elsewhere. Pealing of church bells and singing of Rule Britannia as even the poorest inhabitants forgot their hardships and shouted that they would never, never, never now be slaves.

The camps at Boulogne dispersed as the French troops marched away to their own terrible victory at Austerlitz. The possibility of an invasion of Britain was now seen as remote. In 1806 a return was made for the Farningham Riflemen. It said that the state of their arms was 'serviceable and the men were considered 'fit to act with troops of the line'. However, it now seemed likely that their services would not be needed. They do not appear again in any records after 1806. The Yeomanry Cavalry survived and were used increasingly for state occasions and to quell acts of civil riot. By 1813 it

86–B.Weinreb & C.Hibbert eds, *The London Encyclopaedia* (1983)

appeared that the Farningham Cavalry had been amalgamated with the Dartford troop.

In 1806 Napoleon set up a blockade of British goods. Trade was gradually affected, in particular the price of corn and by 1808 the economic situation was grave. Henry Colyer must have been kept busy because, unusually, he does not appear on the Vestry between 1806 and 1811. The blockade was probably good for Henry's business, also the increase in home wheat production. His sons were not vestry officers either, although Charles and James were active on behalf of the Roper Charity, making journeys to Greenwich to deal with problems on the Roper estate.

Wellington

In 1808 the course of the war moved to the Iberian peninsular. Following Sir John Moore's defeat and death at Corunna a new general, Arthur Wellesley, later to be the Duke of Wellington, took command of the British army. In his own words 'I...went abroad and took command of the Army, and never returned, or even quitted the field, till the nations of the peninsula...were delivered from the French armies; ...till I had invaded France...till the general peace was signed at Paris; and the British...marched home across France and embarked for England...'.[87] Of course the real story was not so easy and it was a broken and penniless army that came home from Waterloo in 1815.

Rifleman Harris saw Wellesley in action in the Peninsular in 1808 during the battle of Vimiero. Maybe Uncle Willy saw him there too. Harris came back to England after the retreat to Corunna and later took part in the disastrous expedition to Walcheren when four thousand men died of fever. It is possible that Willy was there as well, or maybe he stayed to fight with Wellington in Spain, but he was certainly home in England by June 1811 so his army service did not survive until Waterloo.

Back in Farningham in March 1807 John Saunders, the vicar, had died. He was 80 years old and had held the living for nearly 40 years. Much of that time he had conducted a tetchy correspondence with Sir George Yonge over the tithe of hops which belonged to the lease of the parsonage, but that the vicar felt should belong to him. The papers are labelled 'an injured vicar's redress'. In fact there was no redress, the rich and powerful Sir George won the battle over what he described as 'this trifle'. Poor old John Saunders appears to have become very frail in his last years, sometimes signing the vestry book with an X. His dynamic successor, William Van Mildert, arrived in April with a new broom to sweep the parish clean.

Van Mildert was already rector of St Mary-le-Bow and lecturer at St Pauls, when he was collated to the Farningham vicarage. He was obviously destined for higher things and eventually became Bishop of Durham. He lost no time in reporting to Canterbury that his Farningham vicarage was 'old and mean' and extracted a grant of £500 to rebuild it. His report to the archbishop said that his new parish had about 86 houses and 500 inhabitants, no endowed

87-J.Steven Watson, *The Reign of George III 1760-1815*

199

school or Sunday school but a private day school kept by a reputable school-master of the Church of England.

In fact, as S Burgoyne Black points out in her history of the Farningham schools, the census figure for the population of Farningham in 1801 was 397 and in 1811 still only 459. It reached 586 in 1821 and 701 in 1831.[88] She also gives the details of the Sunday school started by Van Mildert himself, at first in the church, but soon in a house leased by himself and under the supervision of the reputable private scoolmaster.

The new Poorhouse

The next improvement the new vicar set in train was to encourage his Vestry to build a proper new Poorhouse. At several special Vestry meetings, presided over by himself, it was decided to erect a small building on a piece of land belonging to Thomas Fuller beside the Turnpike Keeper's house on the Dartford Road. The cost was to be £200, paid off at £30 p.a. from the Roper Charity, with bridging loans provided by Messrs Fuller, Colyer, Cox and Winson. The latter two members of the vestry were Henry, the eldest of the four Cox orphans, who was now aged 21 and in

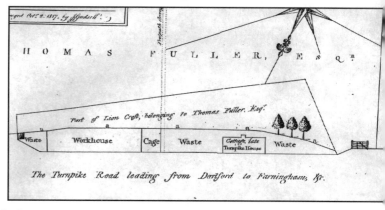

The new Poorhouse, shown as Workhouse on the map. Now known as Roper's Cottages, sited opposite Kings garage

posession of his inheritance of Charton Manor, and James Winson who was the 1804 purchaser of the Croft Farm. Thomas Fuller made the plans for the Poorhouse and it was built by the bricklaying Sharp brothers and the carpenter Jeremiah Sharwood.

Henry Colyer participated in the discussions over the building of the poorhouse between 1809 and its completion in 1811. It was a replacement for the several small poorhouses and lodgings of the past and, although it was sometimes called the Workhouse, it was primarily a place of lodging for the old and infirm, widows, orphans and unmarried mothers rather than a place where paupers were set to work.[89] Occasionally, when space was short, paupers would be sent to the workhouses in Shoreham and Dartford.

One of the first inhabitants was Henry Pounds who lived to be 99 and who on his eventual death was given a wooden memorial at the entrance to the churchyard with the inscription 'Thou shalt Honour the Hoary Head'. In his room he had a stump bedstead, a chaff bed and bolster, 2 blankets, a rug and 2 sheets. 18 people were on poor relief that year and another 16 excused rates because of poverty. The problems of the poor were grave in those years and the list of Overseers went up from two or at most three at the beginning of the war to eleven in 1811.

89–H&W Harding, op.cit, F&ELH Soc.No.9 1994

The rear of The Lion known as the German End as it is today.

Henry was nominated as one of those Overseers at the Easter Vestry that year, but on the 2nd of July he died at the age of 58. He had made his will in 1809 and added a codicil on 21st June 1811.[90] As usual there is no indication of the cause of death. He left his mill with the house, cottages, and 'the house in tenements lately purchased from the heirs of Mrs Smith', to his second son Charles. The house in tenements may have been Lion Cottages which had certainly belonged earlier to the Smiths of the Lion and may only have been leased previously by the Colyers.

He left the Lion and the White House to his third son James, but his 'dear wife' Charlotte was to have the use of the German End, 'that same part that had been heretofore and of old occupied by her father, William Hardyman'. Their two surviving daughters, Charlotte and Sarah, were to live with her and James was to keep the German End in good repair for them. His widow Charlotte was also to have her choice in household goods 'not exceeding £200 in value' and not including 'My Grates' which were to stay in situ.

The German End was the traditional name for the ancient Tudor inn building which still stands at the back of the Lion Hotel. In Robert Smith's inventory of the Black Lion, made in 1690, one of the rooms is called German's Room, but who German was is now forgotten. A 'Jhon German' was recorded in the parish register in 1591 and there was a much later Jarman family in the village. Perhaps we can only assume that German was a favoured customer of the inn who lived there for a long time. Widow Hardyman, Charlotte's mother had lived there after her husband's death and the German End had acquired a garden enclosed by a row of fruit trees.

Charles was to have all the residue of household goods, livestock and business stock including 'all the Gear work and running Tackle' in the mill and the stock of wheat, grain and pulse flour at valuation. Henry's brother Thomas, his brother-in-law John Fuller of Chelsfield and his son Charles were the executors of the will and the trustees of sums of £4000 and £7000 which were to complete the education of twelve year old Sarah and of Thomas, who was still under 21 and was to be put out as Clerk, Apprentice or other wise to any trade, business or profession.

Thomas was also to inherit several small houses in Farningham including the cottages of the carpenters Jeremiah Sharwood, senior and junior, in the Dartford Road. Each of the six children also inherited money. William

90-PRO Prob 11/1526, proved Oct. 1811

201

received £11,000, Charles £8000, James £7,800, Charlotte £4000, Thomas £8,600. The codicil which was made two weeks before his death was witnessed by Ann Pring, and merely exchanged the original houses left to Thomas and James, Thomas receiving extra money to make up for lesser property.

There may well have been a coolness between Henry and his eldest son William because, although William got his fair share of his father's money, he is not otherwise mentioned in the will, neither as executor nor beneficiary, although he may of course, at the age of 27, have been set up already in a house of his own. It seems possible that William had lost favour with his father by his recent conversion from the Church of England to the Eynsford Baptists. Dissent was something new in Farningham and it is doubtful whether Henry's enthusiasm for the fashionable extended to such an unorthodox novelty. As far as William was concerned this was not a passing fancy, he remained a devout Baptist all his life.

William and the Baptists

It is easy to imagine that maybe William had been a budding dissenter and fiery young radical in his youth and that was why he had joined the ranks in the army. Maybe his wartime experiences with wider society had influenced him or it may have been his early association with the Pawley family who also became Baptists. The Eynsford branch of the Strict and Particular (Calvinist) Baptist Church had been brought to the village in 1792 by a workman at the paper mills, Edward Hodges. Many of the paper mills had been founded by Calvinist Huguenots in the 18th century and the paper-millers in Eynsford and Foots Cray remained sympathetic to the Baptist cause. Meetings were at first held in Hodges house until the chapel was built in 1806. [91]

William was proposed as a Baptist in Eynsford on June 9th 1811. On June 16th he related the neccessary experiences of faith to the elders, and it was agreed he should receive baptism, no longer by immersion in the Darent, but in the baptistry of the new chapel. His father died less than three weeks later. However, as Henry made the codicil to his will on the 21st June and did nothing to cut William out, it is possible that he either knew and agreed with his son's conversion, or that he was ignorant of the whole thing. The latter possibility is very unlikely. The doings of the Baptists were watched with great interest and often derision by the local community. But it is possible that Henry also never knew that his third son James was to marry a Baptist, Mary Pawley, later that year.

It was of course not only the difficulties experienced by dissenters, but the loss of what was seen as social status that made the act of crossing over a divisive family issue. Charles of Benenden continued to deny that any of his family had been Baptists more than a hundred years later. When Mrs Glover of Farningham, a descendant of the Eynsford Baptist minister John Rogers, wrote to ask him for information about his uncle William he pretended not

91–Eynsford Baptist Church, 1806-1906, historical booklet (1906)

to understand her. His family all had similar names he declared and there were many Uncle Williams. He blandly ignored all mention of Baptists.

For someone as upwardly mobile as Henry Colyer with his fine house and his garden and grove and grates it may have come as a cruel blow that his eldest son chose to ally himself with what he would have seen as a decidedly socially inferior strata of village society. Baptists at this time were mostly small farmers, tradesmen, craftsmen and labourers. In the list of founder members of the Foots Cray Baptist Church in 1836 Mr W. H. Colyer is the only one described as 'Gent'.

According to a short history of the Foots Cray Baptist Church 'Mr W. H. Colyer, a member of the Eynsford Baptist Church, taking up his residence in Foots Cray in 1812, licenced his house for public worship and gathered together a small congregation which, growing too large for his house, moved in 1814 to the finishing room of the Foots Cray Paper Mill. Returning to Farningham to live he left behind him a company of Christian people who by 1836 had decided to build a church. On March 24th of that year we find our worthy friend Mr Colyer, laying the foundation stone'.

The Mount
Sparepenny Lane
circa 1909

William certainly lived in the Mount, Sparepenny Lane, after his return from Foots Cray. The house was probably built between 1825 and 1828, when he first paid rates for it. It also appears to be true that his brother Charles built it for him as he is the owner and William the occupier in 1840. Henry would have been proud of his sons' taste, it is arguably the most elegant house in Farningham and a fine example of country Regency architecture, most probably built to copybook designs by the Sharp brothers. Their Bricklayer's Arms pub at the end of the lane, which also belonged to Charles, bears strikingly similar features.

Whether the Iron Duke really ever visited Farningham Mill and dandled the miller's baby on his knee is not known. He was certainly often in Kent, and is said to have liked children of all ages. He also liked millers and there is a story about how, on his solitary rides at Walmer where he was to die in 1852, he would knock on the door of Ripple Mill and call up 'That the miller, come down and talk'.[92] Perhaps we will never know.

Henry was buried in a splendid tomb in the churchyard, and Ann Pring, who died thirty years later, lies next door. It was the end of an era, and not just in Farningham. In 1811 George III finally succumbed to madness, and the Regency of George IV was declared. It could be said that, as the first Charles Colyer represented the earlier 18th century of the second and third Georges, and his son Henry the time of George IV, so the new miller, with his qualities of empire building and philanthropy, would come to typify the time of Victoria and Albert.

92-Elizabeth Longford
Wellington, Pillar of State

203

Chapter Twelve

Charles Colyer, Miller1785-1870 / Admiral Bligh /
The Schools / The Last Labourer's Revolt / Thomas Waring /
Miss Anne Colyer / The Trout and the Hare / The Australian Colyers.

Charles Colyer, Miller 1785–1870

Although Charles was the third Charles Colyer of Farningham he was only the second to own and work the mill. He was 26 when he inherited the mill after his father's death in 1811. Presumably father and son had been working together for some years, and so the transition of owners was comparatively easy. His mother Charlotte and sisters Charlotte and Sarah, in accordance with his father's will, moved out into the German End of the Lion Inn, and in two years time Charles married Ann, eldest daughter of John and Rachel Gawan of Dover. The marriage took place at St Augustine's, Old Change in London on February 8th, 1813.[93]

In June1814 there was a great village dinner to celebrate the peace with France. It took place in Thomas Fuller's paddock, known today as Market Meadow.[94] The church bells rang and the village rejoiced. In March 1815 Napoleon returned from Elba and it all started again, but on the 18th of June 1815 the bells rang for the victory at Waterloo and the war was finally over.

On December 16th, 1816, Ann gave birth to the Colyer's only child, another Charles, and on the 20th December she died. This terrible blow appears to have affected Charles for the rest of his life. At his death in 1870, aged 84, he was described in the local newspaper as 'a gentleman of exceedingly retired habits', and a 'generous spirit largely manifested by various acts of benevolence, whose loss would be severely felt by the poor of the village'.

His reclusive nature was remembered in the village a century later by which time much of his benevolence had been forgotten. Indeed he was such a retiring personality that it is difficult to find out much about him. However, Charles of Benenden told a charming story about the way this great-great-grandfather treated his tenants. Every rent day, which was always at or near the quarter days of Christmas, Lady Day, Midsummer and Michaelmas, the tenants of the mill cottages, mostly his own workmen and servants, or the widows and children who were always allowed to stay in their homes, would come to the Counting House to pay their rents. Charles would be sitting behind a table to accept the rent and then, no doubt after a conversation about their welfare and their families and their continuing good behaviour, he would return the money.

There is a cartoon by Rowlandson of a similar scene inside a building very like the Counting House, with the same pointed lattice windows. In the cartoon it is the far from benevolent Lord of the Manor receiving his rack rents

93–F.A.Crisp
Visitation of England and Wales
Vol.4 (1896)
94–Eliza Edmonds,
Notebooks, F&EHSoc.

but, apart from the reversal of fortune, the line of shuffling tenants clutching their bags of money must have looked much the same.

There was no shortage of neighbouring family to support Charles and his child. Charles's brother James had married his childhood friend Mary Pawley, daughter of Henry and Grace Pawley of Sparepenny Lane, in 1811, and they lived in the White House, in the High Street where three of their children were born before they moved to Underriver in 1820. James and Mary both lived into their seventies and had eight children, all brought up as Baptists. Charles's mother, Charlotte, lived in the German End until her death in 1823 aged 66. Her elder daughter Charlotte had died there aged 34, in 1815, and the younger daughter Sarah remained in the German End until her early death in 1827 aged 28.

Charles's Uncle Charles of Horton Kirby had died in 1815, leaving instructions to his nephews Charles and William Hardyman to look after his natural son Henry Jordan and give him a good education in writing and arithmetic, and to bind him apprentice when the time came. This Henry, who kept the name Jordan, later became a collar-maker or saddler, and lived in Farningham for a while in the 1830s.

Of other family members, Charles's brother William Hardyman was still living in Foots Cray in 1816, but their aunt Elizabeth Colyer, widow of James of Dartford Mill, was living in Farningham House in the High Street with her middle-aged son and daughter, James and Ann, who would remain there, unmarried, for the rest of their lives. Their sister Elizabeth had died in 1810 aged 36. Cousin John Colyer was also living nearby in Eynsford with his wife Sarah Godden and their two young sons John and George.

Charles's Aunt Sarah and her husband John Fuller, cousin of the Farningham Thomas Fuller, were living a few miles away at Hewitts in Chelsfield. Most of their children had died young, but two daughters, Mary and Sarah, survived. The Fullers were to build a large family house in Chelsfield called Woodlands for Mary who never married and died there aged 58 in 1842. Sarah married Thomas Waring of Chelsfield in 1803 and started the dynasty of Warings who would inherit all the Fuller properties. Their youngest son William Waring, who was born at Woodlands in 1818, eventually inherited the whole of the Farningham and Chelsfield estates. There was also a large and thriving branch of the Colyer family not far away in Southfleet and Greenhythe. Nevertheless it seems likely that, even though they were surrounded by family and neighbours, the mill might have become a sad and lonely place for the boy and his father.

In 1816 William Van Mildert was replaced by a new vicar, Benjamin Sandford who for reasons of inheritance would change his surname to Winston in 1836. He and his curate Andrew Burnside were to dominate the church and vestry for the next fifty years. Two years later a tribute to the new vicar and his churchwardens, Thomas Fuller and Charles Colyer, was written by two workmen when they worked on church alterations. These included removing the two side galleries and erecting pews paid for by private subscription for the use of the families of Messrs Fuller, Colyer, Cox, Pawley and Burr. The tribute, written on a little piece of paper dated 1818, was found in 1873 under the pulpit stairs.

' John Stockley, painter.
William Turner, carpenter.

THE FARMER'S
MONTHLY VISITOR.

No. IV.]   [APRIL 30, 1848.

THE FARNINGHAM FESTIVAL.

[FARNINGHAM CHURCH, KENT.]

THE little village of Farningham is situated on the Maidstone road, in Kent, about eighteen miles from London, and lies in a somewhat picteresque hollow. The river Darrenth winds through its valleys and affords some good sport to " ye founde lovers of ye piscatorial arte."

Farningham Church in 1848 now showing the addition to the tower which was heightened in 1830.

We hope that all this little scrap who see
May have the powr'to say as much as we
For Parson Sandford is we all declare
As good a man as eer will mount these stairs
And our Churchwardens they are good likewise
May we all meet in peace above the skies.

Mr Fuller,
Mr Colyer, Churchwardens'.

Admiral Bligh

Farningham had acquired its greatest celebrity in 1815 when Admiral William Bligh, 'Bligh of the Bounty', became the tenant of the Manor House. He actually only lived in Farningham for less than three years and died and was buried in London in December 1817. He obviously wanted to make his mark in the village and appears frequently in the Vestry books for those few years. In a schedule of the Manor House made at the time of its sale in 1920 there is a description of 'the South Bedroom, known as "the Admiral's room", with an inset oil painting of a ship said to be the Bounty'. The painting had a hole in it, reputedly caused by a bullet which 'the Admiral in a fit of rage shot at his black servant'. The Admiral, a widower, lived with his spinster daughters who were rumoured to be terrified of him.

In May 1816 Admiral Bligh walked the bounds of his new parish in the company of his landlord Thomas Fuller; the senior and junior William Jessups; the tailors Rickeby and Thomas Wallis; the carpenter Sharwoods; the painter Stockleys; the Petman wheelwrights; the bricklayer Sharps; blacksmith William Gibson, two gardeners and a few agricultural labourers. No women appear on the list and no whipping boys. The two day walk was led by the new vicar Mr Sandford. Charles Colyer, although a regular churchgoer and member of the vestry, did not accompany them. Perhaps he was not very sociable even before his wife's death later that year. He was also of course a busy man. The post- war years were a time of transition in agriculture and milling.

A new doctor, young George Edwards, described as 'surgeon and apothecary', had come to practice in the village in 1813. The vestry employed him to look after the poor of the parish at £10 p.a. He first lived at the house now called Pinehurst which, to judge from its early 19th century appearance, he had possibly commissioned to be built for himself. It was to remain a village doctor's house for nearly a hundred years. James Winson, a farmer who was also a pillar of the church and vestry, lived opposite in the farmhouse which is now the village Social Club. When Winson died, Dr Edwardes bought this property and built a large new house, the Croft, on the land behind the farmhouse.

Other 'Principal Inhabitants' of the village in Charles Colyer's early years as miller were Henry Cox of Charton Manor, who would move to a new estate in Westerham in 1817, John and Henry Pawley of Sparepenny Lane, Lawrence Foster of Chimhams, and all the innkeepers, William Wells at the Lion, George Mandy of the Bull, Abraham Bevins of the Chequers and the bricklayer Sharp brothers in their new pub the Bricklayer's Arms. One of the Sharp brothers, James, was also the Parish Clerk, at a salary of £15 p.a. 'without any further allowance for keeping church and churchyard in order and winding clock etc'. He presumably also still acted as gravedigger, although this is not mentioned in his work schedule. The Sharp brothers had also built the poorhouse in 1810 and in 1815 had added the 'Cage', or village lock-up for offenders, with a room above it 'for purpose of persons out of employ to be employed by the parish Churchwardens and Overseers'.

A significant sign of the times came in 1816 when the vestry decided that 'in consequence of the great influx of paupers in the parish and the want of proper supervision in the poorhouse, certain paupers shall be boarded out in neighbouring parishes'. A special rate was called to raise £100 to enlarge the existing building yet again, and a 'steady woman', Mrs Flewin, was appointed supervisor at a salary of £5 p.a. She was to be allowed 4s. a head weekly for feeding the inmates and two and a half chaldrons of coals and 200 wood bavins to fire a 20 gallon copper boiler, an iron boiler and a 10 gallon oven to keep them warm and clean and fed.

46-CKS P 145/13/4 An inventory of the poorhouse at this time shows sparse furnishings. There were seven basic beds with sheets and blankets, and one tent bedstead with hangings and featherbeds, presumably for the supervisor, one armchair, five other chairs and a few forms and tables. There was also a painted noticeboard with Rules and Articles. Mrs Flewin was to shut and lock the house at nine in the evening in summer, seven in winter and open it again at five in the morning in summer and seven in winter.[95]

In 1817 a piece of ground was rented from the Lion for a poorhouse garden. It was to have a 5ft.6in.fence of oaken palings next to the road with tenterhooks on top to prevent intruders or escapees. Mr Gudsell, the local surveyor, was requested to make a survey of the house and grounds. This was no doubt a garden for potatoes and vegetables, not a place for inmates to play in or sun themselves.

It is good to see that when one unfortunate inmate, Charlotte Heather, ran away and it was resolved not to readmit her, Charles Colyer was one of four members of the vestry who disagreed with this resolution and refused to sign the book. Sad to see a little later that Charlotte had been found other lodging and employment in 'the Stonepitts'. Many workhouse inhabitants, the aged and children included, were still employed breaking stones for the roads in return for a few pennies a cartload.

The Schools

Benjamin Sandford wrote a report on the parish in 1819 for the House of Commons Select Committee enquiring into the education of the poor. He said that there was a population of 459, a day school of 23 kept by a dissenting minister, a boarding school of 20 pupils, a mistress school of 12 children chiefly of tradespeople, a Sunday school of 69 supported by voluntary subscriptions, and a weekly school kept by the master of the Sunday school to which 7 children were sent by aid of surplus subscriptions. He added that 'by the minister's representations, the Roper Charity has placed 20 children at the above, 4 others being placed by the minister himself, 3 by individuals and 16 by their own parents'. The 1821 Census of village inhabitants gives 146 males and females between the ages of 5 and 15 which shows a good proportion of children in school, at any rate for part of the time that might be expected in an agricultural community. Twelve would be the normal school leaving age and children were always needed at seasonal work whatever their age.

For its time Farningham seems to have been well served educationally. The weekly school was kept by the extraordinary Charles Everest who was a wheelwright by trade. He successfully ran the village school until 1850 when he retired and returned to his earlier occupation. He was also, surprisingly, listed in the local directory as a 'patent truss maker'. He had 18 children and one of his many descendants lived in Farningham until recently.

The dissenting minister who also kept a school was John Rogers, minister of the Eynsford Baptist Church from 1802 to 1840. Later, in 1823, vicar Sandford built a thatched schoolroom on his glebe land into which Charles   95-P 145 Vestry book

Everest was allowed to move his school. The history of these schools is well described by Shirley Burgoyne Black in her *Children of Farningham and their Schools.*[96]

The boarding school was Mr Whiffen's 'Gentlemen's Boarding Academy' which, by 1831, had 'upwards of 30 boys'. With all these establishments to chose from it would be interesting to know which, if any, young Charles Colyer attended. Judging by his later career in the legal profession it seems possible that he became one of Mr Whiffin's little gentlemen. Later he may have followed the footsteps of his distant cousin, Henry Cox's younger brother Solomon, who also became a solicitor, by going as a boarder to Sevenoaks Grammar School. Solomon's fees for board and tuition in 1810 at Queen Elizabeth School, as it was then known, were £30 per half year, to include dancing master, writing master, copy books, shoemaker, haircutter, tailor, glover, washing and 10s. 6d. pocket money.

In 1820 Mrs Flewin was offered half the pauper boy's wages in view of 'the greater care required in keeping them decent when at work', but this enticement did not prevent her giving in her notice that year. Perhaps she was too tender hearted for the job or maybe she had saved enough to retire. Mrs Deane, wife of one of the constables, was appointed in her place.

Things were getting harder, and not just in the poorhouse. The 'great influx of paupers in the parish' reported in 1816 was likely to have been caused by unemployed agricultural labourers. Post war depression and inflation devastated the countryside. The infamous Speenhamland system of subsidising wages with a sliding scale of poor relief in proportion to the cost of bread and the size of family was not widely adopted in Kent, but each village vestry had its own way of dealing with labourers who were kept on pathetically low wages by the farmers who knew these would be supplemented by doles from the parish. In most villages, although there was no 'scale' as such, it was

96-S.Burgoyne Black, op.cit

recognised that wages would be 'made up' by poor relief. Work was also concocted for the unemployed such as the 'small scale spade husbandry' which the Farningham vestry asked its members to provide in turn.

It has been observed by countless historians that the gulf between the rich and poor widened drastically in the 19th century. Small farms were eaten up by big farms and many large farmers were now described as gentlemen. William Cobbett, the great champion of the agricultural labourer, accused the farmers of only producing food for the 'Great Wens' of London and other cities. He pointed to how the language used to describe the poor had changed. Once, they were 'the commons of England', now they were 'the lower orders' and 'the peasantry' and, when they met together to demand their rights, they became 'the mob'. 'When farmers become gentlemen' he said, 'their labourers become slaves'. The Farningham mill labourers were very lucky with their benevolent employer.

Another source of distress for the poor was the enthusiasm of the newly rich classes for field sports. Pheasants bred on keeper-protected lands meant increasing punishments for poachers. Sentences of whipping, hard labour and even transportation for frequent offenders became common. An 1820 Act for Malicious Trespass or damage to trees, hedges and underwood meant that even young children could be sentenced to £5 fines or hard labour for collecting firewood. Transportation to the colonies was a new horror for the poor. It was usually a one-way ticket to lifelong exile.

The Last Labourer's Revolt

Cobbett himself was blamed by some contemporaries for blowing the flames of the fires that were soon to be lit in Kent and to spread all over southern England in an uprising that would be known as 'The Last Labourer's Revolt'. In the early 1830s he was touring England on horseback, gathering information on the depressed state of agriculture and the poverty of the labourers, reports which he published as his *Rural Rides*. By 1830 he was on circuit again, giving what were considered incendiary lectures on his findings.

Cobbett, incidentally, was no friend to millers. In his *Cottage Economy,* among household tips to cottagers, he gives instructions on how to avoid the expense of sending wheat to be ground at a mill by the construction of a cheap, do-it-yourself mill which could be turned by a man, a stout boy or a horse. 'My little mill can grind six bushells of wheat a day' he triumphed.

Between 1815 and 1830 relations between the agricultural labourers and their employers deteriorated more and more. The Hammonds, in their study

210

of *The English Labourer,* quote Lord Carnarvon as saying in Parliament that the English labourer had been reduced to a plight more abject than that of any race in Europe.

There were warning signs in Farningham. Conditions in the Poorhouse had worsened. In 1822 Mrs Deane's allowance was reduced to 3s. per head per week for food for the inhabitants, 2s.6d. for provisions and 6d. for herself. The vestry also decided on a new humiliation for 'all single women chargeable on the rates on account of illegitimate children to be ordered into the Poorhouse and the time they are there shall wear a Grey Serge Gown'.

In April 1827 the vestry reported that 'boys and other persons were playing with gunpowder and riotously assembling in the street'. They resolved 'that it is expedient to have a nightly watchman to protect the property of inhabitants from increasing depredations of alarming degree. Likewise to apprehend all idle and disorderly and order all tramps and vagabonds out of the parish or take them into custody'. The Constable, Francis Martin, who was also the butcher, was in future to be assisted by ten wardens, among them Charles Everest, the schoolmaster and James Sharp, the parish clerk.

In the industrial north of England the scene of protest had already been set in 1811 by the Luddite machine breakers. Now discontent was obviously turning to anger in the agricultural south, and the report of boys and other persons playing with gunpowder was a warning of the scenes of arson that were to come. As always, bread and corn were at the heart of things. Millers and farmers with threshing machines which deprived labourers of work were going to be prime targets. In 1827 the first 'malicious fires' were reported in east Kent. 'Nightly depredations', burglary, theft and criminal damage moved to West Kent next year.

The winter of 1829 was especially harsh after a poor harvest. Cobbett was out on lecture circuit that year at Maidstone and Gravesend. In the summer of 1830 the real conflagration started. Of all the southern counties Kent was to have the highest number of fires and machine breakages. The arsonists were very brave, the penalty for firing a rick was death. For destroying a threshing machine the sentence was transportation.[97]

The major uprising started in June in the Sevenoaks and Orpington areas and one of the first ricks to be fired, on July 22, belonged to Charles Colyer of Farningham. A 'threatening letter' was found nearby. These letters, which became a feature of the riots, were often signed by 'Captain Swing', an anonymous figurehead like 'King Ludd'. The letter to Charles Colyer has not survived but a typical 'violent and dangerous paper' received at Mayfield ran as follows, 'Now gentlemen this is wat we intend to have for a married man to have 2s. and 3d. per day and all over 2 children 1s. and 6d. per head a week...and we intend to have the rents lowered likewise...and if ther is no alteration we shall proceed further about it'.

97–E.J.Hobsbawn & G.Rude, *Captain Swing* (1969) Of course there were angrier and nastier letters and many scenes of large 'mobs' that frightened people, but no real violence took place on the labourer's part, and the Last Labourer's Revolt was soon put down by the powerful forces of state and church and the great landowners.

The Duke of Wellington, who was Prime Minister in 1830 although he resigned in November after the troubles had subsided, had little sympathy with the Revolt and denied that the troubles were due to distress. He was very fond of the new sport of fox hunting and his description of how he put down the rioters sounds like someone having a good day at the hunt. 'I induced the magistrates, servants and grooms, huntsmen etc. to mount horseback armed with horsewhips and pistols...to attack the mobs and disperse and confine them'.

Nor were the clergy any kinder. Hobsbawn and Rude in their *Captain Swing* quote from a letter sent to Robert Peel, the Home Secretary, by 'a class conscious clerical magistrate of Farningham' in October 1830 warning that 'if this state of things shall continue the Peasantry will learn the secret of their own physical strength...' and he begged the government to 'sanction the arming of the bourgeois classes by re-establishing the Yeomanry'. (Was the clerical magistrate Mr Winston or Mr Burnside?) He was not alone in hoping for re-arming the Yeomanry but on the whole the farmers were surprisingly reluctant to be re-armed. Many farmers had a lot of sympathy for their workers and asked for a reduction in rents and tithes to make it possible to give a rise in wages. However, Colonel Edmeades in his *History of the West Kent Yeomanry* says that though the regiments had disbanded in 1827, they were in fact called into action again during the 1830 riots. Sir Percy Dyke was in command of the Dartford Troop into which the Farningham Troop had been amalgamated in 1813.

While awaiting transportation, convicts often laboriously ground down bun pennies and engraved them as love tokens for those to be left behind

In addition to the local yeomanry, troops of cavalry were sent into East and West Kent in October. The prisons started to fill to overflowing and by Christmas the labourers' Revolt was over. The Archbishop of Canterbury gave a comunal prayer of thanksgiving, 'Restore, O Lord, to thy people the quiet enjoyment of the many and great blessings which we have received from thy bounty'.

Kent had the highest number of broken threshing machines in the country and also of incendiarism. The trials of captured prisoners started in Kent in October and special commissions went on through the winter. 1,975 prisoners were tried by 90 courts in 34 counties. 19 men and boys were hung and 457 were transported to New South Wales and Tasmania. No free passages home were granted. The labourers were left no better off than before and it was to be a long time before their standard of living improved. The first Reform Bill of 1832 gave the franchise to the middle classes but the rural working classes had to wait for the vote until the 3rd Reform Bill of 1884.

Things were soon back to normal, and in 1834 the Vestry thought it was

time to appoint a Parish Beadle, Thomas May, 'to clear the loads of vagrants'. Next year he was given 'a gould lace hat' so that he could look almost as resplendent as the town beadles. At the same time 'all bastard children receiving 2s. 6d.' were to be reduced to 2s.

After the troubles of the 1830s Charles Colyer began to expand his empire. By 1840 it was said that he and Thomas Waring were the largest landowners in Farningham. They certainly paid the highest rates, although the 1841 tithe map shows several other extensive owners of land.

Thomas Waring

The new squire of the Farningham manor estate, was the son of Dr Richard Waring of St Mary Cray. His mother was Elizabeth Fuller, sister of Thomas Fuller the younger of Farningham. This Thomas Fuller, squire of Farningham since 1788, had no children and so on his death in Suffolk in 1822, his nephew Thomas Waring inherited his property. Thomas Waring was born in 1776 and made a second Farningham connection by marrying Sarah Fuller, daughter of John Fuller and Sarah Colyer, in 1803. So Sarah Colyer's grandson was the new squire. Thomas and Sarah Waring lived at Woodlands in Chelsfield and had eleven children ten of whom died young and unmarried. Thomas was a great sportsman, and a painting of him on horseback with his pack of harriers survives today. He died at Woodlands in 1851.[98]

Although Thomas Waring is often given as the owner and occupier of both Farningham Manor House and Farningham Hill House, he never in fact lived here. Both houses were used by his family at various times, and the Warings did not sell the properties until 1920. His last surviving son, William Waring, who was born at Woodlands in 1818, was living at Farningham Hill in 1841 with his aunt Anne Waring as housekeeper, when Anne died suddenly while walking in Farningham Woods. A window in the church was dedicated to her

98-Geoffrey Copus, Chelsfield historian, pers. com.

memory. Two years later William married Mary Wall Tasker, daughter of the Dartford brewer John Tasker, and three of their twelve children were born at Farningham Hill House.

Charles Colyer's first building in the village appears to have been the Mount House in Sparepenny Lane for his brother William who paid the rates but Charles paid the Land Tax. A document written by his son in 1879 says that Charles was also responsible for building the new Bricklayer's Arms public house.

He described it as 'a new and very substantial building built by my father upon a plan suited for a private residence if it ever ceases to be an inn'. This makes it look as though the Mount, the Bricklayers Arms and the cottages along the London Road were all developed by Charles at the same time and explains the architectural similarities shared by the Mount and the Bricklayers. No doubt they were both built by the Sharp brothers, the bricklayers who leased the inn, probably to designs chosen by Charles from pattern books of the day. There are no records of architects being employed in Farningham before the 20th century.

Top, The Bricklayers Arms circa 1908. The later view below shows modifications including a paved area, facing onto London Road, covered by an awning supported on cast iron pillars.

It became a private house in 1925

Charles next made the very large purchase of a lease of the Parsonage Estate from the heirs of Sir George Yonge. This constituted both the Parsonage house, farm and land, and Eglantine house, farm and land, making a combined total of 220 acres. It also included the so called Folly estate. By the time of the 1841 tithe map Charles is given as the owner of these lands although the Dean and Chapter of Canterbury retained ownership of the Parsonage house and a field of rectorial glebe land. The Folly itself was now a mature beech plantation and is is described on the map as 'Frith Wood', surrounded by the two 'Folly' fields.

Old Parsonage House as it is today

Charles's acquisition of the Parsonage and its land was to lead to a serious altercation with the vicar in 1838 concerning the tithe of hops. Did they belong to Charles or to the vicar? The Revd. Winston declared that Charles 'had made the purchase with his eyes wide open' and that he owed the vicar the traditional tithe of £15p.a. belonging to the property. Charles obviously disagreed and so Mr Winston 'found it his duty to go to law'. Mr Pocock of Lincoln's Inn for the vicar, and Mr Fooks of Dartford for Charles were called to arbitrate and the outcome was that the Dean and Chapter of Canterbury turned down the vicar's claim. It was the old Farningham tithe story of 'an injured vicar' failing to get redress and must surely have led to a coolness between the church and the mill.

Amazingly, in 1840, the Revd. Winston succeeded in reversing the verdict and recovering his tithe, but whether with good or ill will is not recorded. Perhaps Charles, with his notorious benevolence, yielded the argument once he had won his point. This interpretation is strengthened by the fact that Charles's son, Charles junior, was apparently articled at some stage in the 1830s to Mr Pocock, the vicar's solicitor and friend.

By the time of the 1841 tithe map Charles had also acquired the Beesfield farm estate and had become one of the largest landowners in the village.

Beesfield, early 20th century

The 1841 Census shows him living in the Mill House, 'Occupation Independent', with his deceased wife's sisters, Mary Gawan and Maria Hinsby and Maria's daughter, a second Maria. Maybe Mary Gawan, who lived with Charles for the rest of her life, had come to live at the Mill when her sister died and had helped to bring up his son. Maria Hinsby had only joined them recently when she became a widow. The younger Maria died next year in 1841, aged 20. The Hinsbys and Miss Gawan are all buried in the same vault in the churchyard as Charles and his son.

Charles junior is not entered in the Farningham census. He had married his cousin Mary Ann, daughter of Thomas Colyer of Greenhythe, in 1839 and they were living in Dartford. It seems probable that he had finished his articles with Mr Pocock at Lincoln's Inn and was now working with Mr Fooks, the Dartford solicitor. We know this much about the younger Charles's early career from an extraordinary court case brought to contest the will of Miss Anne Colyer of Farningham House in 1847.[99]

Miss Anne Colyer

This story has been told already in the F&EHS paper No 9, so only needs a brief description. Anne and her brother James were the children of James Colyer and Elizabeth Pratt. Both were unmarried and lived in separate halves of their mother's house in Farningham High Street, now called Farningham House. James died intestate in 1839 and Anne as next of kin inherited his estate. She herself died in 1846 leaving two wills which were contested by three interested parties. An Enquiry was held in Farningham parish church on 25th March 1847, later adjourning to the Lion Inn where it lasted several days. First to be heard were the Colyers of Farningham Mill, Charles, James and Thomas who had the claim of next of kin but it appeared that Anne had never liked them and they were not mentioned in either will.

Her first will left her property to the children of her second cousin, Thomas Colyer of Joyce Hall, Southfleet; Edward, Elizabeth and Henry Colyer, who claimed that her brother James had always intended them to be his heirs. The second will included her new friends at Farningham vicarage, the curate Andrew Burnside, his brother Francis and the vicar's sons Charles and Thomas Winston and their friend the solicitor John Pocock.

Charles, James and Thomas who, having been born there, were described as 'of the Mill', claimed that John Pocock had been a complete stranger to Miss Colyer in 1839, when he had become her solicitor 'despite the better qualification of her own cousin Charles Colyer Junior', and that the young men at the vicarage had an undue influence over the lady, borrowing money and drinking all her brother's wines. The Southfleet Colyers claimed that since her brother's death Miss Anne had become mean and stingy but dressed in gay attire, and also implied that she encouraged riotous parties at the vicarage. Burnside, Pocock and Winston in turn claimed that, far from being a stranger, young Charles Colyer had in fact been articled to John Pocock. They

99-H&W.Harding op.cit.
F&ELHS No.9

216

added that Miss Colyer always dressed in black silk and was most generous to all charities, also that she was lonely and neglected by her family.

Fortunately for many charities, including the poor of Farningham, the second will was the one to be proved. The Colyers of Farningham Mill lost their case. But at least we know from the evidence that Charles Colyer junior started his career articled to John Pocock at Lincloln's Inn in the early 1830s. We also know from one of Miss Colyer's codicils that Thomas Winston owed her £5000, so some of the evidence was well founded.

It was a lot of possibly unnecessary litigation and one is left wondering whether perhaps this generation of Colyers of Farningham Mill were rather a touchy lot of people. For all Charles's undoubted benevolence, the few letters that survive from him and Miss Gawan do not indicate much charm. Solomon, the youngest of the Cox family at Charton and a solicitor living in London, kept notes of an exchange of letters with Miss Gawan in 1834. It appeared that Miss Gawan had been to visit Solomon's former guardian Thomas Fuller's widow, in Suffolk and brought back an ear trumpet belonging to the Coxes which she had delivered on Mrs Fuller's behalf to Charton Manor. Solomon thought this a good moment to ask her about a picture of a hare which had also belonged to his family and which he thought Mrs Fuller might now be persuaded to give him, also some missing family papers. He says ingratiatingly 'It is not as good a picture as Mr Colyer's beautiful Trout, but how would Mr Colyer like to see his Trout go out of the family ?'.

He added that 'being of an Antiquarian turn of mind I have sought every Relic of my family and should Mr Colyer favour me with a visit I should be happy to show him my researches connected in part with his own family'. The Coxes and Colyers had intermarried twice in a previous generation and so were cousins.

The Trout and the Hare

'Mr Colyer's Beautiful Trout' was an oil painting of a record 9lb. 2oz. fish that had been caught in the Darent. The same fish was also commemorated by a life sized replica made into a weather vane that still stands above the Mill House stables. Miss Gawan wrote back very tersely to say she had never seen a picture of a horse at Mrs Fullers nor has the lady any papers, and her brother regrets his time in London is too fully occupied with business, nor has he any knowledge of our family pedigrees. She ends 'your humble servant Mrs Gawan' and adds a PS telling him 'you will be kind enough to inform your brother Mr Henry Cox that you have the Ear Trumpet as Mrs Fuller wished HIM to have it'. Poor Solomon, who had an orphan's longing for family solidarity, added a disconsolate note to this collected correspondence saying 'she read my letter wrong I spoke of a Hare and the Ear Trumpet belonged to my grandmother's sister'. It is shocking and saddening to read in the will of Arthur Colyer, Charles's grandson who died in 1920, that he left his paintings of a Trout and a HARE to his son Ernest.

There is an archive of letters and diaries written by the Cox brothers kept

Salmon Trout
9lb.2ozs.caught
in the mill stream
1808.

The painting is now in the possession of Nigel Snelling Colyer who kindly provided this photograph.

for posterity by their great-great-nephew Malcolm Goldsworthy of Charton Farm. Solomon's elder brother Henry kept a 'Journal of Natural Appearances' at Charton Manor from 1808 to 1817 which lists such things as the dates of sowing and reaping, the first frosts and the first swallows. Another series of letters kept by Solomon Cox told the story of his young cousin John Colyer who went out to Australia in 1827. John was the elder son of John Colyer of Farningham and, according to Solomon, had been 'brought up as a surgeon but through neglect of his father and his own inattention, not being able to pass at the College of Surgeons, was fitted out by his father in a very ordinary manner to emigrate to Sidney, New South Wales'.[100]

The Australian Colyers

John embarked on the convict ship Florentia in 1829. (Three years too early to accompany the unfortunate Kentish labourers of the Captain Swing Revolt). An arrangement had been made with the captain that he should act as assistant surgeon with no wages but 'his passage and victuals'. Solomon kept some fascinating letters from this 'Surgeon's Mate' describing the voyage, during which he messed with the carpenter and the boatswain in a canvased space 7ft. by 4ft., living mainly on 'petrous biscuits and a pint of rum'. John's father died in Brussells in 1829 and it took some years of impoverished struggle before the young John received a small legacy of £50, collected by the Colyer and Cox families in Farningham, who also clubbed together to buy him a 'Most Superb Medicine Chest fitted up for Eastern Climates'. An extra £5 each from Charles and William Hardyman Colyer and Mrs Fuller enabled the addition of a small case of surgical implements.

In 1836 John was able to write happily from his new home 'Colyer's Lea' thanking his benefactors for making his marriage possible to a naval surgeon's daughter 'untainted by our convict population. God bless you for ever my excellent and dear cousins'. One of John's letters to his cousins asks to be remembered to 'Your Fire Side Circle', and this charming expression evokes the cosy narrowness of village life. By using a combination of the 1841 census, the 1840 Tithe Map and the notes made by Andrew Burnside on his parishioners in 1838 it is possible to visualise some of these households in the year 1840.

100-Cox family papers, owner Mr Malcolm Goldsworthy

Chapter Thirteen

The 1841 Census / Dissent / The Roper Charity House / The Farms /
Farningham Races / The Fair / Dickens / William Moore, Miller /
The Wesleyan Chapel / Charles Winston, Glasspainter / The Railway /
William Dray's Ironfoundry / The Market / The New Waterwheels /
Farningham Flower Show / Public Health / Marianne Farningham.

The 1841 Census

The 1841 census, the first of its kind, gives the name, age, address and occupation of each person, at each house at home at midnight on Census Sunday. Forms had been previously delivered by employees of the Registrar and were collected by Enumerators on the day itself. Farningham had 121 houses and two Enumerators, one for the east and one for the west side of the river. It must have been a difficult task when many people were surely resentful of this invasion of their privacy, and many people would need help with the forms.

In the Mill House on the 7th of June, Enumeration Day, were Charles and his sisters-in law, perhaps in the fine drawing room with the soldier chimneypieces. In their kitchen were two young maids, Rachel and Emma. Ann Pring, now aged 80, was living in the gardener's cottage and was described by the curate Mr Burnside as an annuitant who would come to church 'whenever gout permits'. We can well imagine that the annuity was a pension from Charles, and we can see from the census that Mrs Pring was able to afford her own maidservant to look after her. Burnside described Charles and his sisters-in-law as 'good church people'.

The next mill cottage was occupied by Michael Deane and his wife, both in their sixties and retired from their labours as constable and poorhouse keeper, and no doubt also on Charles's benevolent free rent list. The other occupants of the mill cottages were Mrs Phillips, widow of a mill worker with five children, 'dissenters' according to Mr Burnside, and a seventy year old widower, Mr Wingate. Evidently nobody was ever turned out of their home. The only active mill cottage inhabitant appears to have been William Longley, described as a 40 year old miller with a wife and three children.

The Manor House was owned by Thomas Waring and inhabited by his senior farm teamsman Stephen Baker, and his wife, probably as caretakers. The Parsonage house was occupied by a wheelwright, James Petman, his mother, wife and children and two young lodgers, the Holland brothers, described as coachmaker and guard. These were the two entrepreneurs who advertised in 1841 'The Farningham Coach will commence running from the Bull Inn...every day, Sundays excepted, at half past seven in the morning, leaves Footscray 8 o'clock and arrives in the Borough at half past nine, Charing Cross

Cross at 10, and will leave the British Hotel, Cockspur at half past three and the Catherine Wheel, Borough, at 4 o'clock in the afternoon'. The coaches were called The Vivid and The Wonder.

We already know about the vicarage circle. The vicar, Benjamin Winston, was for once in residence on the day of census, as were the curate Andrew Burnside and his brother Francis, their friend John Pocock and three servants. We can imagine them sitting by the fire, enjoying a glass of James Colyer's wine. They were resting after a most satisfactory restoration of the church, during which the turret had been raised by 14 feet and battlments added to the tower. A new organ costing 160 guineas had been installed by public subscription, and two fine new windows which had been donated by Miss Colyer in memory of her brother James.[101]

James Phillips, a young farmer who leased land from both Charles Colyer and Thomas Waring, lived in what is now the Bakery with his wife and family. Miss Susanna Peterson, 'Dissenter, sometimes at church', lived next door in Hodsoll House although it was not yet called that nor was she at home on census day. Her 15 year old nephew and niece Richard and Susanna Baker were in residence with a maidservant. Miss Susanna was the daughter of Silk Norman, an earlier prominent well-to-do villager, but why she was called Peterson is a mystery. Silk and his daughters have fine tombs on the left of the path leading to the church west door. Miss Peterson's next door neighbour in Farningham House was that other elderly single lady, Miss Ann Colyer who had four servants to look after her.

Martha Stockley, painter and decorator, a widow aged 65, lived in the house that was until recently Farningham Pine shop with a large family who followed her in the trade. Her great grandson would be the artist known as 'Bus-Driver Stockley'. Mr Burnside noted that she was irregular at church, but that her son John was not only regular but useful in Sunday School. He also 'sang in the gallery'.[102] Charles Everest age 50, still described as schoolmaster, was next door with some of his extensive family. Both Stockleys and Everests were Charles Colyer's tenants.

In the other row of cottages opposite the Bull were a horsekeeper, a hostler, a hairdresser, a cabinet maker and Joseph Hearn, a shoemaker aged 25 with his wife and two apprentices and three children including six year old Mary Ann who later became the poet Marianne Farningham. Some of the fireside circles in these tiny cottages must have been very crowded. Next door to the Hearns lived Rebecca Rogers and her family, widow of the Baptist minister. All these cottages were a hotbed of dissent according to Mr Burnside, but Robert Hayles, the blacksmith in the forge next door and his family of six made up for their neighbours by being 'very regular churchgoers'.

A new surgeon, Frederick Hunt aged 35, whose wife and daughters were away from home that day, lived in what is now Pinehurst with another surgeon, 25 year old Henry Harris, also four maidservants, a manservant and an

101-CKS P145, Vestry Books
102-Andrew Burnside, notebooks, CKS P145/1/8

221

elderly labourer who perhaps drove the doctors on calls. Dr George Edwards, the senior doctor in the village, had moved into the Croft opposite with his wife, two daughters and two maidservants. Another new surgeon Dr Edward Ryan and his assistant William Frowke, both from Ireland, were James Colyer's tenants in the White House. Farningham was always well supplied with doctors.

William Wells junior, now 40, with wife and three children and sundry post boys and ostlers , was still James Colyer's tenant inkeeper at the Lion. Henry Gregory, baker, another dissenter and 'a great humbug' in Mr Burnside's opinion, was a Colyer tenant in what is now Cherry Tree Cottage with his wife Mary and large family.

As they are today, Pinehurst above and The Croft left, were both occupied by doctors in the 1841 census.

Another baker, Thomas Turner, also a dissenter, lived higher up in London Road with a family of six. Francis Martin, the only village butcher, lived in the present day butcher's shop with a wife and three children, 'regular churchgoers'.

John Gandy was the saddler in Saddler's House with a family of wife and ten children and two elderly ladies of independent means who lodged with them.

One of the earliest photographs of Farningham High Street, somewhat later however than the 1841 census. To the right is Waller's shop previously Attwoods. To the extreme left is the Cottage, the 19th century facade behind railings. Centre, Saddler's House and the Chequers.

All 'good church people' and another large fireside circle. There were two more blacksmiths in the High Street. William Gibson, a dissenter with a large family, and Henry Mandy who was possibly a son of George Mandy of the Bull. Joseph Beckley, age 40, another dissenter, who was the assistant registrar of births and deaths, lived in what is now called the Cottage with his wife Phyllis who kept a girl's boarding school.

Jacob Hankins, a watchmaker with a wife and 'a Little Tick of his own' as Mr Burnside indulgently observed, lived in the cottage next door to Thomas Dray, a carrier who ran a weekly service to London. Probably these two worked from the shop and yard which became 'Wakeley's'. Until recently there was an oblong hole in Wakeley's ceiling which, by tradition, had accommodated the watchmaker's high case grandfather clock. Dray's son William was living in London, but would soon come back to live in Mount Pleasant, Sparepenny Lane where he would set up his factory for agricultural machinery.

William Attwood, another dissenter with a young family, was the village grocer and draper running his business from the house later to be Waller's shop, next door to Wakeley's. The Attwoods had three young assistants, a nurse and a maid. Abraham Bevins was the elderly publican at the Chequers opposite, with his daughter, a maid and two lodgers; and Samuel Wallis, aged 45, 'professes himself a churchman', had replaced the Sharps as innkeeper at the Bricklayers' Arms with an expanding family who would continue to run the pub for the next fifty years.

Fernwood House, recently acquired by Charles Colyer, was occupied by one

South Hall as it is today.

of his millers, Charles Payne and family, 'church people'. Several other men giving their occupation as millers were scattered around the parish and may have worked for Charles or for George Whiting at Chimham's windmill. Charles also owned South Hall, then known as Cold Hall, where Mr and Mrs Nash had lived in increasing frailty until 1840 and where Mrs Fellows, widow of the Eynsford miller, now appeared as tenant. Another on Charles's large list of poor widows.

The Sharwoods, a big family mainly occupied as carpenters, lived in London Road. Thomas Sharwood aged 30, one of Charles Everest's star pupils, kept his own small school and was a regular churchgoer approved by Mr Burnside, as were the next door family of stonemasons, the Woolleys, newcomers to the village who would stay for several generations. Burnside later made a note that the Woolley boys who were dabbling with Dissent 'might well be reclaimed'.

Dissent

It is not surprising that Mr Burnside kept such careful notes on his parishioners, he was losing so many to Dissent or apathy. There are many notes such as 'Irregular, Seldom, Occasional, Sometimes and Never'. Dissent in Farningham in 1840 was most likely to mean membership of the Eynsford Baptist church, and it is interesting to see that so many dissenters were 'principal inhabitants' of the village such as tradesmen and craftsmen. 'Scratch a cordwainer (a shoemaker) and you find a dissenter' was a popular saying. They were still only a small proportion of village society, but growing each year.

In his study *The Pattern of Rural Dissent* Alan Everitt says that at the height of their power in the mid-nineteenth century, dissenters probably comprised nearly half the churchgoing population of England. He observes that many of the parishes where dissent found a stronghold were often former medieval market towns where an annual fair was still held such as Farningham, which also enjoyed the ease of communication with the outside world of a village situated at the crossroads of two turnpike roads.

To return to the village census of 1841. James Sharp, described as bricklayer but who was also the Parish Clerk, now aged 55 and no longer publican of the Bricklayer's Arms, was one of Thomas Colyer's tenants in Dartford Road with a wife and six children. The large Flewin family, some of whose descendants live in the village today, also lived in the Dartford Road. The Samuel Shuters, 'dissenters, a wild lot', lived next to the Flewins and the last house in the village was the old poorhouse, occupied by four elderly pensioners.

The 1834 Poor Law Amendment Act had established Boards of Guardians to administrate the Poor Laws and to amalgamate parishes into Unions. Vestry relief was more or less abolished and paupers were herded into the great Union Workhouses. Not only were they exiled from their own villages but men and women and children were segregated. 'It is a prison, with a milder name, which few inhabit without dread or shame' said the poet Crabbe. In fact one Assistant Commissioner is recorded as saying cheerfully 'Our intention is to make the Workhouses as like prisons as possible...as to make them a terror to the poor and prevent them from entering'.

Mercifully for Farningham, money from the Roper Charity had been used to build the village Workhouse in 1810. The Charity estate, prudently invested in houses and land in Greenwich, had been saved from oblivion by the vicar, Benjamin Sandford, who went to great pains to discover the uses that the income could be put to, among them the education and apprenticeship of poor children. In 1836 he anticipated the Board of Guardian's attempt to take over the Workhouse by laying claim to it in the name of Roper's Charity. He said that the charity had paid for the building and if the Guardians wanted it they should pay rent, and if not then it should be let out as cottages to poor people.[103]

The Roper Charity House

On 27th June 1836, in the presence of the Guardian of the Poor for the parish, who was a non-resident, John Pawley formerly of Sparepenny Lane, and the members of the Vestry, vicar Sandford now to be known as Winston, took formal possession of the building and from that date it became a sort of almshouse where deserving poor people could live at low rents. Thanks to

this move and to Charles Colyer's benevolence to his tenants, a number of poor people were saved from the Dartford Union workhouse. 'Farningham Roper's Charity' is still inscribed above the door of the former workhouse.

William Hardyman Colyer, 'Uncle Willy' of the Napoleonic wars, was another benevolent figure in the village. He never married and lived alone in the Mount with a housekeeper and two maids and appears to have been something of a recluse like his brother. He remained a devout member of the Eynsford Baptist Church, and when he died in 1844 he left many bequests to charities and 'a guinea to each of the poor people who dined with me last Christmas'. It is always very difficult to visualise this gentle man as a soldier. There is no indication of a martial past in his will which had been made in Bath, where he apparently often went to take the cure. The Baptist archives have a copy of a charming Ode he once wrote to a member of the congregation 'On hearing a dear Christian friend say "I wish you would mend my Bible for me", which continued 'As if your Bible needed aught to mend or make it better'.[104]

It would be very interesting to know the nature of the 'business in London' which Miss Gawan claimed was occupying Charles at this time. In Miss Anne Colyer's second will of 1842, Charles is described as 'the owner of Farningham Mill but not carrying on the business'. So was the milling now left to his tenant miller William Longley? Charles may have been very involved with his son's family and career. The younger Charles was only twenty three when he married and his wife Mary Anne was nineteen so they probably needed some family support. The first nine of their thirteen children were born in Dartford before they moved to Greenwich in 1855.

By the 1840s the elder Charles appears to have been living the life of a gentleman of leisure. It is most likely that he was following the trend among landowners of the time to speculate in the new railways and other property developments, such as quarrying and brickfields along the Thames where we

104–Property of Mrs Glover of Farningham

know he later owned property. It is possible of course that he had simply become more reclusive and that Miss Gawan had been protecting his privacy. Although he owned land he does not appear to have been actively engaged in farming. He kept some parcels of land in his own name, but most of his Farningham properties were leased to other farmers. James Bellingham and his son Henry were his tenant farmers at Beesfield, and Robert Gibbs, a young farmer who lived in Mount Pleasant, tenanted the Eglantine farm.

The Farms

Other outlying farmers in 1841 were William Crockford, the Pawleys' tenant in Hampton Court. William Waring at White Hill who farmed the Manor estate for his father. Henry Reeves who was Sir Percy Hart Dyke's tenant at Pedham Place. William Smith, aged 30, was the extensive farmer at Chimhams. The Smiths employed seven young men as 'male servants', which indicates that some unmarried men were still known as 'servants in husbandry' and lived in the farmhouse, although it was increasingly the custom for large farms to keep messrooms where unmarried labourers could cater for themselves to avoid unnecessary hob-nobbing with the family. Married farm workers appear on the census as 'agricultural labourers'.

Button Street had a large community of agricultural labourers probably employed by the Hart Dykes or the Warings, or the market gardener John Bath, who owned land and cottages at Mountain Hill in what is now Swanley. The origin of the name Button Street has been lost, possibly the Swanley Village records hold the key. In the eighteenth century it had been called the Old Lane. It included Nightingale Place which had its own beershop, later called the second Hop Pole Inn, run by the Dunmall family who had at least twenty members, although surely not all in the same cottage. The fireside circles in Button Street must have been extremely crowded and hungry, and no doubt the grates were often empty.

Button Street poverty had always been a problem to the Vestry. In 1827 a terrible fire in the farm cottages, possibly connected to the general incendiarism of the time, had led to such generous donations from the village for the sufferers that the vicar Mr Sandford made his famous speech of thanks 'Well done Farningham! Farningham for ever! Huzza!'

An elderly Button Street lady of the 1980s remembered that when she was a child in the 1920s her mother, widow of an agricultural labourer, cooked the entire family dinner in one pot over the fire. This consisted of scraps of meat and vegetable and pudding, all boiled in the same bag. Probably things were much the same in 1841, so long as a fire could be afforded. Button Street was fortunate in its proximity to Farningham Woods which were surrounded by hedgerows and orchards and overrun with rabbits, descendants of the ancient 'coney warren' at Pedham Place. Despite the punitive Game Laws, poaching never ceased to exist, and there are no gamekeepers listed in the 1841 census, although by 1851 William Waring employed William Ashenden as his gamekeeper at Farningham Hill.

Another illicit activity in the 19th century was smuggling, and for many years Calfstock Lane was known as 'Smuggler's Lane'. Edward Cresy of Horton Kirby remembered bands of fifty to sixty horsemen, on their way to London from the coast, 'loaded with packages of all kinds of contraband articles; and frequently, under a maple stub or pollard oak, a keg of Hollands or a parcel of tobacco or tea was left by the smugglers and found its way into my grandfather's house'.[105] It was rumoured that 'Old Killick' the charcoal burner, situated in the middle of the woods, 'died very rich'.

Farningham Races

The first Hop Pole Inn, on the turnpike road at what is now the Swanley interchange roundabout, was the scene of the famous Farningham Races. Horse racing was a fashionable pursuit and the enterprising young innkeeper, William Shenton, who was a tenant of sporting Sir Percy Hart Dyke, started the race meetings in 1835. They continued for ten years until a mixture of corrupt practices, the decline of the turnpike roads and the developing railways brought them to an end.

Thomas Waring gave one of the first silver cups for local farmers on non-thoroughbred horses and no doubt the whole enterprise was an expression of solidarity among local farmers after the troubles of the early 1830s. By the 1840s the races had become

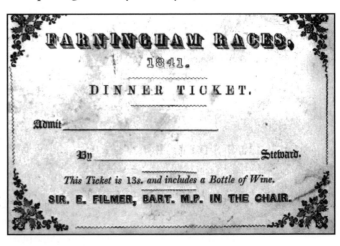

FARNINGHAM RACES,
1841.
DINNER TICKET.
Admit
By   Steward.
This Ticket is 13s. and includes a Bottle of Wine.
SIR. E. FILMER, BART. M.P. IN THE CHAIR.

an upmarket day out for the carriage trade of West Kent, with the Woolwich and Maidstone garrisons competing for 'Military Sweepstakes for officers of the Army on Full Pay'.[106]

A Steeplechase was also held along the Darent valley from Farningham to

105–Edward Cresy, op.cit.
106–H.Harding, Farningham Races, E&ELHS No.

228

Dartford. The local newspaper of Saturday April 16th 1835 reported a record turnout to watch this exciting local event. The line marked off in the valley crossed the river several times and contained about 40 jumps. 'The famous Jim Mason won on Parasol, clearing the 18 foot wide Franks Lane and beating the Marquis of Waterford who fell at Horton Church'.

The Fair

Farningham Fair on Market Meadow. at an unknown later date.

Another great day out for surrounding villages was the annual fair which was held on the 15th October and was now mainly a horse and cattle fair, but had many of the fairground attractions described by Dickens in Greenwich Fair.[107] Wombwell's Wild Animal Menagerie were regular visitors and there were stalls of gilt gingerbread and penny toys, freak shows, brass bands, fast food such as pickled salmon, oysters and whelks, and a huge turnout of coaches, omnibuses, gigs and donkey chaises.

Wombwell's Menagerie travelled all over Britain. The Revd. Kilvert's Diary for 1872 noted them coming from Brecon Fair with an elephant which was advertised to ride on a bicycle. He reported that 'the elephant, a very small one, and three camels or dromedaries, came splashing along the muddy road in heavy rain looking cold and miserable....At six o'clock the wild beasts were ready, and we all went to the show. There was a fair lion and a decent wolf...but the show was small and mean and no bicycle was forthcoming'.[108]

Dickens

Charles Dickens came to Farningham for one of the Good Friday fishing meetings at the Lion Inn and described the visit for his weekly journal, Household Words. This article was not published until after his death in 1870, but in all particulars the event had doubtless been the same for many years.[109] He must have known the village well in the past because he describes the Lion as 'transformed from a little wayside inn to a red brick hotel', which was

107-Charles Dickens, *Sketches bt Boz*
108-*Kilvert's Diary 1870-1879* (1977 ed.)
109-Charles Dickens, *Household Words*

crowded with visitors 'enjoying Mr Wells's hospitality with salmon and soles, home cured ham and new laid eggs, mutton chops and kidneys in relays, flanked as it were by huge joints of cold meat and great edifices of pie crust'. And that was only breakfast. The fishing was a serious business with special flies such as March Browns, Blue Duns, Red Spinners and Alexandras, and was for trout alone. The most prized, and forbidden, 'tit-bit' of water was between the mill and the bridge where 'trout of all sizes from two ounces to three or four pounders may be counted, not by scores but by hundreds'.

William Wells junior had retired in 1843 and put a notice in the Maidstone Journal, as 'the proprietor', of an extensive sale of the contents 'of that long well known established Inn and Post House, The Lion Inn, Farningham, which will be discontinued...in consequence of the extension of the main line of the South Eastern Railroad'.

James Colyer, the owner of the Lion, who was now living in London, was outraged by this liberty and wrote to the same

Charles Dickens circa 1860. Cedric Dickens and his family, Charles' great great grandson lived in Farningham for many years until the late 1980s.

231

paper to say that he, 'as the Sole Proprietor and Freeholder of this old established Inn… finding that his Tenant William Wells had announced that the Inn might be discontinued, he, Mr Colyer, felt himself called upon to make known to the Nobility and Gentry that the House will be resumed with increasing respectability and attention to comfort…'[110]

William Wells countered with a notice 'to offer to the Nobility and Gentry and Public in general of the County of Kent his unfeigned gratitude for the liberal and kind support which has been extended to himself and his late father for a period of nearly fifty years'. No doubt it was all good publicity for the inn.

Other sporting events included the fox hunt and, for a while in the 1840s, the MOH was Mr Tom Colyer of Southfleet. An apocryphal family story says that Tom, who had a fiery temper, once said 'hang the hounds' to his kennel-man who went out and did just that. The Victoria County History says that it was Mr Tom who disappeared mysteriously in 1856, not the hounds which were sold. This may have been the hunt which ran a fox to ground in the vicarage garden, to the indignation of the vicar's wife who was hanging out her washing. The fox was later presumed to have died of fright in the thatched roof of the old schoolhouse where its skeleton was found many years later.

In 1842 Ann Pring died, aged 80. Family history says that she died by falling in the fire. Also that 'she would have it her name was Pringle, not Pring'. Her name is Pring on the good tombstone that Charles put up in her memory next to his father's and his own family stones. 'In Memory of Ann Pring of Aylesbury, Bucks…In Life Valued and Esteemed by the family of Henry Colyer during a long period of service in their House'. Either the stonemason slipped up or weather has worn the stone so that it reads 1812, not 1842. The loss of another link with the past came with the death of Charles's brother William Hardyman Colyer in 1845. He was buried in the churchyard next to his father and Ann Pring.

Some time during the 1840s Charles must have decided to hand over all

110–Gordon Edwards, cuttings collection, pers.comm.

responsibility for the mill to a reliable miller. He would be 60 in 1845 and, as we have seen, was engaged in 'other business'. Perhaps through milling journals, or maybe by word of mouth among the milling fraternity, he contacted a Norfolk miller, William Moore, who was to be the miller of Farningham for the next fifty years.

William Moore, Miller

William Moore was in many ways a surprising choice. He was not from Kent, nor was he of the same faith as Charles who was, according to the vicar's church books and the evidence of his own library, a devout Anglican church-goer. Nor was William a Baptist like Charles's brother William. He was a most fervent Methodist, a preacher himself, who was to build a Wesleyan chapel in Farningham shortly after his arrival here.

William Moore was born in 1819, so he was two years younger than the junior Charles Colyer. He was the son of Robert Moore of Martham, Norfolk, a wherryman on the Broads, and had been apprenticed to a miller, Robert Ferrier of Great Ormsby in 1836. The Moores were Methodists and Robert Moore gave the land for Flegborough Wesleyan chapel in 1841.[111]

William Moore's corn sack stencil

Young William Moore met a draper from Swaffham called William Beswick, surprisingly for a later teetotal the meeting was in an alehouse, and was so impressed by the older man's piety he swore that if Mr Beswick had a daughter he would marry her. The Beswicks had three daughters and in 1845, apparently to the young lady's own amazement, William married their very plain eldest daughter Mary in the Wesleyan chapel in Swaffham.

In 1846 the young Moores moved to Farningham and next year William Beswick and his wife Rebecca retired and came to join them. In the 1851 census the Beswicks and Moores were living together in Charles Colyer's property, Fernwood House in the High Street, with the Moore's young son and daughter who both died in infancy. Three more daughters, Alice, Harriet and Ellen were born between 1851 and 1858.

The Wesleyan Chapel

William Moore became a highly respected member of the village community, as renowned for his straight dealing and philanthropy as Charles Colyer himself. He built the little Wesleyan chapel in London Road at his own expense in 1850 on land he appears to have bought from the Pawley family. Sadly it is now demolished. In just one year the 1851 Census of Religious Worship noted that this Farningham Wesleyan Methodist Chapel had a total of 135 'sittings' with standing room for 25 and was able to report an average atten-

90-PRO Prob 11/1526, proved Oct. 1811

dance since the opening on October 28th 1850 of 70 worshippers in the

afternoon and 80 in the evening. Attendance on census day, the 30th March was 41 in the afternoon and 49 in the evening.

Outside the Wesleyan Chapel.
William Moore, far left. Rosa Marchant, centre left foreground.
Mrs Len Waller with baby, centre.

By contrast Mr Burnside reported in the same census an average attendance at his church of 240 in the morning and 200 in the evening. The actual attendance on census day the 30th March was 242 in the morning and 163 in the evening. In Eynsford, St Martins had an attendance of 150 in the morning that day and 180 in the afternoon. The Eynsford Baptist Chapel had very large congregations with 190 that morning, 160 in the afternoon and 110 in the evening.

William was a zealous old-fashioned Methodist and a strict Sabbatarian. Every Sunday after chapel he carved a huge joint at his table and had the first cuts put in a bowl to be delivered by servants to the homes of the poor. He and his family lived in Fernwood until Charles's death in 1870, after which they moved into the Mill House. Much of the information about William Moore comes from his great grandson, the former Bishop of Taunton, Francis Horner West, who kindly lent family papers after seeing the mill on the cover of Country Life on July 15th 1976.

William Moore appears to have leased the mill from 1847 or 1848. Charles Colyer is still described as 'Miller and Farmer' in Bagshaw's Directory of 1847, but by 1850 he is only entered under the heading 'Gentry' as 'Charles Colyer Esq.', and William Moore appears under 'Traders' as 'Miller and Farmer'. The 1851 census shows him as an active farmer, having leased the Eglantine estate from Charles, and is described as 'Miller and Farmer of 60 acres employing 2

91–Eynsford Baptist Church, 1806–1906, historical booklet (1906) two labourers'.

The late 1840s saw the arrival of a new medical practitioner by the unfortunate name of Dr Slaughter who was to stay in the village for at least three decades and who was followed into the profession by three of his sons. The Slaughters moved into Pinehurst, next door to Dr Hunt who was now living at Hillside. Benjamin Winston at last resigned from ill health and Andrew Burnside took over as vicar in 1848. Winston continued to write cheerful letters about his new life in Wales and in fact outlived his successor. Mr Burnside had recently married Mary Rashleigh of Harrietsham, presumably from the same family as George Rashleigh, vicar of Horton Kirby whose two sons, Charles and William, would live in Farningham in the 1860s and 70s.

Charles Winston, Glasspainter

Benjamin Winston's son Charles became one of the few Farningham people with an entry in the Dictionary of National Biography. Apart from a successful legal practice he was famous for his knowledge of, and skill in painting, church stained glass. Some of his early glass paintings are in Farningham church, one is the little copy of a medieval bishop and the other is of his family coat of arms and includes another bishop, said to be Thomas a Becket, based on a window in Meopham church. He died in 1864 and his widow presented his drawings to the British Museum. A number of his designs are in C.R.Councer's *Lost Glass from Kent Churches*.[112] As one of Miss Anne Colyer's protégées perhaps we have his influence to thank for the copy of medieval stained glass in the East window of Farningham church which she donated in memory of her brother James in 1843.

It is a little confusing to find several other Colyers in Farningham in the second half of the 19th century. Two Richard Colyers, a father and son, were agricultural labourers living and working at Chimhams and Maplescome farms. Both had been born at Kingsdown. There was also William Colyer, saddler and harness maker who had been born in Rochester. Both these families had children with the traditional Colyer names of Charles, Henry, Thomas, Charlotte and Mary, and even the new names of Charles's grandchildren, Ernest and Arthur but it has not been possible to find any family connections with the Colyers of the mill and to have to make the necessary adjustments to the Family Tree.

A newcomer to the village in the 1850s was William Hodsoll, surveyor, auctioneer and land agent. He was a member of the ancient Hodsoll family of Ash, and his own family were to stay in the village for many decades. They lived in Miss Peterson's house which would now become known as Hodsoll House, and both he and his son were land agents to the Colyer family. The Hodsolls and Rashleighs were great cricketers, early members of the Farningham club which was established in 1859 and still plays today on the same pitch in the George Meadow.

112-C.R.Councer, Lost Glass from Kent Churches, KAS Vol.XXII (1980)

The Railway

The Age of the Railways was accelerating fast and by the 1861 census several former agricultural labourers give their occupation as railway employees. Railway labourers from all over England were lodged with various families. Farningham Road Station opened in 1860, and the Swanley to Sevenoaks branch was cut across the Hop Pole race track in 1862. Wellington, who did not die until 1852, used the railway reluctantly to commute from London to Walmer Castle. 'England did not require Rail Roads' he said, 'the English failure to obey orders and show discipline is a defect in the National Character and leads to Rail Road accidents'.

The Duke of Wellington's special carriage.
No wonder he wasn't so keen to travel by rail!

Several proposals for Darent Valley railroads had been made during the 1850s [113] They would all have been very favourable to Farningham Mill and were supported by Messrs Colyer and Moore but were stifled by other landowners. The Farmer's Monthly Visitor pointed out the advantages to the mills along the Darent to have sidings to facilitate the transport of corn and added that 'the capitalist will benefit by the erection of villas at good rentals'. It was envisaged that Farningham would become an important market town, a central depot for the purchase of agricultural produce and machinery and also 'a suburb of the metropolis...studded with villa residences'.

A leading proponent of the Darent Valley Railway scheme was William Dray the ironfounder who by 1855 had set up his factory, the Darent Vale Ironworks, in Sparepenny Lane where he now lived in the Pawleys old house Mount Pleasant. The Farmer's Visitor was published by his company, Deane, Dray and Deane, London Ironfounders. The factory appears to have survived for two decades, but William Dray's fortunes fluctuated. It seems likely that he lost much of his capital in railway speculation, and the failure of the Darent Railway may have hit him hard. The factory appears to have gone out of business by 1880.

93-F.A.Crisp
Visitation of England and Wales
Vol.4 (1896)
94-Eliza Edmonds,
Notebooks, F&EHSoc.

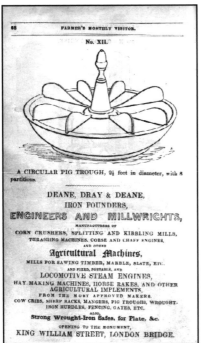

Pages from
'The Farmer's Visitor
and Fires-side
Companion' for 1848,
published by Deane,
Dray and Deane.

William Dray's Ironfoundry

There is a nice description in *The Visitor* for 1848 of a Good Friday day out in Farningham for the London employees of Dray's firm 'who arrive here in the... vehicles so well known in the metropolis and its suburbs...and the good people of the village are enlivened by the merry faces of the denizens of the shops and forges and manufactories of Deane, Dray and Deane'. The day was spent in athletic games and ended with a dinner at the Black Lion, with Mr Dray presiding, where many toasts were drunk and songs sung before the party broke up in time to reel home to London.

The story of Mr Dray and his ironfoundry has been told in *F&E.H.S.paper No29. by Dr W. Duncombe* It represents a very local aspect of the Agricultural Revolution that had been taking place all over England. The years after the repeal of the Corn Laws in 1846 were known by some as the golden age of agriculture, also as the age of 'high farming'. The result of free trade in corn was healthy at first for millers and farmers. The results of high farming with its emphasis on machinery and steam power meant of course the gradual 'flight from the land' of agricultural labourers and the slow death of a thousand year old tradition of rural life. Progressive farmers who flocked to the Great Exhibition of 1850, and all the other fashionable exhibitions of the new agriculture, had a great appetite for Mr Dray's innovative machinery. New methods of stock breeding and feeding, soil management, drainage and fertilizers were discussed in the pages of *The Farmer's Visitor* and at meetings of the Darenth Vale Agricultural Association.

F&ELHS pub.29.
*William Dray of Farningham,
Ironfounder and farmer*
by W.A.Duncombe and
H.Harding

The Market

The revived interest in stock led to a monthly stock market in Farningham, held on every third Wednesday. The market continued for several decades until late in the depression of the 1870s. A weekly corn market was also held for a while at the Lion Inn. There were not only advances in agricultural methods, but milling too was seeing a great change. Steam milling had come in the early part of the century and many mills now flourished without water-ways. After the Industrial Revolution the word mill came to mean a mecha-nised factory. Smeaton and Rennie had both used iron and steam in the Albion and Deptford mills. Iron, the great Victorian building material, would revolutionise the waterwheels.

The New Waterwheels

Two French engineers, Poncelet and Fourneyron, now created new forms of waterwheel. Poncelet's wheels were vertical variations of the undershot and breastshot types, using cast iron and curved metal floats.[114] Fourneyron turned his wheel from vertical to horizontal to make a turbine. Indeed, the word turbine in French meant a horizontal mill. The French had never ceased experimenting with horizontal mills and now, after so many centuries domi-nated by the vertical wheel, the horizontal had come back to stay. Fourneyron patented his turbine in 1832 and by the 1840s they were in use all over Europe and America.

Lewis Mumford said that Fourneyron's turbine was the first prime mover to exceed the capacity of the early steam engines. The advantages of the turbine were its smaller size and smaller cost, less maintenance and the capacity to operate in very little water. A version eventually made its way to Farningham Mill, but as yet we do not know at what date it was first installed.

Milling had become a science and no doubt Charles Colyer and William Moore were aware of this and had read some of the works on the new tech-nology. The American millwright Oliver Evans' *The Young Millwright and Miller's Guide* went into its 15th edition in 1850 and many other works on milling were published by the engineers of the day. William Fairbairn who worked with Stephenson wrote an important *Treatise on Mills and Millwrights* which came out in 2 volumes in 1863. The great Victorian civil engineers were changing the look of England. Fairbairn was said to have built over a thousand bridges.

A crisis of pollution had caused the first cholera epidemic in 1832, and Edwin Chadwick's Report on the Sanitary Conditions of the Labouring Population of Great Britain led to the Public Health Act of 1848. 'What is necessary for a civilized way of life is a pure water supply, sewage and burial arrangements, and the inspection of food'. William Dray observed in 1848 that 'the cholera is slowly but surely wending its way back,...stalking from city to city of continental Europe'. He recommended the use of Dray and

114–Terry S.Reynolds, *Stronger than 100 Men* op.cit.

238

Deane's Air-Tight Cart to remove soil from tanks and cesspools. His prophesy was correct, next year more than 14,000 people died of cholera in London alone. Dr John Snow argued in 1848 that the cause of cholera was in the drinking water and effected the removal of the Broad Street pump, but it was twenty years and another epidemic before he was believed.

Sanitation in the villages was still very primitive. Mr Dray's instructions on the use of his machinery suggests that things had changed very little since Thomas Tusser's rhyming *Good Points of Husbandry* of 1557. His recommendation for November was 'Foul privies are now to be cleansed and fyr'd, Let night be appointed such baggage to hide, Which buried in garden in trenches a-low, Shall make very many things better to grow'. Outdoor ashpit privies were usual, some would be communal for the terraced houses. Larger houses had cesspools, but most liquid drainage went into the river in Farningham. 'Night-soil' collectors would empty cesspits and take the sewage to the fields. Although the water-closet with an overhead cistern and an S bend soil pipe and valve had been invented in the 1770s, many people saw their first version at the 1850 Great Exhibition, and Thomas Crapper's 'certain flush with every pull' mechanism did not appear until the 1860s.

As for the household water supply, although large houses had their own wells and some, such as Charton Manor, had an underfloor reservoir, the majority of people took their water from the river as they had always done. As recently as 1938 Mrs Walter Dunmall, aged 77, remembered her mother paying a penny for every bucket of water drawn from the Darent, but this was probably in a year of drought when the river was low and water was rationed. The mill and mill house presumably still used Henry Colyer's water pump of 1790 to draw water from the river for their household supplies.

Mr Dray was prominent in a lot of pleasurable village activities. The Kentish Agricultural Association had held local ploughing matches since the 1830s, with a dinner afterwards at the Hop Pole, and lately with exhibitions of Dray and Deane's machinery. There were prizes for ploughmen and shepherds and also categories such as 'The Oldest Labourer that has worked for the same family or farm for the greatest number of years', and 'The Labourer that has brought up the largest family and received no Parochial Relief'.

Farningham Flower Show

In 1853 the West Kent Poultry Association, of which William Dray was the treasurer, held its first Flower Show and Poultry Exhibition in Market Field, Farningham. There were prizes for greenhouse plants and fruits such as pineapples and grapes, and a class for cottager's entries of potatoes, parsnips and onions. The show continued for

four days from Tuesday the 14th June. The poultry exhibits included Buff and Cinnamon Cochin Chinas, Single and Rose Combed Dorkings, Spanish Hamburg and Poland fowls. There were ducks, geese, turkeys, game birds, and pigeons such as tumblers, carriers, dragons, beards, baldheads, jacobins and fantails. The best peacock and hen was won by William Dray, and his daughters won prizes for their flowers. Neither Charles Colyer nor William Moore appeared on any of the lists of committee members

or competitors. William probably dis-approved of such frivolity and Charles preferred to stay at home. Maybe he considered the gregarious Mr Dray a bit of a fly-by-night.

The show was such a success it was repeated next year; 'The 2nd Grand Horticultural and Miscellaneous Flower Show', but this time only for two days. The village bridge was 'arched with foliage' and the interior of the marquee 'a perfect California of pendant laburnam'. A musical promenade throughout the day was provided by the Royal Artillery Band. [115]

However, the committee fell foul of their influential patrons by assuming that the patronage extended to financial as well as token support. Acerbic letters were exchanged between the Earl of Darnley in Cobham Hall and the secretary of the committee in the Lion Inn. All the patrons, who included the Lords Stanhope, Sydney and deLisle said that they felt 'mulcted' by the assumption that they would buy tickets as well as lending their noble names which they now withdrew in dudgeon, and the Poultry Association came to a temporary end.

There were great changes in Farningham in the 1850s. The population of the village grew from 698 in 1851 to 944 in 1861. Part of this growth was due to a general rise in population, but the census shows that the main increase came from an influx of railway workers, bricklayers and domestic servants. Much of the increase was temporary, by 1871 the population of the village had dwindled by nearly 100 to 852. Most of the newcomers of the 50s lodged with other families, there were only ten new houses in the twenty

115–Farningham Horticultural Society papers F&ELHSoc property

240

years between 1851 and 1871. In 1821 there had been 97 houses and 171 in 1851.

The bricklayers were part of a building boom in the local towns. The brickmakers of West Kent were busy making the millions of yellow stock bricks to build the London suburbs. Many of the brickfields were along the Thames marshes where Charles Colyer had been buying land. Not only the valuable brickearth deposits and the wharfage available to and from London which supplied the barges of rubbish for the brickfires, but also the possibilities of new railway lines and sea connections must have made the marshes attractive to speculators.

Domestic servants were not a new phenomenon, but the affluent new middle classes now employed a whole range of services previously confined to great houses. Even in Farningham by 1861 there were butlers, footmen, grooms and coachmen, lady's maids, house and parlour and kitchen maids, nurses, governesses, housekeepers and cooks, while the inns and pubs employed waitresses, barmaids, ostlers, porters and potmen. Women in particular, who were gradually being eased off working on the land as an unladylike and harsh occupation, now went into domestic service as early as 12 to live an often harder life away from their families.

There were other new services in Farningham. Six dressmakers and two draper's shops, two new grocers, two hairdressers. All these were signs of prosperity among the incoming professionals; doctors, solicitors, underwriters and civil engineers. There were now two girl's boarding schools, one run by Mrs Beckley in what is now the Cottage, where William Moore's daughters Alice and Harriet aged 9 and 7, are registered as boarding, although they only lived next door, and a second establishment, Mrs Lockyer's Ladies Seminary School, in Croft Cottage. [116]

Far from a flight from the land there appear to have been as many agricultural labourers as ever in 1861. In fact they had increased, as had the shepherds, carters and waggoners. The farmers had more acreage than before under cultivation or pasture. Two Russell brothers from Horton Kirby had moved in to the village, James at the Hop Pole and Robert at Charton. Between them they farmed nearly 2,500 acres and employed 75 men and 28 boys, although this may have included land in Horton Kirby.

Farmers were doing well in this decade before cheap imports from abroad began to spoil their market in the 1870s. Labourers however saw little improvement, their average wage remained between 10s and 12s and, as they followed the national trend for larger families and were healthier than their town counterparts, they had more mouths to feed and so were proportionally worse off. A Kent Agricultural Labourers' Protection Association was formed at Maidstone in the late 1860s, but failed from farmer's opposition. The Kent Labourer's Union of the 1870s was more successful, but had little permanent effect.

116–Census papers, 1850-1890

William Moore increased his holding from 61 to 190 acres in the 1860s, leasing more land from Charles Colyer. Several farmers now employed bailiffs and William himself kept one at Eglantine farm. Some of his adult employees came from Suffolk and Essex but most of his boys were local. Charles Colyer now simply put 'Gent' as his occupation and his brother Thomas, who had come to live in Miss Anne Colyer's old house, put 'Landed Proprietor'

Public Health

Many social changes were taking place in the 1860s and 70s. Cholera epidemics continued but public health took a turn for the better with the 1858 Public Health Act, strengthened by the 1866 Sanitary Act which made authorities liable for prosecution if they failed to provide adequate drainage and water supply. Progress was slow but the North West Kent Waterworks Company supplying the Dartford neighbourhood originated in 1861, and the Sevenoaks Water Company had laid mains through the town streets by 1865. In 1858, after the Great Stink of London when the windows of the Houses of Parliament were hung with lime soaked curtains to counter the smell from the sewage in the Thames, the great drainage schemes for London and the suburbs began. The engineer Bazalgette designed 1,300 miles of brick built sewers, completed in 1875.[117]

The 1872 Sanitary Act and the 1875 Public Health Act saw the appointment of Inspectors of Nuisances and Medical Officers of Health and local authorities began to build sewage farms and to forbid the pollution of waterways. In the 1880s the Darenth Valley sewer was laid from Westerham to Dartford.

The first regular police constable, Thomas Fowle, appeared in the Farningham 1871 census. A paid county police force had been formed in Kent in 1856. The vestry had discussed appointing a paid constable as early as 1850, but decided against it as other villages were not doing so. They continued appointing four unpaid constables each year until the 1870s but Thomas Fowle was probably the first proper village bobby to be seen on the beat in the traditional blue coat and top hat.

Another change in the village came with the death of Andrew Burnside in 1863. He was replaced for three years by Dr John Martine until the appointment of the Revd. William Brewer who would stay until 1891. The widowed Mrs Burnside remained in the village with her son and daughter. It was Mrs Brewer, a commanding lady, who shooed the hunt away when they pursued a fox into her garden.

William Hollands still had his fleet of horse omnibuses. He also ran a bus service to Dartford Railway station. The age of the railway commuters to London had started. By 1867 the railways had destroyed the long distance coach trade and Hollands had a great sale of his last three buses and retired to become innkeeper at the Bull. By 1880 most of the Turnpike Trusts had wound up, killed by the railways and the public resentment at paying tolls.

117-Stephen Halliday, *The Great Stink of London* (1999)

242

One of the earliest photographic images of Farningham depicts Hearn's shop and birth place of his daughter who took the pen name Marianne Farningham. The photograph is undated but the stove pipe hats would suggest around 1870.

Marianne Farningham

The Post Office was still kept by Joseph Hearn and by 1870 he was able to advertise in the local directory as a 'Post and Money Order and Telegraph Office and Savings Bank'. He was no longer helped in the shop by his daughter Marianne who had gone to work in Northampton as a teacher, writer and lecturer on Women's Rights. Her autobiography *A Working Woman's Life* gives the following poetic description of her childhood life in Farningham. 'At the bottom of our garden was a wall...low enough for me to look over...first there was a meadow, in which was a row of magnificent lime trees (were these the vestiges of Sir John Beale's avenue of limes between Farningham and Horton Kirby?)..at the end of this meadow was the river Darent, which made music day and night; in it watercress grew, and such forget-me-nots as are not to be found in the world beside...and over it the willows bent...then far away in the distance were gentle hills and shady woods'.

243

Marianne had been her father's housekeeper from the age of 12 and helped him with the shoemaking and sorting out the mail. Once a year the whole family went hop-picking which she said paid the rent, bought the coals and a set of new clothes for the whole family. The Eastenders came from London, often walking the distance pushing trucks and barrows with necessities for a few weeks stay in the hop-pickers huts down Beesfield Lane. 'Picturesque processions and merry parties' she observed, but not everyone in the village shared her large hearted Christian attitude.

Hop-picking was a great feature of life in Farningham until the mid-twentieth century when hand picking came to an end. Although the Londoners and travellers were not altogether popular, staying as they did in squalid huts or camping out in the woods, many village families were happy enough to join them in the hop-gardens for a profitable day out. It was hard, painful work but plenty of older people in the late twentieth century would talk fondly about the picnics in the fields. According to the 1840 tithe map Charles Colyer grew hops in the river fields near Franks but by the 1920s the Farningham hop-fields were all down the Maplescombe valley.

Being the humble birthplace of an author of renown, the property in Farningham High Street, right, has consistently featured on postcards over the years. Here we see it under various ownerships during the 20th century, the last as commercial premises, being Mrs Atfield's sweet shop of fond memory.

Charles Colyer's last building project, and home to the author for the last fifty years.

In 1866 Charles Colyer commissioned his last building. Bridge Cottage is in fact only a facade, a six foot extension to the terrace of three mill cottages, but it makes an attractive and imaginative finish to the mill buildings. The effect is of a Victorian cottage-orné with elaborate brick and stone work, patterned wooden weatherboarding and pretty 'gothick' window frames. His initials CC and 1866 are carved above the door. Quite why he built it is still a mystery. Perhaps he wanted William Moore to live on the job, and the extension was to enlarge and improve the cottage for the Moore family. Maybe he wanted to make a more imposing entry to the mill drive, with Lion Cottage and Bridge Cottage making the equivalent of lodges relating to each other symetrically on either side of the gate.

It is possible that he made it for himself, so that the Moores could move into the Mill House. Charles was 80 in 1865. Miss Gawan had died, and he lived alone with his housekeeper Rebecca Ashenden and one maid. Bridge Cottage would have given him a continuing eye on the village and the mill without the chilliness of a large empty house. The only problem with this last theory is that the younger Charles and his large family remained very much involved with Farningham and the Mill. Each child who died young, and there were several, was buried in Farningham. Both Charles the elder and younger were active in the Vestry and on the Roper Charity. It seems likely that frequent outings to Farningham took place where the children would have enjoyed the river and the garden and where their grandfather's workmen probably indulged them with rides on horses and waggons, and where they could watch the workings of Mr Moore's mill.

Charles certainly never moved in to Bridge Cottage, because in May 1870 he died, aged 85, and the sale of the contents of the Mill House later that year shows that he was still living there. Apart from a few small bequests he left his entire estate to his 'dear son Charles'. His housekeeper Rebecca Ashenden was to have an annuity of £52, 'so long as she shall remain unmarried'. Her brother, 'my servant Peter Ashenden', was to have an annuity of £25, but only if he were to survive his sister. Two curious clauses. It is even more interesting to see that by the time of the 1871 census Rebecca had moved in to Bridge Cottage with Peter and his wife and son. So perhaps Bridge Cottage was built for the Ashendens to give them a home after Charles's death.

The Ashendens came from Mapledorn in Ash and are buried in Ash churchyard. In the 1871 census Peter described himself as 'Farmer out of business'. Maybe he was one of Charles Colyer's lame ducks, victim of a failing small farm. Peter's wife died in 1873 and Rebecca in 1876 aged 68. The will also gave James Gibson, the mill carpenter, now over sixty and living in one of the mill cottages, an annuity of £13, and the same to another 'old servant' James Woolley the stonemason. William Hodsoll and his clerk witnessed the will, and the sole executor was the younger Charles.

Charles's brother James had died in 1865 aged 79, leaving a large family of five daughters and two sons who continued to quarrel over their inheritance of the Lion Inn and the White House for many years. The two sons went to live abroad, William Hardyman to South Africa and Friend Elisha to New South Wales.

Thomas Colyer, aged 79 in 1871, was not mentioned in his brother's will, but he was a wealthy man in his own right. It would be interesting to know how he came to acquire Mrs Anne Colyer's house over which he and his brothers had quarrelled so violently in 1846. He had never married and lived alone in Farningham House with two elderly maidservants. Presumably Miss Colyer's nephews Edward and Henry Colyer of Southfleet who had been recognised as her heirs, had sold it to him. There was no ill will between them, and when Thomas died four years later he left them each ten thousand pounds.[118]

Thomas also left his nephews, the younger Charles and the younger William Hardyman, twenty thousand pounds each and left annuities to his nieces and, most surprisingly, he left Farningham House to William Waring which, according to later village gossip, was 'in amicable settlement of an old quarrel', but maybe this was a dim memory of the quarrel over Miss Colyer's will. Mrs Burnside and her two children became Waring's tenants in Farningham House cottage.

On June 13th, 1870 the contents of the Mill House were auctioned by William Hodsoll on the premises. A copy of the sale particulars has survived and gives us a good picture of how old Mr Charles Colyer had lived in his last years. The best pieces of furniture were his mahogany four poster bed, a rosewood sofa covered with crimson damask, a rosewood pianoforte, a pair of globes and a barometer and a View of the Voluntary Army of 1805 with Alphabetical List.

It is possible from the particulars to visualise all the rooms, attics, bedrooms, drawing and dining room, kitchens, cellars, dairy, store room, mangle room, bakehouse, knife house and stables. Livestock for sale included 'a Capital Red and White Cow forward in Calf', poultry and a 'Handsome Roan Cob, quiet to Ride and Drive'. In the coach house was a nearly new waggonette and a four wheel chaise. There were also a number of books; *The British Classics in 24 parts, The Faithful Servant in 40 Vols, Dr Gregory's Dictionary of Arts and Sciences, The Encyclopaedia Brittanica in 18 Vols, The Gospel Magazine, Trapp on the Bible, The Churchman's Penny Magazine, and The Gentleman's Magazine.*

William Hodsoll settled in Farningham and developed a thriving business as auctioneer and agent in the second half of the 19th century. Many sales of substance in Farningham and the surrounding area had the benefit of his attention and the auctions, if not on the premises, were often held in The Lion or The Bull inns.

FARNINGHAM, KENT.

A CATALOGUE
Of the Excellent Household

FURNITURE
And Effects,—Comprising
MAHOGANY 4-POST AND OTHER BEDSTEADS,

CAPITAL FEATHER BED
Mattresses, Mahogany and other Chests of Drawers, Wash-Stands,
TOILET GLASSES,
Dining and other Tables, Mahogany Chairs, Sofas ; Excellent

Rosewood Cabinet Pianoforte
BOOKS;
TURKEY AND BRUSSELS CARPETS,
Hearth Rugs, Quantity of Glass and Earthenware, Kitchen and Dairy
Requisites, &c. &c. Also
AN EXCELLENT COB,
Quiet to Ride and Drive ;
CAPITAL MILCH COW, POULTRY.
A NEARLY NEW WAGGONETTE
4-WHEEL CHAISE.
Harnesses, and numerous other Effects.
Which will be SOLD by AUCTION, by

MR. WILLIAM HODSOLL

On Thursday, June 30th, 1870, at 11 o'Clock,
ON THE PREMISES AS ABOVE,
By Order of the Executors of the late CHARLES COLYER, ESQ

May be Viewed on the day prior to the Sale, and Catalogues had Six days
previously, on the Premises, and of
Mr. William Hodsoll, Auctioneer, &c., Farningham, Kent

Dunkin & Co., Printers, High Street, Dartford.

FARNINGHAM, KENT.
TO OMNIBUS PROPRIETORS,
LIVERY STABLE KEEPERS, AND OTHERS.
A CATALOGUE
OF
ALL THOSE THREE VALUABLE

OMNIBUSES,
KNOWN AS
"THE TIMES," "VIVID," & "WONDER,"
WITH THEIR TIMES,
Performing Four Journies Daily from Farningham to Dartford ;
TOGETHER WITH
THE ENTIRE STOCK,
CONSISTING OF
8 USEFUL WORKING HORSES,
A 4-WHEEL BASKET CHAISE,
Pair and Single Harnesses, Riding Saddles and Bridles, Horse
Clothing, Chaff Cutting Machines, 2 Corn Bins, Horse Pails,
10 Young Fowls, &c. &c.,
Which will be Sold by Auction, by

MR. WM. HODSOLL,

At the Bull Inn, Farningham,
On THURSDAY, OCT. 3rd, 1867, at 1 for 2 o'Clock,
Unless previously Disposed of by Private Contract ;
By Order of the Proprietor, MR. W. HOLLANDS,
(who is retiring from the Business.)
May be Viewed One Day prior to the Sale, and Catalogues had
on the Premises, at the Inns in the Neighbourhood, and of
Mr. WILLIAM HODSOLL, Auctioneer, &c. &c.
Farningham, Kent.

Dunkin & Co., Printers, High Street, Dartford.

FARNINGHAM
AND MAPLESCOMB, KENT.

CATALOGUE
OF THE
OAK TIMBER,
COMPRISING
OAK TREES,
189 TELLERS,
Lop, Top, and Bark ; Standing and Growing
Wood," and "Side Hilly Wood."

Trees, and 4 Teller
(Winter Felled,)
all on the Maplescomb Estate, in the Parish
Kingsdown, Kent.
rty of Thomas Colyer, Esq.
ALSO

OAK TREES
325 TELLERS,
large Dimensions, together with their Lop,
ing in "FARNINGHAM WOOD,"—Also
OAK TREES
ch are drawn together and lying close to the
Road, at Farningham Hill,
rty of William Waring, Esq.
be Sold by Auction, by
M. HODSOLL
APRIL 16th, 1858, at Three o'Clock,
INN, FARNINGHAM.
ill be shewn by William Smoker, the Bailiff
and James Dunmull, of Button Street
Timber in Farningham Wood. Catalogues
the Timber ; at the Inns in the Neighbourhood
odsoll, Auctioneer, &c., Farningham, Kent

248

One of the most striking of the timber clad houses in Farningham, Hodsoll House, as it is today, above, shows little or no change from the 1936 exhibition photograph below.

William's son James who succeeded his father as auctioneer and estate agent, played for the Farningham Cricket Club for over 65 years. He lived in Hodsoll House until the second World War

Dr. Tony Cressall, physician and SDC Councillor, lived in the house with his wife Doreen and children John and Lucy from the 1950s to the 1990s.

Chapter Fourteen

The Moores of Farningham Mill / The School / A Mill Wedding /
The Homes for Little Boys / Dartford Corn Market /
Colyer's Mill, Dartford / Steam Technology / Halls of Dartford.

The Moores of Farningham Mill

By census day, April 3rd 1871 William Moore, his wife Mary and daughters
Alice, Harriet and Ellen, a cook-dairymaid and a housemaid had moved in to
the Mill House. No members of the Colyer family were to live there again for
more than a hundred years.

In 1870, after his father's death, the younger Charles showed his continuing
interest in Farningham by becoming actively involved in both the Roper
Charity and in discussions for a new school. The Education Act of 1870 called
for the provision of elementary schools in all areas where schooling was
insufficient, and school boards were to be elected by ratepayers.
The Farningham school, still in its schoolhouse on the glebe land, had come
under criticism for some years. As the Revd.Brewer pointed out in 1869
'Time, the great innovator, has so entirely destroyed the old thatched roof that
it was no longer windproof nor watertight' and a new covering of thatch costing ten guineas had become an unavoidable necessity.

The School

During the rethatching the Dartford Chronicle reported that the vicar's son,
Salisbury Brewer, had found a nest in the old thatch with a mother bird sitting
on four eggs. As it was November perhaps young Salisbury was having a joke,
unless maybe the bird was one of his mother's domestic hens. What with the
bird's nest and the skeleton of the fox also found in the thatch, maybe the dis-
coveries were intended to highlight the unhygienic nature of the roof.

Later that year the Diocesan Inspector, the Revd.Smith, said in his report
'the building is badly lighted and ventilated, poorly fitted up and expensive to
repair. The first step to an improved condition of things must be a new building. No annual grant can be made to the existing one'. The Vestry held a
public meeting in the parochial schoolroom at seven in the evening of 18th
November 1870 and Mr Charles Colyer proposed a motion, seconded by Mr
Rashleigh of the Manor House, that considering the inevitable necessity for
proper school accommodation in this parish, and in order to seize the short
period of Government building grants, efforts should be made by voluntary
subscriptions to go ahead with building a new school.

Mr Waring donated a 1/4 acre site on his private roadway, now known as
Horton Way, and Mr Colyer gave the first £350 subscription. Messrs Rashleigh
and Brewer each donated £15. Tenders were taken and Mr Gumbrell of

*Surprisingly there
appears to be a dearth of
photographs of the school
building. The unusual
view right, is taken from
Horton Way looking
towards the High Street.
The teacher's residence
with its porch and
scullery is clear to the left
and the boundary wall to
Farningham House on
the right.*

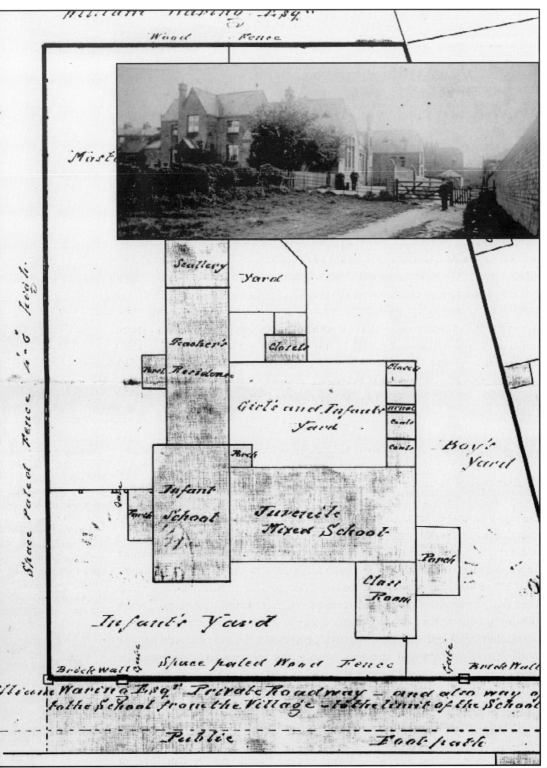

Wood Fence

Master

Space paled Fence 4'6" high

Scullery

Yard

Teacher's Residence

Closets

Closets

Girl's and Infants Yard

Boy's Yard

Infant School

Juvenile Mixed School

Porch

Class Room

Infant's Yard

Brick Wall

Space paled Wood Fence

Gate

Brick Wall

William Waring Esqr Private Roadway — and also way to the School from the Village — to the limit of the School

Public

Foot path

Dartford, having undercut all other builders, was engaged to not only build the new school but also to undertake an extensive rebuilding of the church.[119] The new school had three classrooms and a teacher's residence with its own garden. There was a large boy's play yard, a smaller one for the infants and a very small enclosed yard for the girls.

Mr and Mrs Ragge, the schoolmaster and mistress whose joint annual salary was £85, were able to move in next year. In 1875 they were replaced by Mr and Mrs Richard Edmonds whose daughter Eliza, born in the new schoolhouse in 1876, followed them as infants teacher, only retiring in 1941. She became a keen local historian and was instrumental in setting up and doing much of the research for the earlier Farningham History Society.

The Roper Charity still owned houses and land in Greenwich, where Charles Colyer was now living. He had followed his father on the Board of Trustees of the charity which now met, in 1871, in the Railway waiting Room of Greenwich Station. The Revd. Brewer was in the chair and other trustees

The three ages of Miss Eliza Edmonds.

With a colleague and children in the 1890s. Photograph courtesy of Dr. Gerald Cramp.

Above, with the children in the 1920s and top aged 90 in 1966.

Bottom left, Mr Hetherington with, among others, Robin Roome (nee Donnelly) and the Edwards boys, circa 1920s.

119-S.B.Black, *The Children of Farningham and their Schools*

252

included the Revd.Rashleigh of Horton Kirby and Mr Waring. Mr Colyer's solicitor's clerk took the minutes and, after an inspection of the properties which included some interesting marshland, they all adjourned to Mr Colyer's home, Clifton House in Croom's Hill.[120]

Now that elementary schooling was free the Roper Charity was able to sponsor more apprentices. Several were apprenticed to their own fathers, such as William Woolley, stonemason and James Hales, blacksmith. An example of the usual sum in 1861 was for Thomas Everest to be apprenticed to Joseph Sharwood, tailor, for 1s a week for 7 years and, in 1870, for William Martin 'to learn the art of watchmaking' from Jacob Hankins at a cost of £5.

Mr Gumbrell's next work after he had completed the new school, was the restoration of the church and this took much longer. The grand re-opening took place on the 21st September 1876. We might feel today that the architect, Ewan Christian, went disastrously far with his renovations, but they were the height of fashion in the ecclesiological taste and were received enthusiastically at the time. The galleries, 'which disfigured either end of the nave' were removed, as were 'the high pews and higher pulpit of our forefathers'. The wall painting of Moses and Aaron above the chancel arch was also removed, leaving the walls of the church a nice 'uniform buff tint'.[121]

However, the new South windows in the Decorated and Perpendicular style were maybe an improvement on the former 'square apertures' which are hard to place architecturally. The Colyer family, although no longer living in the village were much involved in the restoration. Mrs Charles Colyer presented a new altar table and her eldest daughter worked the stool for the reading desk. Mr Charles Colyer headed the list of subscriptions with a donation of £100, far in excess of the other subscriptions which ranged from Mr Waring's £75 to Mr Sharwood the carpenter's 5s. The table and its embroidered cover given by Mrs William Waring was considered very fine, as were the new red and black tiles which covered many of the old tombstones in the chancel and nave.[122]

The Bishop of Dover attended the great re-opening and consecrated a new area of burial ground and all the visiting clergy sang as they walked the boundaries. The church was crowded and Mrs Brewer, who was the choir mistress and organist, entertained the visitors to lunch where 'the healths of the Bishop, the Vicar and Mrs Brewer and of the churchwardens' were given with much enthusiasm.

William Dray, who had branched into the Darenth Vale Gas Company, laid on the new gas lighting; 'Two Coronae of great power' in the nave and a smaller light in the chancel. A new organ was now considered a necessity, and a concert in aid of the subscription fund took place in Mr Dray's showroom. 'A brilliant and fashionable audience' was entertained to dramatic readings and songs by Mrs Brewer, Mrs Lockyer and Mr George Rashleigh. Mr Dray's charges included pipes to connect the gas supply to the mains so presumably public street gas lighting already existed in the High Street.

120-CKS P145/25
121-Undated cutting from local paper, Gordon Edward's scrapbooks
122-Restoration report, F&ELHist Soc. archive

The Darenth Vale Gas Co. was amalgamated with the Dartford Gas Co. in 1880. Gas street lighting had already been laid in Dartford as early as the 1830s.

The church had already suffered a drastic exterior alteration in 1830 when the tower had been raised by seven feet and a fourteen foot turret added. The imposing new height of the tower with its crenellated or battlemented parapet, and the new interior restoration unfortunately meant a loss of much of the coherence of the original building.

Lavish entertainment was as popular as ever. A dinner at the Lion in November 1871 reported a bill of fare of 'Mock Turtle, Julienne and Hare soups, Cottelettes de Porc, Ris de Veaux, Vol au Vents, Pâtés des Huîtres, Roast Turkeys, Pigeon Pies, Roast Goslings, Hams, Ducks, Pheasants, Leverets, Wild Ducks, Partridges, Grouse, Plum Puddings, Punch Jellies and Crèmes Francaise'.

Dramatic readings were fashionable in the village. The Darenth Vale Literary Association flourished and gave evening entertainments where there would be chamber music, parlour songs and serious talks on subjects such as 'Women's Rights'. The heightened atmosphere led to the report of a fracas between two members, Captain Grieg of Horton Kirby and Hamilton Cornwall, son of the vicar of Eynsford on the 4.30 train from Victoria. Suburban commuting was becoming dangerous. Other members of the village community were also engaged in violent behaviour. One of Dr Slaughter's sons made the headlines in the case of 'the Student and the Beadle' in 1870, when he and some fellow medical students, 'all in a state of intoxication', were charged at Marlborough Street Police Station with having struck a blow to the head of the Beadle of the Burlington Arcade. John Edward Slaughter was fined 10s. 6d.[123]

More disturbing was the case of the 'Church Loiterers', gangs of 30 to 50 'roughs' who congregated at the gateway of Farningham church in March 1871 and 'seem to delight in making the weaker sex, especially young females, the object of obscene remarks... even following them up the hill'. It would be interesting to know who these large groups were and where they came from. Unemployment should not yet have been severe and the railway 'navvies' and bricklayers appear to have mostly gone home. Looking at the 1871 census for likely culprits, ie males between the ages of 14 and 25, few were born outside Kent. Many young men either belonged to families of village tradesmen or were apprentices or domestic servants, but there are at least 40 agricultural labourers within this group so perhaps they were the disaffected 'roughs'. It does not seem likely that the church loiterers came from the towns, where they could loiter with less effort. Perhaps the agricultural depression had hit Farningham early.

123-Darenth Vale Lit. Soc, papers, F&ELHS

As tradition would have it mother Mary and father William flank the bride and groom. A speculative Charles Colyer, landlord stands behind Mary. Would William's strict sense of the formal have approved of the mad hatter in the back row?

Photograph courtesy Horner West family

124-Local paper cutting from Horner West

A Mill Wedding

On the 27th April 1874 the Mill House enjoyed its greatest festivity for many years, when the Moore's eldest daughter Alice was married to Frank Horner from Dublin. The local paper reported the event at length. 'The village was decorated with flags and flowers, and a line of triumphal arches was erected in front of the Mill House... for the young bride whose sunny smile and heart-felt sympathy has made her dear to every cottage home'. They added that she wore white silk and orange blossoms and was attended by six bridesmaids in blue silk.[124]

The ceremony was naturally held in the Wesleyan Chapel and conducted by three Methodist clergymen. Flowers were scattered in front of the couple on the pathway home where the wedding party of 44, many of whom had stayed

in the Lion overnight, 'sat down to an elegant dejeuner'. Mr Moore had asked the vicar whether the church bells might be rung and the aimiable Mr Brewer had no objection, but his wife, who must have been a formidable lady, was outraged and locked the belfry door before going out for the day with the keys in her pocket. However, the bellringers of Eynsford 'whose sectarian principles were over-ridden by their love for the bride', brought their hand bells and 'rang a hearty peal on the steps of the Mill House'. The brass band from the Homes for Little Boys also played in the mill grounds all day.

Top left, Alice Moore, daughter of William and Mary.
Above, Mary Moore (nee Beswick)

Below, the Farningham Band from the homes for Little Boys, Farningham and Swanley.
It is interesting to note that the tables also carry a large array of hand-bells.

The Homes for Little Boys

The Farningham Homes for Little Boys were actually in Horton Kirby but presumably took their name from the nearby Farningham Road Station. The Homes had opened in 1867 and were a fine experiment in the new cottage style living intended to replace the great Dickensian orphanages. Originally there were five cottages with workshops, classrooms, a chapel and 19 acres of farmland. The aim was to 'feed, clothe, educate and train to industrial work

homeless and destitute boys'. The first batch of boys arrived in 1867 from their earlier orphanage in Tottenham and marched from the station to their new home behind their own brass band. A former Little Boy, Patrick Roast, has written a description of the home in his autobiography, *A City Set on a Hill*.[125]

Alice Moore's new husband was also concerned with orphan boys. The Horner family came from Ireland but Frank worked in his father's business in London. Like the rest of his family he was a devout Methodist, and his great interest was in mission work among young people in the London slums, especially in a hostel for homeless boys run by his friend

William Moore and grand children circa 1895

125–Patrick Roast,
A City set on a Hill (1996)

257

The Homes for Little Boys at Farningham and Swanley
1. The Boys' Village, Farningham. - 2. The New Building at Swanley - 3. The Stores, Farningham
4. The Band Room, Farningham. - 5. Shoemakers. - 6. The Little Boys' Composing Room, Farningham.

the Revd. T.B. Stephenson. William Moore, who often put up visiting preachers in the room his daughters described as 'the Prophet's Chamber', heard about the enterprise and invited a party of the boys to spend a day at the Mill, and Frank came as one of their mentors.

Bishop Horner West described the course of his grandparent's courtship. Frank's increasingly frequent visits to the Prophet's Chamber. Alice's fears that perhaps he preferred her sister Harriet. How Alice watched for Frank through the little shuttered windows by the front door. It is a nice story with a happy ending. The Horners had eight children and lived in a house called Farningham Lodge in Beckenham. Their children were to remember visits to their grandparents in Farningham all their lives; fishing and punting on the river, playing in the stables and harness rooms and in the gardens and paddocks. Old Mr Moore was a strict Sabbatarian and on Saturday nights all toys and books not about religion were put away. Theatre-going and dancing were always prohibited, even playing cards was forbidden. The whole family were teetotal and the children wore blue ribbons to show that they had signed the pledge, although a little whisky was kept for the family physician.

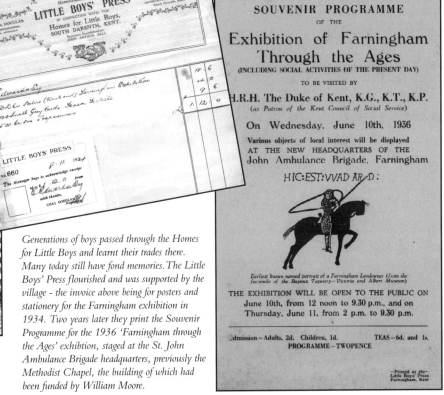

Generations of boys passed through the Homes for Little Boys and learnt their trades there. Many today still have fond memories. The Little Boys' Press flourished and was supported by the village - the invoice above being for posters and stationery for the Farningham exhibition in 1934. Two years later they print the Souvenir Programme for the 1936 'Farningham through the Ages' exhibtion, staged at the St. John Ambulance Brigade headquarters, previously the Methodist Chapel, the building of which had been funded by William Moore.

A new general practitioner had come to live in the village and was the Moore's family doctor and friend. Dr. William Ashurst had arrived from Anglesea in the late 1850s. He was a tenant of the Colyers in the White House and was to remain in the village until his death seventy years later,

The White House (1743) as it is today, left. In 1936 above, vision to the site was easier, with less foliage and fencing.

aged 97. Several visiting members of the Horner family stayed with him for the wedding and reported on the doctor's eccentricities, one of which was to keep little parasols over his rosebushes which he turned every day to protect the roses from the sun. Dr Ashurst appreciated his tot of whisky and was once watched in horror through the little hall windows by a teetotal grandchild who expected him to fall down the steps dead drunk on his way back to his pony and trap. One of the earliest Farningham photographs is of the doctor on his rounds in this same trap.

William Moore, 'that fiery old Methodist' as his Anglican great grandson described him, was a match for Mrs Brewer in intolerance. Once, top hatted and frock coated on a Sunday afternoon's walk with a grandchild, he climbed up on a fence to shout 'Thou shalt keep holy the Sabbath' at a tennis party and got the reply 'Thou shalt mind thine own business old man'. The tennis party was likely to have been in the Manor House garden where the sport loving Rashleighs had one of the first tennis courts in the village.

Dartford Corn Market

Another miller, S.K.Keyes, includes a description of the Dartford Corn Market in 1877 in his collection of historical notes. The market took place in the yard of the Bull Hotel which had been covered to make 'the excellently commodious Corn Exchange. Here are rows of stands at which traders post themselves to do business... Mr William Moore, the extensive miller of Farningham and at Shadwell. Mr G.Parker, corn and coal merchant at Farningham Road Station. Mr Alfred Wallis, corn and hay dealer of Farningham. Mr Thomas Wood of Crockenhill. Mr Bellingham, corn and seed dealer of Farningham and, (among many others), Messrs Samuel Strickland and Son of Dartford who hold extensive stores of grain and deal largely in cattle food[126]. Most of the farmers of the neighbourhood visit the Corn Market at some periods of the year and Mr Hodsoll of Farningham is among the auctioneers'.

Thomas Hardy gives an enjoyable description of a similar scene in *Far from the Madding Crowd* where the heroine, Bathsheba Everdene, who had inherited her uncle's farm, goes to the exclusively male Corn Exchange to buy corn. Corn Markets were a sight that would not often be seen again after the end of the century. Mr Keyes adds that the Dartford Corn Market was well attended when he himself re-started Colyer's Mill in 1887 and became a stall holder, but that the market closed in the early 1890s.

William Moore's business at Shadwell is another story. Shadwell is in Stepney on the North bank of the Thames, a long way from Farningham by horse transport. Tower Bridge had not yet been built in 1877 and, although there were ferries, and the Thames Tunnel had opened to the underground railway in the 1860s, the journey would still have taken several hours. Moore had in fact bought the lease of a corn mill in Shadwell in the 1870s. The implications of this will be examined later.

126-S.K.Keyes, *Further Historical Notes* (1938)

The other Farningham corn dealers were Alfred Wallis, son of Samuel Wallis of the Bricklayer's Arms; John Bellingham, who ran his business from a shop in the village now known as the Bakery, and Thomas Wood of Crockenhill who was to set up an iron foundry and traction engine business which is still kept alive today by the fourth generation of his family. The Stricklands were highly reputed seed merchants of Dartford, and Donald Strickland, Samuel's grandson, later lived in the house behind King's Garage, Crossways, in Farningham.

Sidney Kilworth Keyes, who made the historical notes about Dartford, was one of the most successful millers in the county. He patented the famous Daren Flour, and Daren bread became a rival to

Hovis, indeed the golden letters of its logo closely resembled that of Hovis. Until the 1960s the Daren sign stood above the Farningham Bakery and can still occasionally be seen above baker's shops in Kent, although the bread is no longer made. 'Colyer's Mill' in Dartford, which S.K.Keyes acquired in the 1880s, was of course the first Charles Colyer's Dartford Mill which he had purchased in 1768 and left to his son James and which had been sold after James's early death. Miss Anne Colyer of Farningham, James's daughter, still owned some of his land in Dartford marshes in 1840. Keyes later moved his business to a larger mill on the Dartford marshes, where he had a wharf and Thames barges with the Daren sign on the sails. The mill had been brought back into the family by Thomas Colyer of Joyce Hall, Southfleet, whose younger son Henry had inherited it in 1835.

262

Colyer's Mill, Dartford

Henry and his elder brother Edward and their sister Elizabeth were Miss Anne Colyer's heirs after the notorious law suit. Henry had settled down as the miller of Colyer's Mill but died unmarried and intestate in 1877, and Edward became his heir. After Edward's own death at Joyce Hall in 1886 he left 'All my corn mill, Royal Victoria Mill and 12 acres belonging, and the adjoining Acacia Hall' to his nephew Charles Snelling Colyer. This is of some interest to Farningham because today, Charles Edward Snelling Colyer's geat grandson Nigel is the present owner of Farningham Mill. The Snelling connection with the mill goes back to the 1720s, before the first Charles Colyer's arrival in Farningham when a John Snelling shared the rent of the mill with John Kemp.

'Acacia Hall' was the new name for Colyer's Mill. The adjoining Royal Victoria Mill, which had only been purchased by Edward Colyer shortly before his death in 1885, had earlier been known as Hard's Mill until its owner, James Hards, obtained a Royal warrant to supply the bread for Buckingham Palace. Together, Colyer's Mill and the Royal Victoria made a most valuable property. A superbly illustrated Estate Book was made of all Edward Colyer's properties at the time of his death. They included the Mates Farm estate with the old Mates farmhouse, home of the first Charles Colyer, and the lands of the Manor of Poole in Southfleet and Stone. The Lordship of the Manor of Poole had been purchased by Thomas Colyer, Edward's father, as had Joyce Hall which Thomas had built for Kitty Snelling when they married in in 1801. The estate included the ancient Roman site of Springhead and the Harrow Inn at Southfleet, now called the Colyer's Arms; the Court lodge farm estate, also in Southfleet; seven large areas of marshland along the Thames, and the two adjoining corn mills opposite Dartford church, the Royal Victoria Mill and Colyer's Mill, or Acacia Hall. There was also a house called Bridge House, still to be seen opposite the church, linking the two mills, and extensive gardens and meadows along the river Darent.

In 1879 Charles Colyer made some notes about his own estate. There had been many sad changes in his family life. Four of his children had died as infants, also a daughter at twelve and a son at 17. Another daughter and son were to die at 40. It is a hard record even for the late 19th century. Mary Ann, Charles' wife, also died comparatively early, aged 56 in 1876.[127]

At the time of her death the Colyers were living at Clifton House in Greenwich. This fine late Georgian house at the top of Crooms Hill has since been demolished. One son, Arthur Henry, had married in 1868 and a daughter, Caroline Rosabelle, had married the son of the vicar of Greenwich in 1875. This left three unmarried daughters and one son, Francis James, at home. Charles himself married again in 1878. His second wife was another cousin, Elizabeth Jane Colyer, daughter of John Colyer of Welling, and after their marriage they went to live at 38 Dorset Square, Regent's Park.

127-Nigel Snelling-Colyer, pers. comm.

Elizabeth was 38 and Charles was 62. The three daughters later married but Francis James died unmarried, and aged only 40 in 1885, leaving Arthur Henry the only suviving son. Arthur's own son Ernest, who would later inherit Farningham Mill, was born in Greenwich in 1869.

'As to my own estate' Charles wrote in July 1879, 'some portions of this estate may with advantage be sold at early opportune times, but not hastily or without good advice...'. Among those to be retained he recommended the Eglantine and Beesfield estates 'upon which there are many most commanding and eligible building sites'. He also considered the Eglantine Lane and Maidstone Road fields, the Eynsford Road land and the Folly land suitable for development and it is good, from today's point of view, to note that of these only the Eynsford Road land has been built over in the last hundred years. Especially in the light of his comments on the fields above Eglantine farm which he considered might include 'large plots for buildings of a superior class, or for any public buildings'.[128]

The maintenance of old timber buildings is an ongoing and expensive business.

Below, a relatively recent view of the interior top floor of Farningham Mill.

Right, ground floor interior, circa 1902.

'Concerning the Mill Estate' he continued, with a typical lawyer's caution,...'there may be much to be thought of its retention...and much on the opposite view. If any of the younger of my descendants should be likely to take on the business of a miller as a pursuit...that business in former bygone years held its own well to the benefit of the Colyer family,...but on the other hand I know my father pronounced in his later time the class of men such as Bakers were most difficult and unpleasant people to deal with,

...on the other hand others have successively and successfully carried on that business, Mr Moore likewise, and the late Mr James Colyer, Mr Henry Colyer and Mr Edward Colyer and other millers have all done well at such business'.

'Further, as to the fabric of the Mill itself, altho' now in course of being put into as perfect and substantial and complete order as practicable, yet it is to be born in mind that it is in the main a timber building and a very old one and constantly liable to heavy repairs. In the future a new brick building might be an essential, and with steam power added...'. So, in 1879 the mill was 'in the course of being put into as perfect and substantial and complete order as practicable', but not yet 'with steam power added'. William Moore was obviously a progressive miller. He had taken a lease of the Shadwell mill by 1872, but obviously not at the expense of the Farningham mill. Could this have been

128-C.Colyer notebooks, property of Nigel Snelling-Colyer

264

the time that the turbine was added? It also appears that the small Victorian outhouse to the right of the mill was built in the following years to house a steam engine.

Charles added a few more notes on the disposal of the Mount House and the Bricklayer's Arms and the house adjoining, Fernwood, then occupied by a Dr Tucker, also directions about the disposal of his properties in Southfleet, Darenth Wood, Greenhythe and Stone. Among these informal notes there is an 1872 draft rental with the names and rentals of Charles's tenants. This shows that William Moore was paying £50.10s.per quarter for the Mill and £2.10s p.q. for one of the mill cottages. Moore also paid £51.10s p.q. for lands in Farningham and Eynsford including Eglantine Farm, and £1.5s.3d for the rectorial tithe of the Parsonage.

Other tenants included Samuel Wallis who paid £25 per half year for the Bricklayer's Arms. William Austin in the Mount paid £25 p.q. Mr Whitlock paid £6.10s. per half year for the Cottage. Everest and Marchant, the wheelwrights in the Parsonage and carpenter's shop, paid £6.17s.6d. per half year. A Mr Clarke paid £5 p.a. for a fishing licence, and Joseph Woolley and James Gibson had their rent set off against their wages. Rebecca Ashenden and 70 year old John Pratt were to be rent free, but to pay one penny a week.

The last decades of the 19th century saw a complete change in the fortunes of water corn mills. Free Trade and the new steamships in conjunction with the opening up of the prairies and the new railroads meant that cheap imports of wheat were flooding into the country from America. Much of this was a hard variety of winter wheat which was difficult to grind on the old mill stones. The Americans had developed a new method of grinding by rollers which produced a very popular uniformly fine white flour. Great commercial roller mills were set up at ports and the little riverside country water corn mills began to close. Many adapted to grinding animal feed but the majority, including Farningham were to go out of business by the end of the century.

The whole romantic story was coming to an end. As Elizabeth David says in her book on Bread 'The ancient rituals of ploughing and sowing and reaping, the gruelling work at harvest time, the thanksgivings and feastings when the corn was safely gathered in, ...the millstreams running dry so that no grain could be ground, the tales of dishonest millers, the portrayals of the poor humble gleaners bent double over their task of scratching the few last ears of wheat from the cornfields after the landlord's grain had been harvested...all these are more or less familiar to us through the works of our poets and writers'. But now the only writing was on the wall.

The golden age of farming was over too. By the 1880s depression and drought, added to the cheap imports by rail and steamship meant that many farmers were bankrupted by the 90s. The labourers were worse off than ever, many evicted from their cottages, many forced off the land to the cities or to colonial migration. This was the real 'Flight from the Land'.

William Moore's workmen outside the mill.

Top, left to right
George Errey
C. Glazebrook
Charles Hawley
John Waller
in the bowler hat, unknown
Front row
Ted Cornell
unknown
Ted Baker

Below, at a slightly later date
left to right
Ted Baker
John Waller
George Errey
Charles Hawley
Ted Cornell

Steam Technology

S.K.Keyes was at the forefront of milling progress. Two other Dartford citizens had been pioneers of the new technology of steam in the earlier part of the century; John Hall, an ironfounder and his protégé the famous Richard Trevethick. Keyes originally worked the two mills leased from the Colyers with traditional water-milling machinery, but in the late 1880s, when he moved to a disused mill at the head of Dartford Creek, he installed rollers driven by a steam engine, and his barges delivered flour direct from the docks to his mill.[129]

This was the factory where he added wheat germ to the soulless white American flour to make the light but enriched Daren bread. Clever marketing with little loaf shaped vans and the golden logo on top no doubt helped sales. It was sad that Daren bread never became as famous as Hovis which was a similar bread invented at about the same time and marketed with a similar golden logo.

Halls images courtesy of Halls of Dartford 1785-1985 by Harry Miller

Halls of Dartford

John Hall of Dartford was another enormously successful entrepreneur. He was a millwright by trade who started his own smithy in Lowfield Street in 1785. In 1791 he moved to larger premises in Waterside. At the time of his death in 1836 his business had grown to include steam engine manufacture, iron and brass foundry, engines for steam vessels and machinery for milling oil, corn, paper, sugar and gunpowder.

Richard Trevethick, the Cornish inventor, who is believed to have designed the world's first steam locomotive in the early 1800s, came to work for Hall in 1831 after losing his fortune in the Peruvian silver mines. He lived in the Bull Inn in Dartford and died there, penniless, in 1833. During his time at Halls Trevethick designed a steam turbine or 'whirling engine', also prototypes of screw and water-jet propulsion for ships, and predicted the design of the 'artificial cold' or refrigeration engines into which Halls diversified in the second half of the century.

John Hall employed many skilled engineers and designers. A Hall's billhead of the mid 1830s advertises 'Patent Steam presses for Oil Mills and Rolling Mills'. Halls continued pioneering work on steam engines until they moved

129-E.Martin,
DHA Newsletter, No.25 (1988)

FROZEN MUTTON FROM THE FALKLAND ISLANDS,

Per S.S. " Selembria," fitted with

J. & E. HALL'S COLD AIR MACHINES.

S.S. "SELEMBRIA"—3041 TONS REGISTER.

on to the petrol driven engines for which they became famous in the early 20th century.[130] After John Hall's death the firm was inherited by two of his sons, John and Edward, and became known as J. & E. Hall's, but the business deteriorated, until it was reanimated by Everard Hesketh in the 1880s. Under Hesketh it became a private limited company and moved into the new refrigeration technology which would contribute so brilliantly to the national economy but so disastrously to British agriculture by making possible imports of frozen meat from Australia, New Zealand and South America. Several J. & E. Hall people had Farningham connections including Hesketh himself and John Ward, who followed him as company chairman in 1921 and who was to live at Farningham Mill for the first part of the 20th century.

William Moore had also branched into steam technology. The mill he had acquired in Shadwell, the Globe Flour Mills in Narrow Street, had the advantages of steam and wharfage. He continued with this and another Globe Flour Mills in nearby Ratcliff until the late 1890s. Quite how he managed the two businesses so far apart is a mystery. The Thameside mills were quite small, not on the scale of Mr Keyes in Dartford, but were obviously moneyspinners. Even so, the journey, possibly by carriage or on horseback, maybe by Holland's horse omnibus to Dartford, then the East London railways and the Thames underground tunnel, would have been taxing, especially for a man no longer young.

Presumably he had good mill managers and staff. It seems very likely that he added a steam engine to Farningham Mill at this time. The engine house is still there beside the mill and the line of its tin roof can just be seen behind Mr Moore and his family as they pose for a photograph in about 1895.

In the Dartford Library archive of the Dartford mills there is a broadsheet

130-Adrian Herbert, *DHA Newsletter, No25* (1988) that must have been written at about this time. It is about the Death of

Shooting Money, that perk given by the farmers to the mill workers when they unloaded the grain. Although the names of the people accused are left blank someone has obligingly pencilled them in and they are all of late 19th century local farmers. Some of the verses are given below.[131]

POOR
SHOOTING MONEY,
Its Death and Burial.

'Who kill'd Shooting money?
I, said Josiah B——h,   (Bath, of Swanley)
With a merry laugh
I killed Shooting Money
Who saw it Die?
I said Mr Rus—ll   (Russell, of Horton Kirby)
After a strong tussle
I saw it Die
Who caught its Blood?
I, said the Miller
That bag'd the siller
I caught its Blood
Who'll be Chief Mourner?
I, said Mr M——re, (Moore, of Farningham)
Because I'm losing score
I'll be chief Mourner.
Who'll toll the Bell?
I, said Mr D——ke, (Dyke, of Lullingstone)
I can make it strike
So I'll toll the Bell'.
...etc

In the 1871 census William Moore is simply described as 'Miller'. In 1881 he is described as 'Corn Flour Miller, employs 30 men and 4 boys. In 1891 he is down as 'Miller and Merchant'. In the trade directories he is usually described as 'Miller', but in the Electoral Roll of 1894 he is entered as the occupier of 'house, mill and land' and the qualifying property is given as 'the Folly', so it appears that he was farming the Parsonage estate. This might explain why he employed as many as thirty four men and boys which seems excessive for Farningham mill, although perhaps the Shadwell millers are included.

Chapter Fifteen

Farningham in the Eighties and Nineties / Fashionable Farningham /
Sporting Farningham / The Charities / Last Days of the Working Mill /
Death of Charles Junior /
The End of the Vestry and the First Parish Council / Fort Farningham /
Public Health

Farningham in the Eighties and Nineties

In 1938 and 1939 the Kentish Times published a series of interviews with
Farningham people who had been born in the last decades of the 19th
century. It is good to hear the voices for the first time of people who do not
usually get a chance to tell their story. They have been G.K.Chesterton's
famous silent people. 'Smile at us, pay us, pass us; but do not quite forget/
For we are the people of England, that have never spoken yet'. It took a
world war for these Farningham voices to be heard.[132]

Inventories and wills and court proceedings have sometimes given us an
insight into people's possessions, and ways of life and very occasionally we
hear them speaking at second hand, dictating a will or being quoted in court.
The vestry records and the charity books told us a little about ordinary
people's behaviour, so did the vicar's comments on their churchgoing habits.
Unfortunately even the literate elite have not left us much in the way of
written testimonies. No diaries and few letters. Marianne Farningham's
anecdotes, Henry Cox's nature observations, Solomon Cox's family history
and Charles Colyer's plans for the future were almost unique. The census told
us the bare bones of people's circumstances, but this is the first time they get
a chance to speak for themselves.

Mrs Walter Dunmall appeared to enjoy being interviewed. She had been

born at Chimhams in 1861 and was the daughter and wife
of agricultural labourers. Her father, James Gould was one
of the four parish constables in the 1870s and she told a
story about the day two army deserters came to their door
asking for food. Her mother, a kind lady who had a son in
the army herself, made them a parcel of food and sent them
packing quickly before the constable came home and had to
take them into custody. This mother, Bridget Gould, was the
lady mentioned earlier who remembered paying a penny for

132-*Kentish Times,*
'Farningham' 1&2 Dec 30
& Jan 13 1938/1939

271

each bucket of water taken from the river. Her daughter, Mrs Dunmall had gone into service at an early age and became a housemaid to Dr Slaughter's family. In the 1881 census she is still 19 year old 'Ann Gould, housemaid'. She related memories of the doctor's sons, all medical men. Dr.Slaughter was 'a lovely man and ever so kind'. It is a pity that the first voices to speak to us are often a little obseqious. Anecdotes about the naughty young Slaughters as medical students might have been more amusing.

Mrs Dunmall's husband Walter worked all his days on the Manor Farm estate as an agricultural labourer. In the 1881 census he was working for William Waring at White Hill. One of his jobs was to collect the entrance money on market day at the gate of Market Meadow. A particular joy in reading the census returns is to see who is going to marry whom, how many children they will have, where they will live and what they will do with their lives. To see these people, so long dead, as children, adults and old men and women and to wonder how their lives must have crossed and how they must have all known each other, at least by sight.

 Mr William Bates, aged 80 in 1938, had come to Farningham from Boughton Malherbe at the age of 18 to be coachman to Dr Ashurst. He lived as a boarder with a family in the High Street and it is interesting to see in the census that one of Dr Ashurst's live-in servants was Bridget Gould, Mrs Dunmall's mother, who at the age of 57 had left her husband and younger children at Chimhams, but whether from necessity or choice we will never know. Her youngest daughter Jane was perhaps now old enough at 14 to look after their employers, the Smith family who had farmed at Chimhams for several generations and still had five live-in farm servants.

William Bates reminisced about harnessing the cob and trap for the doctor at all hours of the day and night. One night, in mid-winter, they were called out to a delivery in Fawkham where Mr Bates and the cob had to wait in a snowstorm until half past four in the morning, only revived by a kind neighbour with a glass of brandy. His son Albert, who lived with him in Oliver Crescent, had been captain of the Farningham bellringers since 1916, and in 1908 had conducted the first peal on six bells, a new bell having been donated by Mr and Mrs Fisher of the Mount that year. The peal took three hours to ring. Mr Bates's memory was slipping a little because the placards in the belfry say that the Fisher's gift was in 1904 and the peal of Bob Minor, 5040 changes, conducted by Albert Bates took 2 hours and 39 minutes. But that is a minor quibble. Albert Bates's expertise gave pleasure, not always unalloyed, to the village for at least three decades, for jubilees and coronations, funerals and festivities. He also taught new generations of bellringers including his own daughter Betty Bates, who was ringing until the 1990s.

The histories of the church, the manor and the mill, all within sight and

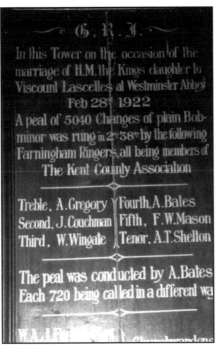

earshot of each other have been closely interwoven for two thousand years. The sound of the mill wheel and the church bells in a quiet world were familiar for many centuries. Many well known village personalities have been bellringers. Jesse Couchman, son of the famous Farningham blacksmith Thomas Couchman, was a ringer for fifty years and said in 1939 that 'the nearest approach to the ideal of the brotherhood of man in my opinion is to be found at the meetings of ringers. If the nations had some of the spirit of goodwill to be found there, there would no longer be talk of war'.

Several of the Everests, whose family had lived in the village since the 16th century, were bellringers. Fred Everest, son of Thomas Everest the wheelwright, was interviewed in 1938. He was born in Kingsdown and came to Farningham as a child, where his first job was scaring birds for 4d a day. In the 1881 census he was aged 24 and living in South Terrace with his wife and son, almost next door to his father's family. His memories in 1938 were of Holland's coaches, 'my how he could handle the horses'. Mr Everest was a carter all his life and, like Mr Bates, said that the winters were much colder in his youth. 'We looked for snow or frost by the middle of October and it was nothing to get fourteen or fifteen weeks of frost right off the reel...it was possible to walk to Kingsdown or Maplescombe over the hedges', and his wife would have to thaw the ice off the buttons of his greatcoat before he could undo it.

He also remembered Farningham Fair, which was held in the Bull Meadow up White Post Hill in those days, and how for five or six weeks before October 15th the horse dealers would congregate in the village and, from the moment of their arrival, would start showing off their horse's paces. A Russian contingent came every year. He also rembered the market every third Wednesday when there was precious little room to move in the High Street, and Guy Fawkes night when the daredevil Flewins used to roll lighted barrels of tar through the village.

Mr Bill Reeves, born on the Franks estate in the 1860s, was first employed as a shepherd boy for 2s a week and then came to work for Mr Moore the miller as a gardener. However, after buying a cow and starting a milk round he gradually prospered enough to become the tenant of Eglantine farm.

He too had memories of the Fair and of fiddlers playing in the Chequers while Pearly Kings and Queens, down from London for the day, danced in the street and bare-fist fights were a popular entertainment. He also remembered as a boy of five sitting on an uncle's shoulder to watch the Farningham to Dartford steeplechasers jump across Frank's Lane.

Walter Whitehead, watchmaker son of the old watchmaker, was born in Farningham in 1860 and was interviewed in his 'dim, low ceilinged, old-fashioned shop' with a fine grandfather clock behind him. Then Herbert Thomas, postmaster son of John Thomas the postmaster who had succeeded Joseph Hearn, told his story. His father had come to work for Hearn in 1865 and was estimated to have walked 273,750 miles with the post in the following fifty years. He first boarded with the Hearns, then married and went to live in the new Post Office in South Terrace where his son and daughters Eva, Jenny and Lottie would all follow him in the job.

The post had always been delivered on foot. The London to Maidstone road had never been a Mail Coach route and Farningham was a receiving station

Above. The very clock that used to grace Mr Whitehead's shop, still on the premises and now in the care of Martin and Pamela Finch, together with the postmans alarm clock that once resided at South Terrace right.

Left. Mr Alfred Gregory, Postman, and Mrs Eldridge at White Post Cottage (now demolished)

Right. Mr Thomas and family of the Farningham Post Office at No 1 South Terrace. Here was housed the telephone exchange which covered Eynsford and Lullingstone as well as Farningham.

for post on the cross route from Dartford to Sevenoaks. In the 1850s the innkeeper at the Lion sorted and redistributed the mail as it came in from Dartford, then Joseph Hearn had taken on the work from his own house. His successor John Thomas used to walk to deliver letters as far as Kingsdown even on Sundays. Telegrams were taken by special delivery on horseback.

Mr Alfred Gregory, aged 78 and the son and grandson of Farningham bakers, had seen no future in baking after the war and had succeeded Mr Thomas as village postman. In the early days he had covered the whole of Farningham and Maplescombe from six in the morning to nine at night. 'There was no need to put names or numbers on any of the houses...I knew everyone in the village' he said. He remembered his parents telling him that in the old days servants and labourers were hired for the year at the annual fair in the village, which is the first confirmation that the event also served as a Mop or Hiring Fair.

The Gregory family, who were Colyer tenants, baked bread in the bakehouse behind Cherry Tree Cottage and sold it from the front room. When Alfred turned postman he used to deliver bread with the letters. His sister, Lily Cross, continued baking until the 1930s when she sold out to Morleys who continued the business in the house still called the Bakery opposite the church. Most older people in the village remember the early morning queues outside the shop under the gilded Daren sign, the smells of fresh bread and the enjoyable conversations.

Mrs Caroline Smith lived in Elizabeth Place and was the champion hop-picker of Kent in 1921. She had lived in the village for over forty years. Despite her dark complexion and her gold ear-rings she hastened to say that she was not a Romany. She and her daughter Jane had picked 600 bushells of hops in one week. Miss Eliza Edmonds came next. She was the schoolmistress daughter of the village schoolteachers and had been born in the schoolhouse in 1876. She was living in Farningham House Cottage when she was interviewed in 1937 and had a strange story to tell about 'old Mr Colyer', a famous recluse, who had also

lived in Farningham House. She believed him to have been crossed in love, and also to have been haunted by remorse for having knocked down and killed a villager.

Miss Edmonds was a great romantic and not an entirely reliable historian. She went on to say that Mr Colyer's two sisters lived next door to him in her present cottage so it is hard to know whether she meant Mr James Colyer, brother of Miss Anne and collector of books and fine wines, who had died there a hundred years earlier in 1839, or Mr Thomas Colyer, Charles's retired farmer brother, who had lived there in the 1870s. Both men were unmarried and apparently fairly unsociable, so fitted the possibilities of the story. The traffic accident remains a mystery.

Another important village personality in the late 19th century was Henry Marchant, of Everest and Marchant the wheelwrights who leased the Parsonage house and yard and carpenter's shop from Charles Colyer, whose notes made in 1879 say that they paid a rent of £6.17.6. per half year. Henry Marchant had come to the village in the 1860s and joined Thomas Everest, father of Fred, in this highly successful village industry which continued into the 20th century. Their billhead for 1890 advertises 'Coach, Cart and General Builders, Steam Saw Mills Etc'. In Kelly's Directory of 1907 Henry Marchant is also listed as Undertaker. This is a new term in the village, the Everests and other carpenters had always made the coffins, and generations of village women had always been called in to lay out the dead, but this would now increasingly be the work of professional undertakers.

Charles Colyer of Benenden had fond childhood memories of a cart made

for his pet goat by 'Old Marchant'. Henry Marchant and his family lived in the Parsonage and he later built a house, Hillfield, now demolished, on the old Bull Meadow next to Braeside. His daughter Miss Rose Marchant lived there until her death in 1939. She was a member of Mr Moore's Wesleyan Chapel and can be seen in the foreground of a photograph of the congregation taken in the late 1890s. Henry became very rich and has a fine obelisk memorial in the churchyard.

Another neccessary village service in the 1880s and 1890s was provided by the plumber, glazier and painter William Mason and his sons. They lived in Laurel Cottage, the first house in London Road on the corner of Sparepenny Lane. This old house, about which very little is known as yet, belonged to the Waring's manor estate. One son, Alboin Mason, who was later a Parish Clerk, was still living there in 1934 when he had his photograph taken at his garden gate.

Another thriving business was that of John Gandy the saddler, who had been succeeded by his son John. Also in Saddlers House on census day 1881 was another son Charles who gave his occupation as photographer. Maybe he was responsible for some of the early Farningham photographs. William Colyer, the other saddler, lived in one of two cottages in 'Gandy's Yard', and was presumably the 'one man' stated to be employed by Gandy. Gandy must have demolished these cottages in 1883 when he built Rablus Place which he named after his wife's family. By the 1891 census William Colyer had moved in to one of the Rablus place cottages. The younger members of this other Colyer family had grown up by the 1880s, Arthur was a 'Boots at Hotel' and Lindsey a 'House Boy in Gentleman's family'. It has not been possible to establish a relationship between the two Colyer families.

John and Charles's Gandy's sister, Louisa, still ran the grocery and drapery shop in the High Street in the 80s. She was assisted by her nephew Charles

Hook who later took over the shop. Next door was the other village grocer, Arthur Reynolds. A third village grocer and haberdasher was Miss Sally Mummery who kept her shop in Joseph Hearn's old house. Other new shops in the High Street in the 1880s included a greengrocer, a china shop and a druggist or chemist.

William Woolley, the stonemason, was living in his father Joseph's house in the London road in the 1880s, next door to Thomas Couchman the blacksmith. The Woolley's weatherboarded cottage and mason's yard are still there

at the top of London Road. The Woolleys were Colyer tenants and did a lot of work for the mill. Perhaps they used to cut the millstones, although this was usually a job for skilled itinerant craftsmen. William's father Joseph had built the wall to the churchyard in the 1870s. Before that time there was a picket fence and sheep used to graze in the graveyard. Thomas Couchman's son Adam was reputed to have been the last boy to tend sheep there. William Woolley's grandsons, William and Harold continued the masonry and builder's business until the mid 20th century, living first in the White House and later in South Hall.

On the other side of Couchman's forge lived William Wickenden, Mr Moore's coachman and gardener, who moved

The Waller brothers, Leonard and Herbert. Leonard enjoyed a reputation as an accomplished cellist. Waller's emporium sold everthing from boot laces to elephants, and was the nearest thing to a department store in Farningham, before or since. With careful study of the facia boards at 7 High Street, the name Waller can still be detected under multi-layers of paint.

into one of the mill cottages in the 90s. Bishop Horner West took a photograph of 'Old Willie Wickenden' and his wife at their garden gate in the 1930s, but that must have been the Wickenden son who was born in 1880.

In addition to Thomas Couchman there were two other blacksmiths in the village in the 1880s and 1890s. George Hales at the South Terrace forge had died and left a widow Julia who still described herself in the census as 'Blacksmith employing 2 men'. The third blacksmith was Samuel Gibson, working the forge behind the butcher's shop.

Two important and popular village personalities who unfortunately failed to be interviewed in 1938 were the Waller brothers who would take over Louisa Gandy's shop and remain there for many years. They not only kept groceries and haberdashery, but also sold second hand furniture and other useful things. Many people in the village in the mid 20th century had furnished their houses at 'Waller Brothers'. The brother's father, John Waller, had arrived in the village to work at the mill for William Moore in the 1860s. He and his wife and three of their children lived in one of the mill cottages in 1871 but by the time of the 1881 census had moved to a house in London Road, where John is described as a 'journeyman miller' and where two more sons, the future grocers, Leonard Fickes and Herbert Charles had been born in 1875 and 1877.

In 1881 William Moore's manager and foreman was still Frederick Thacker who was now 66 and still lived in one of the mill cottages. Several other mill employees, such as George Errey, are described, like John Waller, as 'journeymen millers'. This is a new description in the census although it is a very old term for someone who has finished their apprenticeship. One of the earliest photographs of the mill shows John Waller, George Errey and others standing on the bridge above the mill leat.

The occupants of the mill cottages in 1881 indicate that Charles Colyer and William Moore continued the earlier Charles's benevolence to pensioners. Widowed Mrs Gibson still lived in one cottage on an annuity, and Peter Ashenden, whose wife and sister had died in the 1870s, was still in Bridge Cottage although he was now described as a farm bailiff, perhaps working for Mr Moore. His daughter Harriet had married John Thomas the Postmaster and lived in the new Post Office in South Terrace although two of their daughters had been born at her parents home in Bridge Cottage.

This Mrs Thomas was interviewed by the Kentish Times, in 1938 on the sixtieth anniversary of her years as postmistress. Her husband had died in 1926 but her son Herbert who was also interviewed, and two of their daughters would continue to run the post office until they too retired. She had memories of her schooldays at Mrs Lockyer's 'dame school' across the road at Croft Cottage and, best of all, she was able to identify that village landmark, the cast iron owl above the butcher's house which she said her father Peter Ashenden had brought with him from his farm in Ash in the 1860s. Louisa Lockyer might not have been pleased to hear her 'Ladies Seminary' described as a dame school. She was the widow of an insurance agent and had been running a successful little boarding school since the 1860s. In 1881 she had at least ten boarders from as far away as London, Middlesex and Surrey and employed a teacher and a servant.

The Farningham Owl, still guarding the door, if a little coyly, from behind his master's floral extravaganza.

A Chat with the Farningham Owl

First published in the Dartford Chronicle, April 1930 Author anonymous

What is your age, you quaint old bird?
And who first perched you there?
And why so lately roughly moved?
These answers now declare.

Well, as to age I cannot say,
With truth, when I was born,
I hear it said some seventy years
Have been since then and gone;

I know for over forty years,
I sat in quiet here.
A well-known sight alike to all
Who pass from far and near.

My present master Mister Dell
With whom I've lived five years,
Has always treated me right well.
I had no cares or fears.

I never wished to fly away,
Was happy all day long,
Until a rough hand seized on me,
As though I had done wrong.

Yes! One dark night, not long ago,
I never shall forget,
I had the fright of all my life,
The mem'ry haunts me yet.

The coward hugged me rudely down,
It made me sadly think
A man who could so madly act
Must be the worse for drink.

But luckily help was at hand
(altho' I had not hollered)
A neighbour had been watching all,
And now the thief he collared.

Guess our surprise, quite unabashed
He said "I don't regret,
I wagered I would have him down,
And I have won my bet."

"I'll put the old owl back again,
And pay all it may cost,
I'm sorry for my foolish act,
But glad I have not lost."

The neighbour said "What will you do?
Your case is very clear".
But Mister Dell said "I won't charge
The chap had too much beer".

He proved to be a student young
(of medicine I think)
And owned he made his foolish bet,
When he was full of drink.

I hope his let-off teaches him,
Such folly is absurd,
And heed this warning
"When drink's in, Wits out" says this old bird.

So I'm perched up here again,
To watch all passers by,
My master's made me safe from harm,
Whatever thief may try.

So here I stand, and watch events,
And guard my masters door,
The village Owl at Farningham,
Just as I was of yore.

Fashionable Farningham

During the 1880s the Lion Hotel, as it was now called, increased its reputation with people from London in search of a fashionable country weekend. Most would come in their own carriages or by train but there was also a short lived coach service to the Lion from Hatchett's, Piccadilly in the early 1880s. Hatchett's had formerly been known as the White Horse Cellars and was one of the most famous terminals for coaches. The heroine in Charles Dickens' *Bleak House* was to be met at the White Horse Cellars when she arrived by coach from Reading.

The popular Victorian writer F.C.Philips wrote a novel, *As in a Looking Glass,* set partly in Farningham. It is a racy story of adultery and intrigue with a twice married heroine who has found a prospective third husband to pay her casino debts. The couple come to Farningham where she stays at the Lion and he at a nearby farmhouse. She goes to London by train to get a marriage licence and then they wait for the banns to be called in the village church. A jealous former lover arrives, intent on blackmail, but they are married in Farningham and then escape to the husband's ancestral home in Scotland where the story ends, as perhaps contemporary morality demanded, with the wife's suicide. The book went into a special edition illustrated by George du

MISS STELL HAYDON

MR GEORGE EDWARDES

MR JOHN HOLLINGSHEAD

PARTING WORDS

SIR HENRY IRVING

MISS FLORENCE ST JOHN

MR HAY COFFI

Maurier and dedicated to Sarah Bernhardt; famous names of the day.

The Lion enjoyed its enhanced reputation. It had been popular among theatrical people since the 1870s when Madame Adelina Patti the opera singer used to visit and, a little later, Sunday lunch at the Lion became fashionable among Gaiety Girls and their admirers.[134] The Mill itself was used as a backdrop for the musical The Quaker Girl. Later still, in the 1920s and 30s, a number of retired theatre people came to live in Farningham, among them the Albery family.

Sir Henry Irving, was indirectly responsible for the naming of Irving's Corner, the litle garden of quiet relaxation immediately opposite The Lion Hotel.
Here he leads the singing at the last night of the Old Gaiety Theatre.

Sporting Farningham

The solid county sporting fraternity still accounted for much of the clientele of the Lion and the Bull. In 1878 the Lion Hotel advertised itself as 'an easy distance from the West-Kent Foxhounds, the Mid-Kent Staghounds, Messrs Lubbock's Harriers and the Woolwich Arsenal Draghounds which frequently start from the hotel. Stabling is of the best quality for sporting gentlemen'. The West Kent Foxhounds hunted all over Lullingstone and Farningham Woods, and their followers often lunched afterwards with 'that worthy squire of Woodlands' William Waring, now living at Woodlands in Chelsfield. In 1895 Mr Waring's sporting friends gave him a dinner at the Lion and presented him with a silver foxhound.

William Waring's second son Arthur Thomas lived at Farningham Hill House from 1877 until his father's death in 1904. His elder brother William, who had been born at Farningham Hill, had died in 1871 so, when their father died, Arthur inherited the Chelsfield property and his younger brother Herbert

134-Nancy More, ex-Gaiety Girl, pers. com.

Farningham Hill House around the turn of the twentieth century and below as it is today.

inherited the Farningham manor estate. Arthur had married Agnes Birkett in 1877 and their two sons were born at Farningham Hill.

Arthur was a barrister and a JP and was a member of the first Kent County Council. He was also a great local and family historian.[135] He was credited by F.W.Snaith, Farningham vicar from 1911 to 1922, with having compiled the list of vicars from 1284 which hangs in Farningham church. Unlike his father and grandfather Arthur does not appear to have been much of a sportsman.

135-Geoffrey Copus, Chelsfield historian, pers. com.

285

John Fuller = **Sara Colyer**
of Hewitts
Chelsfield

Mary Fuller

Sarah Fuller = **Thomas Waring**
1776 - 1851
of Hewitts and later of Woodlands

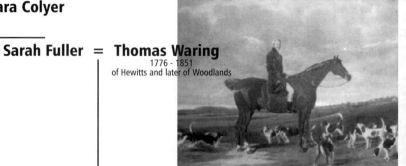

William Waring = **Mary Wall Tasker**
1818 - 1904
Recipient of the silver foxhound

Arthur Waring = **Agnes Birkett**
1851 - 1920

Of Farningham Hill House
(circa 1876-1904).
Inherited Chelsfield
Woodlands in 1904 on
fathers death.
Barrister and J.P. and
member of the first KCC
and first Farningham Parish
Council.
Family historian who
compiled the list of
Farningham vicars from
1284.

Herbert Fuller Waring = **Alice Maye Anderson**
1859 - 1919

Inherited Farningham
Manor House in 1904 on
fathers death.
From 1908, Walter Wilson
the inventor was his tenant
there. He described Waring
as "the bearded and auto-
cratic landlord who took a
poor view of his (Wilson's)
scientific activity on his
property".
Quote from (Walter Wilson,
portrait of an Inventor) by
his son Gordon Wilson.
Herbert was living in
Farningham Hill House in
1907.

Alison Mary

Born 1890.
Married in Farningham
Church, Walter Howard.
Sold Farningham Manor
House to Irving Albery in
the early1920s.

Elizabeth Maye   Nancy   Susan

Alison Mary and Nancy
with their Uncle Arthur
and Aunt Agnes at
Farningham Hill House.

The Mid-Kent Staghounds met at the Lion on Boxing Day 1884 for what the Kentish Times described as 'the usual high jinks where every horse that could wear a saddle had...been dignified by the name of "hunter". Sightseers accumulated on the hill by Charton farm. Hounds arrived at the Lion lawn and speeches were made by hunters and farmers about the excellence of the sport, and then 'Lady Mansell, a fine red hind who has given her field many a good run', was uncarted and allowed 20 minutes to get away. Lady Mansell was soon lost in the fog but was followed by hounds from Farningham Woods to Pedham Court and eventually took shelter 'in cottage buildings near Button Street'.

Presumably she was then carted away for another day's sport. The hunt next put up a 'natural' deer in Horton Wood which took everyone for a long ride round the Homes for Little Boys, then down to Court Lodge, 'as if to thank Mr Robert Russell for feeding it the past month', then away to Dartford and eventually 'housed itself' in Old Bexley before being carted back to Horton Wood. These were apparently very domesticated deer.

In November 1888 there was another meet of the Mid-Kent Staghounds at the Lion. The Master, 'the gallant Colonel North' had laid on a champagne lunch in the 'large assembly room' and 'streams of persons on horseback and in carriages poured in to the quiet little village...The coachmen and servants of the visitors as well as the labourers of the place were also partakers of the good Colonel's liberality'. This time the stag, after a good run around the Fawkham valley, was allowed to escape to 'its old quarters' near Wateringbury. Perhaps the deer were in on the secret that the hunt could not afford to kill them, although it is hard to imagine that they enjoyed the 'good run'.

Hunting of course was not the only entertainment in the village in the late 19th century. Sport in fact was a new craze in England, steadily filtering down the social scale from the upper classes and their traditions of 'blood sports', through the new middle classes with the novelties of tennis and golf, to the working classes, who also enjoyed blood sports such as bare knuckle fighting, badger baiting, cock fighting, and ferreting and whose traditional 'games and pastimes' would now become organised. Association football started in the 1870s and became professional in the 1885. Fishing continued to be as pop-

ular as ever until the arrival of the tarmac bypass road in 1928 is believed to have killed off the trout. The Invicta Bicycle Club made Farningham its destination for their 25 mile rallies and many other Londoners enjoyed the same route, ending at the Lion for tea and taking their bikes home from Farningham Road station.[136]

Although predominantly agricultural villages such as Farningham were suffering from the Great Depression, or general decline, in agriculture in the 1880s and 1890s, those labourers who still had work and a place to live were marginally better off than before. The cost of living had come down and people in a prosperous village like Farningham with its increasing population of suburbanised middle class residents were more likely to find work as gardeners and grooms or domestic servants. There was also growing employment in the nursery garden businesses opening in what is now Swanley.

Sport also provided a financial outlet for young working men. Jesse Couchman, a gardener all his life, became a famous cricketer with the Farningham Cricket Club in the days when players were paid. They could earn 10s a match in the 1860s, as much as a gardener's weekly wage. Bernard Drew, who wrote *A Hundred Years of Farningham Cricket* in 1957, says that there was a country house flavour to the matches in the late 19th century. It was no village club, practically all the members lived miles away, some in London, and they would arrive in traps and 'four-in-hands'. There were marquees in the George Meadow and dancing in the evening with fairy lights strung along the Lion lawn where a temporary bridge led across to the cricket field.

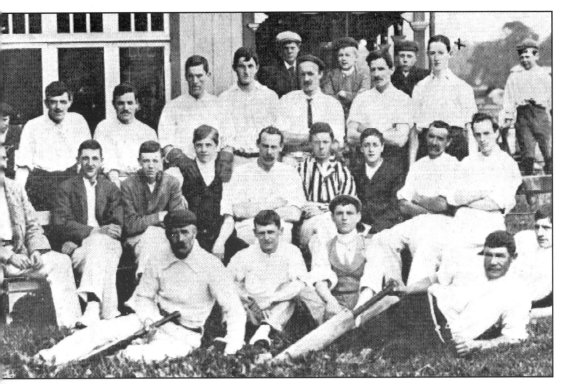

Life was very rich and enjoyable for the new middle classes. Edward Prince of Wales, the new Prince of Pleasure, was setting a fashion for hedonism that contrasted with the austere last years of his mother's reign. Gargantuan meals were eaten, elaborate fashions worn, holidays taken by the sea and abroad, and the cult of the house and its decoration became important in the smallest suburban homes.

The first Annual Rose Show was held in the Manor House garden in 1879 and again every following year in Market Meadow, until 1914. This was a successor to the ill-fated Flower Shows of the 1850s and predecessor of the Farningham Horticultural Society. Military bands played at the Rose Shows and visitors and exhibits came from all over Kent, Canterbury, Bexley, Maidstone and even Colchester. Londoners too came to enjoy the rustic spectacle.

Entertainment for poor people, apart from watching the rich at play, was still provided once a year by the Farningham Fair and by the three-weekly cattle market. There were also the annual outings organised by the church and chapel and of course the agricultural year, however diminished, still had hop-pickings and harvest suppers. Hops in fact were one of the few thriving industries. The poor in Farningham were not as badly off as in many other villages. Not only were there comparatively benevolent landlords such as Moore and Colyer and the Warings, but the local charities were able to contribute significantly to welfare problems.

The Charities

The Roper Charity had lost their Greenwich properties in 1881, when the South Metropolitan Gas Company made a compulsory purchase of their lands as suitable for development for 'Dock and Railway, Tramway, Subway and Steam Ferry'. The Trustees, including Charles Colyer, William Waring and the Revd.Brewer, who all negotiated vigorously, eventually accepted £11,827 for the properties. The money was well invested and in 1886, Farningham's share of the Roper Charity income was £66, in 1888 it was £90 and by 1894 it was £242. The doles to the poor were distributed at the church door after Sunday morning service and there are many sad stories of hardship in the lists of applicants.[137]

William Sharp, 'cripple from birth and Parish Clerk and Sexton for 44 years, at wages of £10 p.a.', who was living with his wife in the Roper Almshouse in 1889, both of them 'sick and nursing', received 19s. 6d; the saddler's widow, Ann Colyer, 'old and helpless', 7s., 'Pyke, for a Mechanical Boot, 10s.', 'Mary O'Brian for a finger amputation, 5s.', and poor 'Old Helvie, distressed, lost his purse, laid up', was given 11s.6d. William Bates was given 5s. for 'Railway to hospital' and old Helvie got another 4s. for 'Decrepitude'.

By the 1890s the Roper Charity was able to add a Prize Fund to their assisted school fees which gave rewards to children for regular attendance. Miss Ann Colyer's Charity also provided £70 p.a. for a Shoe Club in the 1890s, giving half the price of a pair of shoes for every child in the National School, and Mrs Nash's Charity provided about £10p.a. in the 1890s which was distributed as tickets to be exchanged at the draper's shop for clothes.

Late Victorian England, for all its moralising and paternalism towards the poor was a time of great philanthropy, private and unrecorded, as well as in subscriptions to the new organisations and foundations, There was a great new wave of charity. 'He who dies rich dies disgraced' said the American philanthropist Andrew Carnegie.

Last days of the working Mill

In 1886 William Moore's wife Mary died aged 56. 'After much suffering' is written on her gravestone. William stayed on in the Mill House, looked after by his daughter Harriet. There are a few photographs of him with his grand-children in the mill gardens in the last years of the century; also one of the last photographs of the working mill with Mr Moore and a waggon with sacks of corn. The gardens look well kept and full of flowers, but the Folly appears overgrown. Perhaps Mr Moore had no time for follies.

Eliza (Nina) Edmonds, who had known the village since her birth in the 1870s, wrote in her 1930s history of the village that several older residents remembered the working mill with its four horse waggons loaded with sacks of flour setting off for London. This is confirmed by a centenary publication of Stricklands, the seed merchants of Dartford. Samuel Strickland, who

*The Mill around 1900,
still working,
but not for long.
William Moore and
daughter Harriet in the
foreground*

founded the firm in 1851, used to do business at the Mark Lane Corn Exchange in London. For fear of foot-pads on the way home he banked his money at the Bank of England before returning. His friend William Moore, who did not have a London bank account, after delivering flour to bakers in South London and 'finding himself with a weight of cash in gold and silver', would pay his money in to Mr Strickland's account and, 'in due course', reclaim it in Dartford.[138]

Here then we have a nice picture of William Moore delivering flour to South London bakers and, since he would probably also visit his London mill and rather than go home with an empty waggon, would he not, like Samuel Strickland, combine the journey with buying grain from Mark Lane?. The medieval corn market at Cornhill had been supplanted by the Mark Lane Exchange in 1749 and enclosed and enlarged in the second half of the 19th century. Surely Mr Moore knew it well.

138–W.G.G.Alexander
A Farming Century
(1991)

291

Death of Charles Colyer Junior

On the 22nd of June 1887 Charles Colyer died aged 70 at 38 Dorset Square, London and was buried in Farningham the following week. With him died much of the Colyer family's active participation in Farningham life. His only surviving son Arthur inherited his estate, but Arthur was a nomadic figure, never staying at one address for more than a few years. According to his grandson Charles Colyer of Benenden he moved house 16 times during his married life.

The two Arthurs, Colyer and Waring, are described in Kelly's Directories as the principal landowners in Farningham at the turn of the century. Arthur Colyer and his wife, Elizabeth Kemp Matson, had four children; Ernest, born in Greenwich in 1869, Eva, Harold Arthur, and Mary Constance. The eldest son, Ernest, would inherit the mill estate on his father's death in 1920. Arthur and his sisters donated the money for a parochial room or vestry to be built on the south side of the chancel in their father's memory in 1888.

In 1891 the Revd. Brewer died and the Revd. Joseph Williamson, a relative of the Waring family was appointed to the living. Although the gift was with the archbishop of Canterbury, no doubt family influence played some part. Joseph's grandmother, Elizabeth Waring, was a sister of Thomas Waring of Chelsfield and Farningham. Elizabeth had married William Woodbridge Nash, descendant of the Farningham Nash family. She and her husband have commemorative brass plaques in Farningham church. Their son Edwin was a well known architect who designed Crockenhill parish church, and their daughter Emma, who had married Joshua Williamson, was the mother of Joseph and his sister Anne who now both came to Farningham vicarage. Joseph had been curate at Sellinge in Kent from 1864 to 1874 and was now in his mid-fifties. Neither he nor his sister, who kept house for him, ever married and when she died in 1905 he resigned the living and went to live in London where he died in 1909.

The end of the Vestry and the first Parish Council

The Local Government Act of 1894 brought the work of the Vestry to an end. County Councils had been established in 1888 and now Rural and Urban District Councils were created, and rural parishes of more than 300 inhabitants would transfer the work of the Vestry to a Parish Council.

The first Farningham Parish Council meeting was held on Tuesday December 4th, 1894, at the National School. William Moore was there and seconded the unanimous proposal that Mr Arthur Waring should chair this first meeting until a parish chairman was elected. There were eleven candidates for the Council, seven of whom were then elected by a show of hands. The highest vote of 85 hands went to a comparative newcomer to the village, Mr John Camden Hayward of Dartford, who had recently become the tenant of Charton Manor and would stay there until his death in 1912. Son of Mr

John Hayward, a Dartford solicitor, Mr J.C.Hayward was already Clerk to the Board of Health, and to the Magistrates, and was the first Town Clerk of Dartford Urban District Council. He was obviously thought a most useful addition to village society and a week later, at the second Parish Council meeting, he was elected the first Chairman.[139]

Other councillors elected at the first meeting were the Revd.Williamson

The first meeting, December 1894, of the Dartford Urban District Council. Third from the left, back row is J.C.Hayward, Town Clerk.

with 71 hands; James Lines, proprietor of the Bull, with 64; Thomas Vaughan, market gardener of Button Street, with 58; H.E.Reynolds, grocer, 55; George Errey, miller, 52; James Maloney, bricklayer, 32. Francis Gandy with 32 votes, and Herbert Wood with 26 and Walter Dunmall with 3 were not elected. Mr Stephen Davis, manager of the London and County Bank was appointed Treasurer with no remuneration, and Mr Richard Edmonds, the schoolmaster, was appointed the first Parish Council Clerk at £20 pa. Mr George Solomon was appointed Waywarden and Arthur Pipon of the Mount and Charles Stone of the Lion were appointed Overseers for the Dartford union, posts that were not abolished until 1927. The Revd.Williamson became Vice Chairman to J.C.Hayward.

The business of the Parish Council went on in much the same way as the business of the Vestry had done. Roads, Bridges, Transport, the Poor, the Church and the Charities were all to be joined by newer subjects such as Planning, Footpaths, Recreation, Street lighting, Festivals, Refuse and Litter, Pollution and Dog Fouling, Traffic Calming, Gypsy Sites, Health and Safety and Social Services and the literally endless search for a Playing Field. Everything would be discussed, sometimes fruitfully, sometimes in vain, over the next hundred years.

Fort Farningham

Everything relating to the village, that is, matters of wider, national importance do not appear in the minutes. One Farningham phenomenon of the 1890s which did not appear in the Council minutes was the building of 'Fort Farningham' at Pedham Place. Although this is now demolished, it appears on many maps and causes curiosity. This was not a fort but an armoured storehouse for amunition and supplies, one of a defensive line of similar buildings erected along the North Downs against a possible invasion of England by unnamed hostile enemy forces.[140] Volunteers were to man the fortified storehouses which were surrounded by banks and ditches for machine gun emplacements. Only 15 were built and they were abandoned, curiously enough, before the first war. The Farningham one was not considered suffi-

139-CKS P145/29/1
140-Victor Smith, 'Maginot Line at Farningham' *Kent Archaeological Review* No 27 (1972)

ciently important to merit a preservation order and was buried under a golf course in the 1990s.

At the second meeting Dr Ashurst and Mr Whitehead, the clockmaker, were appointed to the Roper Charity and Dr T.F.Hugh Smith, a most important new arrival in the village, proposed a vote of confidence in the new Council and approval of the course they had taken so far. The first complaint to the Council was made by Mr Albert Bates who said that 'certain persons in the employ of the Darenth Valley Sewerage Board had emptied the contents of the sewer passing through the village into the river on the 26th March 1894'. The 1865 Sewerage Act had created sewer authorities and the Sanitary Act of 1866 had made local authorities responsible for providing drainage, water supplies and 'removal of nuisances'. The river was no longer to act as a sewer, although a water supply to each house and drainage into a public sewer was still some way into the future. The Darent Valley Sewer Scheme had authorised a sewer to be laid from Westerham to Dartford as early as 1878 but the work took many years to complete.

Fort Farningham

Public Health

The Public Health Acts of 1872 and 1875 established the appointment of Medical Officers of Health and Dr Thomas Frederick Hugh Smith, FRCS, 'surgeon, medical officer and public vaccinator', was the first in Farningham. He and his son, Sumner Hugh Smith, were to serve the village for the next half century as much loved general practitioners as well as MOsH. Dr Ashurst would be increasingly retired until his death, aged 97 in 1929. On leaving the White House he moved into a large house named the Beacon which he had built on the site of William Dray's ironfoundry. There was quite a stir at his death, because he left much of his considerable estate to his housekeeper, Mrs Saxe-Park, in a will contested by his niece. He also left £100,00 to local and national charities.

Dr T.F.H. Smith came to the village in 1890. He married a Farningham girl, Florence, daughter of the farmer James Russell. Her brother, Robert Russell was house surgeon at King's College Hospital at the time T.F.H. was a registrar. The Smiths were an old medical family, T.F.H.'s father, Professor Henry Smith had been a surgeon and lecturer at Kings before him. The Hugh Smiths first lived at Fernwood and, after Florence's death in 1904 he remarried and built himself Braeside on Gorse Hill. His son, Sumner, later came to live and practice at Fernwood again.

After service in the first World War, Dr. Sumner Hugh Smith came to Fernwood around 1920 and was a Colyer tenant. The freehold was not acquired until 1937. The porch to the left was the entrance to the surgery which comprised, waiting and consulting room and dispensary. Medicines were dispensed and left for collection on the shelves in the porch, which are still there today.

Pictured above, Dr. Smith M.C. (Military Cross) with the rank of Major in W.W.2

Right, Dr. Ashurst died in 1929 aged 97.

The village doctors have been very important in the history of Farningham. Early doctors, such as the infamous Dr Harris who as 'surgeon and apothecary' was possibly licenced by the Society of Apothecaries, and good Dr Nash who appears to have trained by apprenticeship alone, were possibly not very highly qualified. Later doctors, such as Dr Slaughter and Dr Ashurst, were able to put MD after their names.

These doctors, as we have seen, treated patients privately but also were retained, first by the Overseers and later the Unions, to treat the poor in the village. In 1894 the first publication of a Parish Magazine gives details of a Medical Club in the village, possibly initiated by Dr T.F.H.Smith. A man and his wife paid 8d. per month and 3d. per child or widow. Payments were to be made at the schoolroom on the 1st Monday of each month between 4. and 4.45.pm. The new Parish Magazine cost 1½d. and 150 copies were sold in its first month.

295

Chapter Sixteen

*The Mill Closes / The Wards of Farningham Mill / Motorised Traffic /
Electric Light / Walter Wilson, Inventor / The Golf Course /
The First World War / The Nursery and Market Gardens / The Tank /
The Village Hall / The Social Club / The Manor House sale /
The First, Second and Third Farningham Exhibitions /
The Village in the 1930s, World War Two / The Last Sixty Years.*

The Mill closes

Farningham Mill closed for business in 1900 and William Moore went to live
with his daughter Harriet in Wimbledon. He died two years later, and the
whole family came to his funeral service in the Wesleyan chapel followed by
burial in the churchyard. Only three members of the Moore family ever
came back to visit the village, the two eldest Horner children in 1926 and
William Moore's great grandson, Bishop Frank Horner West, whose curiosity
about his old family home had been revived by the photograph of the Mill
House on the cover of *Country Life* on July 15th 1976.

Arthur Colyer's elder son Ernest, wrote to Thomas Colyer Fergusson, the
family historian, in 1902 giving him news of the birth in November the
previous year, of his elder son and heir. 'Our boy's name is Charles Ernest,
baptised at St James's Church, Gravesend'. This boy was to be Charles of
Benenden who would own the mill estate from Ernest's death in 1951 to his

*Charles Colyer of
Beneden, brother Billy
centre and sister Evelyn,
mother of Vvyyan,
recent owner of the Mill.
See Colyer family tree,
page 179.*

own in 1993. Ernest himself inherited the estate at Arthur's death in 1920.

Alice Horner died in 1925, and the son and daughter who visited next year reported that the mill 'had been let to rich Americans who, of all things, had converted the great mill chamber into a dance hall with what would now be called a cocktail bar'. Allowing for the outraged sensibilities of Alice's bereaved children, who had after all known the mill as a place of industry as well as pleasure and had been brought up in a very puritanical household, there was just a grain of truth in the report.

The Wards of Farningham Mill House

Charles and Ernest Colyer

In 1900, after William Moore had left the Mill House, Arthur Colyer had rented the whole property on a long lease to Herbert John Ward and his wife Alice. Herbert would live there until he died in 1940 and Alice, until she went to live in St Margaret's Bay in 1945. Herbert came from Lennoxvale, Belfast. He was born in 1870 and trained as a marine engineer and naval architect. In 1900 he was living in Liverpool where he was in charge of construction for Elder, Dempster & Co, working on the design of banana ships fitted with refrigeration plant by J.&E. Halls of Dartford.[141]

Halls appear to have snapped up this clever young man who came south to join their company that same year. His expertise in marine refrigeration and his obvious managerial skills meant that he became a director in 1910 and succeeded Everard Hesketh as chairman in 1921. Harry Miller, in *Halls of Dartford 1785-1985*, says that he 'had great charm but a frail constitution on which the strain of the Depression years took its toll, and he retired in 1939 and died in 1940'. His wife Alice was the daughter of Alexander Guthrie

141-Harry Miller Halls of Dartford 1785-1985

Top left, the Ward family, Herbert, Alice, Jack and Caroline.

Top, Herbert's father John Ward, in the garden of The Mount 1909

Left, Jack and Caroline and Nurse, who is showing some concern at the proposed descent.

There is no doubt the Wards were in the vanguard of motoring enthusiasts in the early 1900s. It is not certain whether these were all owned simultaneously

of Liverpool and the granddaughter of Thomas Guthrie, a well known Scottish Presbyterian preacher and philanthopist, quite probably as strict a puritan as William Moore. She had however spent some of her youth in America, and maybe it was a trace of this in her accent and her taste in interior decoration which so upset her Horner visitors.

The Wards were undoubtedly ruthless in their clearance of all the mill machinery, but they respected the exterior of the building and the maintenance and upkeep of the buildings and garden. It is probable that they built the walled kitchen garden, because it does not appear in the Moore's photographs, but that might be looked on as an improvement. In fact they must have been model tenants, the photographs taken of the mill during their occupancy show a beautifully kept house and grounds. It is surprising that Arthur Colyer allowed the mill itself to be gutted but these were days before there was much interest in industrial archaeology.

The main floor of the mill was converted not exactly into a dance hall, but a very large living room which, with its parquet floor, could undoubtedly have been a ballroom. The Ward's granddaughter, Kate Kavenagh, who lived in the mill house with her grandparents in the late 1930s, remembered a magical Mill Room as it was called, with a great inglenook fireplace, built by the Wards who had also installed central heating, rugs, sofas, a grand piano and a billiard table and countless beautiful objects and cabinets full of curiosities.

The Wards had two children, Caroline born in 1904 and Kate's father, John or Jack as he was usually called, in 1909. The house and gardens were immaculately kept by a large staff of servants. Alice Ward had proverbialy good taste and was a stickler for order. All the woodwork inside the house was painted dark red, traces of which can still be seen, and the walls covered with pale grey tweedy wallpaper.

Herbert Ward's father, John Ward, came to live at the Mount in Sparepenny Lane and Michael Donnelly came from the family home in Ireland to act as gardener, handyman, and originally as coachman, but later as chauffeur. The Donnellys lived in one of the Mill Cottages and had four children. They became very integrated with village life and their two daughters still lived here in 2002. When Mike Donnelly died in 1947, aged 78, he had spent 53 years as 'faithful and beloved friend of John Ward of Lennoxvale and of Herbert and Alice Ward of the Mill House'. He and his two sons became loyal supporters of the Church, the St John's Ambulance, the Cricket Club and the Working Men's Club. The Wards also employed a cook, a parlourmaid, a house-maid and a kitchen maid and later a cowman, George Talbot, who lived in the Gardener's Cottage with his wife and twin daughters and looked after the Guernsey cows.

The Arthur Waring's ex-governess, Miss Alice Smith from Yorkshire, later to become a well known village personality, came to teach the Ward's children and started a little school to include neighbour's children which she ran from the Counting House. She specialised in the Latin and French neccessary to get little boys into prep and public schools. The Wards were joined in Farningham by other family members. Herbert's brother Harry came to live in Lavender Bank, and his sister Edith and her husband Guy Evans, who also worked at Halls, came first to the Mount with their father and later, after Herbert Waring died, they lived at Farningham Hill House.

A most important arrival in the village was Alice Ward's half brother Gordon

 Guthrie who came from Liverpool in 1908 to work for his brother-in-law at Halls. Gordon first lived at the Lion, then as a lodger with Mrs Handsley in Bridge Cottage, and then, when he came back from the war in 1919, he bought Hampton Court House from Dr Ashurst. This was Edward Hampton's little farmhouse of the 1750s to which the Guthries would add extensively in the 1930s. Gordon married Christina (Kirstie) Stevenson in 1924 and they had four daughters. He spent the rest of his working life at Halls, becoming a director in 1945. He lived to be a hundred in 1985 and cele-brated his birthday by planting the Metsequoia tree beside the bridge. Kirstie died in 1998 aged 97. She had been a pivot of village life for many years.

This nucleus of related families, the Wards, Guthries and Evans, living so close together, remained united for the first half of the century. Alice Smith's school moved out of the Counting House and into Sancton, a converted army hut in Horton Way. She kept rabbits and fed the children on rabbit stew and wore a rabbit fur coat which gave her a reputation for eccentricity but she is

The extension to Hampton Court House built by the Guthries.

remembered by some of her pupils, now in their seventies, with admiration and awe. Although she only ever lived in a caravan at the back of the school, she became a surprisingly rich woman and owned several houses in the village.

Farningham moved slowly into the twentieth century. Life remained very much the same until the first World War. The same families stayed on and did many of the same things. An exciting innovation was the arrival of the telephone, and the Thomas family of the Post Office installed a switchboard in 1904 to serve the first 12 subscribers. The greatest change of course was the arrival of motor vehicles. Edward Shuter, of the family of carpenters, became the manager of the first Farningham Motor Bus Company in 1902. The bus had 10 seats and left the Bull yard at 8.30 arriving at Dartford at 9.15. Fare 1s.6.

Early motor cars in the Bull yard circa 1904.

Motorised Traffic

The internal combustion engine had been invented as early as 1885 but private motoring had developed slowly in England, mainly because of the 1865 'Locomotives on Turnpike and other Roads Act' which imposed a 4 m.p.h limit and the necessity to have a man with a red flag walking in front of the vehicle, which was not repealed until 1896 with a 12 mph limit. The speed limit was increased to 20 m.p.h. in 1903.

*The Hallford No 1 outside
the Mill House;
chain driven and of robust
construction.*

*An open top bus built on a
Hallford chassis outside the
Bull.*

The Royal Army Medical Corp visit to Farningham in 1905, the transport section being billeted and entertained by Herbert Ward at the Mill House.
Note the group of house maids in the doorway of the house, no doubt enjoying the occassion.

Below, in the field adjacent to the cricket pavilion.
Photograph courtesy of Dr. Gerald Cramp

Halls of Dartford did not venture far into the private car industry but became increasingly involved in the production of commercial vehicles. 'Hallford' lorries and buses became famous. There is a photograph of a Hallford bus with an open top deck taken outside the Bull in 1911. Guy Evans was in charge of the motor vehicle division from the start and Halls directors were quick to move into private motoring. One of them owned a 1900 belt-driven Benz which may be one of the cars photographed outside the Mill in the early days of the century. The most interesting photograph is of a Hall's No.1 Chain Drive tractor. Herbert Ward was driven by Michael Donnelly in a series of Wolesleys. The dashing Guy Evans drove an Arrol-Johnson with a Beadle cabriolet body.

Motorised traffic became a most vexatious problem for the Parish Council.

303

By 1910 speeds of up to 25 m.p.h. were reported through the village despite the 8 m.p.h. restriction signs. Heavy traffic problems increased due to troop movements during WW1, after which the peace-time pleasure seekers came bowling through the village with the same enthusiasm as the drivers of barouches and four-in hands on the Turnpike roads a century earlier.

There had been earlier troop movements at the mill in 1905 when the RAMC performed a route march from Woolwich to Farningham of about 300 men, officers and instructors with horses, cycles, a horse drawn ambulance waggon, a motor ambulance, 2 service waggons and a dressings cart. The photographs taken in the village and outside the mill to commemorate the day have caused much speculation about how and why war had come to Farningham at such an early date. Herbert Ward billetted the Transport Section in his stables and entertained the men 'at a smoking concert in the mill adjoining the house which had been lighted by electricity for the purpose'. An electric generating plant had been installed by Bob Smith of Halls who had fixed a flat belt drive from the old mill spur-wheel driven by the existing turbine in the river to the generator, possibly producing the first electric light in Farningham.

We may complain about speeding 'through' traffic today but the top end of the High Street was just as dangerous, if not more so, in 1921. The by-pass was obviously much needed.

Two crashes created serious damage to property, the first nearly demolishing Furlonger's and the paper shop, and the second involving a steam lorry which lost power and ran back into Fernwood House. Luckily the doctor's porch had not yet been added.

Left, Furlonger's shop before the accident and during subsequent reconstruction.

Electric Light

Electric light would not be connected to the village until 1930. One man who was instrumental in bringing electricity to people's houses was Mr John Crowhurst, one of nine children of the farming family at Charton and Hever in Kingsdown.[142] John was born in 1905 and was to initiate the first electric services in the village. Maybe Major Wilson, his father's neighbour at Charton, had alerted him to the emerging importance of electricity. John Crowhurst started a flourishing business in the 1920s, first from the little shop, now a hairdresser's, opposite the Lion and later from the former Pine Shop opposite the Bull which he named the Darent Valley Battery Service. Apart from making and selling radios he would tour on his motor-bike to wire the houses and change and re-charge the batteries. John and his wife, who was a grand-daughter of the wheelwright Henry Marchant, were two of several people in the village whose lives would span nearly the whole of the 20th century.

It is always interesting to note the different uses of the same buildings over the years. Being a modern man, John Crowhurst has installed a plate glass window, replacing that of the boot repairers of an earlier time.

William Waring had died in 1904 which meant that Arthur Waring and his family went to live at Chelsfield and his younger brother Herbert, with his wife Alice and four daughters, came to live at Farningham Hill House. Herbert had a reputation for irascibility, and his gamekeepers kept a close watch on poachers in Farningham Woods, so he was not the most popular new squire. He leased the Manor House to the engineer and inventor Walter Wilson in 1908. Wilson knew the neighbourhood well, having collaborated with Percy Pilcher on the ill-fated 'soaring machines' which they tested at Eynsford in the 1890s. Had it not been for Pilcher's accidental death Walter Wilson's aircraft engine might have beaten the Wright brother's first powered flight by four years.

142-Zena Bamping, *West Kingsdown* op.cit.

306

Walter Wilson, Inventor

The Wilson-Pilcher motor car was one of the first British designs but it was a very small business and Wilson had been forced to sell out his share. He now joined Halls of Dartford to work on the design of the Hallford lorry. So now the three neighbours, Herbert Ward, Guy Evans and Walter Wilson drove, or were driven, to work in Dartford every day in their amazing new motor cars. Walter Wilson's son Gordon, in his memoir of his father, remembers that his father's Darracq car made such a distinctive noise that Patch, the Clumber spaniel, started barking when Wilson reached the Bricklayer's Arms.[143]

Driving a private motor car was still the prerogative of the rich. Despite Gordon Wilson's claim that his parents did not regard themselves as particularly well off, their life in the Manor House was supported by a multitude of servants; cook, kitchen maid, housemaid, parlour-maid, nurse, nursery maid, gardener, garden boy and a groom who was later to act as a very nervous chauffeur.

A small golf course was built on the fields below Sparepenny Lane between Farningham and Eynsford in 1912. These were the fields once known as Sheeplands and, in 1841, had belonged to John Pawley, grandson and heir of Edward Hampton. No records of the Golf Club have come to light, but a 1912 prospectus of 'The Hampton Court Estate' has a map showing the golf course and the club house which was more or less opposite the Eynsford paper mill. The Hampton Court Estate was a project to build an estate of houses and bungalows on the fields above Sparepenny Lane. This had also been John Pawley's land, known in 1841 as Hanging Hill. All these lands had earlier belonged to the Bosvilles of Eynsford and were the lands leased by John Kemp of Farningham Mill. John Pawley's heirs had been his sister Mary Colyer and her husband James who was Henry Colyer's third son, so these were now Colyer lands.

There is map of 1861 showing the same Hampton Court estate as the property of James Colyer, who died in 1866.[144] His heirs were his eight quarrelsome children but which of them sold the land and to whom has not yet been discovered. The new houses were to be built 'from a cost of £600 upwards', each house with views across the Darent Valley and 'the Estate regulations will prevent freeholders having their property spoiled by unsightly or low-class buildings on adjoin-

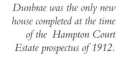

Dunbrae was the only new house completed at the time of the Hampton Court Estate prospectus of 1912.

143- Gordon Wilson, *Walter Wilson, Portrait of an Inventor* (1986)
144-CKS U36 T30

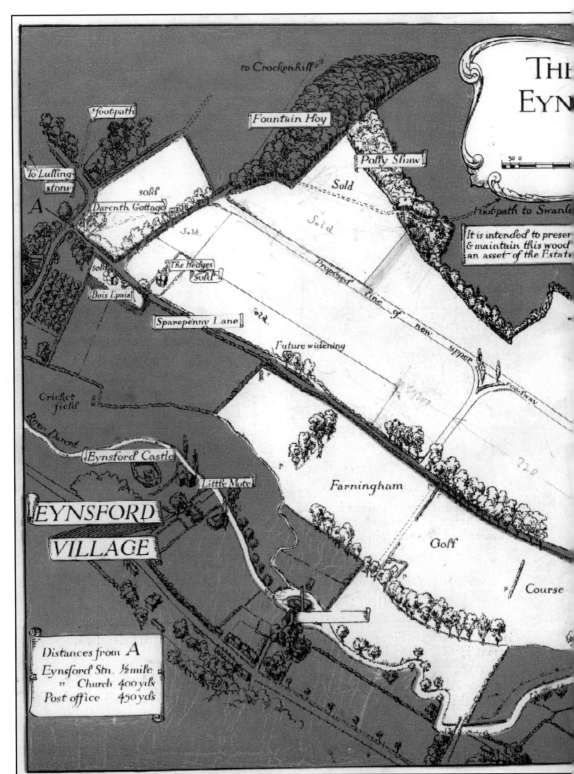

to Crockenhill

THE
EYN

50 0

footpath

Fountain Hoy

Polly Shaw

To Lulling
stone

Sold

Darenth Cottage

sold

footpath to Swanle

Sold

A

Sold

It is intended to preser
& maintain this wood
an asset of the Estate

sold

The Hedges
sold

Bois Epais

Proposed line of new upper

Sparepenny Lane

sold

Future widening

foot-pay

upper

Cricket
field

River Darent

220

Eynsford Castle

Little Mote

Farningham

EYNSFORD
VILLAGE

Golf

Course

Distances from A
Eynsford Stn. ½ mile
" Church 400 yds
Post office 450 yds

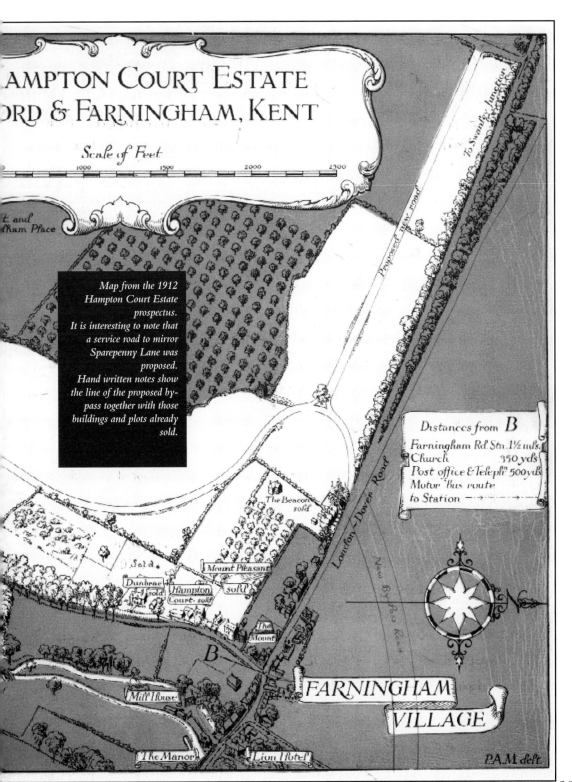

HAMPTON COURT ESTATE
ORD & FARNINGHAM, KENT

Scale of Feet

| 1000 | 1500 | 2000 | 2500 |

t. and
ham Place

Map from the 1912
Hampton Court Estate
prospectus.
It is interesting to note that
a service road to mirror
Sparepenny Lane was
proposed.
Hand written notes show
the line of the proposed by-
pass together with those
buildings and plots already
sold.

To Swanley Junction

Proposed new road

Distances from B
Farningham Rd Stn. 1½ m/s.
Church 350 yds
Post office & Teleph" 500 yds
Motor 'bus route
to Station ———→

London—Dover Road

New By-Pass Road

N

The Beacon
sold

Sold

Mount Pleasant
sold

Dunbrae
sold

Hampton
Court- sold

The
Mount

B

Mill House

FARNINGHAM
VILLAGE

The Manor

Lion Hotel

P.A.M delt.

309

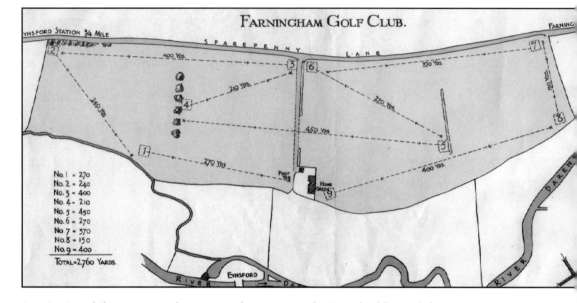

No.1 = 270
No.2 = 240
No.3 = 400
No.4 = 210
No.5 = 450
No.6 = 270
No.7 = 370
No.8 = 150
No.9 = 400

TOTAL = 2760 YARDS.

ing sites', and there were to be 'positive bars against the jerry-builder and the purveyor of eccentric or inartistic designs'. Under the title 'amenities' it was noted that 'Harrods deliver daily', so this was obviously to be an upmarket development. The Estate architects were Messrs Gripper and Stevenson of Cannon Street, London and the agent was William Hodsoll of Farningham, and from the proprietorial description in the estate brochure it seems likely that the golf course had been built by the developers to attract customers for their houses. Fortunately perhaps, for the overdevelopment of the valley, the houses were never built, due maybe to the approach of war. It is possible that Dr Ashurst who, like Miss Smith, was investing in property in the village and owned Hampton Court House until he sold it to A.G.Guthrie in the late 1920s, had bought the whole Hampton Court estate. The classy new name of 'Hampton Court' for Edward Hampton's farm must have been thought up by the speculative builders.

The Golf Course

The golf course however, had already been built and, although it went into hibernation during the first war, it was revived by the Wards of the Mill and the Daniels of Lavender Bank in the early 1920s and became very popular until the land was needed for arable fields again during the second war.[145] The club house had a verandah overlooking the course, there was a professional, Mr Tindall, and there were the usual cups and trophies. Herbert Ward and Irving Albery were both presidents and credited with saving the course from several more attempted incursions by speculative builders. The 1932 Town and Country Planning Act would later set out proceedures for submitting and approving planning schemes and for preserving historically valuable buildings.

145–*Kentish Times* 13/1/1939

The First World War

The Parish Council had little to say about the course of the First World War. In 1914 they were most concerned about the installation of gas street lighting which seems curious in the light of possibile enemy air raids. Allotments were offered for rent in Wested Lane to encourage self sufficiency. In 1915 the chief discussion was the shortage of tobacco in the village shops. However, the village constable was to be provided with a shrapnel helmet for Air Raid Protection.

This is not to suggest that the people of Farningham knew nothing of the horror of the war. Many had friends or family who never came home and many who did return were disabled for life. The huge psychiatric hospital at Stone was home to several local men traumatised by their experiences in the trenches. The Couchmans, Mills, Dunmalls, Wingates, Flewins and Gregorys all lost sons as did the parents of the fifteen other men listed on the War Memorial. Dr Sumner Smith, who served in the RAMC in both wars, was awarded the MC for attending and removing wounded men from under fire in the front line.[146]

Life was very hard for the poor after the war. The Parish Council discussed the 'starvation wages' of agricultural labourers, and it must not be forgotten that a huge percentage of the rural population was still employed in agriculture. 25s. a week was the minimum wage set by Lloyd George but local farmers were not keeping to it and were deducting 2s.3d. to 3s.3d. a week for rents of their tied cottages. 'Homes for Heroes', or 'Houses for the Working Classes' were debated, as was an Arterial or bypass road and a War Memorial. By 1922 the Arterial Road, now the A20, was constructed but the council houses at Oliver Crescent were not built until 1927. The houses were rented by the DRDC at 9s. p.w. for parlour type and 7s.6d. non-parlour. The parlour type, as recommended by the Government in 1918, were to have 3 ground floor rooms with 3 bedrooms above and a larder and bathroom. The non-parlour, which proved the most popular in Farningham, had 2 bedrooms and saw the beginning of the demise of the parlour, that often unused showroom of the house.

The Liberal Governments of 1905-1915 brought many social welfare reforms. Lloyd George's 'People's Budget' of 1909 raised money to pay for the first National Insurance scheme and the first Old Age Pensions. Both were modest in scope, but as the Parish Magazine said 'God Bless Lloyd George'. The Poor Law was to be renamed Public Assistance and the destitute would be called the 'necessitous'.

The new bye-pass nearing completion in 1921/2. Nestling against the trees in the centre of the picture is the old cricket pavilion.
Photograph courtesy of Dr. Gerald Cramp

146-Mrs H.D.Caldicott, daughter, pers. com.

311

The Old Age Pensions Act of 1908 provided a pension of five shillings a week for people over 70 with an income of less than £31.10s p.a. The National Insurance Act of 1911 established health and unemployment insurance to be paid for by contributions from the State, employers and employees. The scheme...was compulsory for all employees earning less than £160 per year (raised to £250 in 1919 and £420 in 1942).[147] The worker paid 4d., the State 2d. and the employer 3d.; the famous 'Ninepence for Fourpence'.[148] The services of a 'panel' family doctor was provided but there was no cover for dependents or right to hospital care or medicines.

Top left. The view up Farningham Hill prior to the construction of the arterial road in 1922.

Above. With such a spacious junction, some traffic confusion would be inevitable. Perhaps this accounts for the heavy presence of the St, John Ambulance Brigade.

The Nursery and Market Gardens

New sources of employment were provided for local people by the great nursery and market gardens at Swanley.[149] Several prominent people in Farningham's later 20th century history were born or brought up in what is now Swanley, as the children of men who worked for Cannell's nurseries. They lived in Cannell's Highcroft Cottages, opposite the bus station and went to school at the Farningham Hill School next to the present day Swanley interchange of the motorways. This part of the village, known as Farningham West, was not transferred to Swanley until 1955.[150]

Mrs Nora Ward (Auntie Norah as she was known to several generations) was the eldest of eight Cronk children who lived here and later moved to Farningham. Her life also spanned nearly the whole century and she had many memories such as walking down to Farningham Fair where traders would have pushed their barrows all the way from London. The last Fair was held in 1915. Horace (Rog) Rogers, chairman of the Parish Council from 1968 to 1983, was also born here, although at a later date. His father, James or Jimmy, was a Farningham Parish Councillor from 1924 to 1955 when Rog joined in his place. Between them father and son chalked up over sixty years of service to the village.

147-Michael D.Warren, *A Chronology of State Medicine, Public Health, Welfare and related services in Britain 1066-1999,* (2000)
148-Nicholas Timmins, *The Five Giants, a Biography of the Welfare State* (1996)
149-W.G.Duncombe, 'Cartwheels and Chrysanthemums, Cannells, Nurserymen of Eynsford' F&ELHSoc.No7
150-Parish Council Minutes

The two lonely St. John Ambulance huts were abandoned in 1935 in favour of new headquarters at the old Methodist Chapel in London Road.

Motor traffic accidents increased and 1926 saw the foundation of the Farningham Division of St John's Ambulance to deal with the casualties. At first the Ambulance men were stationed in huts on the Arterial road but after 1936, when William Moore's Wesleyan Chapel closed, they made their headquarters in the old chapel.[151] By 1928 the provision of a mortuary for Farningham to deal with the fatalities on the road was proposed but it was agreed that the one for Sutton-at-Hone in Swanley could be used. Norah Ward's husband was an instructor in First Aid at the St John Ambulance HQ, and the Donnellys, father and sons and Mr Talbot of the mill were voluntary members. Some worked with bicycles and Billy Donnelly attended on his motor bike.

151–Gordon Edwards (of White House) scrapbooks of newspaper cuttings

The Tank

In 1919 the War Office presented the Parish Council with the 'War Trophy' of one of the fighting tanks designed by Walter Wilson and William Tritton in 1915. The Wilsons had moved from the Manor House to Charton Manor where some trials of the tank had taken place.[152] A Mr George Eves gave the Kentish Times two memories of this tank in 1976.[153] The first was from 1915 when he had been driving a threshing machine along Eglantine Lane and this extraordinary machine, 'the first Mark Four (tank) ever built', appeared from Farningham Road Station and drove across the river and fields to Charton for testing. The second memory was of the self same machine driving down into the village in 1919, 'under the watchful eyes of the Waller brothers outside their general store, Mrs

Gregory outside her sweetshop...the two venerable figures of the Whitehead twins...and the sturdy figure of Mr Furlonger' (the blacksmith)...clattering on past the Lion Hotel to 'opposite old Granfer Marchants's timber yard' where it settled on its concrete standing 'under the eyes of local dignitaries and the famous Major in person'. It should be added that this account varies slightly from other people's memories.

Arthur Colyer died in 1920 and was followed as landlord of the mill estate by his son Ernest. The estate still consisted of the mill and mill house and cottages and several houses in the village. Herbert Waring also died

in 1920 and there was a great sale of the manor estate. The 480 acres, and the houses, shops and cottages were sold in 10 lots. The fields are all amazingly similar to those on the Hanger map of 1693, so it seems that the manor lands had changed very little. Lot number 3, the Manor House, with 16 acres land, was sold to Mr (later Sir) Irving Albery who belonged to a famous theatrical family and was named after his godfather Henry Irving. He was married to Jill Jones, daughter of the playwright Henry Arthur Jones and they had three children, Jessica, Michael and Peter. Irving Albery became the Conservative MP for Gravesend in 1924 and was knighted in 1936.

In 1921 the tank, never an entirely popular addition to the village scene,

Two views of the famous tank together with the offending chain link fence around the Manor House lawn, and the telephone pole that proved the point.

152-W.G.Duncombe, 'Walter Gordon Wilson' F&ELHSoc Pub22
153-*Kentish Times* 22/1/1976

was the centre of controversy when Mr Albery erected posts and chains to fence off not only the tank but also the whole of the green outside his house. Parishioners believed, with some justification, that this was the village green and common ground. Mr Albery, already a politician, said that it was not his wish to debar the public from use of the green, only to beautify and add to the picturesqueness of the village and to protect the tank. Mr Rashleigh, solicitor to the deceased Mr Waring, was consulted and said that as Mr Albery received way-leave rent on the telegraph pole outside his house the land was his. The matter rumbled on for some years with many complaints about people falling over the chains on their way to church, also about the risks of being run over, which seems to indicate that there was no pavement on the other side of the road.

A few years later, in 1927, Mr Albery appeased the village with the offer of a portion of his paddock, (Market Meadow), for the long needed playing field. Although profuse votes of thanks were passed, for some reason this never happened. Two years later the Parish Council were discussing proposals to buy the cricket field or the vicarage meadow for the same purpose, but with no success. Negotiations and arguments continued through the whole of the 20th, century and into the 21st, but a playing field was never built. Eventually, ten years later in 1937, Sir Irving was able to fill his role as public benefactor by giving the land in Market Meadow as a site for a proposed Village Hall, so long as his conditions for the design were observed.

The Village Hall

Jessica Albery, aged 21, with brothers Peter and Michael in the Manor House garden, 1929.

Funds for building the hall were raised partly from the War Memorial Association which had been formed in 1919 with the intention of building a village hall if the building costs had not proved too great. Instead, the Association had bought Croft Cottage in 1919, the former farmhouse on the High Street which had remained standing in 1836 when Dr Edwards built his 'Grecian style' villa, the Croft, on the land behind it. This house was then to house the already existing Working Men's Club and the newly founded Women's Institute. Both organisations paid rent to the Association for their premises. This was never an entirely happy combination of uses and in 1937 the WI were only too pleased to sell their room in Croft Cottage to the Men's Club and put the proceeds towards the new Village Hall. With a grant from the Carnegie Trust and many voluntary contributions, and many special Parish meetings which attracted record attendances, the appointment of Miss Jessica Albery as architect was approved and the building went ahead. It was agreed that the new hall should be vested in the Parish Council and managed by a Management Committee.

Although there may have been some initial criticism of the

315

The newly built Village Hall in 1938. Donald Strickland's house, situated behind the garage can be seen in the background.

choice of such a young and inexperienced architect (it was rumoured that this commission was a 21st birthday present from her father, although in fact she was nearly thirty), the village eventually realised its luck. Jessica Albery built a fine hall, in the style of the day but with sensitive acknowledgement to the Tudor barn next door and the other houses in the village. At the opening ceremony in May 1938, A.G. Guthrie, as the chairman of the Building Committee, took the chair, handing over to Herbert Ward of the Mill to declare the Hall open. Mr Ward had been instrumental in raising the Carnegie grant, and as a former Parish Council chairman and resident of the village for 37 years he had been thought the most suitable person to perform the ceremony. Sir Irving Albery proposed a vote of thanks to Mr Ward for his untiring work for the village. Jessica then handed the keys to Mr Alban Rogers, the Chairman of the Parish Council. That evening saw the first concert in the new Hall with Gordon Guthrie at the piano and songs by the Folly Singers and others.

The Social Club

The 'Farningham Social Club and Institute' as it was first called, although it became known as the 'Working Men's Club' for many years before it reverted to its proper name, had been founded in 1911. An entrance fee of 6d. was charged and Mr Edmonds the schoolmaster was in the chair.[154] Mr John Ward, Herbert's father, was the first president and 'a great benefactor'. 'No intoxicants were served, members drank mineral waters, Oxo or Bovril...or nothing'.

Croft Cottage was rented by the club but the advent of war and depletion of members meant that the lease was sold and the house used as a hostel for land girls. Then, in 1918, the club was reborn thanks to the generosity of farmer Harry Jackson of Beesfield who lent the furniture and paid the rent until the War Memorial Association stepped in next year. By the time the

154–*Kentish Times* 13/1/1939
Farningham No2

Village Hall was built the Social Club had become so successful they were able to buy the clubhouse for themselves, (and the teetotal rules were lifted).

Mr Edmonds had retired as village schoolmaster in 1912, and Mr John Hetherington had taken his place. Miss Eliza (Nina) Edmonds stayed on as teacher of the infants. John Hetherington became an enormously successful and popular headmaster. He also worked hard in the village community, becoming a member, and later chairman, of the Parish Council, secretary of the Cricket Club and also of a Tennis Club which existed between the wars at the end of Horton Way. He was also secretary of the Social Club, a trustee of the War Memorial Association and probably took part in half a dozen other activities. The inter-war years were a time of great community solidarity.

Mrs Hetherington was a founder member of the WI which enrolled 35 members at its first meeting. It is interesting to see that they are all listed without first names and by their title of Mrs or Miss, except for younger daughters such as Miss Rose and Miss Alice Mills. The list of members of the first Village Hall Committee in 1938 gives the women's names in full, but they are identified by their husbands, and qualified by the husband's occupation, unless they are simply identified as 'Spinster'. This seems surprising today, but the ladies on the committee must have felt that these were their correct and polite titles.

A, presumably welcome, development in 1917 was the establishment of a District Nurse Service. It is possible that those who hated change mourned the loss of the old village midwives and resented having to allow strangers into their homes. A national District Nursing Association had existed for fifty years but this was the first appointment to serve the villages of Farningham, Eynsford and Horton Kirby. Alice Ward was president of the 'Farningham and District Nursing Association', and meetings were often held in the Mill House. Several nurses came and went in quick succession but by 1924 Nurse Hemsley had settled into the post and she and her partner Nurse Elvery each served for 14 years. The nurses were provided with a new Austin 7 at a cost of £100, although Nurse Hemsley, having had a traffic accident, was told to take further lessons and get a certificate of efficiency from the AA.

The Manor House Sale

At the 1920 sale of the manor lands it appears that Herbert Ward bought the Farningham half of the woods. At any rate it was he who sold them to Dartford Rural District Council in 1930. He, or his brother-in-law Guy Evans also bought Farningham Hill House where the Evans family were to live. Presumably both men enjoyed shooting and kept up the Waring's game preserves. Herbert Ward's health began to fail in 1926 when he had to resign his chairmanship of the Parish Council and Guy Evans had financial difficulties which maybe explains their later sale of the woods.

The Manor House Sale of 10th May 1920 had been conducted by Messrs Dann and Lucas at the Cannon Street Hotel, London, and had included the

Colyer's old Farningham House, which had been so mysteriously left to Thomas Waring by Thomas Colyer. This was now bought by Mr Ernest Morgan who would live there until the 1960s. Miss Edmonds was the sitting tenant of the cottage next door at 6s. p.w. Lot No 2 which included the George Barn and 105 acres of land was at that time in the tenancy of Mr Murray Wood of Swanley and appears to have been bought at the auction by Lord Bathurst who had come to live at his old family house of Franks Hall from 1910 to 1923. In 1925 Mr William Alexander of Eynsford took over the lease and in 1933 bought the property. His son William described the estate later as 'a compact dairy farm with reasonably suitable buildings comprising a tithe barn which could house 32 cows, a cart lodge and two farm cottages'.[155]

The other cottages auctioned in 1920 as part of the manor estate included the house now known as the Bakery with stable and coach house let to William Alcock, a cabinet maker, at £30 p.a. The house and shop at the corner of Sparepenny Lane was let to Mr Mason at £16 p.a. The Masons were plumbers and glaziers, and Alboin Mason was Parish Clerk for many years, while Mr Edmonds was Clerk to the Parish Council. There was also a row of shops at the top of the High Street which included Waller Brothers, let at £36 p.a, a bakers shop and Walter Dunmall's cottage.

Farningham had a new link with the outside world with the arrival in August 1921 of the first London motor-omnibus service, the 21B from Wood Green (the Wellington), in North London to Farningham (the Bull). The journey time was 153 minutes, the service every 60 minutes and the through fare was two shillings. A famous London bus driver who lived in both Eynsford and Farningham was the artist Henry Stockley who worked from the Swanley Bus Garage from 1925-57.[156] He was born in Eynsford in 1892, lived in Oliver Crescent in Farningham and sadly died in a psychiatric hospital in Dartford in 1982. His paintings, of the 'naive, Sunday painter' school have been exhibited in galleries and museums, especially the

London Transport Museum. He was one of a large family of Farningham Stockleys who had been painters and signwriters for more than a hundred years. 'Martha Stockley, painter' appeared in the 1841 census, and 'John Stockley, painter' was one of authors of the little rhyme found under the pulpit stairs in 1873. There is a painting of Farningham Mill by a Robert Stockley who was probably one of Henry's ten siblings.

155-William G.G. Alexander, *A Farming Century* (1991)
156-John Walker, 'Against Despair-Busdriver Stockley' F&ELHS No20 (1997)

A far more important artist than bus-driver Stockley, who also lived in the village in the 1920s, was Graham Sutherland. He and his wife Kathleen, a fellow Goldsmith's College student, came to live in the White House in 1927. They left in 1931 after the death of their only child in 1929, a loss which probably brought about a complete change of style in his work. Until this time he was producing a series of etchings in the idyllic, pastoral style of Samuel Palmer. Wood Interior (see illustration page 335) was made in 1929 when he was living in the White House within sight of Farningham Woods.

Left. The picturesque qualities of the Mill were fully exploited by poster artists to promote the new routes terminating at the Bull

Right. An early bus operating from Farningham. George Fuller is the driver and Frank Bowler is the conductor with his ticket pouch and punch.

Far right. This group going hop picking by bus from the Bull, Farningham seem to be defying gravity on the top deck!

Left. Farningham Mill, a 'naive' oil painting on canvas by Robert Stockley dated 1933.

The Farningham Club as it is today. Possibly the Nash Farmhouse in earlier times, it later became Croft Cottage when the elegant Croft was built on the land behind. Under its various names it has been the home of the Farningham Club since 1911. Farningham WI spent its formative years there until moving to the new Village Hall in 1938.

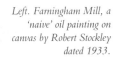

319

1. Doris Gates (Mrs Mills) 2. Gordon Edwards 3. Millie Couchman (Mrs Smith)
4. Winifred Chinery (Mrs Rainsley) 5. Douglas Leigh 6. Vernon Edwards 7. Roy Wellard
8. Percy Warner 9. Joan Edwards 10. Margarie Chinery (Mrs Cameron) 11. Sylvia Munn
12. Not known 13. Not known 14. Peggy Munn (Mrs Eves) 15. Kitty Martin (Mrs Potter)
16. Ivy Martin 17. Tom Hodge 18. Roy Martin 19. Eddie Mason 20. Barbra Bryant (Mrs Woolley)
21. Joe Munn 22. Sidney Gates 23. Fred Martin 24. Mrs Turner 25. Leslie Martin
26. Fred Wickenden 27. Jack Wickenden 28. Not known 29. Katie Pankhurst 30. Elsie Talbot
31. Not known 32. Not known 33. Mrs Copeland

Farningham and Eynsford hop pickers, circa 1920s, with many familiar names and faces.

The First, Second and Third Farningham Exhibitions

In 1934 the village put on an exhibition in celebration of local history. This seems to have been instigated mainly by Major Everard Goldsworthy of Charton Manor (a descendant of the earlier Cox family), and an energetic newcomer, Edward Edwards of the Cottage. Miss Edmonds appears to have done much of the work of gathering information and writing up the notes and minutes which would later be collected together in her history of the village.[157] The exhibition, called 'Farningham Past and Present' took place in the WI room of the Social Club.

Encouraged by the success of the first, a second, more ambitious exhibition, 'Farningham through the Ages' was held in the St John Ambulance HQ, Mr Moore's old Wesleyan chapel, in 1936 and was honoured by a visit from the Duke of Kent. Many years later a third exhibition, 'Farningham Past, Present and Future', was opened by Mrs Christopher Soames in the Village Hall in

157-F&ELHSoc. archives

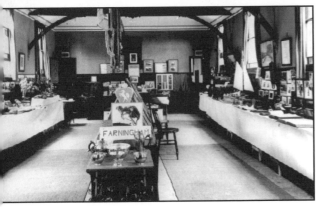

1958. A fourth exhibition and festival 'This is Farningham', would be opened by Charles Colyer of Benenden on June 27th, 1973.

Herbert Ward died in 1940. His wife Alice stayed on at the mill until 1945 when she went to live at St Margarets Bay. They had both been active and generous members of the community. Their son, who became Sir John, had a distinguished career in the Diplomatic Service, becoming British Ambassador to Argentina from 1957-61 and Ambassador to Rome 1962-61. In 1940 he brought a Foreign Office Platoon to join the Farningham Volunteers, later called the Home Guard. A photograph was taken of the battalion in front of the mill where they often performed their manouvres. They are seated and standing under the inscription in the brickwork which commemorates Henry Colyer's Volunteer Riflemen of 1804. The HQ was at the Lion Hotel and the CO. was Lt.Col O.H.Moseley, of the Folly who was later to lose a son and a daughter in the Armed Forces. (the family appears to have had no relationship to the fascist Oswald Mosley).

In the tradition of Mr Burnside successive Farningham vicars have left valuable information about their parishioners, although some information must be taken with a pinch of salt. Some people, myself included, when confronted unexpectedly by this figure of spiritual, moral and intellectual authority, tended to tell him tall stories. Donald Campbell, vicar from 1957 to 1973, kept a scrupulous account of each pastoral visit he made with comments, some in code, on the household, the member's names and ages, occupation, state of health, family and extended family relations, even the names of their dogs and cats.[158]

He is not so concerned as Mr Burnside with their churchgoing habits, unless those are recorded in the coded marks, nor is he judgemental about their characters. He must have been a wonderful parson. He was the last vicar to live in the vicarage which he filled with so-called paying guests, partly to contribute to the costs of such a big house, partly in the old tradition of looking after the homeless. The three benefices of Eynsford, Farningham and Lullingstone were to be united under one rector, who would live in Eynsford, in 1974.

The Revd.Snaith, vicar from 1911 to 1922 left an excellent description of the church, with some fine photographs of the font, but no notebooks about his parishioners. The Revd.Scott Wilkinson, presumably his curate, seems to have stood in for him on the Parish Council and social occasions. The Revd. Frederick Wiltshire however, who came after them from 1929 to 1949, left some useful notes on who was living where and their occupations in the mid 1930s.

The Village in the 1930s

Mr Wiltshire's list is more a directory than a commentary, but gives an indication of the changing population of the village between the two wars. There was still a small core of farm labourers, living presumably in tied farm cottages, a very large percentage of middle class people such as civil servants, engineers, retired service officers with, again presumably, a large unnamed population of domestic servants, many gardeners, possibly some employed by the nursery gardens but most by private households, a few employees of the paper mills at Eynsford and Horton Kirby, a few bus and lorry drivers and many small shops and businesses.

There were still two grocer's shops, Penny Son and Parker with Mr Jack Wakeley, the manager who would later own the shop and serve the village for 62 years, and next door were the Waller brothers who were coming to the end of the many years they had served in their shop and were living in the White House. These two sons of John Waller, miller to Mr Moore, were men of many talents; Leonard who was in charge of the bacon counter was a cellist, and Herbert, who looked after the second hand furniture, was the village photographer.

Next door again were the two aged Whitehead brothers, watchmakers and jewellers and next again were Mr and Mrs Glen with a library and stationer's shop in today's Post Office. The Furlonger brothers now had both forges in the village, the one next to Glens where they also had an ironmonger's shop, and one at the end of South Terrace. The Gregory's were still the

Glen's Library in the 30s at the site of the current post office. Mr Waller may have been the village photographer but Glen's did a roaring trade in film processing and printing. The invoices below relate to the 1934 and 1936 exhibitions

322

bakers in Cherry Tree Cottage where their family had baked bread since 1840, although Mr Gregory had now become the postman and his daughter Lily Cross was the baker.

All the different shops begin to sound like an old-fashioned game of Happy Families in an ideal old-fashioned village, with Mr Dell the butcher and opposite Mr Youe the draper, Mr Welham the shoemaker, and Mr Bailey, the last saddler and harness maker in Saddler's House. Mr and Mrs Brooks the greengrocers were opposite Wakeley's with Mr and Mrs Baldwin's sweetshop next door. Messrs Shuters, the carpenters lived in Lion Cottages and had their wood yard in the garden at the back. Mr Dolley, another baker, had taken Mr Alcock's house which would from now on be called the Bakery and Lily Cross would sell out her business to him. Messrs Woolley the builders, had their stone-masons yard and business premises in the weather-boarded cottages at the top of London Road.

Down at the other end of the village were Mrs Oxtoby and her daughter Mrs Atfield with their sweetshop in Marianne Farningham's old home. Mr Crowhurst had his wireless and electric shop. Mr Jeffs, a retired journalist, lived in Sandhurst (as Pinehurst was called) in part of which his wife ran a teashop. There were also Mr and Mrs West with another tea-shop and restaurant at the end of Horton Way, or School Lane as it was called, and Miss Bertha May with a café in the Bull yard where Mrs Robinson also had a fishmongers stall. Mr Barrett had recently opened a grocer's shop, Barrett's Bull Stores in the Bull yard which would remain there until 1996. Mr, Mrs and Miss Thomas still had the Post Office in South Terrace with Mr Horne the chemist at the other end of the terrace.

The Furlonger brothers at work in the 30s. The forge is situated at the end of the alley between the butchers and their then shop, and is still flagged by a plough suspended over the alley.

Welhams footwear service in the High Street shop to the right of the passage to Elizabeth Place.

There were Mrs Webb and Mrs Wingate the dressmakers, Mr Hodsoll the surveyor and estate agent at Hodsoll House, Messrs Ray and Easter at the White Post Motor Service Station and there were the doctors, Dr Smith at Fernwood, Dr Ockwell at Hillside and Dr Rogers at Braeside. The farmers were the Woods of Pedham Place, the Alexanders of the Manor Home Farm, the Rogers of Maplescombe, the Crowhursts of Charton, the Palmers of Eglantine, the Hankins of Chimhams.

There was the school, with the teachers, Mr Hetherington and Miss Edmonds. There were the District Nurses, Hemsley and Elvery. There was Sergeant Rowden, the policeman who lived in Mary Villas and Mr Lambourne, the wheelwright and timber merchant who lived in Elizabeth Villas with his

work-yard next door. Mr Alban Rogers was the proprietor at the Chequers, Andy Clements of the Lion, William Bryan at the Bull and John Murphy at the Farningham Hotel. Lastly there were the ancient William Bates the undertaker and Adam Couchman the sexton. It might almost be one of those self-sufficient villages of an earlier age.

The village changed greatly between the wars. Many new houses were built on land that would probably no longer be considered suitable for development such as along the Dartford and Eynsford roads, up Calfstock Lane and along Beesfield Lane. Horses began to disappear as tractors and motor vehicles took over their work, and small craftmen such as saddlers and harness makers and blacksmiths either closed down or adapted to the new technology. Shoemakers, dress-makers, carpenters, would all begin to loose custom to cheaper manufactured goods.

The Farningham Police Force in the 1930s, outside the Chequers public house.

By 1938 the Parish Council, holding its first meetings in the new Village Hall, were soon debating issues such as trenches and air raid shelters, ARP wardens and the Home Guard. There was the campaign to Dig for Victory and most of the iron railings and gates went in a salvage drive for scrap-iron for munitions factories as did the now very rusty Tank. There were invasion precautions, sandbags and ditches, the Spitfire Fund, pig swill collections, potato harvests.

Farningham Parish Council in 1936.
L to R back row;
Mr C.B.Searle, Clerk
Mr H.C.Waller
Mr E.Edwards
Mr J.Rogers
Front row"
Mr J.W.Hetherington
Mr A.G.Guthrie
Mr Alban Rogers,
Chairman
Col. Clapham
Vice Chairman

Col. Clapham lived at Pinehurst in the High Street (previously known as Sandhurst). He changed the name because it reminded him too much of the army.

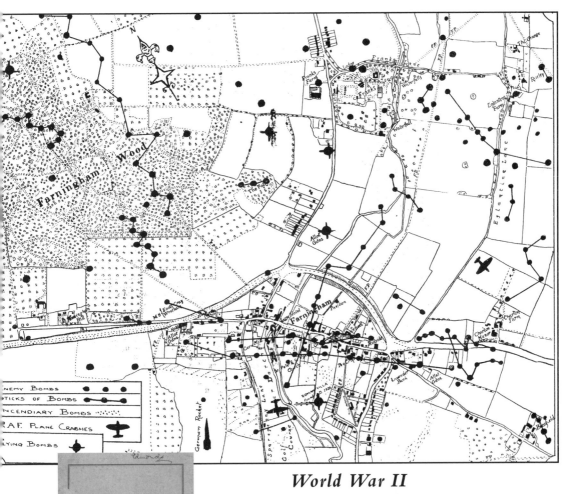

World War II

Farningham was heavily bombed during the war but, amazingly, nobody was killed. Bernard Drew, a newspaper editor and a great new addition to village life, had come to live in Vicarage Cottage and published a history *'Farningham Against Hitler'* in 1946 describing the course of the war in the village with a map showing where the two hundred or more bombs fell. Mrs Ann Lacy, another important newcomer who was to live at the Croft with her family for many years, was Head ARP Warden among other wartime activities. The WVS gave lectures on gas and first aid, and ran an emergency canteen in the village hall for the men who manned the Barrage Balloons stationed in the Mill field in Sparepenny Lane. Nearly every house suffered damage and the manor house was almost completely destroyed by a bomb in 1941. Over a hundred villagers served with the forces and the War Memorial gives the names of seven who never came back, including Billy Donnelly of the Mill, and young Cecil Dunmall, who had joined the Merchant Navy as a galley-boy and whose

MGM ran picture shows at the village hall during the war. Captain Corageous showing on this occassion.

The original Farningham Home Guards who served throughout the war.
L to R back row;
Gordon Wood
W.E.Hawkins
F.S.Mills
Donald V.Strickland
J.G.Ward
S.D.S.Bramer
L to R front row;
R.J.Strawson
F.A.Mitchell
Stephen Hartfield
W.H.Cheeseman
P.Copeman

Special Constables 1939-1945
L to R back row;
W.Wingate
L.Rutter
W.Langridge
A.Gould
A.G.Guthrie
E.Brown Jeffries
W.Manville
G.Talbot
L to R front row;
W.Elliott
S.Furlonger
H.Welham
W.North
J.Crowhurst

A Farningham coach trip in the 1950s, by whom and to where?

last letter home said 'Keep the old horses a-going...I shall be home at Christmas'.

In 1945 the Victory celebrations meant that the church bells, silent for the war years, could be rung again and no doubt Mr Albert Bates and his team made a tremendous and joyful noise. When he died in 1967 it was noted in the Parish Magazine that he had been ringing the bells for 60 years. Journeys to London were organized to see the festive lights and Miss Edmonds was sent on one of the coach trips with special thanks for 'Standing Firm in the Twilight of Life'. The village also had their own celebrations for the Festival of Britain 1951, and in 1953 there were more bells and bonfires and souvenir mugs for the schoolchildren to celebrate the Coronation of Elizabeth II, who was also commemorated by a new window in the church which, some might think strangely, shows the new queen kneeling next to the ill-fated Charles I. Charles Colyer of Benenden, still involved in village affairs, was invited to unveil the window.

Probably, if one were to visit Farningham in the 1950s and 60s one would see very little apparent change. Many of the little shops would still be here. Mr Wakeley behind his bacon counter, Mrs Brooks in her greengrocer's shop and Mrs Baldwin next door with her sweets. Mr Howe, repairing, if not making, shoes and Mrs Howe with 'draperies and haberdashery'. Mr Macdonald with mother, wife and five children in the Post Office. Mr Warren was the butcher, Mr and Mrs Bartowiak, the bakers, with their early morning queues for poppy seed loaves and Scottish baps and, at harvest time, their intricate glazed bread plaques with scenes of loaves and fishes and harvest sheaves.

Down the road were still Barrett's Bull Stores and Mrs Attfield's sweetshop. Mr Alexander's cows still plodded home from the field for milking in the manor farmyard where a prize bull lived in isolation in his stall. The school was still there with Miss Regan and Mrs Dilys Rogers in charge. Mike and Eve Reed ran a very upmarket pub in the Lion with their famous smoked salmon sandwiches and Jack and Gwen Chitham ran an even more popular pub at the Bull. Both Jack and Mike were deeply involved in village life and both were Parish Councillors.

Jack Wakely served the village, from behind his bacon slicer, for 62 years. He is remembered with great affection for his dedication.

The fields and woods themselves, still much the same as in the 1841 tithe map, would not have looked very different. At harvest time there might still have been a few sheaves and stooks of corn in some fields as well as the tidy bundles thrown out by the combine harvesters and, although there were no more hand reapers or gleaners there were still great hay and straw stacks in some farm yards. Even a few of poor Cecil Dunmall's horses were still 'a-going', but not many of the great working horses remained.

The Last Sixty Years

Springfield and Summerfield in Horton Way, designed by Jessica Albery

Only a brief chronology of events in the village for the last sixty years is possible. In the 1950s Jessica Albery designed and built Springfield and Summerfield along Horton Way and, later in the 50s, she and her business partner Muriel (Moly) Nutting were responsible for the houses beyond the Cottage on the Hill in Sparepenny Lane. She also rebuilt the bombed manor house and built Miss Smith a house behind Sancton just before the latter's death in 1965. In 1953 a new Council estate was built in Beesfield Lane and named Alban Crescent after that long serving 'Father of the Parish Council', Alban

Rogers. In 1955 the part of Farningham West beyond Pedham Place was lost to Swanley and the last part of Oliver Crescent came to Farningham from Eynsford, and in 1957 a private development of 20 houses was built on the site of the old Hillside house and named after its predecessor.

On the evening of September 5th, 1958 the 300 year old chesnut tree crashed to the ground.

Minnie Ling planting the replacement tree on April 4th 1959.
L to R
Minnie Ling
Jack Chitham
Tom Starbuck
Arthur Overington
F.G.Smith
Mike Reed
'Uncle' Woodie

In 1958 a 'Phenomenal Storm and Flood' brought down the 300 year old chestnut tree at the Lion and inundated the Mill estate.[159] The next year a new tree, a rare yellow chestnut, was ceremoniously planted by Mrs Minnie Ling, JP, Bernard Drew's mother-in-law, in the roots of the old one. The result is a most unusual grafted chestnut, half white, half yellow. In 1959 the village street lights were at last converted from gas to electricity and in 1960 the first Conservation Area was designated. In 1968 the river flooded again, sweeping water and mud through the mill and cottages to a height of four feet or so. In 1970 Dutch

159-Kentish Times Elm Disease struck the village, changing the landscape in many places, espe-

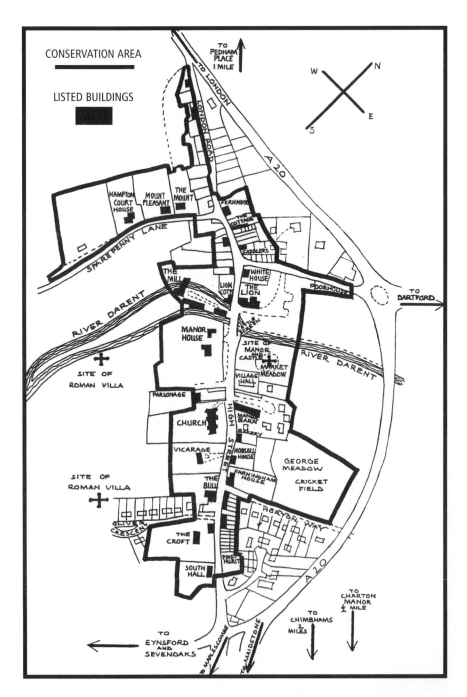

CONSERVATION AREA

LISTED BUILDINGS

TO PEDHAM PLACE 1 MILE

TO LONDON

A 20

TO DARTFORD

HAMPTON COURT HOUSE

MOUNT PLEASANT

THE MOUNT

FERNWOOD

THE COTTAGE

SPAREPENNY LANE

SADDLERS

THE MILL

LION COTT

WHITE HOUSE

THE LION

POORHOUSE

RIVER DARENT

MANOR HOUSE

SITE OF MANOR AND CASTLE

MARKET MEADOW

RIVER DARENT

SITE OF ROMAN VILLA

PARSONAGE

VILLAGE HALL

CHURCH

HIGH STREET

MANOR BARN

BAKERY

VICARAGE

HORSOLL HOUSE

GEORGE MEADOW

SITE OF ROMAN VILLA

THE BULL

FARNINGHAM HOUSE

CRICKET FIELD

OLIVER CRESCENT

ASHTON WAY

THE CROFT

PINEHURST

SOUTH HALL

TO CHARTON MANOR ½ MILE

TO EYNSFORD AND SEVENOAKS

TO MAPLESCOMBE

TO MAIDSTONE

TO CHIMBHAMS 2 MILES

cially along Sparepenny Lane where the famous elms had made an arched canopy. In 1972 the school closed and Anthony Roper was commemorated by naming the new school in Eynsford after him. The next year Farningham lost its vicar and vicarage when Donald Campbell left and Dennis Sweetman was appointed rector of the three parishes with a rectory in Eynsford. This was the year that local government changes meant that Farningham was no longer part of Dartford Rural District Council but now belonged to Sevenoaks District.

In 1973 Charles Colyer of Benenden opened the last of the three Farningham Exhibitions in the Village Hall. He had always retained a great love of the village and the mill estate and was a benevolent landlord in the tradition of his great grandfather. In the same year Brian Philp and his Archaeological Rescue team discovered the walls of 'Farningham Castle' while excavating in the path of the sewer being laid across Market Meadow. In 1976 and 77 those parts of the new motorways, the M25 and M20 that cut across Farningham parish, were opened leaving behind a landscape changed more completely than by that of the ravages of the elm disease. In 1978 Tilmans Mead, another private development of 42 houses was built. In 1979 the Lion became a Chaucer Inn, a chain of popular steak-houses although the hotel rooms continued until they were found a financial burden. In 1983 the decaying manor barn was converted to four houses. In 1985 Gordon Guthrie celebrated his 100th birthday by planting a Metasequoia, or 'Living Fossil, like myself', tree beside the bridge.

Gordon Guthrie planting a Metasequoia beside the bridge in 1985 to celebrate his 100th birthday.

In 1986 the Lion changed again to a Harvester Inn. In the same year there was a Public Enquiry where the Davids of the Parish Council fought the Goliaths of big business to prevent the construction of a Motorway Service Station and Hotel at Pedham Place, and won their case. In 1987 Charton Manor was completely demolished, and in 1987 the terrible Hurricane changed the landscape yet again and the beeches in the Folly and much of the woodland was lost. In 1988 the Darent Riverside Path from Dartford to Westerham was constructed and a footpath made through the Lion grounds with a new footbridge connecting the fields with the High Street. In 1989 Jessica Albery opened the little garden for quiet relaxation in her family's Market Meadow which was named Irving's Corner after her father.

In 1995 a low cost housing unit was built on the site of Braeside and called Centenary Court in honour of the hundredth anniversary of the Parish Council, and in 1996 new brick and stone pavements were laid along the whole High Street. In 1998 Market Meadow was acquired by a consortium of villagers for the village to use in perpetuity. In 1999, in honour of the Millenium Year, a Village Sign showing Wadard at the Battle of Hastings was erected. In the year 2000 a startling notice was given by the rector and Parochial Church Council that the church would have to close for lack of funds and a meeting attended by more than 150 anxious parishioners ensured enough funds to postpone this sad fate for the time being.

Fortunately for Farningham the DRDC had managed their half of the woods well and they had been declared a Site of Special Scientific Interest in 1951. They remained a safe and beautiful place for the village to enjoy until 1971 when local government reorganisation transferred them to Sevenoaks District Council. By that time lack of funds for maintenance, added to the loss of revenue from the dying woodland industries such as coppicing for hop-poles, hurdles, charcoal, basket and broom making had led to serious neglect. There had also been a disastrous sale of 8 hectares of woodland for felling and conversion to orchards, at the back of Hill farm in 1970.

In the new climate of interest in ecological movements and raised awareness of the environment, the possibility of the woods becoming a Nature Reserve began to be discussed by the Parish Council from 1977 to 1980 and, in 1983 the SDC, in conjunction with the Kent Trust for Nature Conservation and the Farningham Parish Council, designated their half of the woods, about 83 acres, a Nature Reserve, which was opened by Sir David Attenborough on the 20th September 1986. In the speech he made that day he said 'This is as near as you will find in the whole of this country and the whole of this kingdom of the ancient woodlands that were here when the Anglo-Saxons were here...this...with all its richness of birds and insects and plants and mosses and funghi...this is the ancient woodland of England and there is not much of it left...'. The woods are a rich inheritance for Farningham. In 1987 the second, Franks', half of the woods was acquired from John Palmer of Eglantine Farm, the then owner, making a reserve of 175 acres.

Sir David Attenborough at the opening of the Farningham Nature Reserve in 1986. Wilfrid Harding, Chairman of the Parish Council in the background.

Although the village and the woods are now an island in the middle of motorways, there is still a visitation of native and migrant birds, recorded each day by the ornithologist Ted Saxton who also writes a monthly review of the fauna and flora in the woods and surrounding fields. It is sad that the stewardship of the woods has allowed such radical opening up of woodland paths in the sacred name of biodiversity. The woods are small and enclosed by motorways and the chainsaw has not only destroyed much of the historic scenery but also allowed in an increase of motorway noise that can only disturb the resident animal population. As Auden said, 'The trees encountered on a country stroll / reveal a lot about a country's soul/...A culture is no better than its woods'. Perhaps the woods will recover, as they have in the past.

There have been several tenants of the millhouse since the Wards. First came Dr Grainger and his wife Iris, a daughter of Morris Wheeler of Franks Hall. Then, from the early 1950s Dr Gleadow and his family lived here for about 20 years. His hobby was duckbreeding and for a while the river was full of exotic diving and dabbling Californias, Pintails and Mandarins. Then Lino Ferrari, a newspaper editor, and his family lived here until his untimely death in 1982. The Ferrari's son Simon became a much loved village personality, active in the church and the Cricket Club and running 'Simon's shop' in the High Street until his own early death in 2002.

After the Ferraris came Jim and Sue Haskins and their children. Jim ran his architect's office from the old Mill ballroom. After Charles Colyer's death in 1993, his niece Vyvyan Sandford inherited the mill estate and came to live here until her own early death in 1999. Now the mill is owned by Nigel Snelling Colyer whose branch of the family were the owners of Colyer's Mill in Dartford in the 1890s. Nigel and his wife Kay have two young sons, one of whom will be yet another Charles Colyer of Farningham Mill.

There have been many more changes in the village in the last twenty years. Most of the shops have closed, unable to compete with the supermarkets. The only shops catering to everyday needs are the butcher's and the Post Office. There is also a bank, a bookshop, three hairdressers, two antique shops and an Indian restaurant as well as the four pubs, and there is a partnership of three doctors with a surgery and pharmacy. However, it seems a miracle in the light of repeated hold-ups by vicious masked criminals that Phil and Kim, the owners of the Post Office, continue to serve the village so bravely.

Eddie and Christine at the butchers and Phil and Kim at the Post Office are the only survivors of the old village retail businesses to make it into the 21st century - long may they prosper!

There is still a small nucleus of families whose parents and even grandparents were born here or in the neighbouring villages, but their children are seldom able to afford the inflated prices of housing here and are forced to move away. The council houses have mostly been sold, and there is little to rent. However, the Housing Association is at present converting the Farningham Hotel into small units for first time buyers. Questions of security have led to an increase of high fences with remote controlled electric gateways, giving the village a strangely enclosed appearance. Until the 1960s many people never bothered to lock their front doors, but surely, if asked, all the past residents of the village would be happy to lock their doors in exchange for clean tap water, main drainage, flush toilets, electric light and gas cookers, not to mention radio, TV and computers, telephones, refrigerators, vacuum cleaners and central heating and the omnipresent motorcar.

Reading the Parish Magazine, it is clear that there is still a strong feeling of community for those who want one. As well as the Church itself there is the Parish Council, a Horticultural Society, a Local History Society, the Women's Institute, the Riverside Players, a private Kindergarten and Toddlers group. There are Scouts, Guides, Cubs, Brownies, Beavers, Colts, Venturers and Rangers. There is the Cricket Club, the Social Club, the Guitar Club and the

Bellringers. There is Line Dancing, Tea Dancing, Keep Fit and Aerobics. The Bull and Chequers still have strong local attendance and the Village Hall has a rota of local events as well as outside bookings and there are outdoor events in Market Meadow and a Craft Fair on the Manor House Green. The church may not have a big membership but it is still used by a large percentage of villagers for those rites of passage still considered a necessary part of life such as weddings, christenings and funerals. And the churchyard is still a quiet and peaceful place where the history of the village lies comparatively undisturbed and one ancient hollow yew belongs to an earlier time than any of the houses.

The river itself still flows past and under the mill and is clean and full of fish, and there are still herons and kingfishers. It has been served much more sensitively and happily than the woods. The Darent River Preservation Society (DRiPS) has done much to prevent over-extraction of water and there are now boreholes to augment the supply, when summer drought threatens to dry out the river bed as it did in 1976, 1990-92 and 1996.[160] The DRiPS works with the Environment Agency to keep the river healthy and encourage the return of lost fauna such as otters, water voles, native crayfish and brown trout. However, it can only be expected that climate change will affect the river, as well as the woods and the landscape as a whole.

Nigel Snelling Colyer, the present owner and custodian of Farningham Mill, with his wife Kay and boys Charles and Toby.

Farningham Mill, like so many other English water corn-mills, ceased grinding in 1900, more than a hundred years ago. All the people who knew it, or who worked there, are now dead and gone. Ecclesiastes, who spoke of the day when 'the grinders cease because they are few', added 'then shall the dust return to the earth as it was'.

Erratum
We must apologise that, owing to a printer's error, the final illustration on
page 335 was omitted

Wood Interior 1929
a signed limited edition etching by
Graham Sutherland
made during his residence at the White House in Farningham.
From the authors collection.
By permission of the Sutherland estate.

The End

Index

**Abreviations
used throughout this book.**

Agricultural History Review (AHR).
Archaeologia Cantiana (Arch Cant).
British Museum (BM).
Centre for Kentish Studies (CKS).
Canterbury Cathedral Library (CCL).
Dartford Historical and Antiquarian Society
Newsletters (DHASN).
Dictionary of National Biography,
compact edition (1975) (DNB).
Farningham and Eynsford Local History
Society (F&ELHS).
Her Majesties Stationery Office (HMSO).
Kent Archaeological Society (KAS).
Lambeth Palace Library (LPL).
Public Record Office (PRO).
Transactions of the Dartford and District
Historical Society (TDDHS).

Bibliography

Accado, L. & Boni, P. & Palmeri, S. *I Mulini di Calatofimi* (1996)

Adler, M. *The Jews of Medieval England* (1939)

Alexander, W.A. *A Farming Century* (1991)

Aspinall, A. ed. *English Historical Documents Vol XI 1783-1832*

Backhouse, J. *The Luttrell Psalter* (1989)

Baker, A. Some Fields and Farms, *(Arch. Cant. CCXXX)* (1965)

Balls, H. Typescripts in Dartford Reference Library

Bamping, Z. *West Kingsdown* (1983-91)

Barber, R. *The Pastons, a family in the Wars of the Roses* (1981)

Bartlett, R. *The Norman and Angevin Kings* (2001)

Bede, A *History of the English Church,* trans L.Sherley Price (1995)

Belcher, K. *Kentish Brasses* (1904)

Bennett, J.A. Tallis Patron, *Proceedings of the Royal Musical Association*

Bennett, R. & Elton, J. *History of Corn Milling, 4 vols.* (1898-1904)

Blake, P, The Early Derings *(Arch. Cant. CCXII)* (1993)

Bloomfield, P. *Kent and the Napoleonic Wars* (1987)

Burgoyne Black, S. *The Children of Farningham and their Schools* (1982) *Farningham Crossroads* (1984)

Burrell, A. trans. William Langland, *The Vision of Piers Plowman* (1912)

Byng, J. *The Torrington Diaries 1781-94*

Campbell, M. *The English Yeoman* (1942)

Cave-Brown, Rev. *The History of the Parish Church of All Souls, Maidstone* (1889)

Chalklin, C.W. *Seventeenth Century Kent* (1965)

Chambers, R. *Thomas More* (1935)

Charles Wall, J. *Porches and Fonts* (1919)

Churchill, W.S, *A History of the English Speaking Peoples, Vol 3* (1957)

Clark, P. *English Provincial Society from the Reformation to the Revolution* (1977)

Clarke, D. & Stoyel, A. *Otford in Kent* (1975)

Clifton Taylor, A. *The Pattern of English Building* (1972)

Cockett, R. trans. *Calendar of Patent Rolls* (1555)

Cooper, W.D. Jack Cade's Followers in Kent *(Arch. Cant. CVII)* (1868)

Copus, G. *Chelsfield Chronicles* (2004)

Councer, C. Lost Glass from Kent Churches *(KASR XXII)* (1980)

Cresy, E. *Horton Kirby* (1857)

Crisp, F.A. *Visitation of England and Wales Vol 4* (1896)

Crossley Holland, K. *The Anglo-Saxon World* (1982)

Cumberland, A. Saxon Cemetery at Riseley *(TDDAS No8)* (1938)

Cunliffe, B. *Iron Age Britain* (1995) *Iron Age Communities* (1974)

David, E. *English Bread and Yeast Cookery* (1977)

De Jersey, P. *Celtic Coins in Britain* (1996)

Detsicas, A. & Yates, N. *Studies in Modern Kentish History*

Dickens, A.G. *The English Reformation* (1964)

Dickens, C. *Sketches by Boz. Household Words*

Douglas, D.C. & Greenway, G.W. *English Historical Documents Vol 2.* (1953)

Du Boulay, F.R.H. *The Lordship of Canterbury* (1960)

Duncombe, W.G. The Boundaries of the Parishes of Farningham and Eynsford, *(F&ELHS No.14)* (1995) The Bridges of Farningham and Eynsford, *(F&ELHS No.33)* The Hearth Tax Returns for Eynsford, Farningham and Lullingstone, *(F&ELHS)* Cartwheels and Chrysanthemums, *(F&ELHS)* Walter Gordon Wilson, *(F&ELHS)*

Dyer, C. *Everyday Life in Medieval England* (1994)

Earle, P. *The Making of the English Middle Class* (1987)

Edmeades, Lt.Col. *Some Historical Records of the West Kent Yeomanry 1994-1909* (1969)

Edmonds, E. *(F&ELHS)* Notebooks

Ekwall, E. *English Place Names* (1936)

Emsley, C. *British Society & the French Wars 1793-1815* (1974)
Everitt, A.M. *The Community of Kent and the Great Rebellion 1640-1660* (1969)
Continuity and Colonization; the Evolution of Kentish Settlement (1986)
The Making of the Agrarian landscape of Kent *(Arch.Cant. XCII)* (1976)

Farrer, W. *Honour's and Knight's Fees Vol.3* (1925)
Fell, C. *Women in Anglo-Saxon England* (1984)
Ferris, C. *The Badgers of Ashcroft Woods* (1994)
Fielding, H. *Tom Jones* (1749)
Filmer, R. *Hops and Hop Picking* (1982)
Flaherty, F. The Great Rebellion in Kent, *(Arch,Cant, III)* (1860)
Flight, C. Four vernacular texts *(Arch.Cant, CXV)* (1995)
Fortey, R. *The Hidden Landscape* (1993)
Fraser, Sir J. *The Golden Bough* (1922)
Friend, A. Master Odo de Ceriton, *Speculum 23* (1948)
Furley, R. *History of the Weald of Kent* (1871)

Gardiner, D. *The Oxinden Letters 1604-1642* (1933)
Gelling, M. *Signposts to the Past, Place Names and the History of England* (1978)
Gomme, G. *Topographical History of Kent* (1895)
Goose, N. Wage-Labour on a Kentish Manor: Meopham, 1307-75 *(Arch.Cant. XCII)* (1976)
Gordon, R.K. *Anglo-Saxon Poetry* (1954)
Graves, R. trans. *Apuleius, The Golden Ass*

Hall, H. Select cases of the Law Merchant Vol 2, *Selden Society 46* (1929)
Hallam, H.E. *Rural England 1066-1348* (1981)
Halliday, S. *The Great Stink of London* (1999)
Hammond, J.L. & B. *The Village Labourer 1760-1832* (1911)
Hancock, G. *Fingerprints of the Gods* (1995)
Harding, H.&W. Pubs of Farningham *(F&ELHS No. 19)* (1996)
The Charities of Farningham and Eynsford *(F&ELHA No.9)* (1994)
Hardy, T. *The Trumpet Major*
Hartridge, R. *A History of Vicarages in the Middle Ages* (1936)
Harvey, I.M.W. *Jack Cade's Rebellion of 1450* (1991)
Hasted, E, *The History and Topographical Survey of the County of Kent (1778-1801)* (reprint 1973)
Herbert, H. Aviation and Steam in Dartford *(DHAS)* (1988)
Hibbert, C. *The Recollections of Rifleman Harris* (1970 ed)
Hilton, R. *Bondmen Made Free* (1973)
Hindley, G. *A History of Roads* (1971)
Hinton, D. *Alfred's Kingdom* (1977)
Hobsbawn, E.J. & Rude, G. *Captain Swing* (1969)
Holt, R. *The Mills of Medieval England* (1989)
Homans, G. *English Villages of the 13th Century* (1975 ed.)
Hoskins, W. *The Making of the English Landscape* (1955)
Hull, F. John de Berwyke and the Consuetudines Kancie *(Arch.Cant. XCVI)* (1980)

Jekyll, G. *Old West Surrey* (1904)
Joliffe, J.E.A. *Pre-Feudal England, the Jutes* (1933)
Jordan, W.K. Social Institutions in Kent *(Arch.Cant.LXXV)* (1961) *The Charities of England* (1959)
Jusserand, J.J. *Wayfaring Life in the Middle Ages* (1889)

Keith-Lucas, B. *Parish Affairs, the Government of Kent under George III* (1986)
Kentish Cartulary *(KASRXI)*
Kerling, N. *Cartulary of St. Bartholomew's Hospital* (1973)
Keyes, S. *Further Historical Notes* (1938)
Kilvert, Rev. *Kilvert's Diary 1870-1879* (1977 ed.)
King, M. *Sundridge, a Brief History* nd.
Kitchinham, *DDAG Under Your Feet*, The Saxon Period (1993)
Knafla, L. *Kent at Law* (1994)

Knocker, H.W. The Manor of Sundrish *(Arch. Cant. CXLIV)* (1932)

Lacey, R.& Danziger, D. *The Year 1000* (1999)
Lambarde, W. *A Perambulation of Kent 1570* (1970 ed.)
Lambeth Palce Library)LPL)
Laslett, P. *The World we have Lost* (1971)
Lawson Dick, R. ed. *Aubrey's Brief Lives* (1962)
Lennard, R. *Rural England 1086-1183* (1959)
Lewis Butler, Lt. Col. *Annals of the King's Royal Rifle Corps* (1923)
Loyn, H.R. *Anglo-Saxon England and the Norman Conquest* (1962)

Mabey, R. *In Pursuit of the Wild* (1987)
Mattingley, trans, Tacitus, *The Agricola* (1970)
Meates, G.W. Farningham Roman Villa II *(Arch. Cant XXXVIII)* (1973)
Early Christianity in the Darent Valley *(Arch. Cant C)* (1984) *Lullingstone Roman Villa* (1955)
Melling, E. ed. *Crime and Punishment in Kent*
Miller, H. *Halls of Dartford 1785-1985*
Mitchell, S. *(DDAG) Under Your Feet* (1993)
Moore, N. *St. Bartholomew's Hospital* (1918)
More, T. *Utopia*, trans P. Turner (1965)
Moritz, L.A. *Grain Mills and Flour in Ancient Antiquity*
Morlock, P. The Elizabethan Religious Settlement *(KAS Newsletter 2002-3)*
Morris, J. *Domesday Book, Kent* (1983)
Moseley, C. *News from the English Countryside 1750-1850*
Mumford, T. *Technics and Civilization* (1934)
Mundil, R. *England's Jewish Solution* (1998)
Myres, J.N.C. *The English Settlements* (1986)

Nettel, R. ed. Carl *Philip Moritz, Journey of a German through England 1782* (1965)

Oman, C. *The Great Revolt* (1906)

Page, R.L. *Life in Anglo-Saxon England* nd.
Parker, R. *The Common Stream* (1975)
Penn, W.S. The Roman Town at Springhead *(Gravesend Hist. Soc.)* (1966)
Philipot, J. *Villare Cantium* (1776)
Philp, B. Excavations in the Darent Valley (1984) *Archaeology in the Front Line* (2002)
Philp, B.&E. *Archaeological Excavations in the Darent Valley* (1973)
Porter, R. *English Society in the 18th Century* (1982)
Postan, M. *The Medieval Economic Society* (1972)
Pouter, J. *Anglo-Saxon Riddles* (1995) R.Page, *Life in Anglo-Saxon England* nd.
Powicke, M. *The Thirteenth Century* (1962)
Priest, S. & Cumberland, A. Farningham Roman Site *(TDDAS)* (1931)
Pugh, R.B. *Imprisonment in Medieval England* (1970)

Rackham, O. *Ancient Woodland* (1980) *The History of the Countryside* (1986)
Radley, J. Holly as Winter Feed *(AHR IX)* (1961)
Rahtz, P.A. Medieval Milling, *Council for British Archaeological Research Report 40* (1981)
Razzell, P. *The Conquest of Smallpox* (1977)
Reynolds, E.E. *Margaret More* (1960)
Reynolds, T.S. *Stronger than 100 men* (1983)
Richardson, J. *The Local Historian's Encyclopedia* (1974)
Rose, M. Further on the Lodwyk Theewes Harpsichord, *Galpin Society Journal* (2002)
Roth, C. *A History of the Jews in England* (1964 ed.)

Salway, P. *Roman Britain* (1981)
Salzman, S.I. *Building in England down to 1540* (1952)
Sawyer, P. *Anglo-Saxon Charters* (1968)
Selden Society Yearbooks, *The Eyre of Kent 1313* (1970)

Shrewsbury, J.D.F. *A History of Bubonic Plague in the British Isles* (1970)

Sinclair Williams, C. Codification of the Customs of Kent *(Arch.Cant. XCV)* (1970)

Smith, N.A.F. The Origins of Water Power, *Transactions of the Newcomen Society 55* (1983)

Smith, R.A.L. *Canterbury Cathedral Priory* (1943)

Smith, V. The Maginot Line in Farningham *(KAR 27)* (1972)

Smith, T.P. The Roper Gateway *(Arch.Cant. CVIII)* (1990)

Snaith, R. *Farningham Church Guide* (1913)

Spain, R. Romano-British Watermills *(Arch.Cant. C)* (1984)

An 18th Century Corn Watermill *(Arch.Cant. LXXXV)* (1970)

The Len Watermills *(Arch.Cant. XXXII)* (1967)

Spray, M. Holly as Fodder in England *(AHR 29)* (1981)

St.Clare Byrne, M. *Elizabethan Life in Town and Country* (1961)

Steinman, G. Some Account of the Manor of Apulderfield, *The Topographer & Genealogist* (1858)

Stenton, D.M. *English Society in the Early Middle Ages* (1962)

Stenton, F.M. *Anglo-Saxon England* (1971)

Stephen Watson, J. *The Reign of George III 1760-1815*

Swanton, M. trans. *Anglo-Saxon Prose* (1993)

Tate, W.E. *The Parish Chest* (1946)

Thirsk, J. ed. *The English Rural Landscape*

Thomas, E. *Richard Jefferies* (1978 ed.)

Thorpe, J. ed. *Custumale Roffense* (1769)

Thrupp, S. *The Merchant Guilds of Medieval London* (1948)

Timmins, N. *The Five Giants, a Biography of the Welfare State* (1996)

Tyler, S. Anglo-Saxon Settlement in the Darent Valley *(Arch.Cant. CX)* (1992)

Unwin, G. *Guilds and Companies of London* (1908)

Vince, J. *Discovering Watermills* (1987)

Wall, J.C. *Porches and Fonts* (1919)

Wallenberg, K. *Kentish Place Names* (1931) *The Place Names of Kent* (1934)

Walter, J. Against Despair, Bus Driver Stockley *(F&ELHS 20)* (1997)

Ward, G. The Making of the Great Park at Otford *(Arch.Cant. XLI)* (1929)

The List of Saxon Churches in the Textus Roffensis *(Arch.Cant. XLIV)* (1932)

Warren, M. *A Chronology of State Medicine, Public Health, Welfare and Related Services in Britain 1066-1999* (2000)

Watson, B. Typescript (CKS)

Watts, M. *The Archaeology of Mills and Milling* (2002)

Webb, S.&B. *The Story of the King's Highway* (1913) *English Poor Law* (1927)

Webster, B. The Community of Kent in the Reign of Richard II *(Arch.Cant. C)* (1984)

Wedgwood, C.V. *The King's Peace* (1955)

Weinreb, B. & Hibbert, C. eds. *The London Encyclopedia* (1983)

Weldon Finn, R. *Domesday Book, a Guide* (1973)

Westlake, H. *The Parish Guilds of Medieval England* (1919)

Whitelock, D. ed. *English Historical Documents Vol.1*

Wilson, A.N. *A History of Colyer's School* (1965)

Wilson, D.N. *The Anglo-Saxons* (1972)

Wilson, G. *Walter Wilson, Portrait of an Inventor* (1986)

Wilson, P.N. Watermills, an Introduction *(SPAB)*

Witney, K.P. *The Jutish Forest* (1976) Kentish Land Measurements of the 13th Century *(Arch.Cant. CIX)* (1991)

The Kingdom of Kent (1982)

Wood, M. *In Search of the Dark Ages* (1981)

Zell, M. *Early Modern Kent 1540-1640* (2000)

Ziegler, P. *The Black Death* (1969)

List of Subscribers

Sincere thanks to our subscribers, whose enthusiasm and pre-production support, has made possible the realisation of this book.

Cyril Edward Goodearle	Kerry Silcox-Butt
Peter & Pat Doye	Phillip & Stella Baggaley
Cheryl Holdsworth	Clive & Pamela Davy
Peter & Teresa Dzierzek	Donald Rayfield
Linda Mergell	Ralph Daniel
Jack & Caroline Gould	Mr & Mrs Weaser
Pearl Turrell	Vincent Gianonni
Christina Arnold	George & Barbara Cooper
Jonathan Histed	Beryl Saunders
Peggy Wood	Monica Lacy
Sylvia Mackenzie	Doreen James
Mike & Franny Swann	Doreen Parmenter
Geoff & Lesley Burr	Margaret Wyatts
Helen Glaister	Doreen Bowles
Terry & Wendy Divers	Kay Kitto
Barbara Cannell	Doreen Hustwick
Steve Isaacson	Marylyn Redelmeier
Andrew Towers	Ted & Grace Saxton
Frances Simpson	Gerald Cramp
Sheila Bennett	Barry & Rosamund Morgan
Jean Armstrong	Jennifer Gough-Cooper
Vic Clarke	Vivian Gough-Cooper
Philip & Dorothy McGarvey	Garry & Lee Mullins
Jim Robb	William & Diana Alexander
Paula Callum	Mary Berdinner
Janet Gasson	Betty Hutt
Robert Morris	Phillip & Martine Meakin
Henry Cooper	Bruce Hamilton
Veronica Sheppard	Maria Martin
Sara Corall	Paul Jarvis
Barrie Payne	Peter Chinery
Paul Fletcher	Eddie & Christine Bainbridge
Janet Dugdale	L.M.Blake
Lynn Cooper	T.W.Mills
Rachel Tann	Mr & Mrs L.Allen
Beth Powell	Mrs J.Hall
David & Janet Pritchard	Neil & Pauline Lucas
Ruth Peet	Mrs Maureen Elliot
Brian Clarke	Andrew & Fran Dunk
Margaret Cutler	Don & June Evans

Ray & Julie Bainbridge
Mr D.A.Royce
Mrs S.R.Crosby
Valerie Doust
R.Saxby
Mrs Christine Smith
Viv & Chris Chilton
Teresa Roberts
Mrs Ellen Hedges
John & Janet Cook
Mr T. Moore
Mr & Mrs Owen
Betty Wright
Joan Bowring
Rodney & Annie Cooper
Carolyn Lewis
John Curry
Jonathon Curry
John & Dorothy Richards
Brian Flewin
Dominic Flewin
Jason Flewin
Jon & Jackie Carr
Fiona Learmond
Mrs J.D.Parsons
Julia Chamberlain
Elizabeth Oakes
R.Warrick
Mr F. Gray
Brian & Irene Staples
Stephen Preston
David & Helen Horobin
Derek Lampkin
Peter Selby
Mrs Jane King
Fiona Scott Gordon
Mrs Davida Baker
Tony Corbett
Mrs G. Clegg
Peter Page
Phil & Kim Barratt
Joan Peck
Harry Palmer
Julia Cooper
Jean Lawrie
Ben & Tricia Garrad
P. Elliman

Heidi Parker
Karen Jefferies
Sue Hutchings
Linda Fitzsimons
G.E.T. Granter
Mrs B.A.Sloper
Mr & Mrs J. Saunders
Joan Everitt
Ray Tyalke
Susan Pittman
Mollie Bersett Lee
Pauline Penney
Susan Williams
A.L. & M.J. Bradshaw
Derek Humphrey
Joyce Everest
Mr & Mrs Rose
Dr. Nigel Perry
Harvey Langman
Nigel Handley
Mrs D. Hucker
Mrs Diane Metcalfe
Steve Earl
Elizabeth Roberts
Barry Quinn
Darren Blake
Miss K. Spencer
Tony Morgan
Marjorie A. Pratt
Stanley & Maureen Shand
G.C.A.Bergne & Co.
Carol Salmon
Jackie Wainwright
R.G.Wenham
Susan Drury
Suzanne Williams
Gillian Darley
Reg Nightingale
Malcolm & Pat Gale
Jenny Spring
Mr & Mrs P. Slinger
Peter Silley
Paul Telford
R. Foard
Georgina Hearne
Rodney Burton
Mrs Joan Atkins

Mrs D.E. Sage
Mrs P. Sanders
Dr. Andrew & Mrs Wendy Nicolson
Trevor & Brenda Beech
Lady Ann Reid & Mr Donald Reid
John & Shelagh Longstaff
Lee & Sandra Thomas
Peter & Rosemary Beasley
Mrs J. Down
Andrew & Lisa Thomas
John A. Meakins
John & Mary Hood
Mrs J.M. Renshaw
Hazel J. Cutten
Jonathan Chapman
Gillian Clarke
Mr & Mrs N. Casey
Richard Falconer
Stewart & Sheila Grainger
Ian & Alice Herve
Mr & Mrs J. Taylor
Miss Ann Carreck
Colin Marsh
Vera Nicholls
Mrs Carol Ann Kemp
John Clay
J. Stacey
Sue Harris
Catherine R. Ross
Richard Ellingworth
Dr. W.G. Duncombe
Mr & Mrs A. Noble
Robert Ward
Michael Thomas
Mr & Mrs Derek Britton
Terry Chisholm
Roy Phillips
Chris & Rosie Walker
Michael & Marianne Cook
Mrs P. Rising
Duncan & Kath McNair
Mrs C. Goldsworthy
Mrs Gwen Francis
Sheila Ireland
Ian Boyd
Elizabeth Purves
Mr & Mrs Hamish Maxwell

Mrs Val Brooman
Mrs G. McAndrew
Frank & Zena Bamping
Mr & Mrs Cerely
Lady Best Shaw
Mr T.G. Booer
Mrs Sue Ray
Robin Thew
Mrs L.E.F. Knight
Maria Friend
M.T. Hodges
David Willis
M.W. Rich
Linda Mullis
Ron Burnett
Ann Cowper
W.C. Ward
Godfrey Smith M.B.E
John O'Sullivan
Neville machin
Cheryl Mitchinson
Bryan & Marie Wolfe
David R. Ward
David Thornwell
Guy & Sara Hart-Dyke
Tom & Anya Hart-Dyke
Mary Hart-Dyke
A.J. Harris
K.H. Saunderson
Mrs P. M. Annett
Anthony Croucher
Kate & Andy Merritt
D.G. Mollon
Mrs Audrey Gee
Mrs Marie Garrett
Bridget Wilcox
Mr R.L. Ribbens
Roger Gough
Tanya Sheridan-Boulton
Bernard Ducker
Mrs J. Douglas

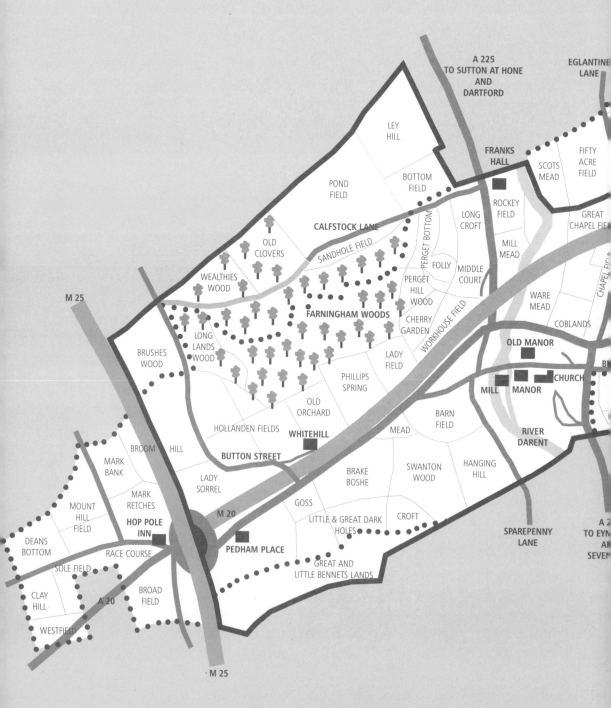